For more information

on all our products, along with the most up-to-date news on releases, series announcements, and contests, please visit us at:

SUBLIME MANGA

W9-AYY-963

The World's Greatest First Love:
The Case of Ritsu Onodera

Volume 6
SuBLime Manga Edition

Story and Art by **Shungiku Nakamura**

Translation—**Adrienne Beck**
Touch-up Art and Lettering—**NRP Studios**
Cover and Graphic Design—**Fawn Lau**
Editor—**Jennifer LeBlanc**

SEKAIICHI HATSUKOI ~ONODERA RITSU NO BAAI~ Volume 6
© Shungiku NAKAMURA 2011
Edited by KADOKAWA SHOTEN
First published in Japan in 2011 by KADOKAWA CORPORATION, Tokyo.
English translation rights arranged with KADOKAWA CORPORATION,
Tokyo.

ASUKA
COMICS
CL^D_X

Printed in the U.S.A.

Published by SuBLime Manga
P.O. Box 77010
San Francisco, CA 94107

10 9 8 7 6 5 4 3 2 1
First printing, April 2017

 PARENTAL ADVISORY
THE WORLD'S GREATEST FIRST LOVE is rated M for Mature and is
recommended for mature readers. This volume contains graphic
MATURE imagery and mature themes.

www.SuBLimeManga.com

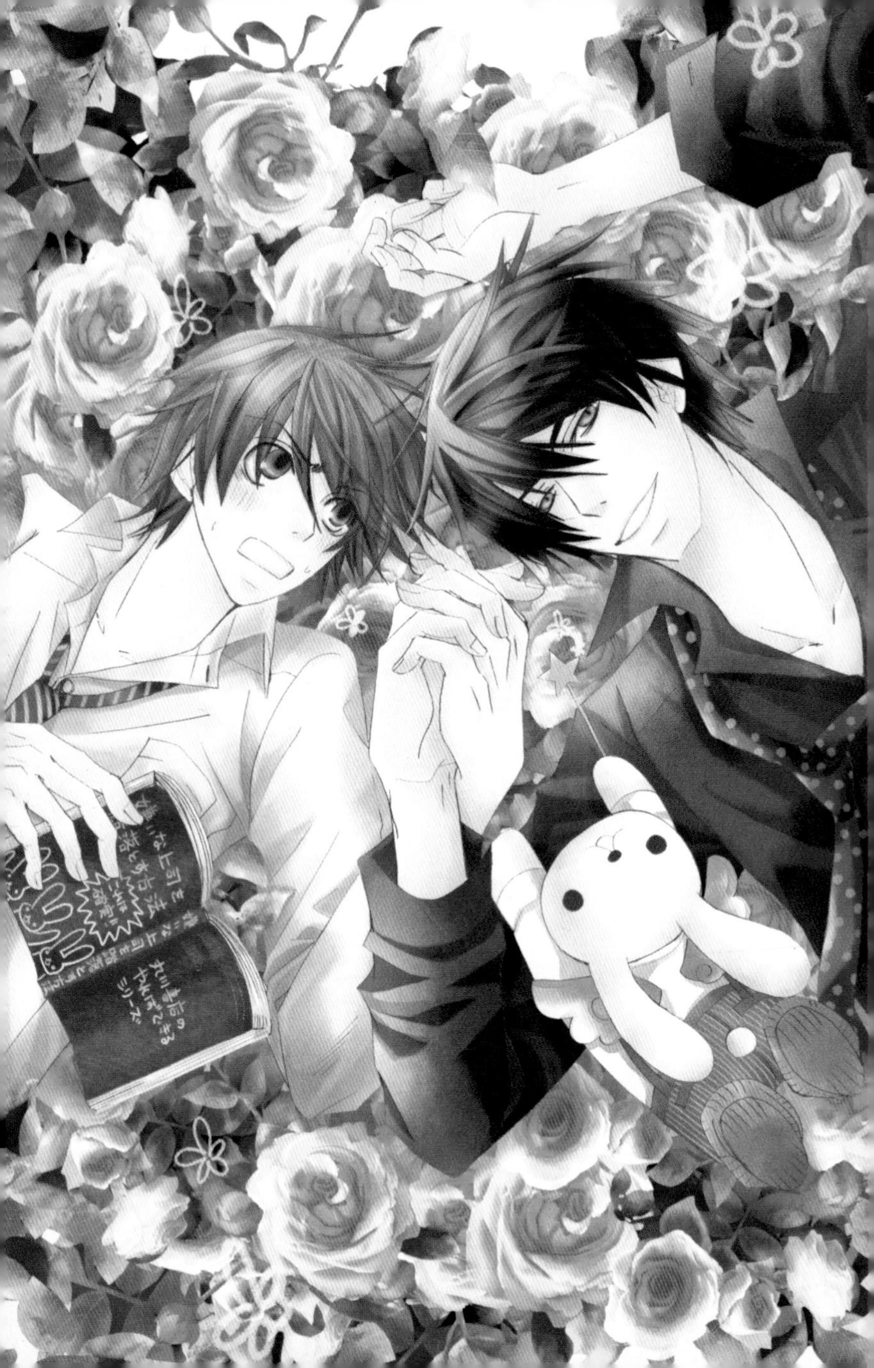
嫌いな上司を
落とす方法
丸川書店の
やればできる
シリーズ

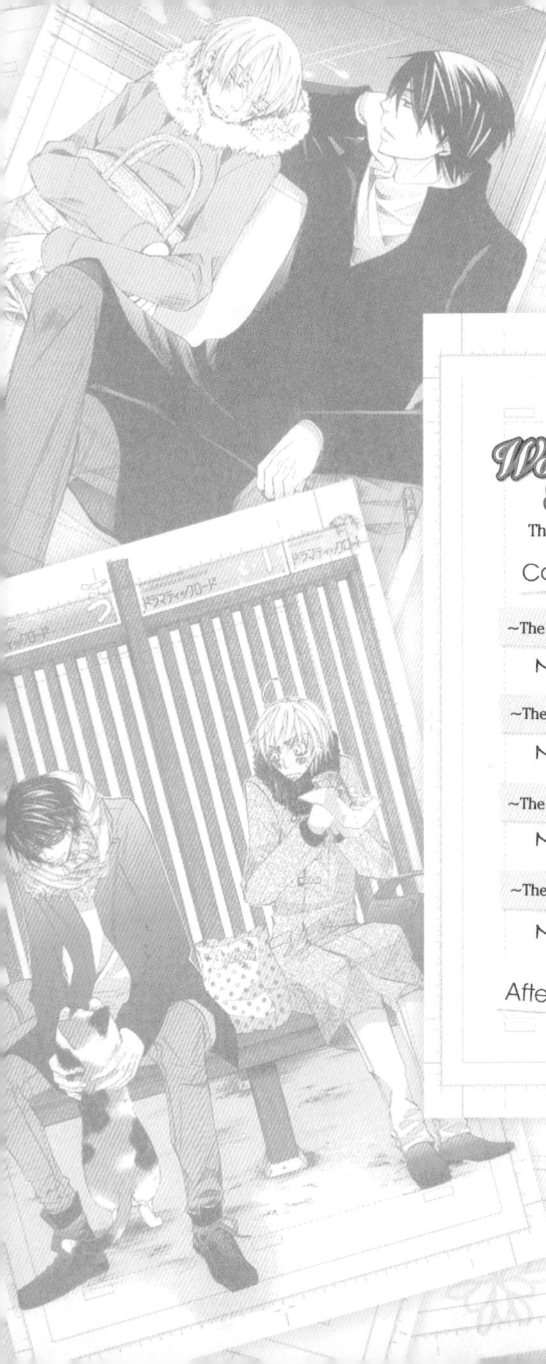
ドラマティックロード

The World's Greatest First Love

The Case of Ritsu Onodera *6*

Contents

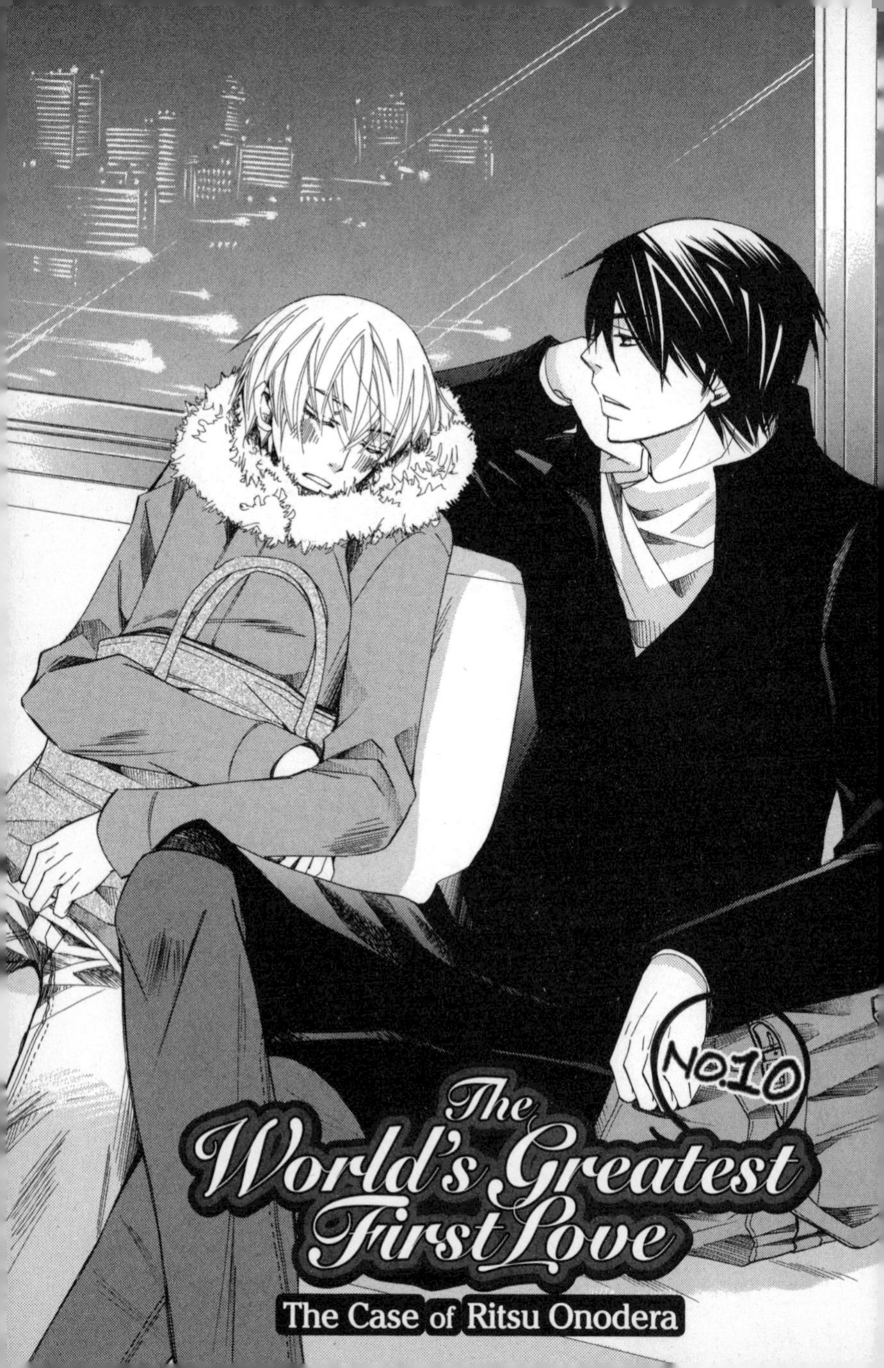
No.10
The World's Greatest First Love
The Case of Ritsu Onodera

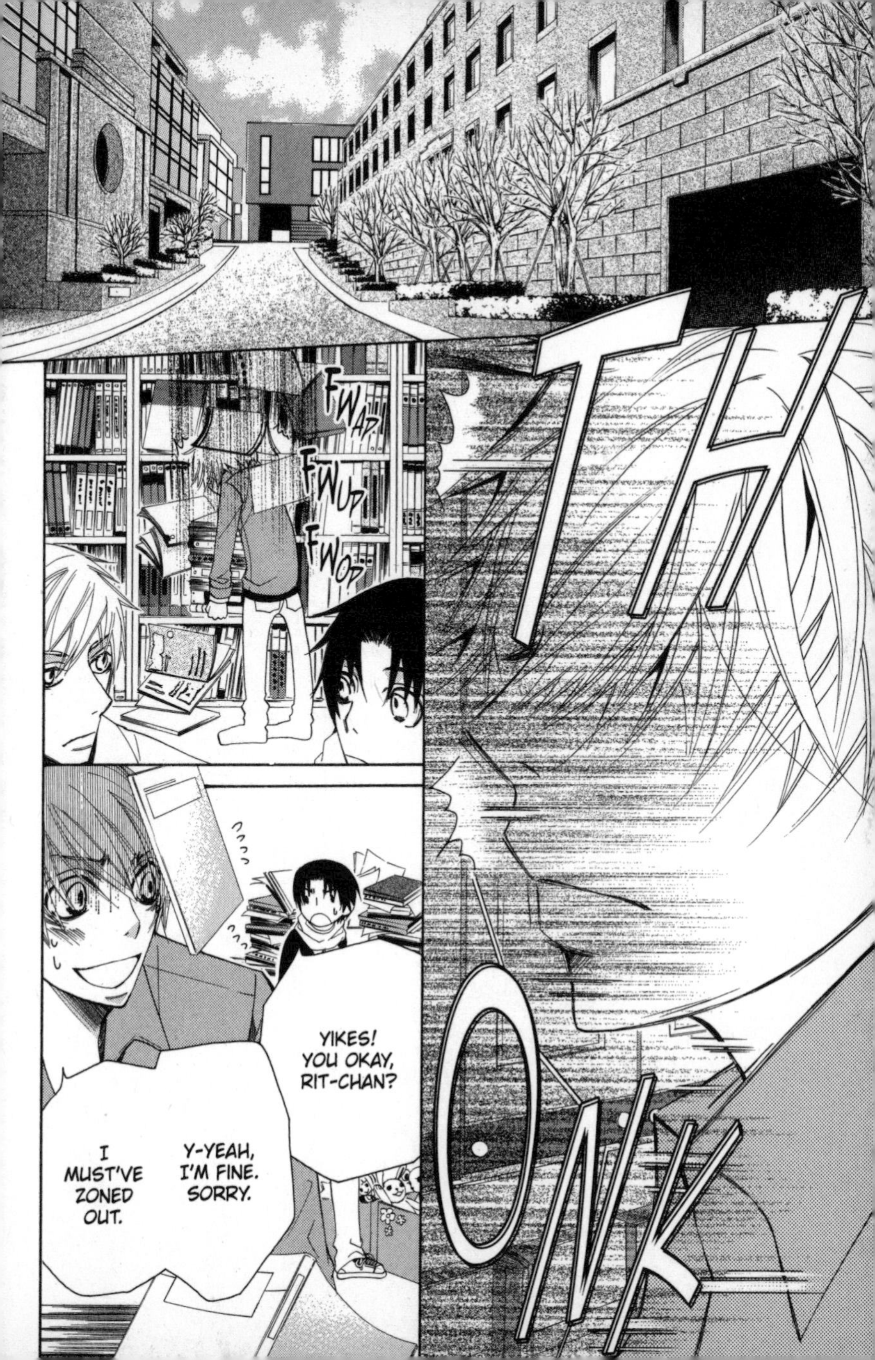
THONK
FWAP
FWUP
FWOP
YIKES! YOU OKAY, RIT-CHAN?
Y-YEAH, I'M FINE. SORRY.
I MUST'VE ZONED OUT.

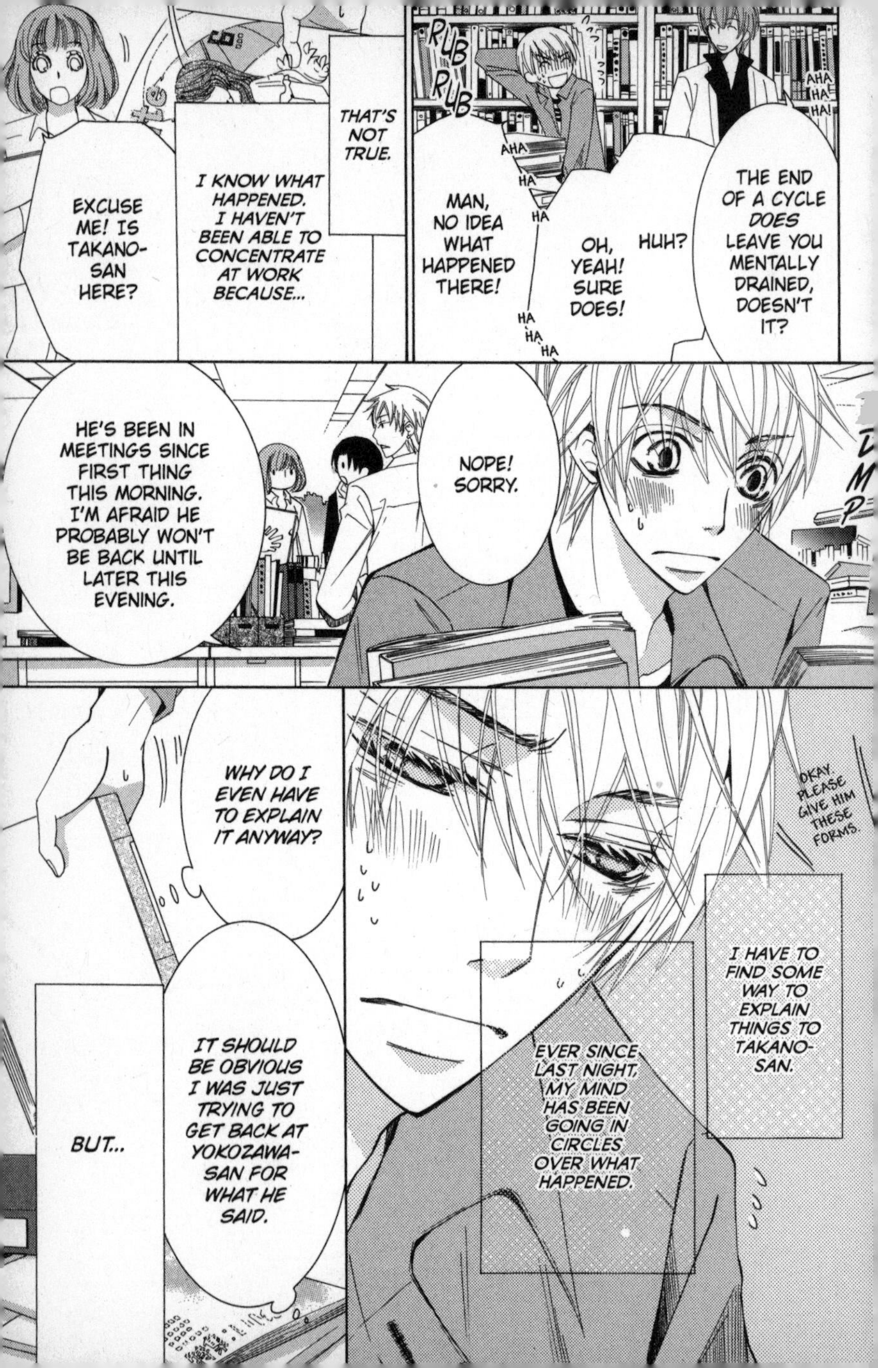
AHA HA HA!
THE END OF A CYCLE DOES LEAVE YOU MENTALLY DRAINED, DOESN'T IT?
HUH?
OH, YEAH! SURE DOES!
RUB RUB
MAN, NO IDEA WHAT HAPPENED THERE!
AHA HA HA HA HA HA
THAT'S NOT TRUE.
I KNOW WHAT HAPPENED. I HAVEN'T BEEN ABLE TO CONCENTRATE AT WORK BECAUSE...
EXCUSE ME! IS TAKANO-SAN HERE?
NOPE! SORRY.
HE'S BEEN IN MEETINGS SINCE FIRST THING THIS MORNING. I'M AFRAID HE PROBABLY WON'T BE BACK UNTIL LATER THIS EVENING.
OKAY. PLEASE GIVE HIM THESE FORMS.
I HAVE TO FIND SOME WAY TO EXPLAIN THINGS TO TAKANO-SAN.
EVER SINCE LAST NIGHT, MY MIND HAS BEEN GOING IN CIRCLES OVER WHAT HAPPENED.
WHY DO I EVEN HAVE TO EXPLAIN IT ANYWAY?
IT SHOULD BE OBVIOUS I WAS JUST TRYING TO GET BACK AT YOKOZAWA-SAN FOR WHAT HE SAID.
BUT...

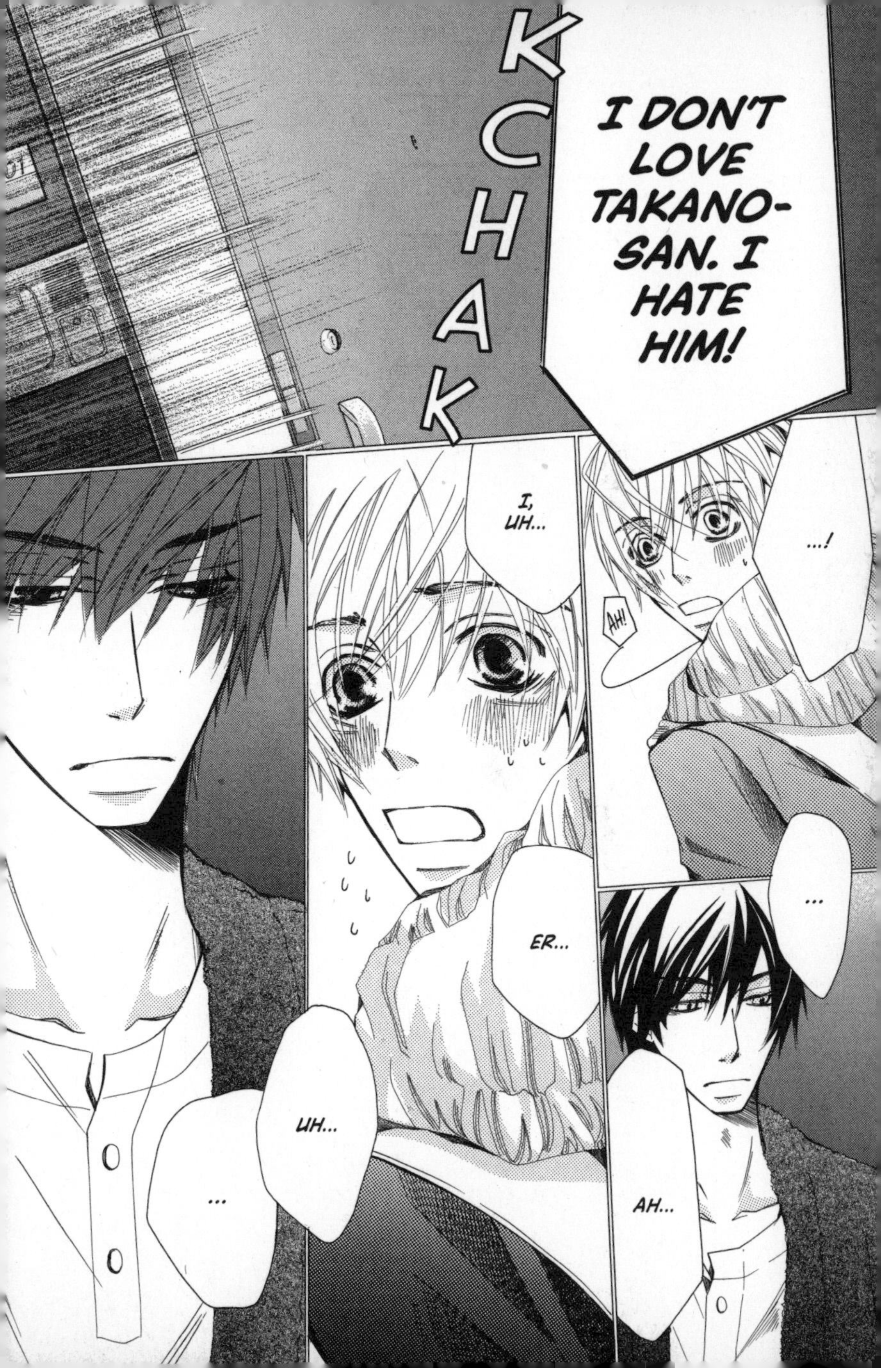
I DON'T LOVE TAKANO-SAN. I HATE HIM!
KCHAK
...!
AH!
...
AH...
I, UH...
ER...
UH...
...

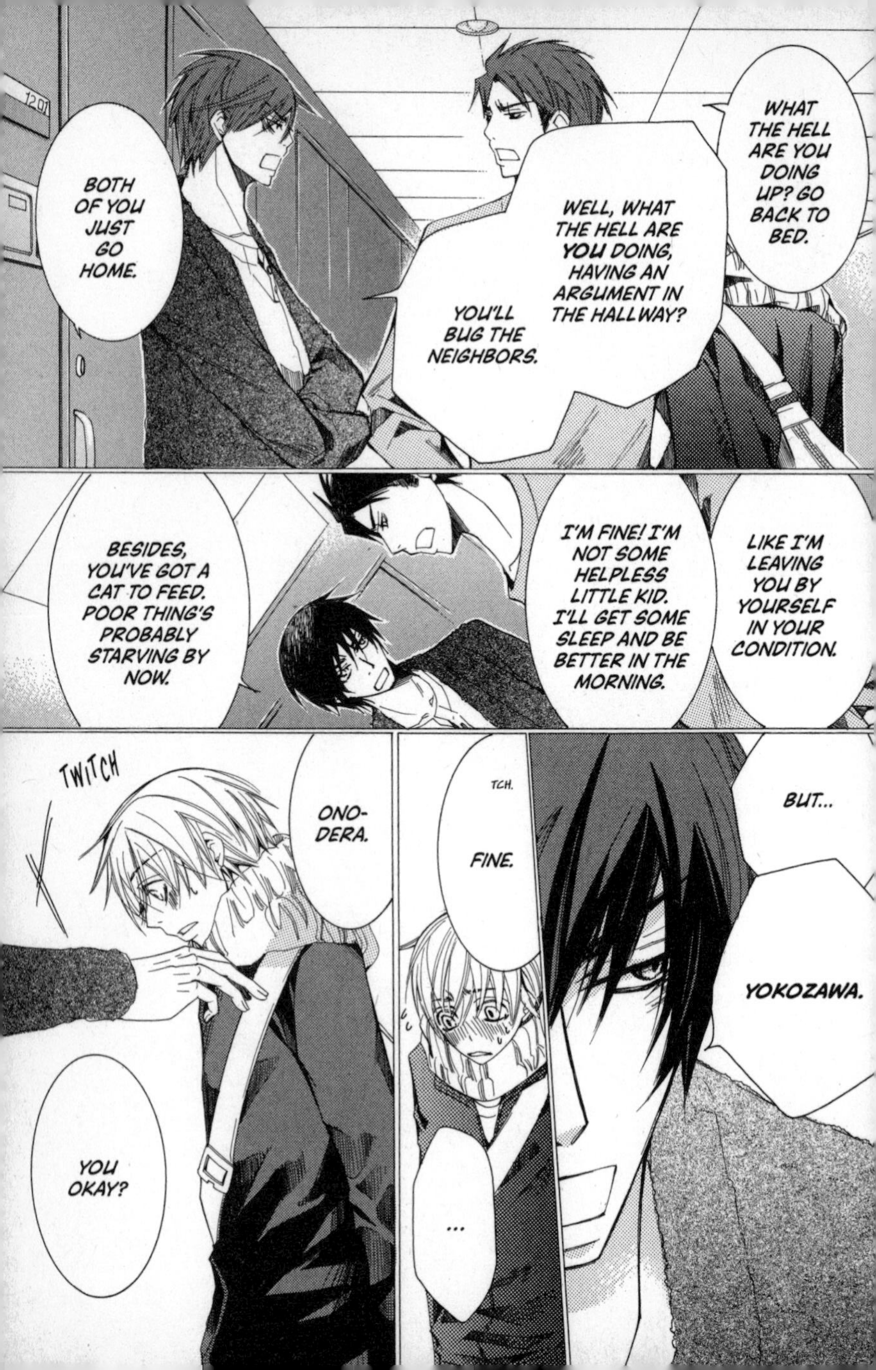
WHAT THE HELL ARE YOU DOING UP? GO BACK TO BED.
WELL, WHAT THE HELL ARE YOU DOING, HAVING AN ARGUMENT IN THE HALLWAY?
YOU'LL BUG THE NEIGHBORS.
BOTH OF YOU JUST GO HOME.
LIKE I'M LEAVING YOU BY YOURSELF IN YOUR CONDITION.
I'M FINE! I'M NOT SOME HELPLESS LITTLE KID. I'LL GET SOME SLEEP AND BE BETTER IN THE MORNING.
BESIDES, YOU'VE GOT A CAT TO FEED. POOR THING'S PROBABLY STARVING BY NOW.
BUT...
YOKOZAWA.
TCH.
FINE.
...
ONO-DERA.
TWITCH
YOU OKAY?

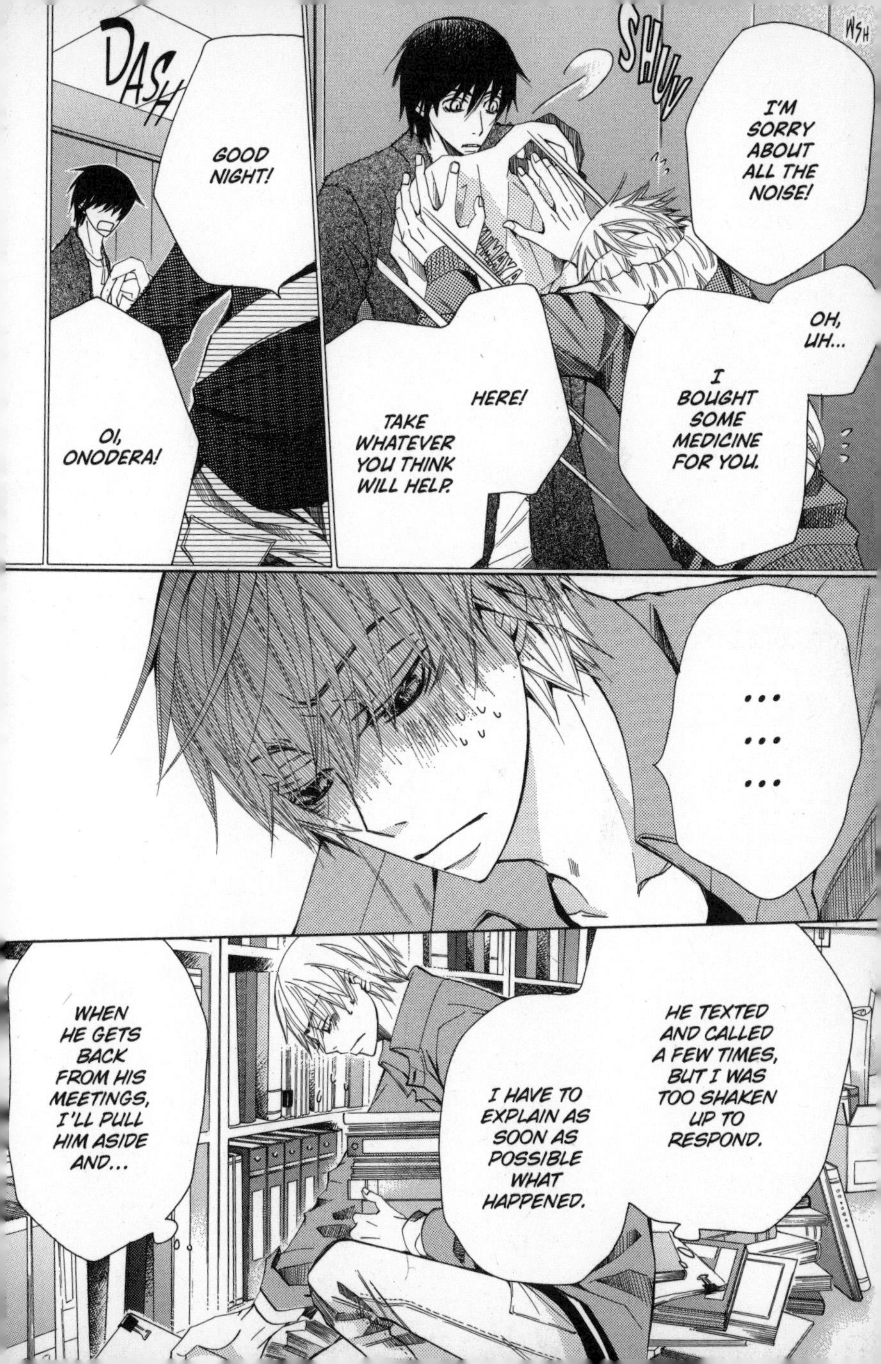
WSH
SHUW
I'M SORRY ABOUT ALL THE NOISE!
OH, UH...
I BOUGHT SOME MEDICINE FOR YOU.
HERE!
TAKE WHATEVER YOU THINK WILL HELP.
DASH
GOOD NIGHT!
OI, ONODERA!
...
...
...
HE TEXTED AND CALLED A FEW TIMES, BUT I WAS TOO SHAKEN UP TO RESPOND.
I HAVE TO EXPLAIN AS SOON AS POSSIBLE WHAT HAPPENED.
WHEN HE GETS BACK FROM HIS MEETINGS, I'LL PULL HIM ASIDE AND...

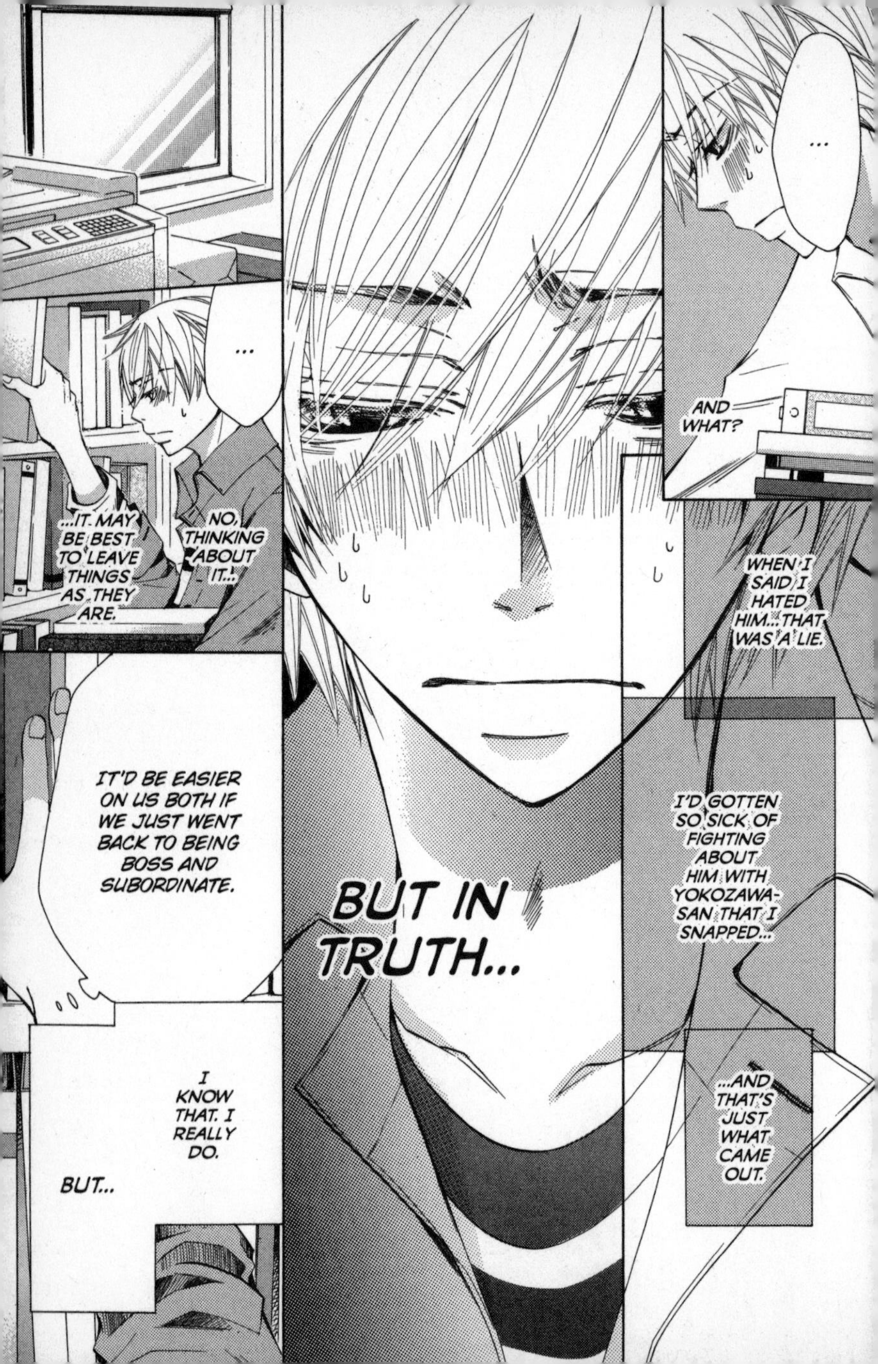
...
AND WHAT?
WHEN I SAID I HATED HIM... THAT WAS A LIE.
I'D GOTTEN SO SICK OF FIGHTING ABOUT HIM WITH YOKOZAWA-SAN THAT I SNAPPED...
...AND THAT'S JUST WHAT CAME OUT.
BUT IN TRUTH...
...
NO, THINKING ABOUT IT...
...IT MAY BE BEST TO LEAVE THINGS AS THEY ARE.
IT'D BE EASIER ON US BOTH IF WE JUST WENT BACK TO BEING BOSS AND SUBORDINATE.
I KNOW THAT. I REALLY DO.
BUT...

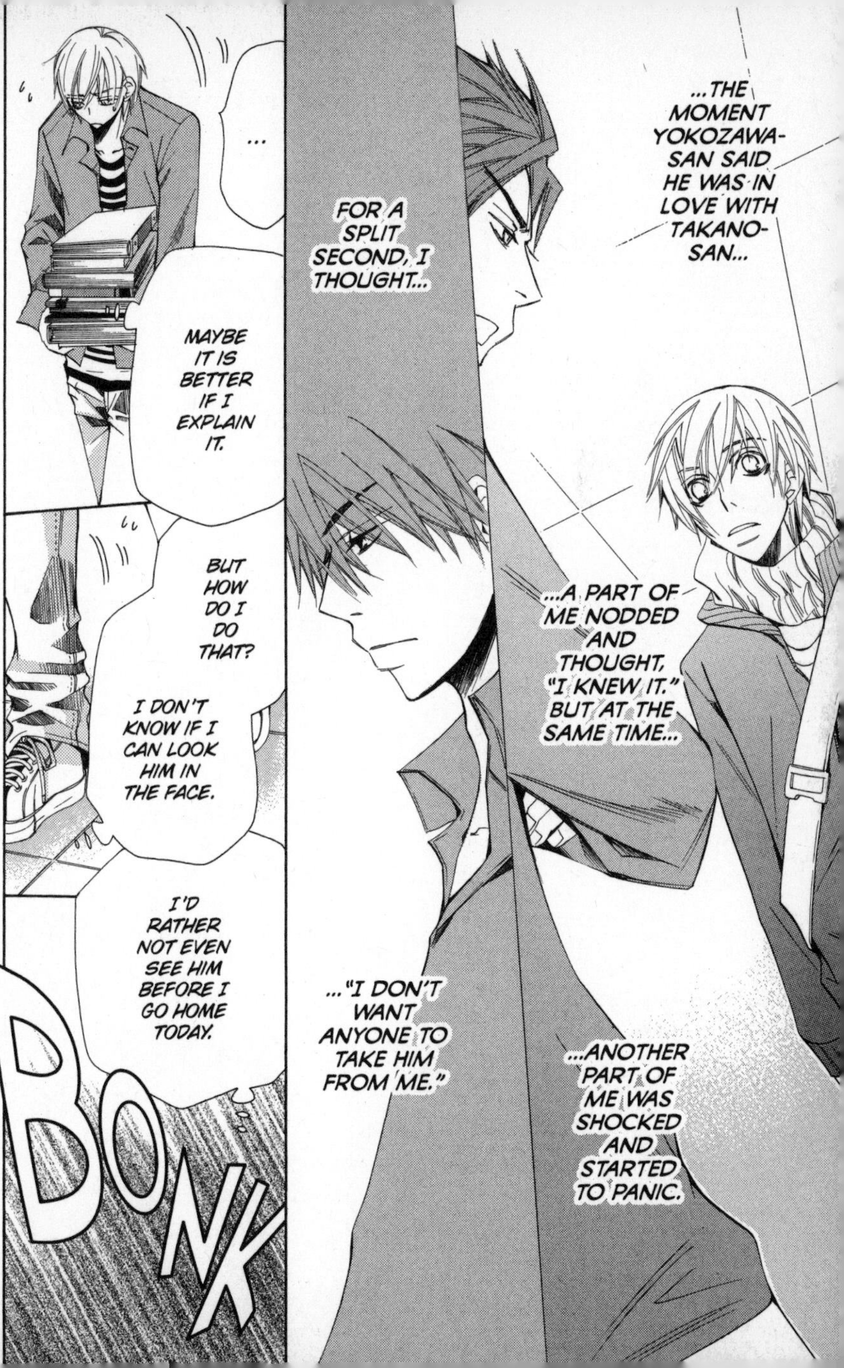
...THE MOMENT YOKOZAWA-SAN SAID HE WAS IN LOVE WITH TAKANO-SAN...
...A PART OF ME NODDED AND THOUGHT, "I KNEW IT." BUT AT THE SAME TIME...
...ANOTHER PART OF ME WAS SHOCKED AND STARTED TO PANIC.
FOR A SPLIT SECOND, I THOUGHT...
..."I DON'T WANT ANYONE TO TAKE HIM FROM ME."
...
MAYBE IT IS BETTER IF I EXPLAIN IT.
BUT HOW DO I DO THAT?
I DON'T KNOW IF I CAN LOOK HIM IN THE FACE.
I'D RATHER NOT EVEN SEE HIM BEFORE I GO HOME TODAY.
BONK

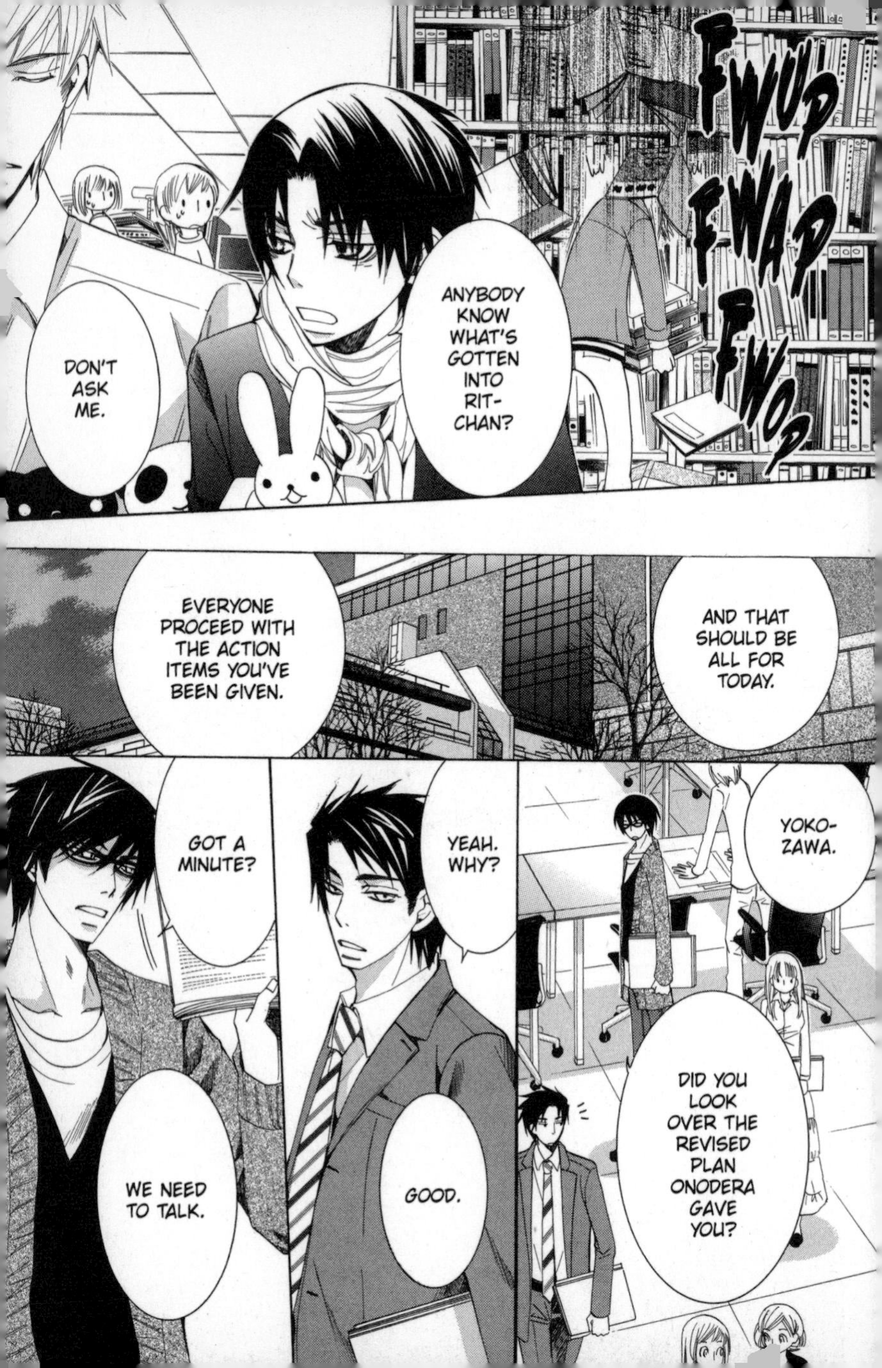
FWUP FWAP FWOP
ANYBODY KNOW WHAT'S GOTTEN INTO RIT-CHAN?
DON'T ASK ME.
AND THAT SHOULD BE ALL FOR TODAY.
EVERYONE PROCEED WITH THE ACTION ITEMS YOU'VE BEEN GIVEN.
YOKO-ZAWA.
DID YOU LOOK OVER THE REVISED PLAN ONODERA GAVE YOU?
YEAH. WHY?
GOOD.
GOT A MINUTE?
WE NEED TO TALK.

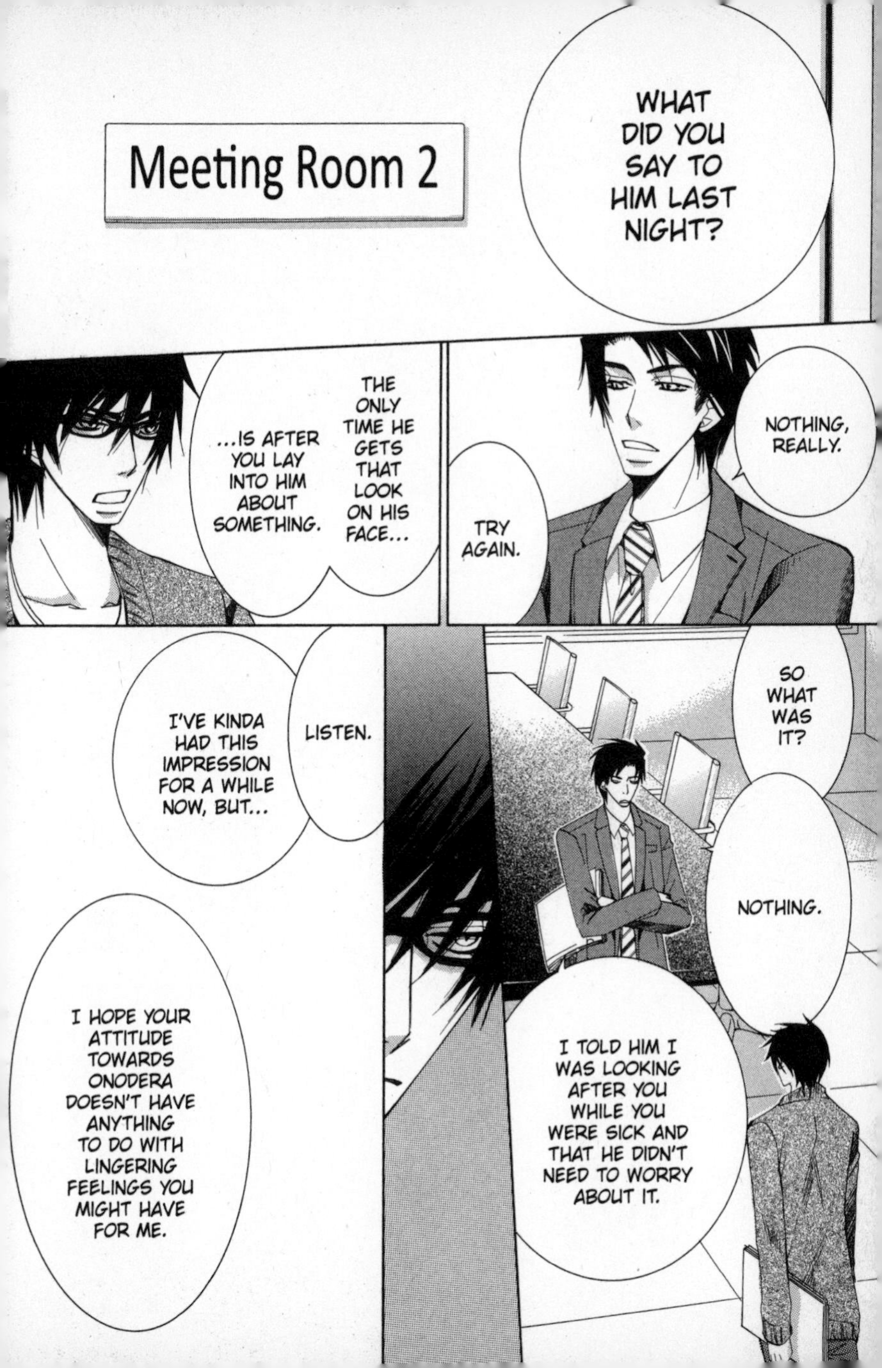
WHAT DID YOU SAY TO HIM LAST NIGHT?
Meeting Room 2
NOTHING, REALLY.
TRY AGAIN.
THE ONLY TIME HE GETS THAT LOOK ON HIS FACE...
...IS AFTER YOU LAY INTO HIM ABOUT SOMETHING.
SO WHAT WAS IT?
NOTHING.
I TOLD HIM I WAS LOOKING AFTER YOU WHILE YOU WERE SICK AND THAT HE DIDN'T NEED TO WORRY ABOUT IT.
LISTEN.
I'VE KINDA HAD THIS IMPRESSION FOR A WHILE NOW, BUT...
I HOPE YOUR ATTITUDE TOWARDS ONODERA DOESN'T HAVE ANYTHING TO DO WITH LINGERING FEELINGS YOU MIGHT HAVE FOR ME.

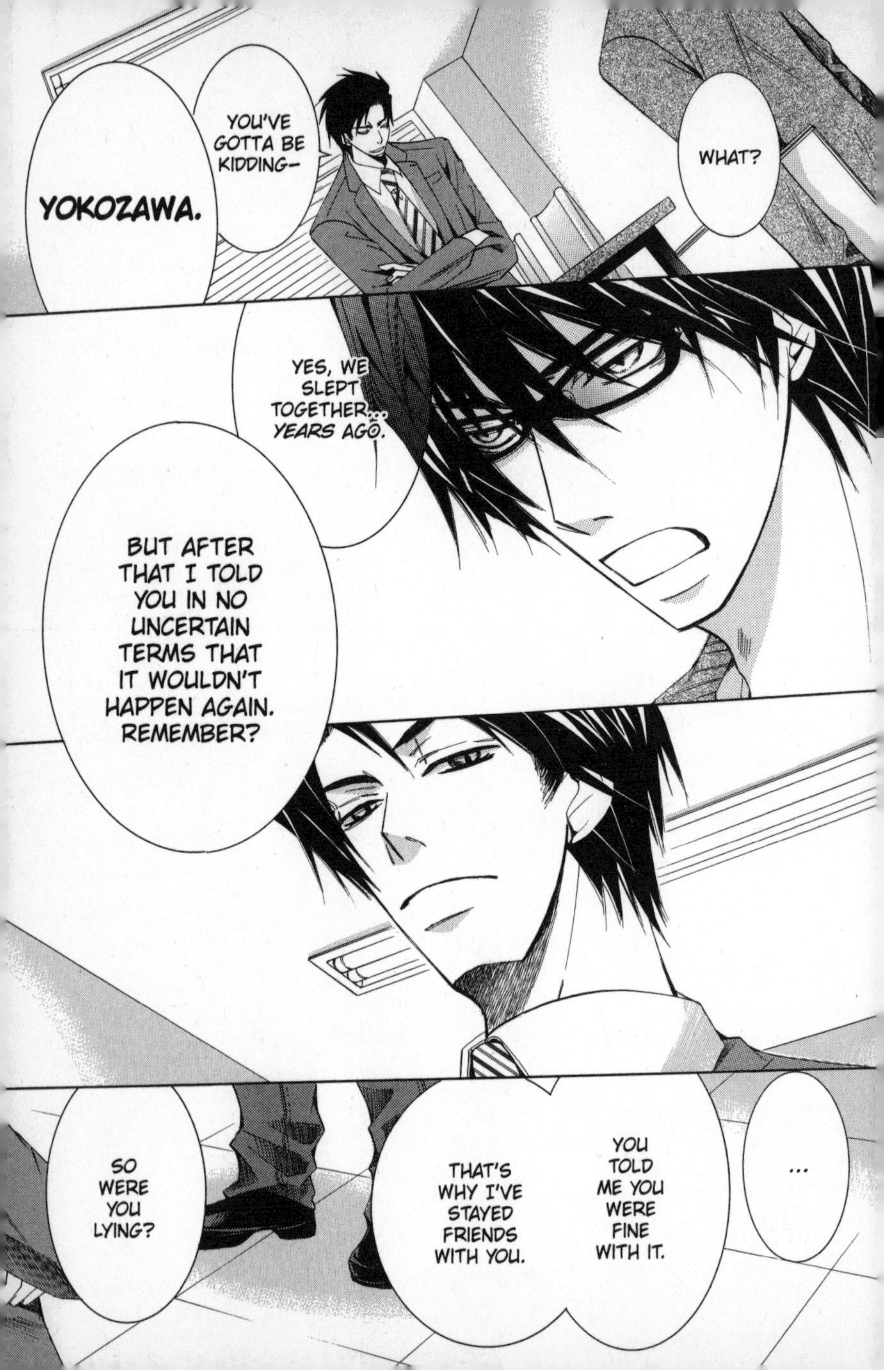
WHAT?
YOU'VE GOTTA BE KIDDING–
YOKOZAWA.
YES, WE SLEPT TOGETHER... *YEARS AGO.*
BUT AFTER THAT I TOLD YOU IN NO UNCERTAIN TERMS THAT IT WOULDN'T HAPPEN AGAIN. REMEMBER?
...
YOU TOLD ME YOU WERE FINE WITH IT.
THAT'S WHY I'VE STAYED FRIENDS WITH YOU.
SO WERE YOU LYING?

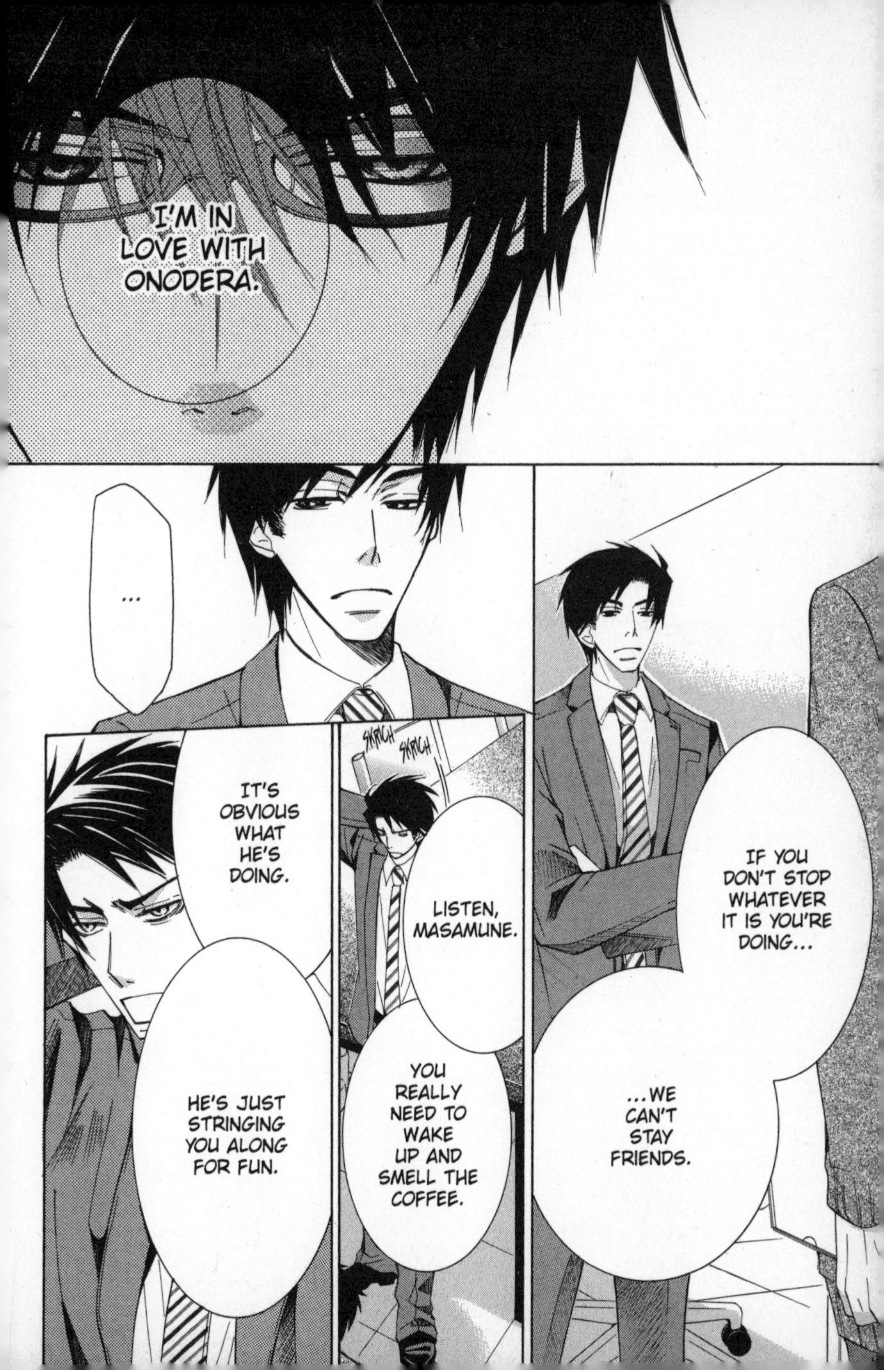
I'M IN LOVE WITH ONODERA.
IF YOU DON'T STOP WHATEVER IT IS YOU'RE DOING...
...WE CAN'T STAY FRIENDS.
...
SKRICH
SKRICH
LISTEN, MASAMUNE.
YOU REALLY NEED TO WAKE UP AND SMELL THE COFFEE.
IT'S OBVIOUS WHAT HE'S DOING.
HE'S JUST STRINGING YOU ALONG FOR FUN.

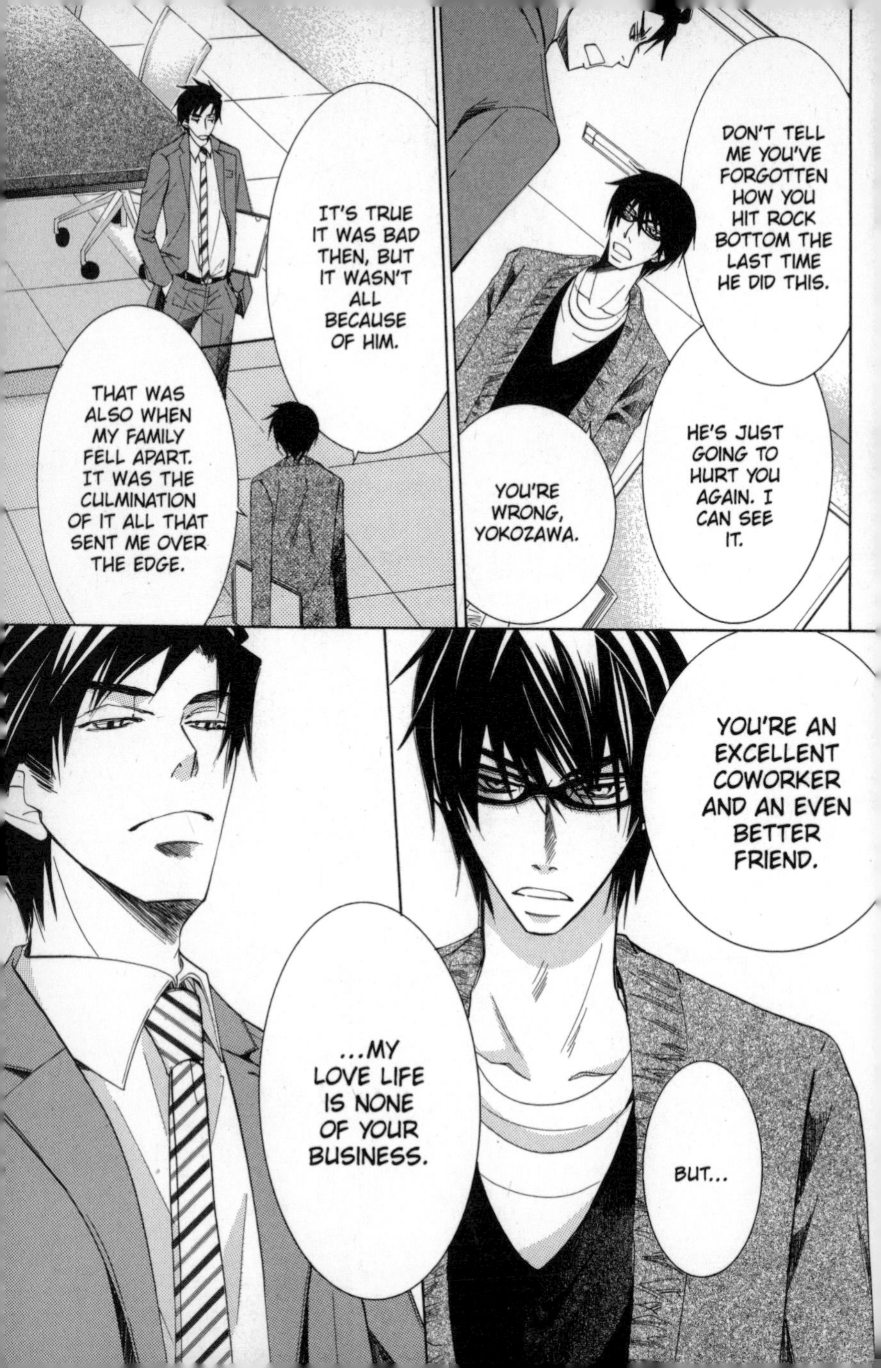
DON'T TELL ME YOU'VE FORGOTTEN HOW YOU HIT ROCK BOTTOM THE LAST TIME HE DID THIS.
HE'S JUST GOING TO HURT YOU AGAIN. I CAN SEE IT.
YOU'RE WRONG, YOKOZAWA.
IT'S TRUE IT WAS BAD THEN, BUT IT WASN'T ALL BECAUSE OF HIM.
THAT WAS ALSO WHEN MY FAMILY FELL APART. IT WAS THE CULMINATION OF IT ALL THAT SENT ME OVER THE EDGE.
YOU'RE AN EXCELLENT COWORKER AND AN EVEN BETTER FRIEND.
BUT...
...MY LOVE LIFE IS NONE OF YOUR BUSINESS.

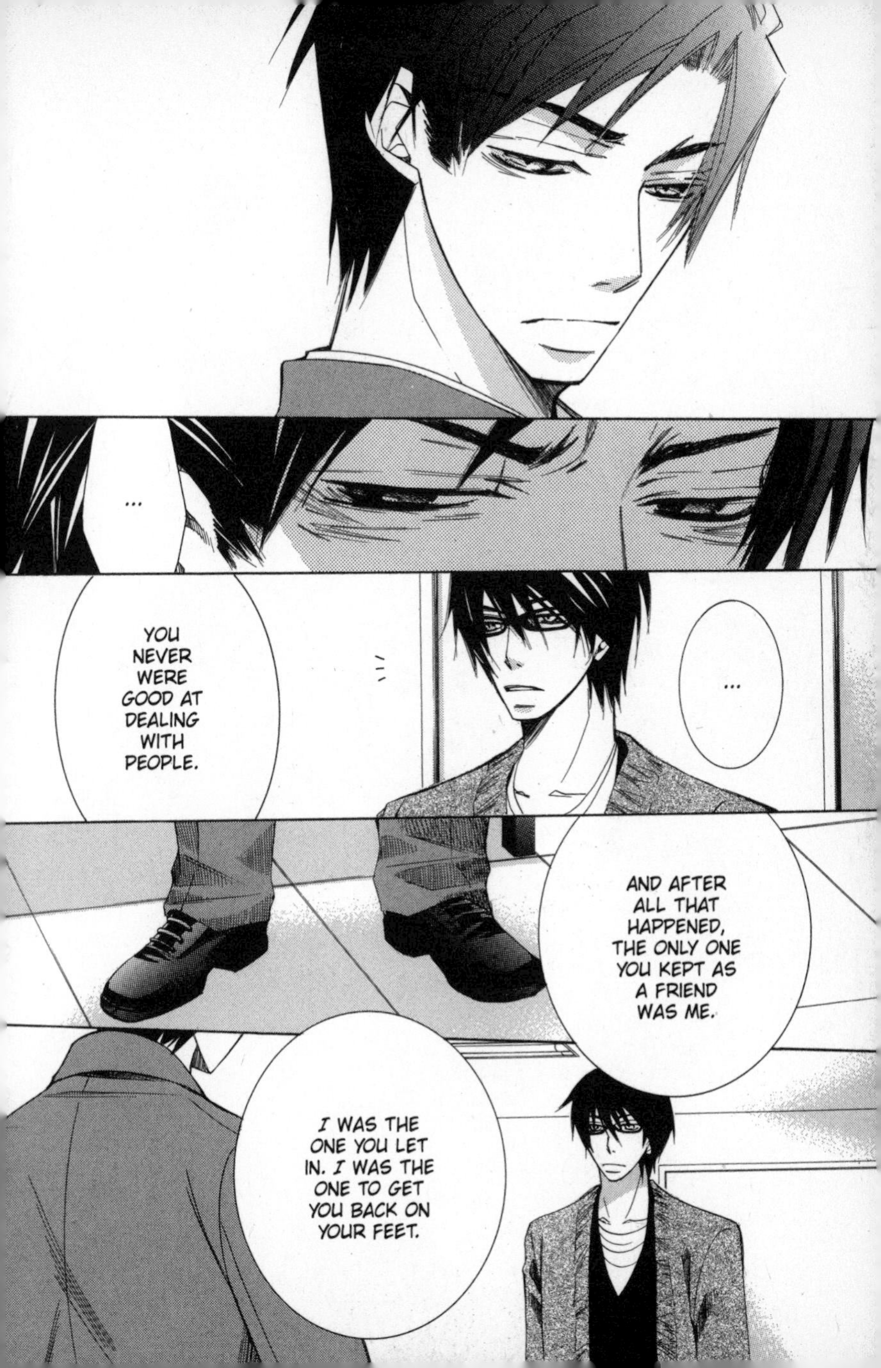
...
...
YOU NEVER WERE GOOD AT DEALING WITH PEOPLE.
AND AFTER ALL THAT HAPPENED, THE ONLY ONE YOU KEPT AS A FRIEND WAS ME.
I WAS THE ONE YOU LET IN. *I* WAS THE ONE TO GET YOU BACK ON YOUR FEET.

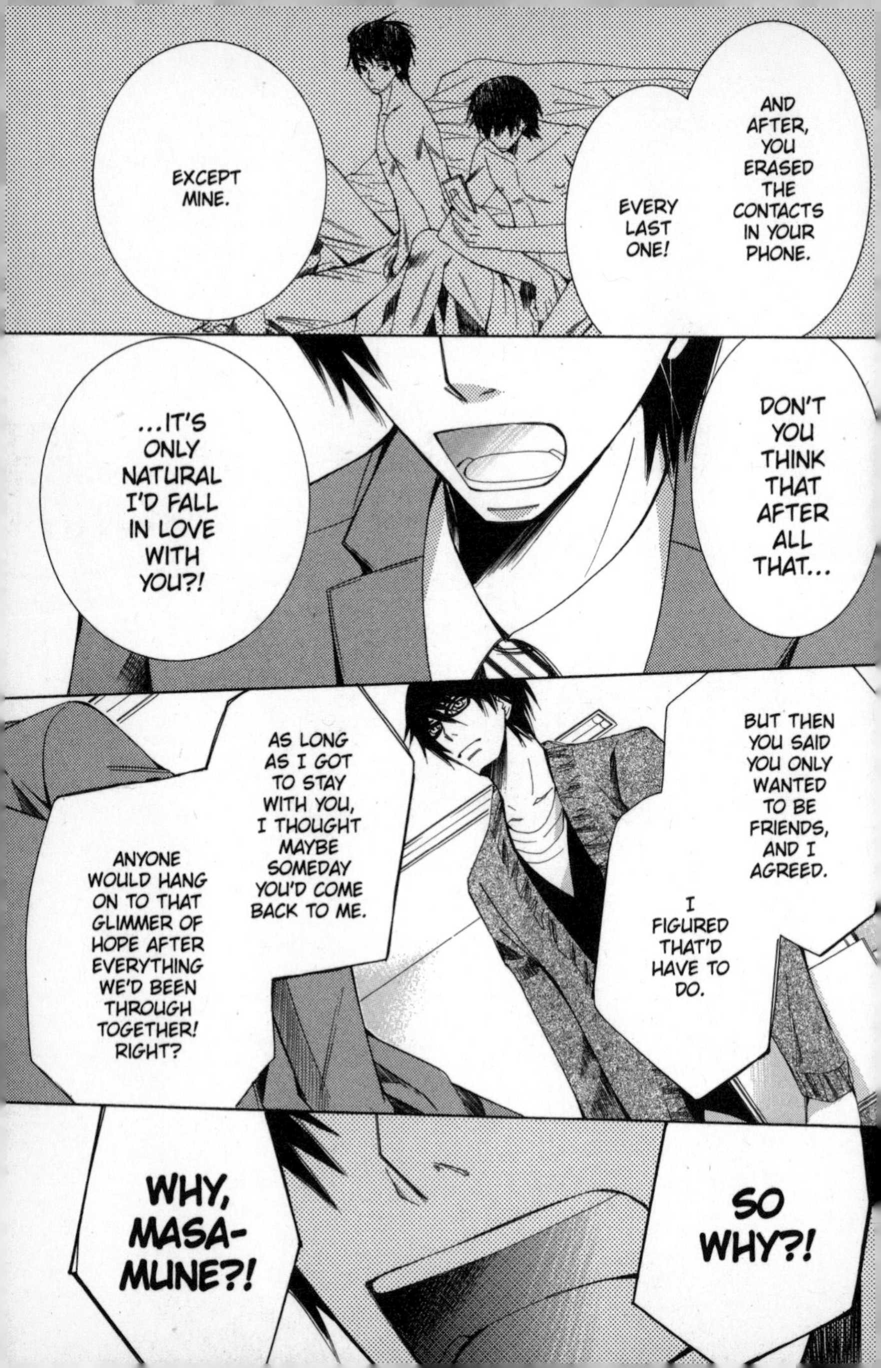
AND AFTER, YOU ERASED THE CONTACTS IN YOUR PHONE.
EVERY LAST ONE!
EXCEPT MINE.
DON'T YOU THINK THAT AFTER ALL THAT...
...IT'S ONLY NATURAL I'D FALL IN LOVE WITH YOU?!
BUT THEN YOU SAID YOU ONLY WANTED TO BE FRIENDS, AND I AGREED.
I FIGURED THAT'D HAVE TO DO.
AS LONG AS I GOT TO STAY WITH YOU, I THOUGHT MAYBE SOMEDAY YOU'D COME BACK TO ME.
ANYONE WOULD HANG ON TO THAT GLIMMER OF HOPE AFTER EVERYTHING WE'D BEEN THROUGH TOGETHER! RIGHT?
SO WHY?!
WHY, MASA-MUNE?!

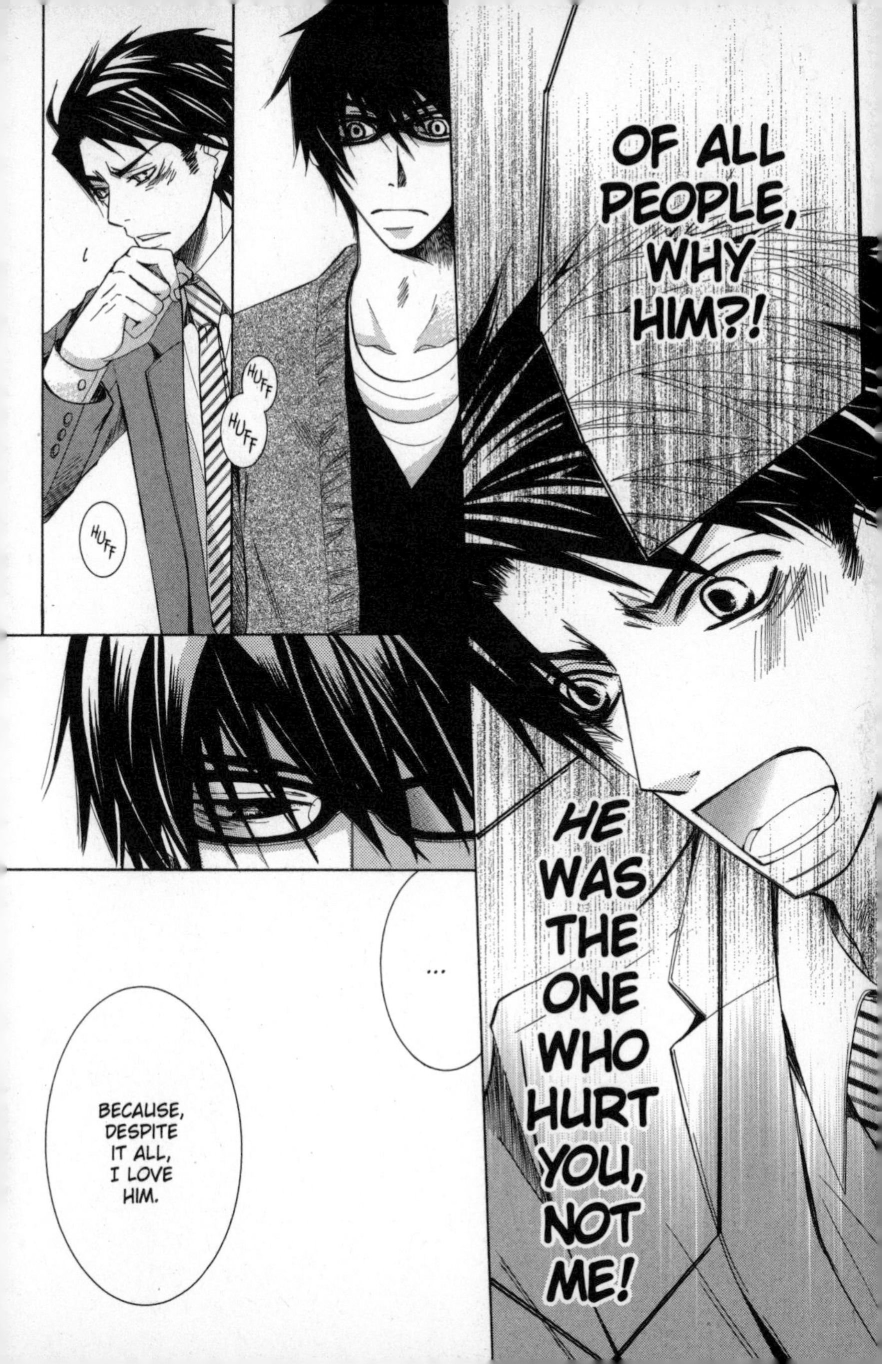
OF ALL PEOPLE, WHY HIM?!
HE WAS THE ONE WHO HURT YOU, NOT ME!
HUFF
HUFF
HUFF
...
BECAUSE, DESPITE IT ALL, I LOVE HIM.

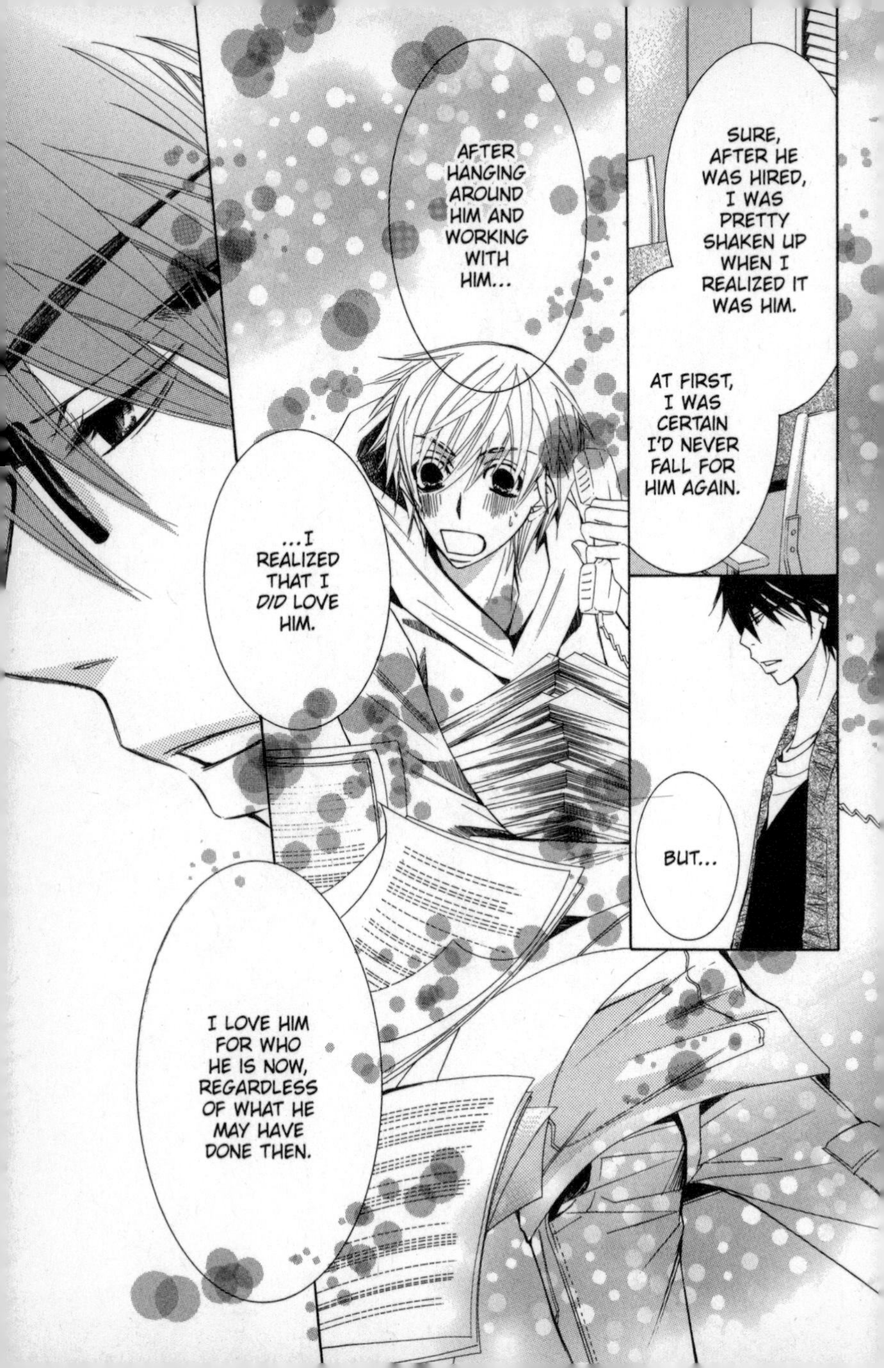
SURE, AFTER HE WAS HIRED, I WAS PRETTY SHAKEN UP WHEN I REALIZED IT WAS HIM.
AT FIRST, I WAS CERTAIN I'D NEVER FALL FOR HIM AGAIN.
BUT...
AFTER HANGING AROUND HIM AND WORKING WITH HIM...
...I REALIZED THAT I *DID* LOVE HIM.
I LOVE HIM FOR WHO HE IS NOW, REGARDLESS OF WHAT HE MAY HAVE DONE THEN.

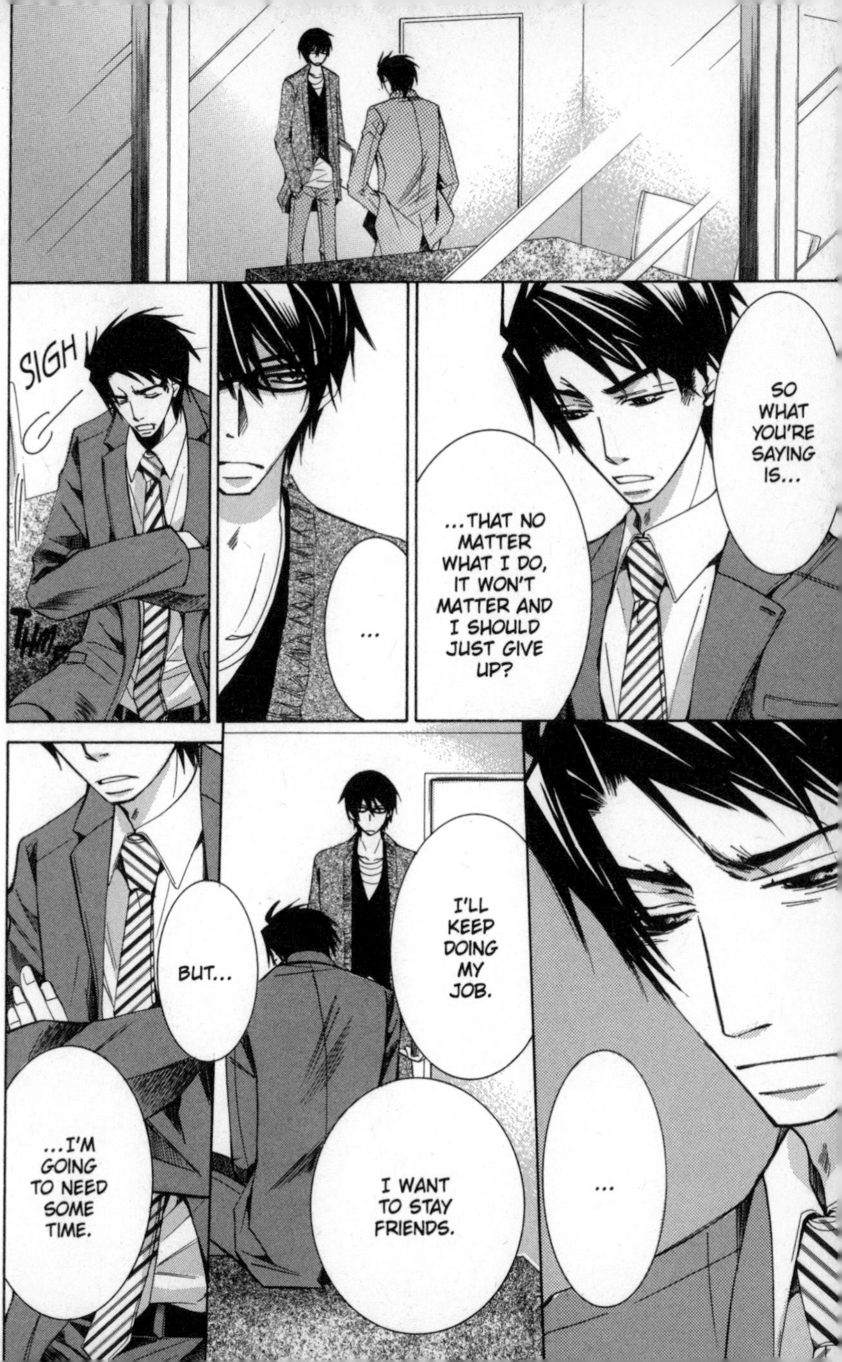
SO WHAT YOU'RE SAYING IS...
...THAT NO MATTER WHAT I DO, IT WON'T MATTER AND I SHOULD JUST GIVE UP?
...
SIGH
THM
...
I'LL KEEP DOING MY JOB.
I WANT TO STAY FRIENDS.
BUT...
...I'M GOING TO NEED SOME TIME.

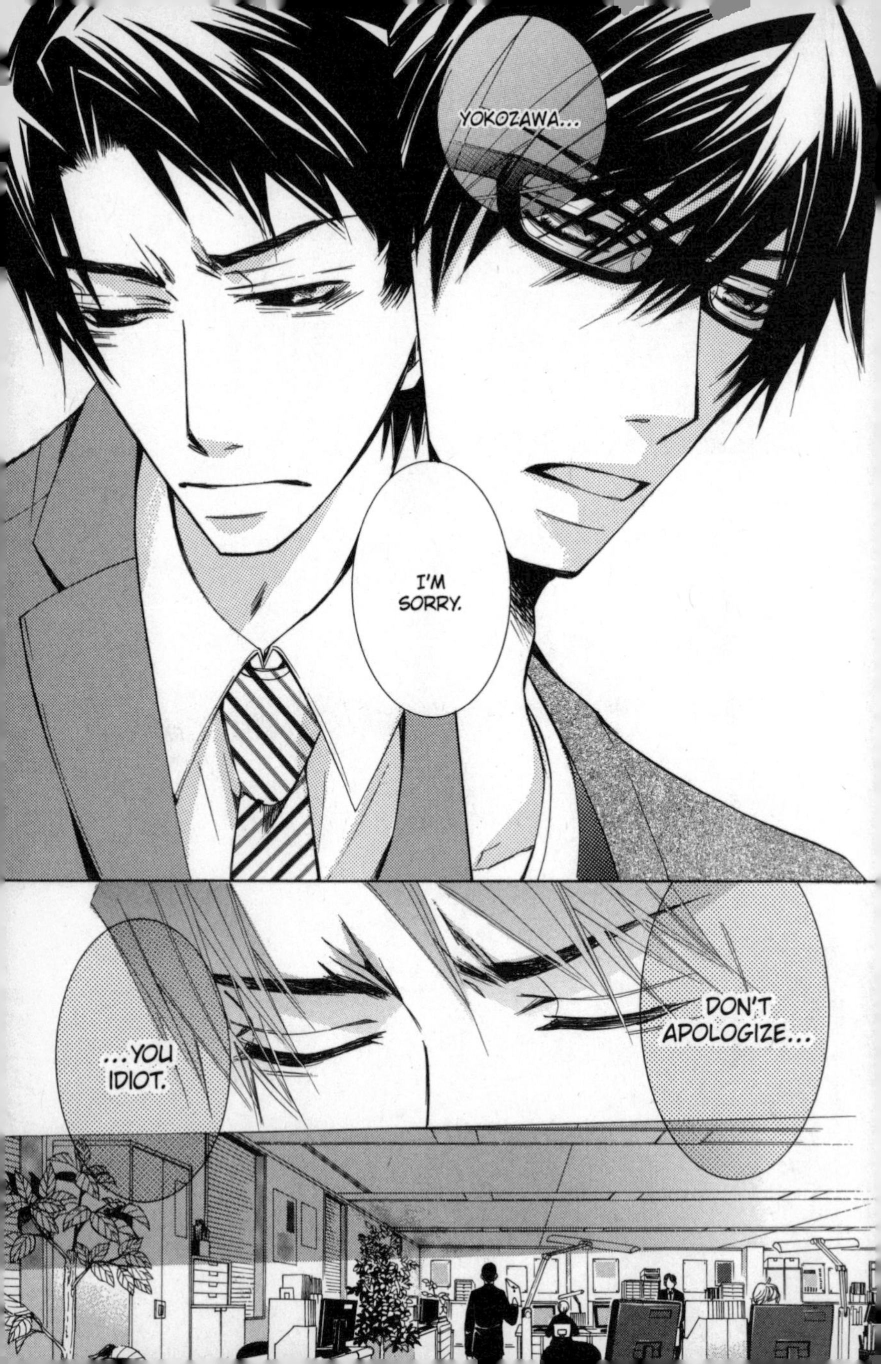
YOKOZAWA...
I'M SORRY.
DON'T APOLOGIZE...
...YOU IDIOT.

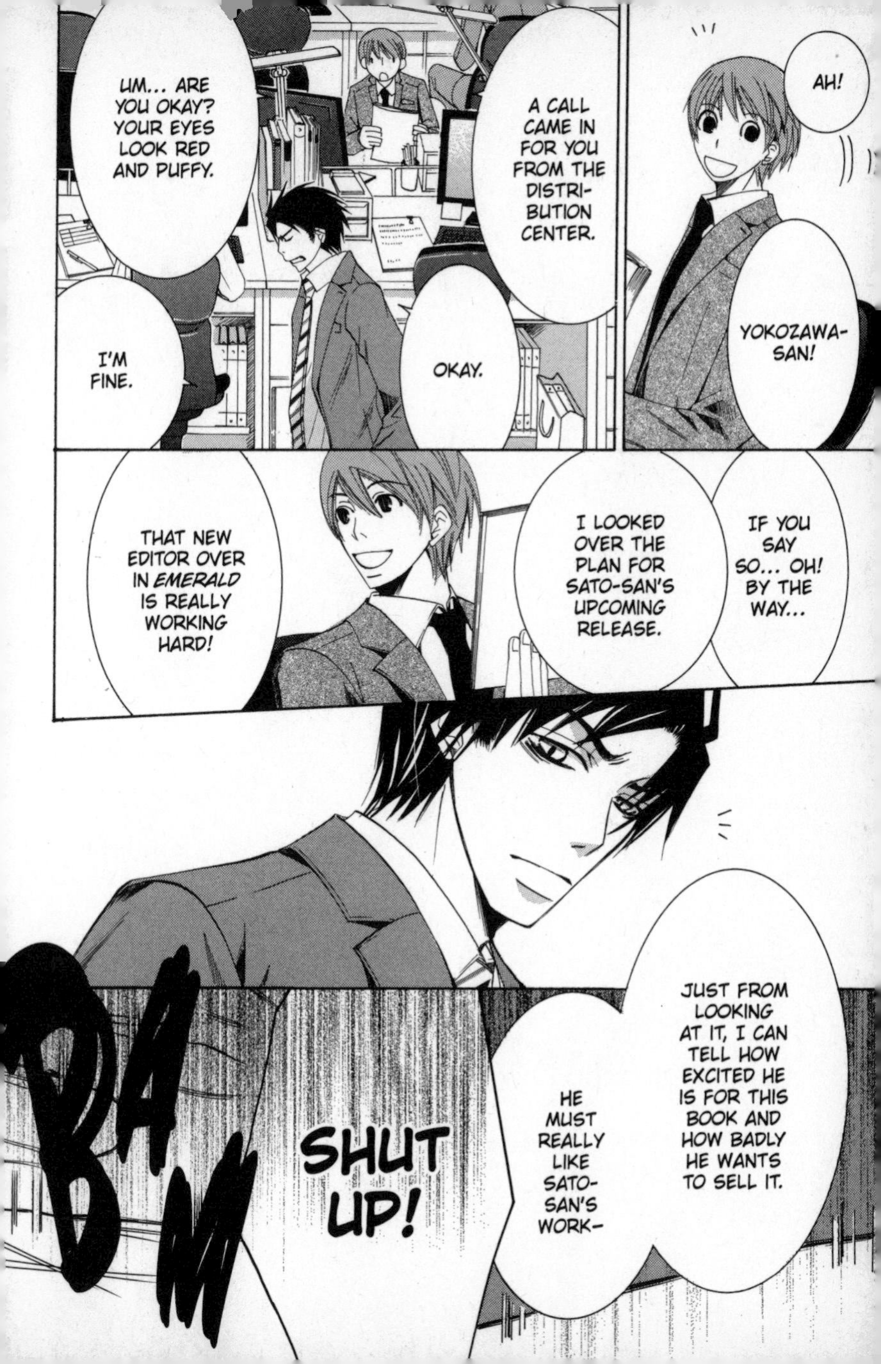
AH!
YOKOZAWA-SAN!
A CALL CAME IN FOR YOU FROM THE DISTRIBUTION CENTER.
UM... ARE YOU OKAY? YOUR EYES LOOK RED AND PUFFY.
OKAY.
I'M FINE.
IF YOU SAY SO... OH! BY THE WAY...
I LOOKED OVER THE PLAN FOR SATO-SAN'S UPCOMING RELEASE.
THAT NEW EDITOR OVER IN *EMERALD* IS REALLY WORKING HARD!
JUST FROM LOOKING AT IT, I CAN TELL HOW EXCITED HE IS FOR THIS BOOK AND HOW BADLY HE WANTS TO SELL IT.
HE MUST REALLY LIKE SATO-SAN'S WORK-
SHUT UP!
BAM

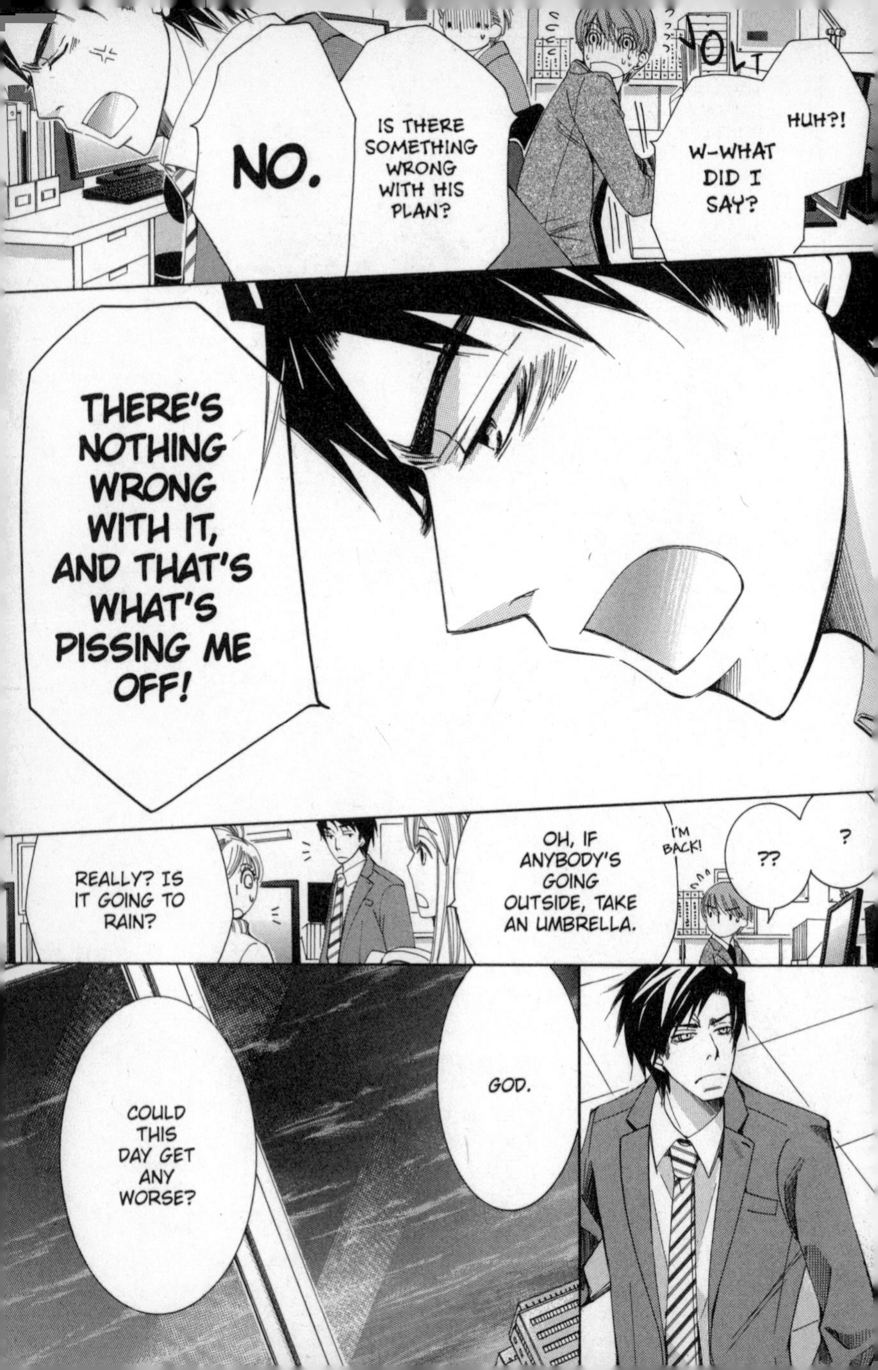
IS THERE SOMETHING WRONG WITH HIS PLAN?
NO.
JOLT
HUH?!
W-WHAT DID I SAY?
THERE'S NOTHING WRONG WITH IT, AND THAT'S WHAT'S PISSING ME OFF!
?
??
I'M BACK!
OH, IF ANYBODY'S GOING OUTSIDE, TAKE AN UMBRELLA.
REALLY? IS IT GOING TO RAIN?
GOD.
COULD THIS DAY GET ANY WORSE?

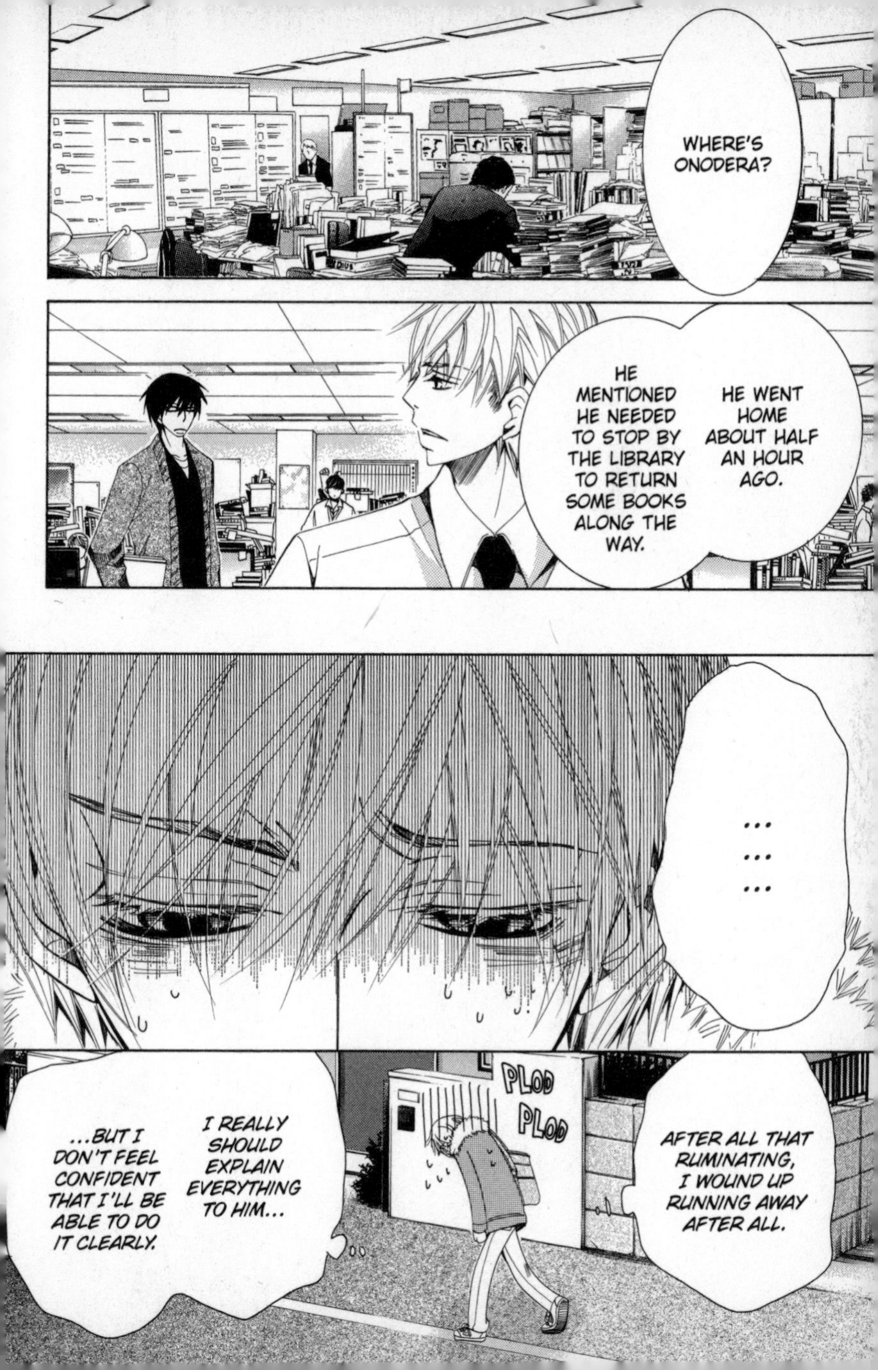
WHERE'S ONODERA?
HE WENT HOME ABOUT HALF AN HOUR AGO.
HE MENTIONED HE NEEDED TO STOP BY THE LIBRARY TO RETURN SOME BOOKS ALONG THE WAY.
... ...
AFTER ALL THAT RUMINATING, I WOUND UP RUNNING AWAY AFTER ALL.
PLOD PLOD
I REALLY SHOULD EXPLAIN EVERYTHING TO HIM...
...BUT I DON'T FEEL CONFIDENT THAT I'LL BE ABLE TO DO IT CLEARLY.

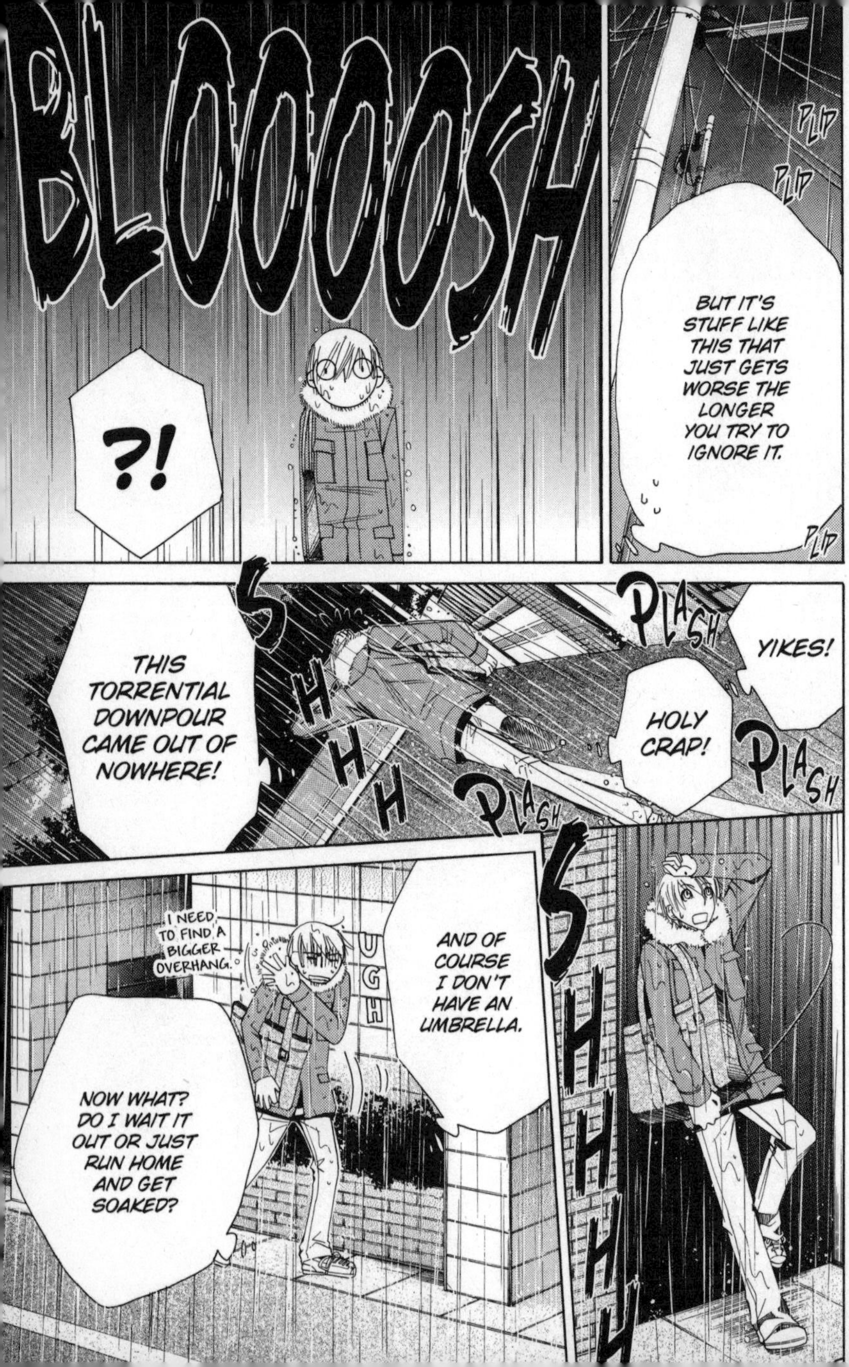
PLIP
PLIP
BUT IT'S STUFF LIKE THIS THAT JUST GETS WORSE THE LONGER YOU TRY TO IGNORE IT.
PLIP
BLOOOOSH
?!
PLASH
YIKES!
HOLY CRAP!
PLASH
PLASH
SHHH
THIS TORRENTIAL DOWNPOUR CAME OUT OF NOWHERE!
SHHHH
AND OF COURSE I DON'T HAVE AN UMBRELLA.
UGH
I NEED TO FIND A BIGGER OVERHANG.
NOW WHAT? DO I WAIT IT OUT OR JUST RUN HOME AND GET SOAKED?

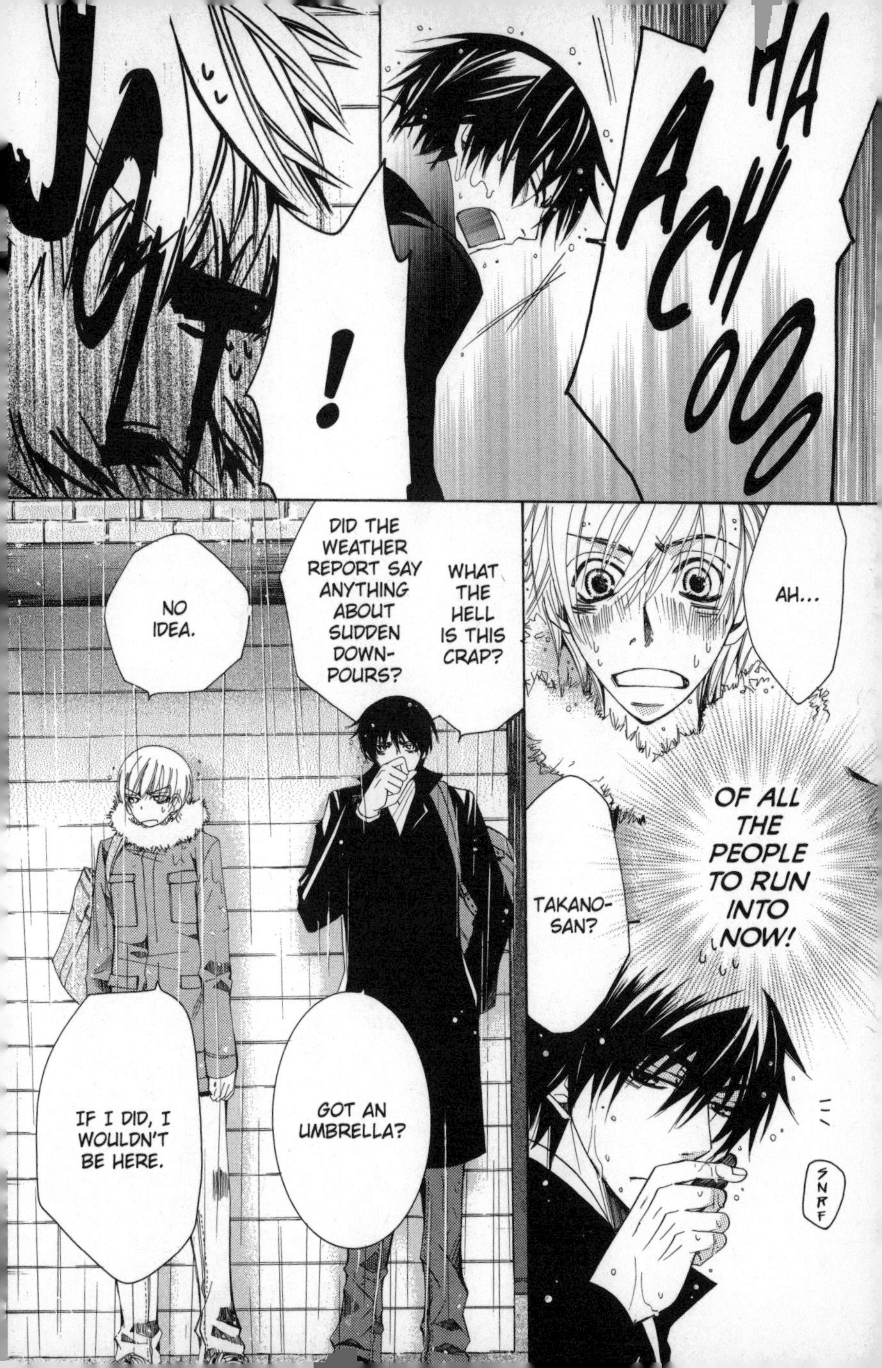
HA ACH OOOO
!
JOLT
AH...
OF ALL THE PEOPLE TO RUN INTO NOW!
TAKANO-SAN?
SNRF
WHAT THE HELL IS THIS CRAP?
DID THE WEATHER REPORT SAY ANYTHING ABOUT SUDDEN DOWN-POURS?
NO IDEA.
GOT AN UMBRELLA?
IF I DID, I WOULDN'T BE HERE.

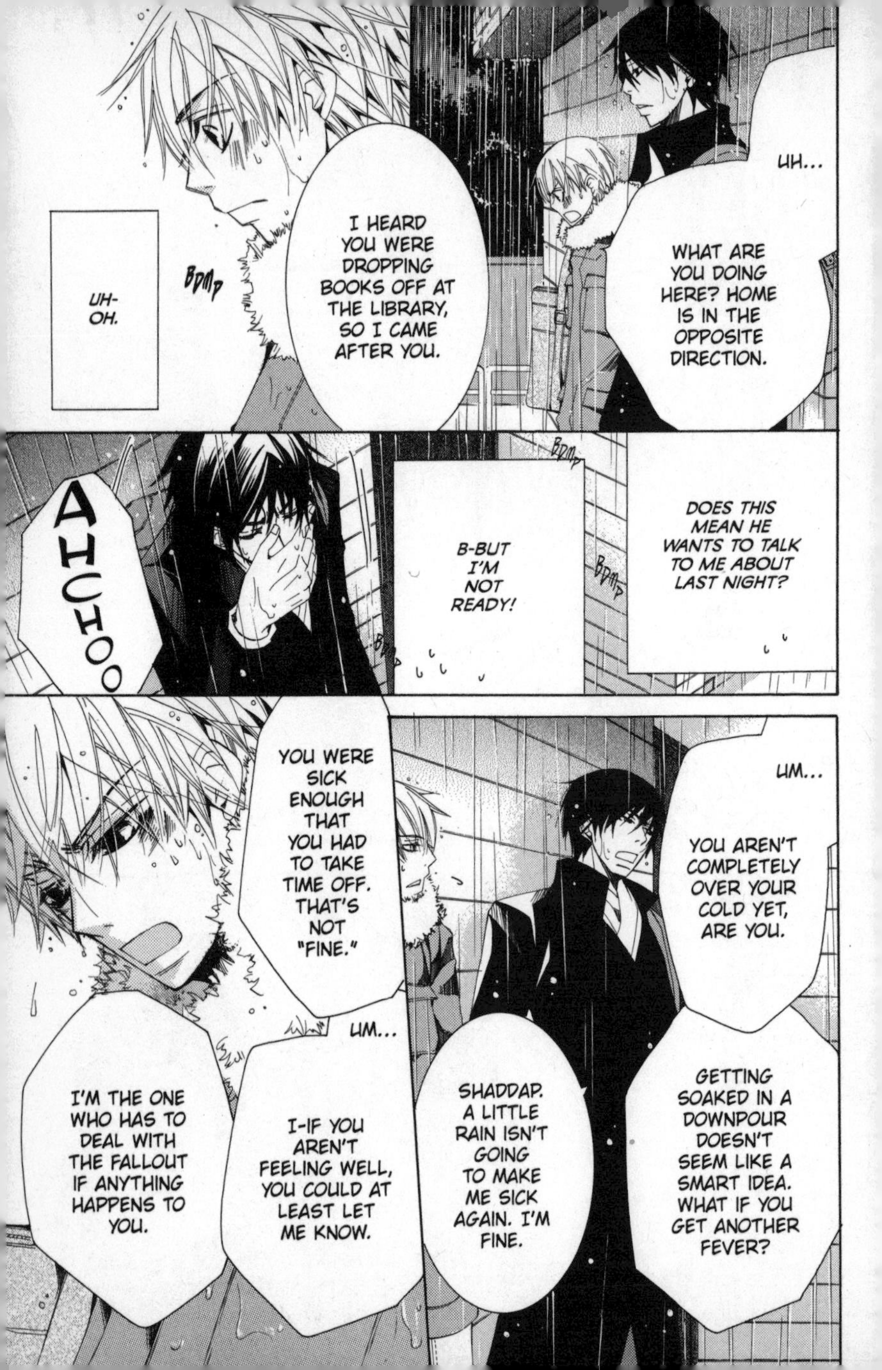
UH...
WHAT ARE YOU DOING HERE? HOME IS IN THE OPPOSITE DIRECTION.
I HEARD YOU WERE DROPPING BOOKS OFF AT THE LIBRARY, SO I CAME AFTER YOU.
BDMP
UH-OH.
DOES THIS MEAN HE WANTS TO TALK TO ME ABOUT LAST NIGHT?
BDMP
B-BUT I'M NOT READY!
BDMP
AHCHOO
UM...
YOU AREN'T COMPLETELY OVER YOUR COLD YET, ARE YOU.
GETTING SOAKED IN A DOWNPOUR DOESN'T SEEM LIKE A SMART IDEA. WHAT IF YOU GET ANOTHER FEVER?
SHADDAP. A LITTLE RAIN ISN'T GOING TO MAKE ME SICK AGAIN. I'M FINE.
YOU WERE SICK ENOUGH THAT YOU HAD TO TAKE TIME OFF. THAT'S NOT "FINE."
UM...
I-IF YOU AREN'T FEELING WELL, YOU COULD AT LEAST LET ME KNOW.
I'M THE ONE WHO HAS TO DEAL WITH THE FALLOUT IF ANYTHING HAPPENS TO YOU.

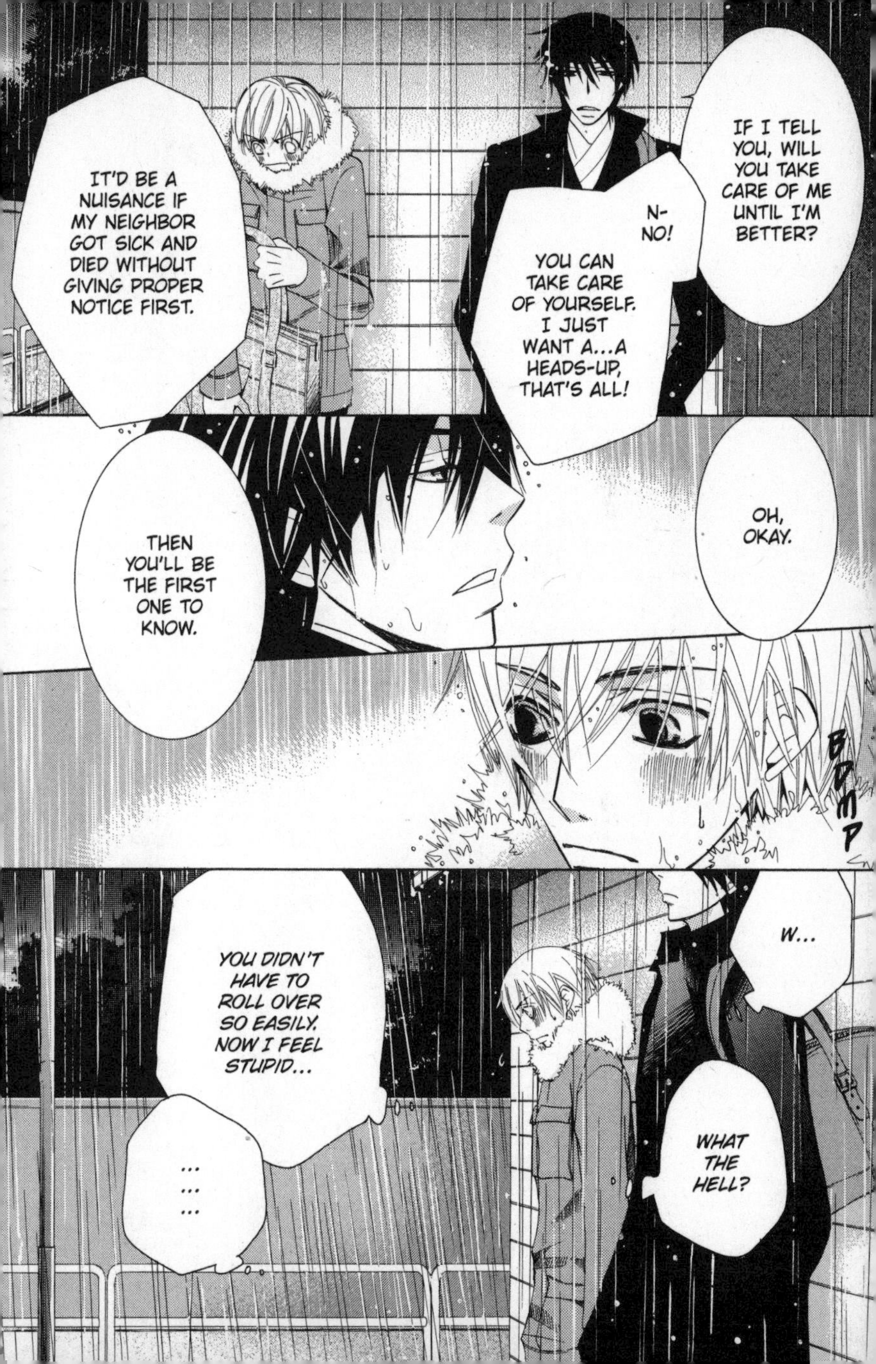
IF I TELL YOU, WILL YOU TAKE CARE OF ME UNTIL I'M BETTER?
N-NO!
YOU CAN TAKE CARE OF YOURSELF. I JUST WANT A...A HEADS-UP, THAT'S ALL!
IT'D BE A NUISANCE IF MY NEIGHBOR GOT SICK AND DIED WITHOUT GIVING PROPER NOTICE FIRST.
OH, OKAY.
THEN YOU'LL BE THE FIRST ONE TO KNOW.
BDMP
W...
WHAT THE HELL?
YOU DIDN'T HAVE TO ROLL OVER SO EASILY. NOW I FEEL STUPID...
...
...
...

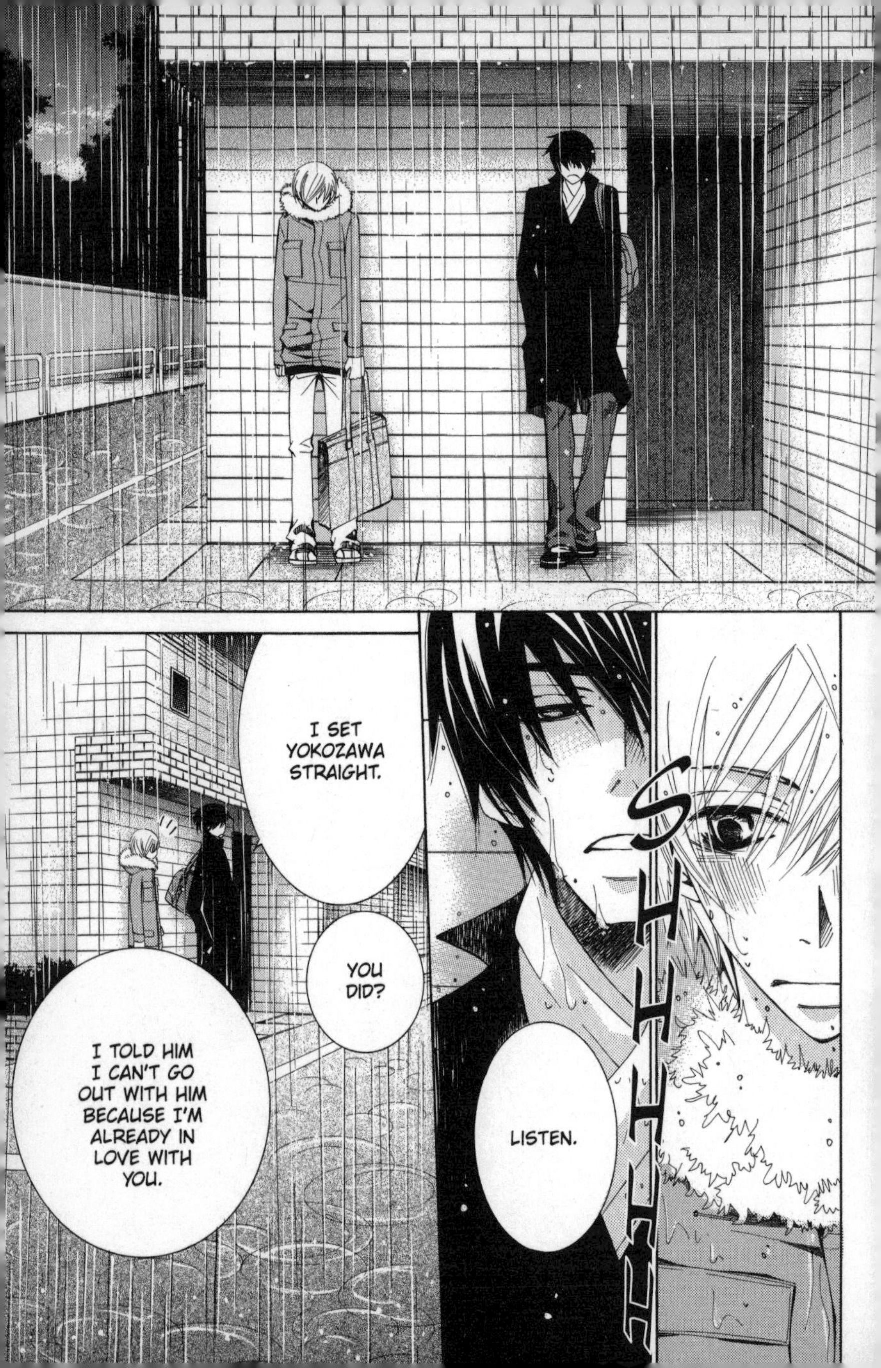
SHHHHH
LISTEN.
I SET YOKOZAWA STRAIGHT.
YOU DID?
I TOLD HIM I CAN'T GO OUT WITH HIM BECAUSE I'M ALREADY IN LOVE WITH YOU.

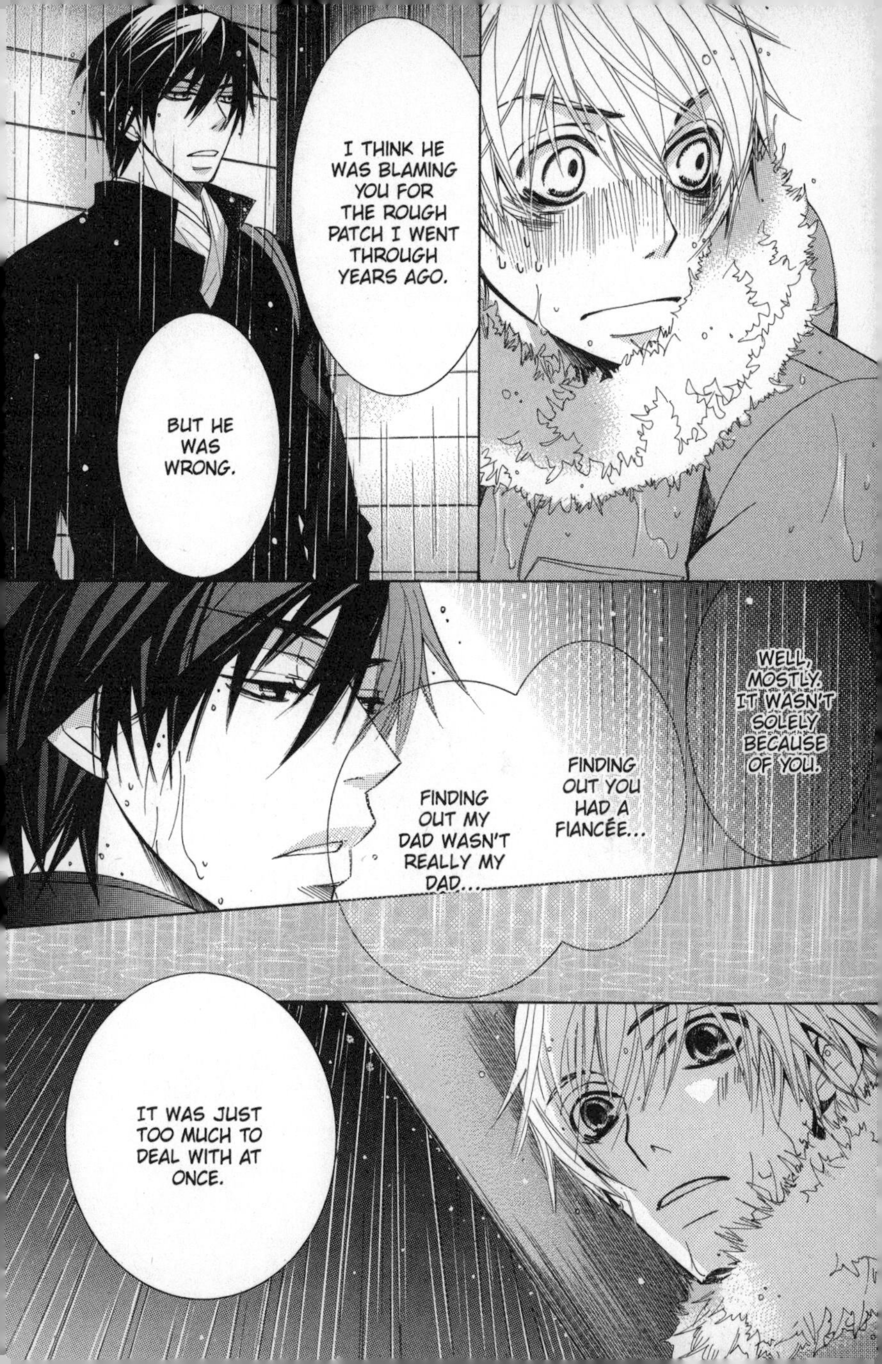
I THINK HE WAS BLAMING YOU FOR THE ROUGH PATCH I WENT THROUGH YEARS AGO.
BUT HE WAS WRONG.
WELL, MOSTLY. IT WASN'T SOLELY BECAUSE OF YOU.
FINDING OUT YOU HAD A FIANCÉE...
FINDING OUT MY DAD WASN'T REALLY MY DAD...
IT WAS JUST TOO MUCH TO DEAL WITH AT ONCE.

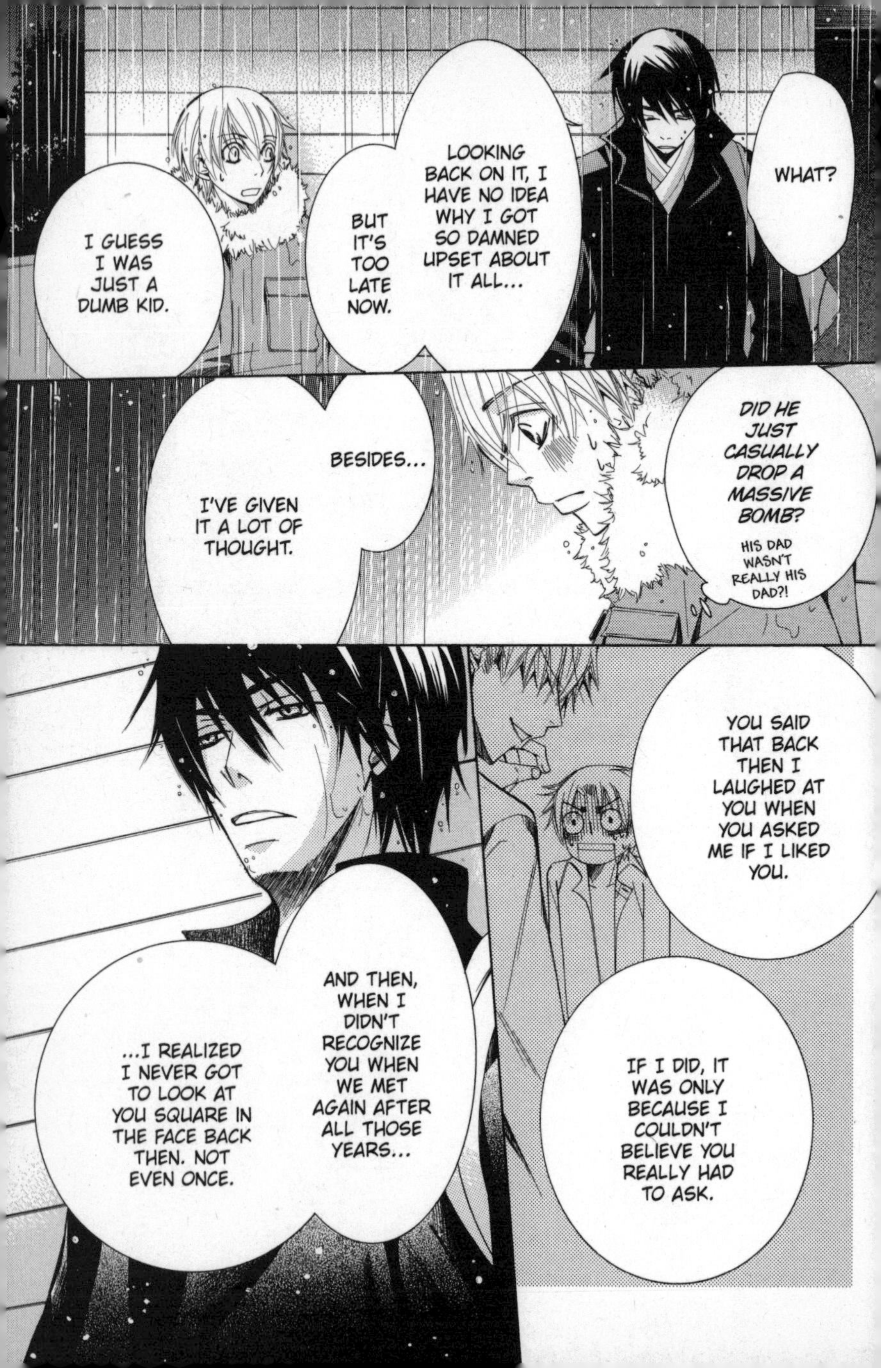
WHAT?
LOOKING BACK ON IT, I HAVE NO IDEA WHY I GOT SO DAMNED UPSET ABOUT IT ALL...
BUT IT'S TOO LATE NOW.
I GUESS I WAS JUST A DUMB KID.
DID HE JUST CASUALLY DROP A MASSIVE BOMB?
HIS DAD WASN'T REALLY HIS DAD?!
BESIDES...
I'VE GIVEN IT A LOT OF THOUGHT.
YOU SAID THAT BACK THEN I LAUGHED AT YOU WHEN YOU ASKED ME IF I LIKED YOU.
IF I DID, IT WAS ONLY BECAUSE I COULDN'T BELIEVE YOU REALLY HAD TO ASK.
AND THEN, WHEN I DIDN'T RECOGNIZE YOU WHEN WE MET AGAIN AFTER ALL THOSE YEARS...
...I REALIZED I NEVER GOT TO LOOK AT YOU SQUARE IN THE FACE BACK THEN. NOT EVEN ONCE.

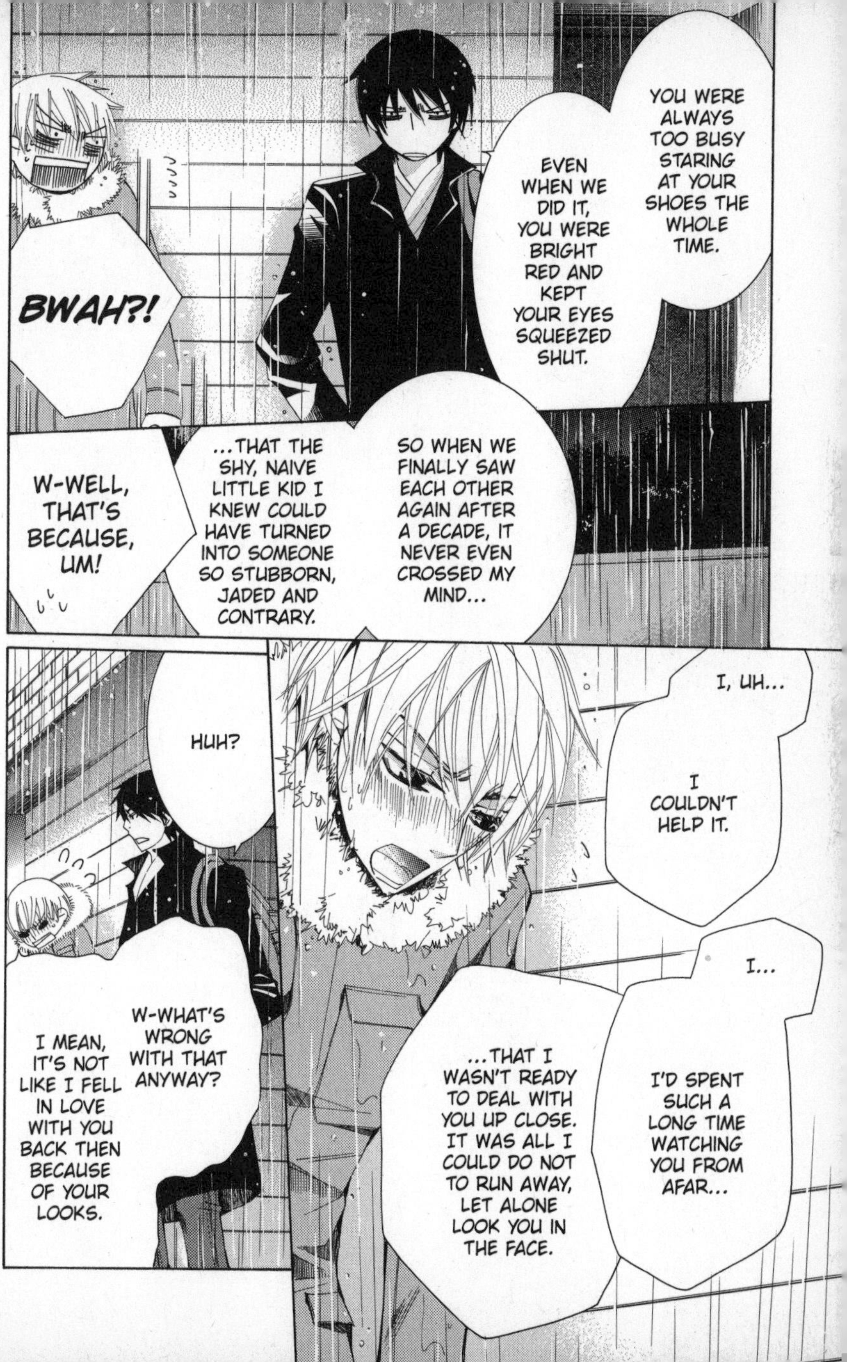
YOU WERE ALWAYS TOO BUSY STARING AT YOUR SHOES THE WHOLE TIME.
EVEN WHEN WE DID IT, YOU WERE BRIGHT RED AND KEPT YOUR EYES SQUEEZED SHUT.
BWAH?!
SO WHEN WE FINALLY SAW EACH OTHER AGAIN AFTER A DECADE, IT NEVER EVEN CROSSED MY MIND...
...THAT THE SHY, NAIVE LITTLE KID I KNEW COULD HAVE TURNED INTO SOMEONE SO STUBBORN, JADED AND CONTRARY.
W-WELL, THAT'S BECAUSE, UM!
I, UH...
I COULDN'T HELP IT.
I...
I'D SPENT SUCH A LONG TIME WATCHING YOU FROM AFAR...
...THAT I WASN'T READY TO DEAL WITH YOU UP CLOSE. IT WAS ALL I COULD DO NOT TO RUN AWAY, LET ALONE LOOK YOU IN THE FACE.
HUH?
W-WHAT'S WRONG WITH THAT ANYWAY?
I MEAN, IT'S NOT LIKE I FELL IN LOVE WITH YOU BACK THEN BECAUSE OF YOUR LOOKS.

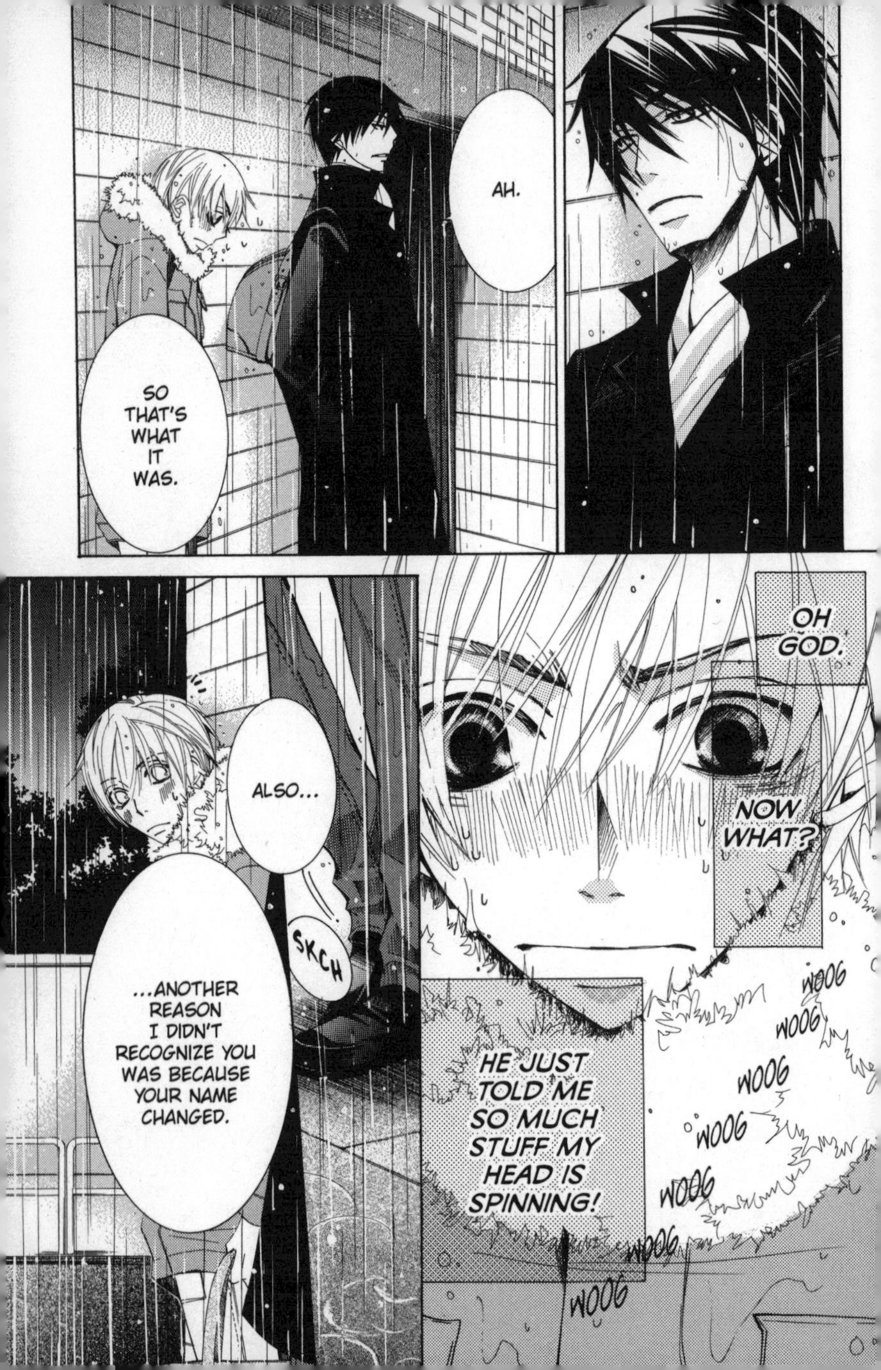
AH.
SO THAT'S WHAT IT WAS.
OH GOD.
NOW WHAT?
HE JUST TOLD ME SO MUCH STUFF MY HEAD IS SPINNING!
WOOG WOOG WOOG WOOG WOOG WOOG WOOG
ALSO...
SKCH
...ANOTHER REASON I DIDN'T RECOGNIZE YOU WAS BECAUSE YOUR NAME CHANGED.

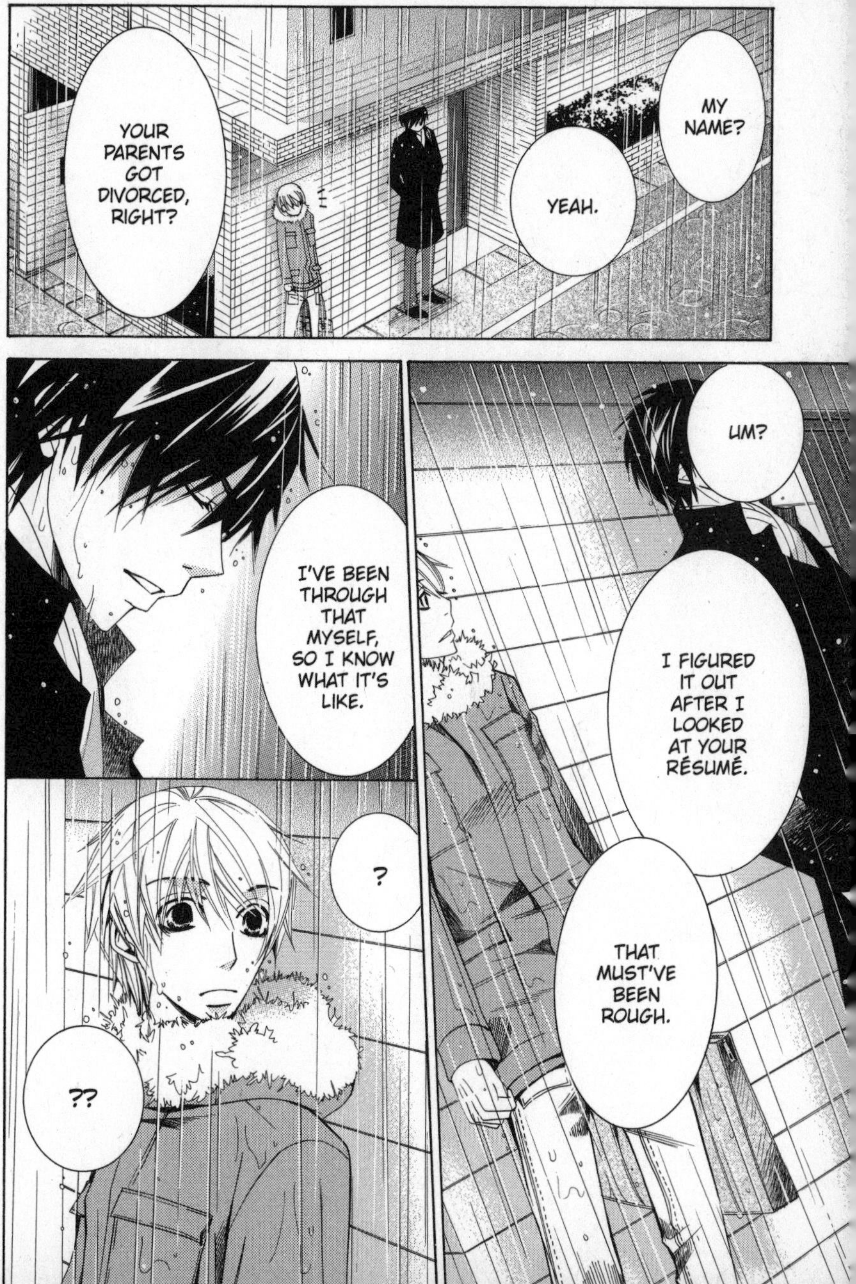
MY NAME?
YEAH.
YOUR PARENTS GOT DIVORCED, RIGHT?
UM?
I FIGURED IT OUT AFTER I LOOKED AT YOUR RÉSUMÉ.
THAT MUST'VE BEEN ROUGH.
I'VE BEEN THROUGH THAT MYSELF, SO I KNOW WHAT IT'S LIKE.
?
??

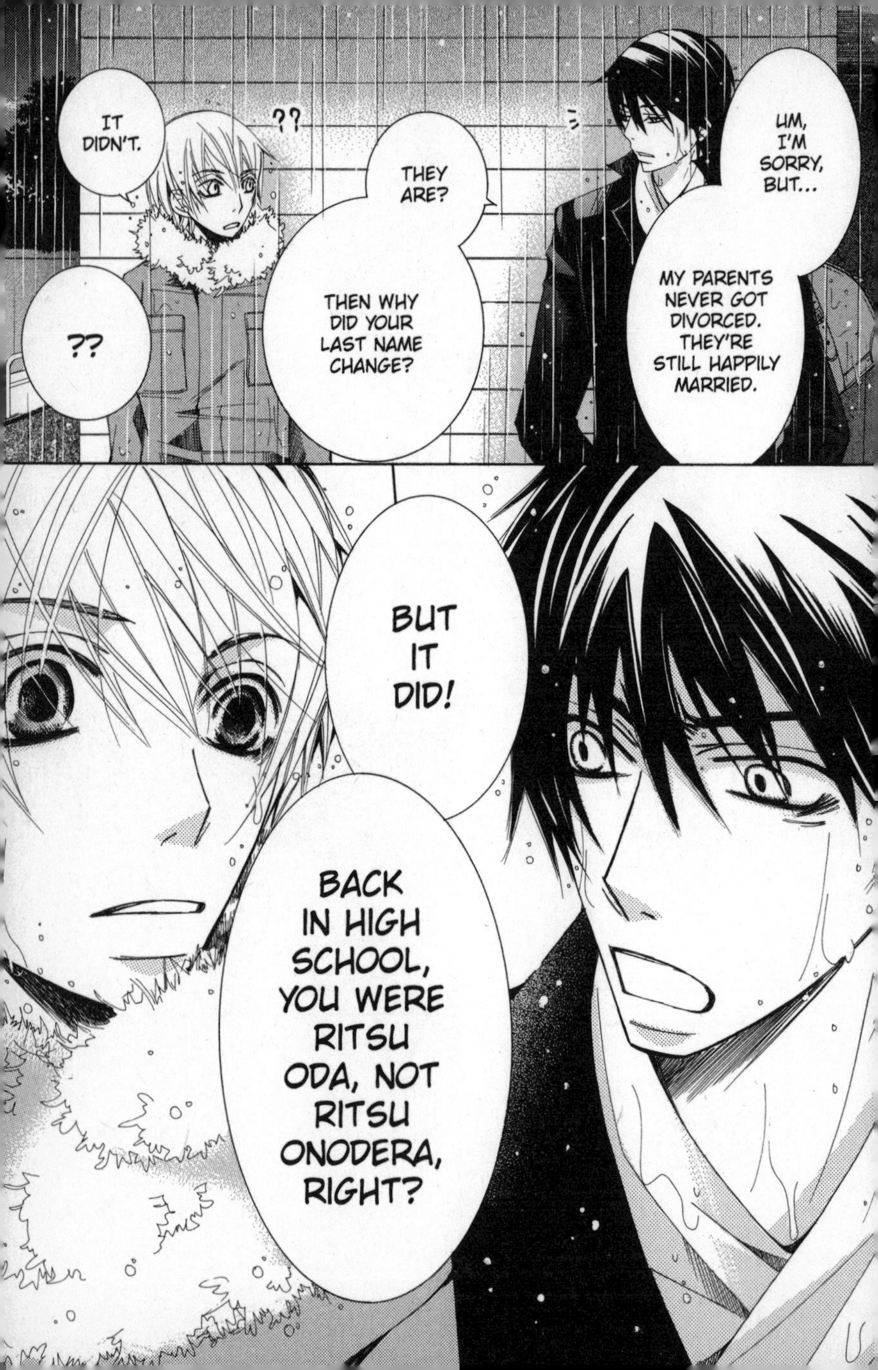
UM, I'M SORRY, BUT...
MY PARENTS NEVER GOT DIVORCED. THEY'RE STILL HAPPILY MARRIED.
??
THEY ARE?
THEN WHY DID YOUR LAST NAME CHANGE?
IT DIDN'T.
??
BUT IT DID!
BACK IN HIGH SCHOOL, YOU WERE RITSU ODA, NOT RITSU ONODERA, RIGHT?

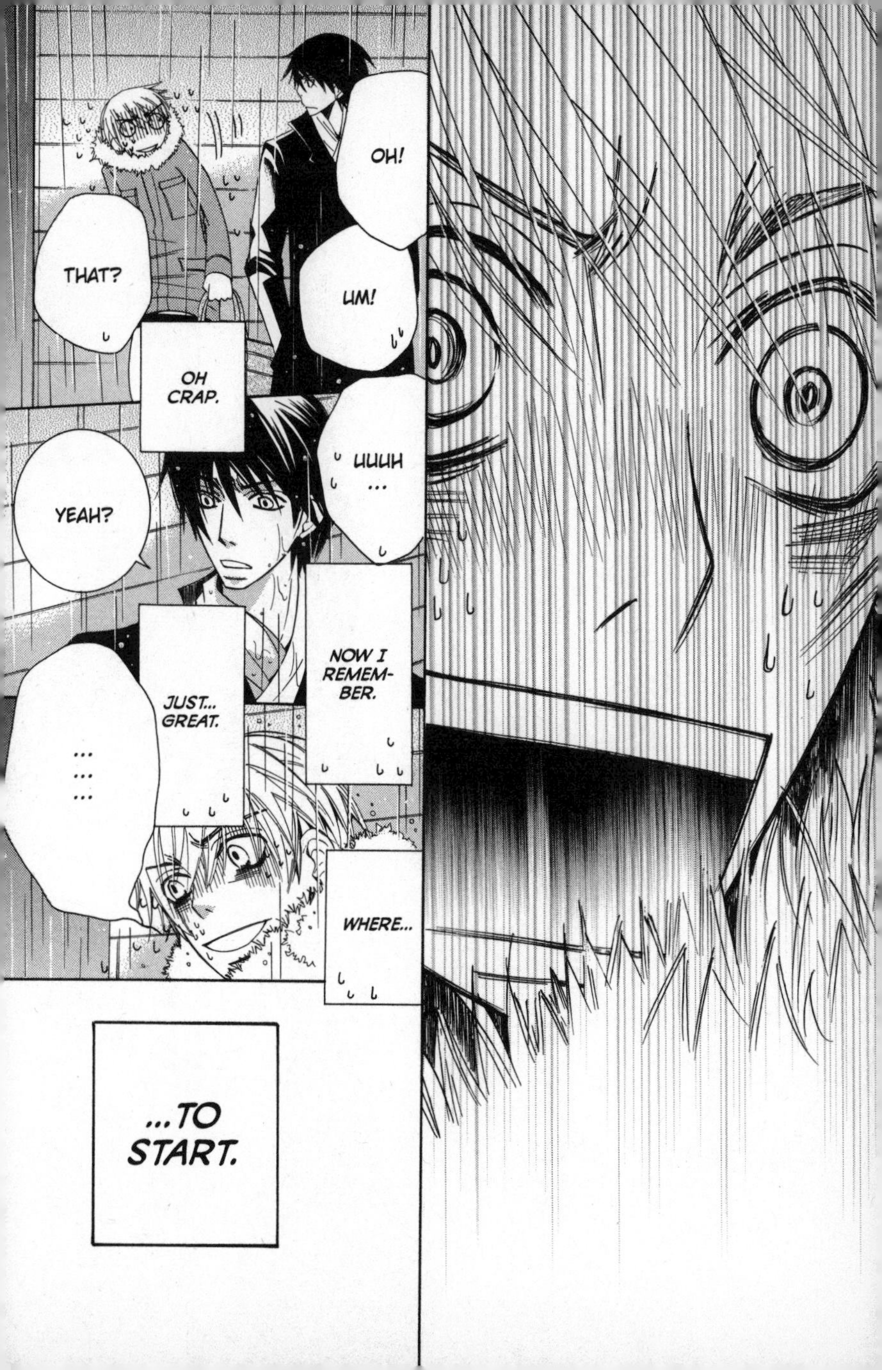
OH!
UM!
THAT?
OH CRAP.
UUUH ...
YEAH?
NOW I REMEMBER.
JUST... GREAT.
WHERE...
... ...
...TO START.

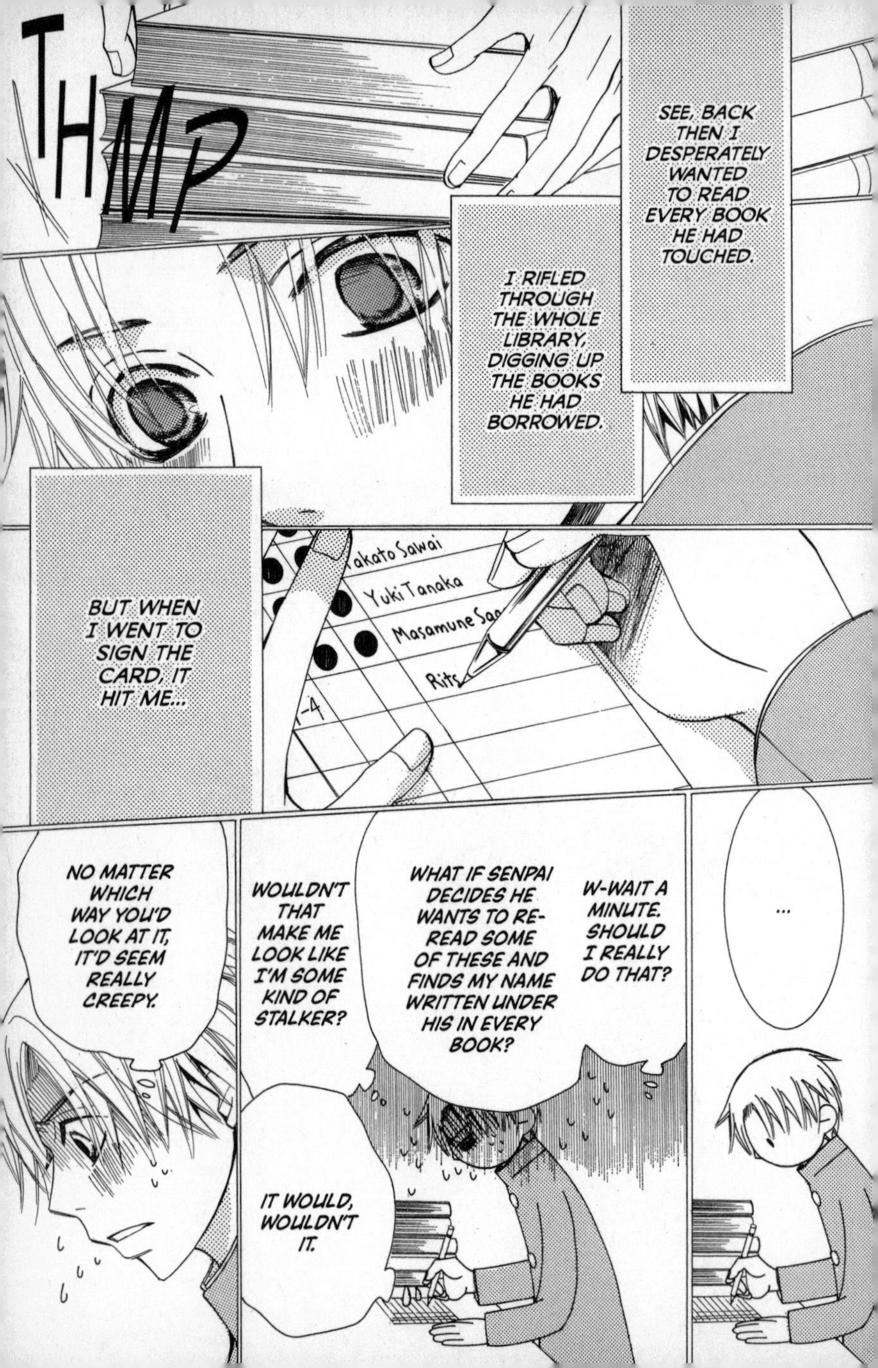
SEE, BACK THEN I DESPERATELY WANTED TO READ EVERY BOOK HE HAD TOUCHED.
THMP
I RIFLED THROUGH THE WHOLE LIBRARY, DIGGING UP THE BOOKS HE HAD BORROWED.
Yuki Tanaka
BUT WHEN I WENT TO SIGN THE CARD, IT HIT ME...
...
W-WAIT A MINUTE. SHOULD I REALLY DO THAT?
WHAT IF SENPAI DECIDES HE WANTS TO RE-READ SOME OF THESE AND FINDS MY NAME WRITTEN UNDER HIS IN EVERY BOOK?
WOULDN'T THAT MAKE ME LOOK LIKE I'M SOME KIND OF STALKER?
IT WOULD, WOULDN'T IT.
NO MATTER WHICH WAY YOU'D LOOK AT IT, IT'D SEEM REALLY CREEPY.

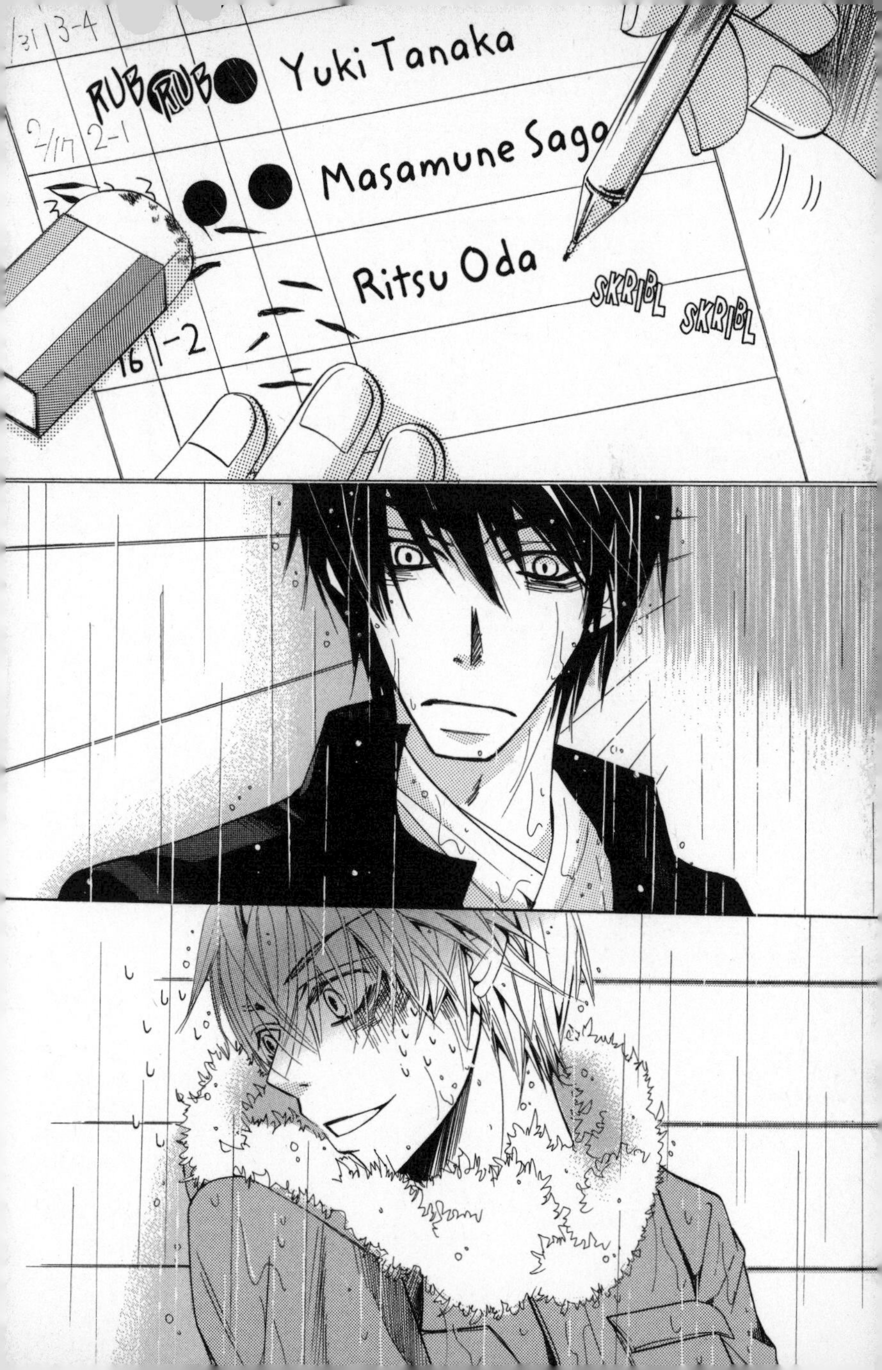
SKRIBL SKRIBL
Yuki Tanaka
Masamune Saga
Ritsu Oda
RUB RUB
3-4
2-1
1-2

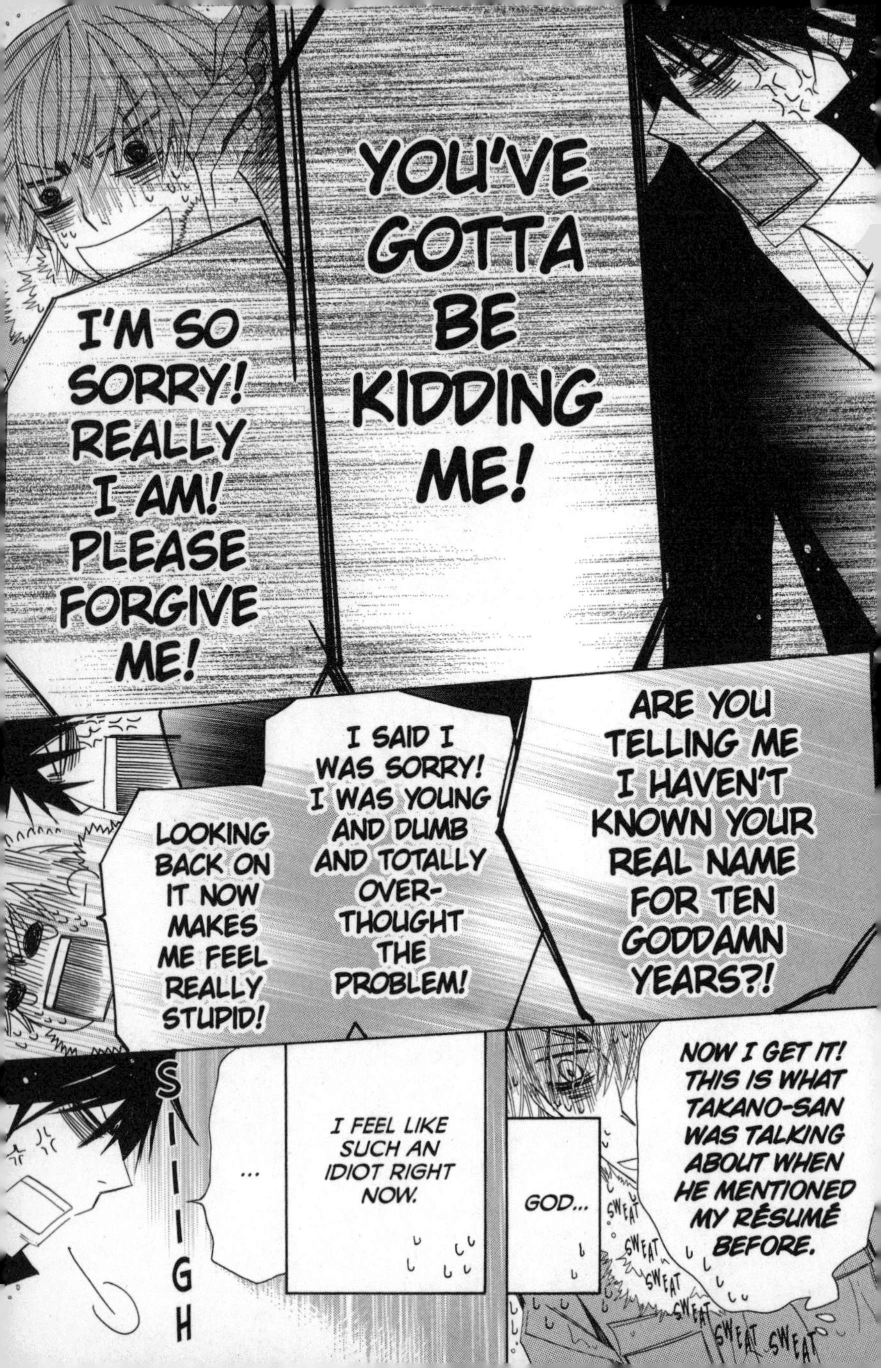
YOU'VE GOTTA BE KIDDING ME!
I'M SO SORRY! REALLY I AM! PLEASE FORGIVE ME!
ARE YOU TELLING ME I HAVEN'T KNOWN YOUR REAL NAME FOR TEN GODDAMN YEARS?!
I SAID I WAS SORRY! I WAS YOUNG AND DUMB AND TOTALLY OVER-THOUGHT THE PROBLEM!
LOOKING BACK ON IT NOW MAKES ME FEEL REALLY STUPID!
NOW I GET IT! THIS IS WHAT TAKANO-SAN WAS TALKING ABOUT WHEN HE MENTIONED MY RÉSUMÉ BEFORE.
SWEAT SWEAT SWEAT SWEAT SWEAT SWEAT
GOD...
I FEEL LIKE SUCH AN IDIOT RIGHT NOW.
...
SIIIIGH

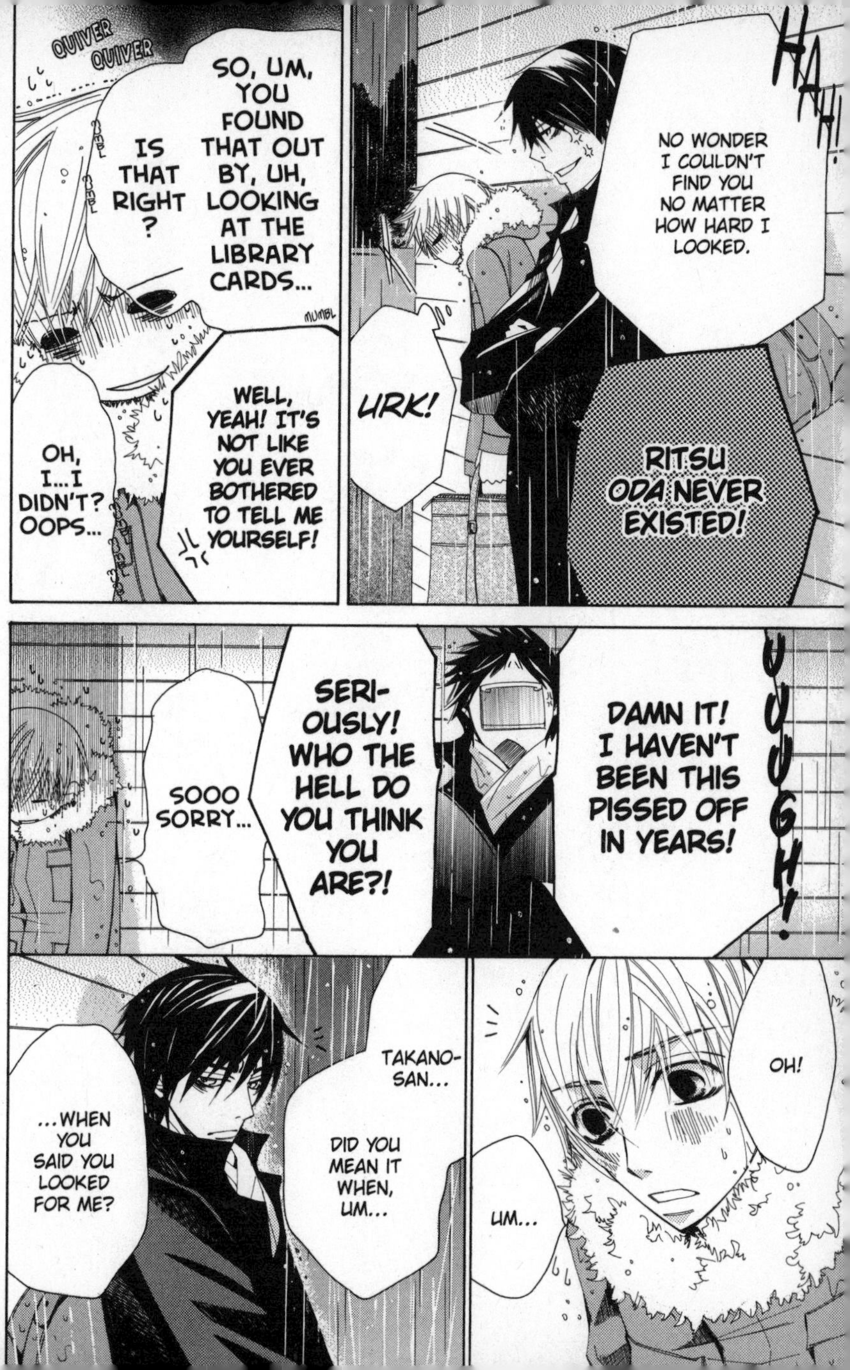
HAH!
NO WONDER I COULDN'T FIND YOU NO MATTER HOW HARD I LOOKED.
RITSU ODA NEVER EXISTED!
URK!
QUIVER QUIVER
SO, UM, YOU FOUND THAT OUT BY, UH, LOOKING AT THE LIBRARY CARDS...
IS THAT RIGHT?
MUMBL
MUMBL
MUMBL
WELL, YEAH! IT'S NOT LIKE YOU EVER BOTHERED TO TELL ME YOURSELF!
OH, I...I DIDN'T? OOPS...
UUUGH!
DAMN IT! I HAVEN'T BEEN THIS PISSED OFF IN YEARS!
SERI-OUSLY! WHO THE HELL DO YOU THINK YOU ARE?!
SOOO SORRY...
OH!
UM...
TAKANO-SAN...
DID YOU MEAN IT WHEN, UM...
...WHEN YOU SAID YOU LOOKED FOR ME?

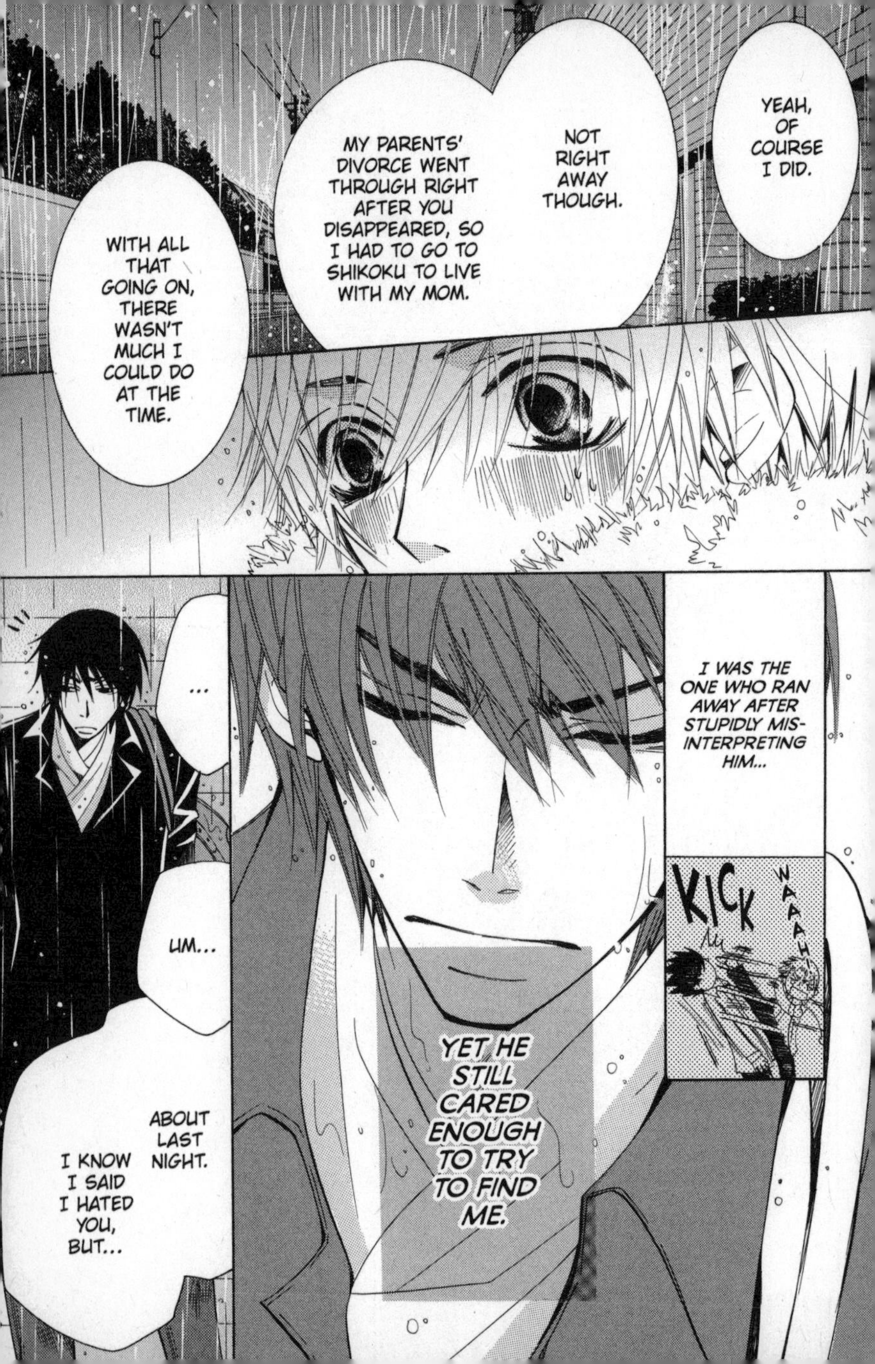
YEAH, OF COURSE I DID.
NOT RIGHT AWAY THOUGH.
MY PARENTS' DIVORCE WENT THROUGH RIGHT AFTER YOU DISAPPEARED, SO I HAD TO GO TO SHIKOKU TO LIVE WITH MY MOM.
WITH ALL THAT GOING ON, THERE WASN'T MUCH I COULD DO AT THE TIME.
I WAS THE ONE WHO RAN AWAY AFTER STUPIDLY MIS-INTERPRETING HIM...
KICK
WAAAH!
YET HE STILL CARED ENOUGH TO TRY TO FIND ME.
...
UM...
ABOUT LAST NIGHT.
I KNOW I SAID I HATED YOU, BUT...

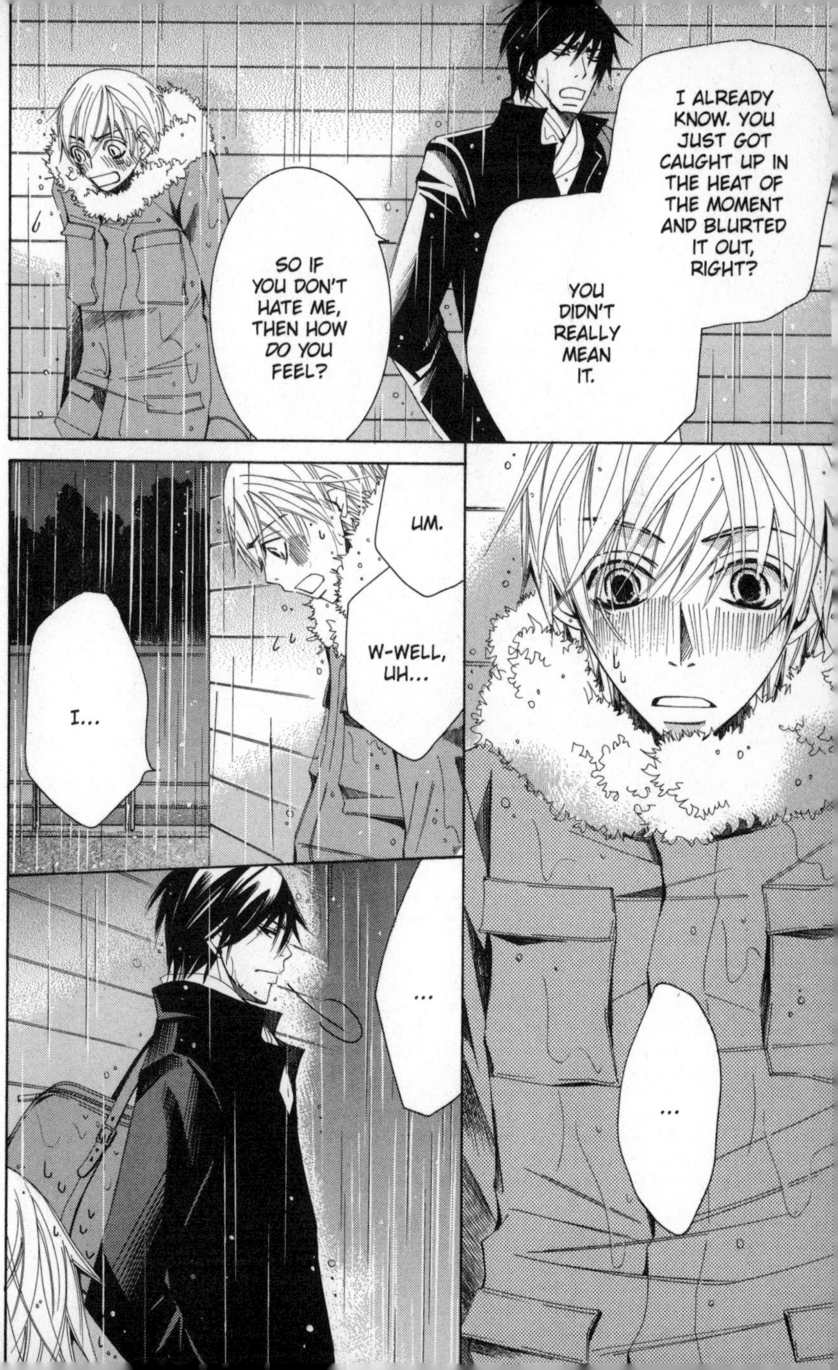
I ALREADY KNOW. YOU JUST GOT CAUGHT UP IN THE HEAT OF THE MOMENT AND BLURTED IT OUT, RIGHT?
YOU DIDN'T REALLY MEAN IT.
SO IF YOU DON'T HATE ME, THEN HOW *DO* YOU FEEL?
...
UM.
W-WELL, UH...
I...
...

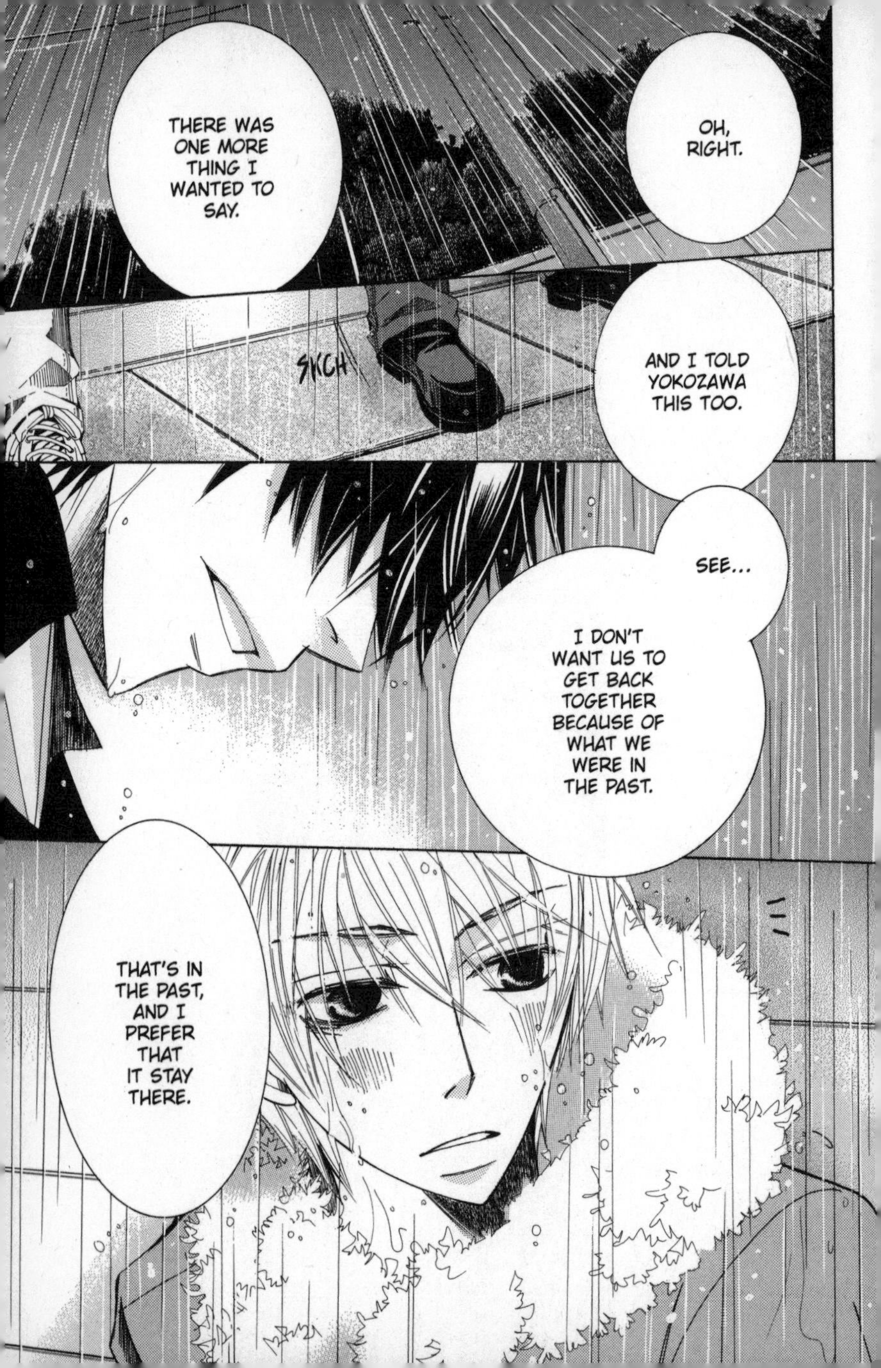
OH, RIGHT.
THERE WAS ONE MORE THING I WANTED TO SAY.
SKCH
AND I TOLD YOKOZAWA THIS TOO.
SEE...
I DON'T WANT US TO GET BACK TOGETHER BECAUSE OF WHAT WE WERE IN THE PAST.
THAT'S IN THE PAST, AND I PREFER THAT IT STAY THERE.

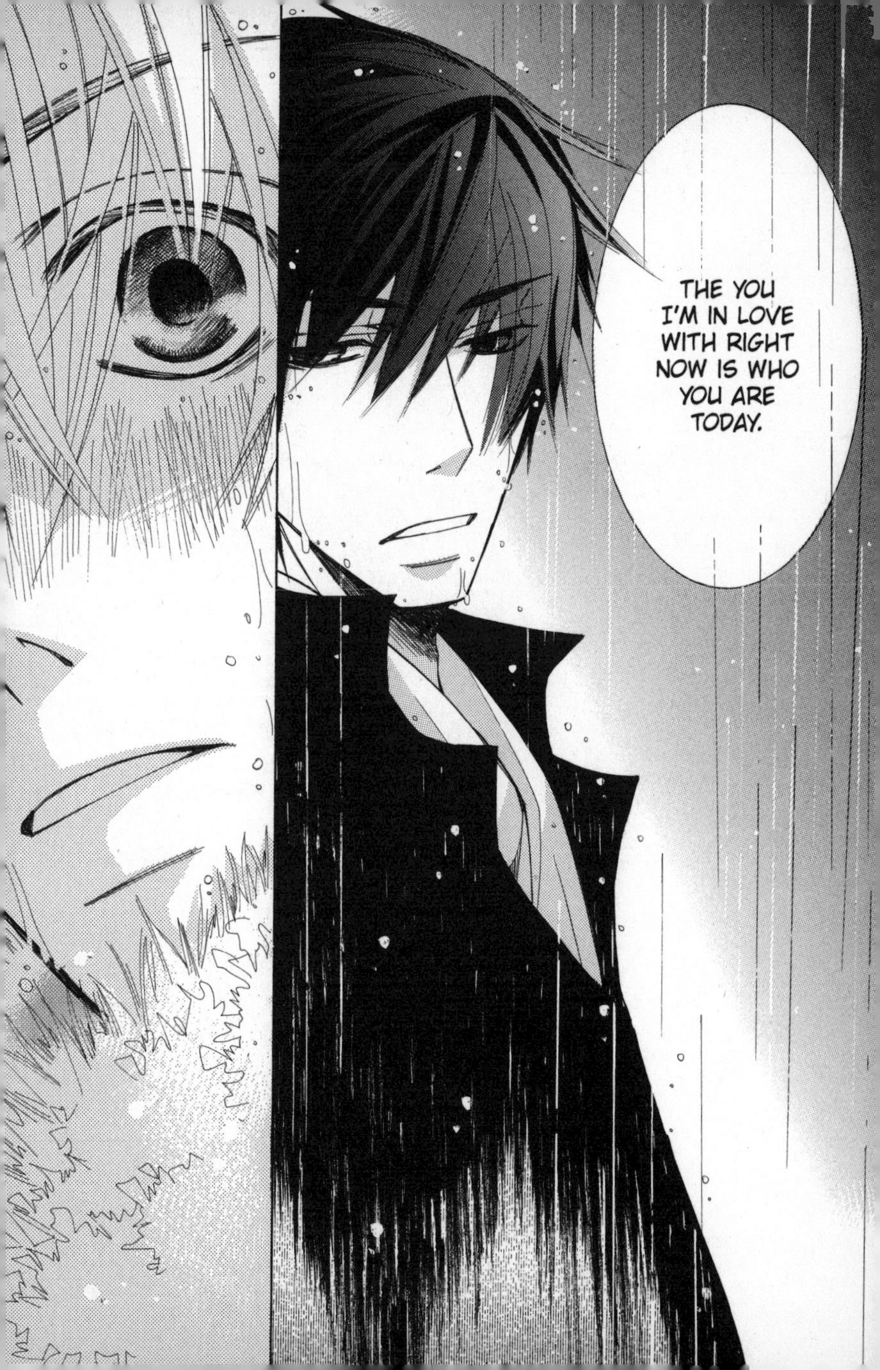
THE YOU I'M IN LOVE WITH RIGHT NOW IS WHO YOU ARE TODAY.

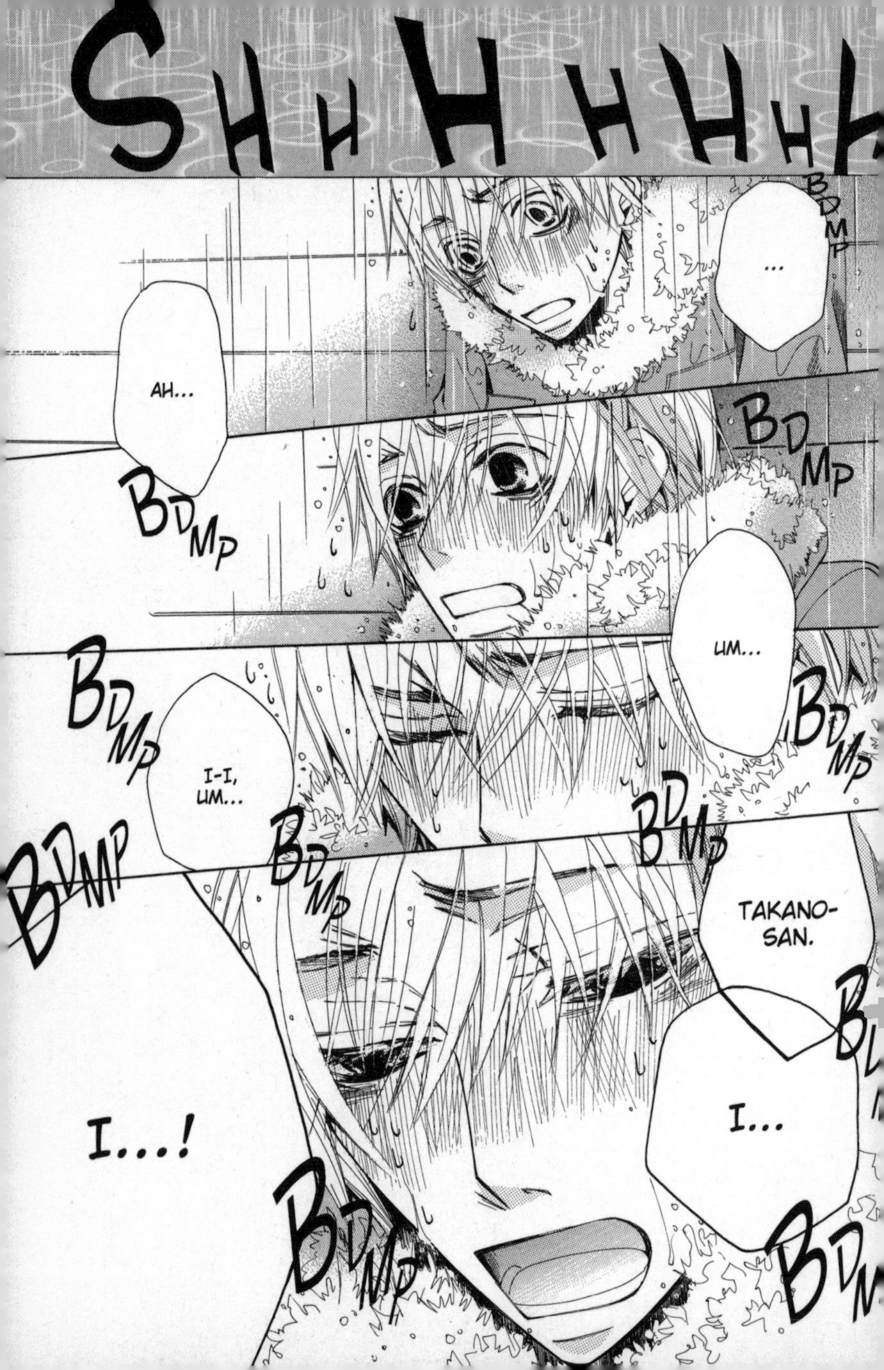
SHHHHHHHH
BDMP
...
AH...
BDMP
BDMP
UM...
BDMP
BDMP
I-I, UM...
BDMP
BDMP
BDMP
TAKANO-SAN.
I...
I...!
BDMP

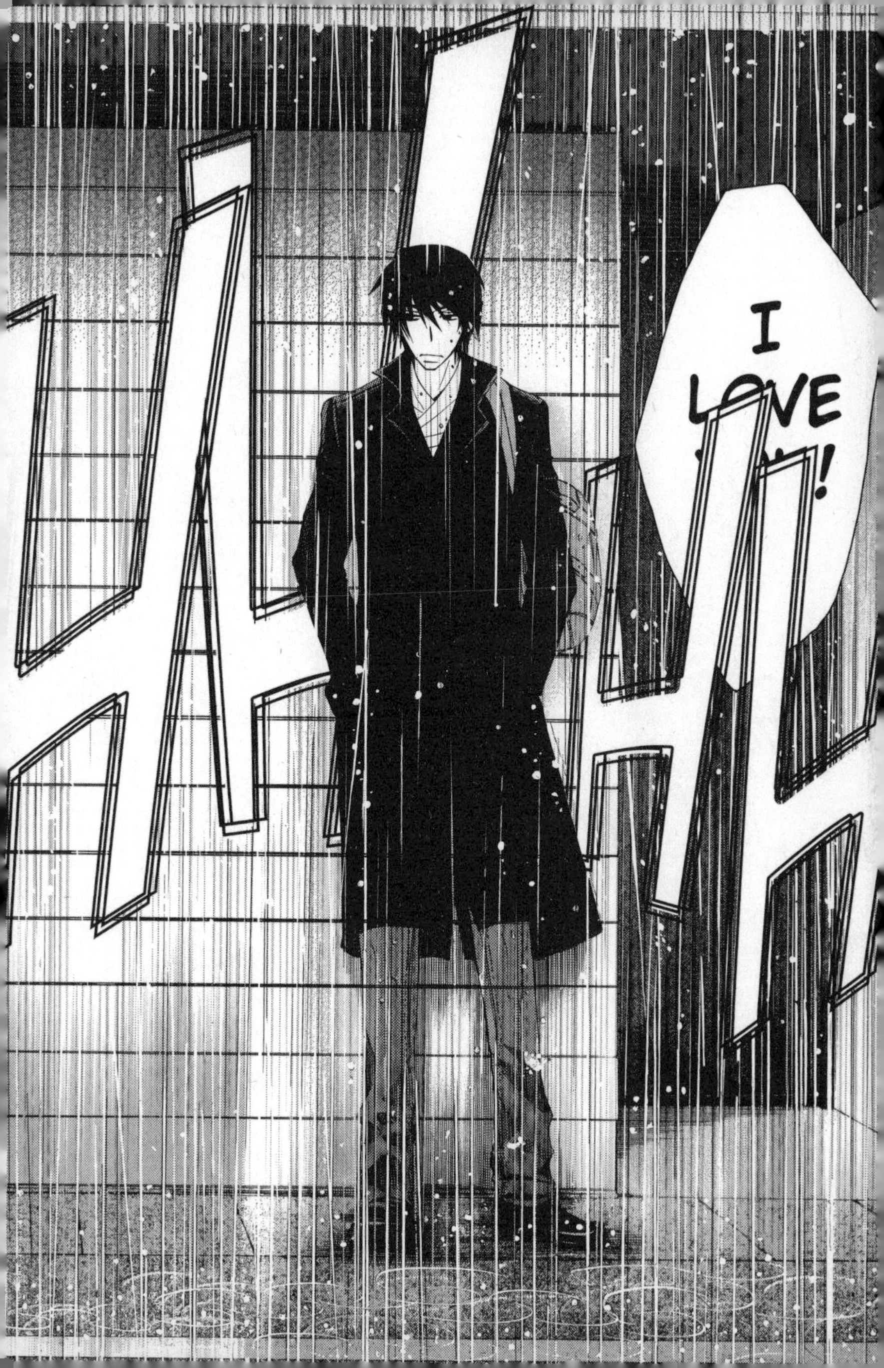
I LOVE !

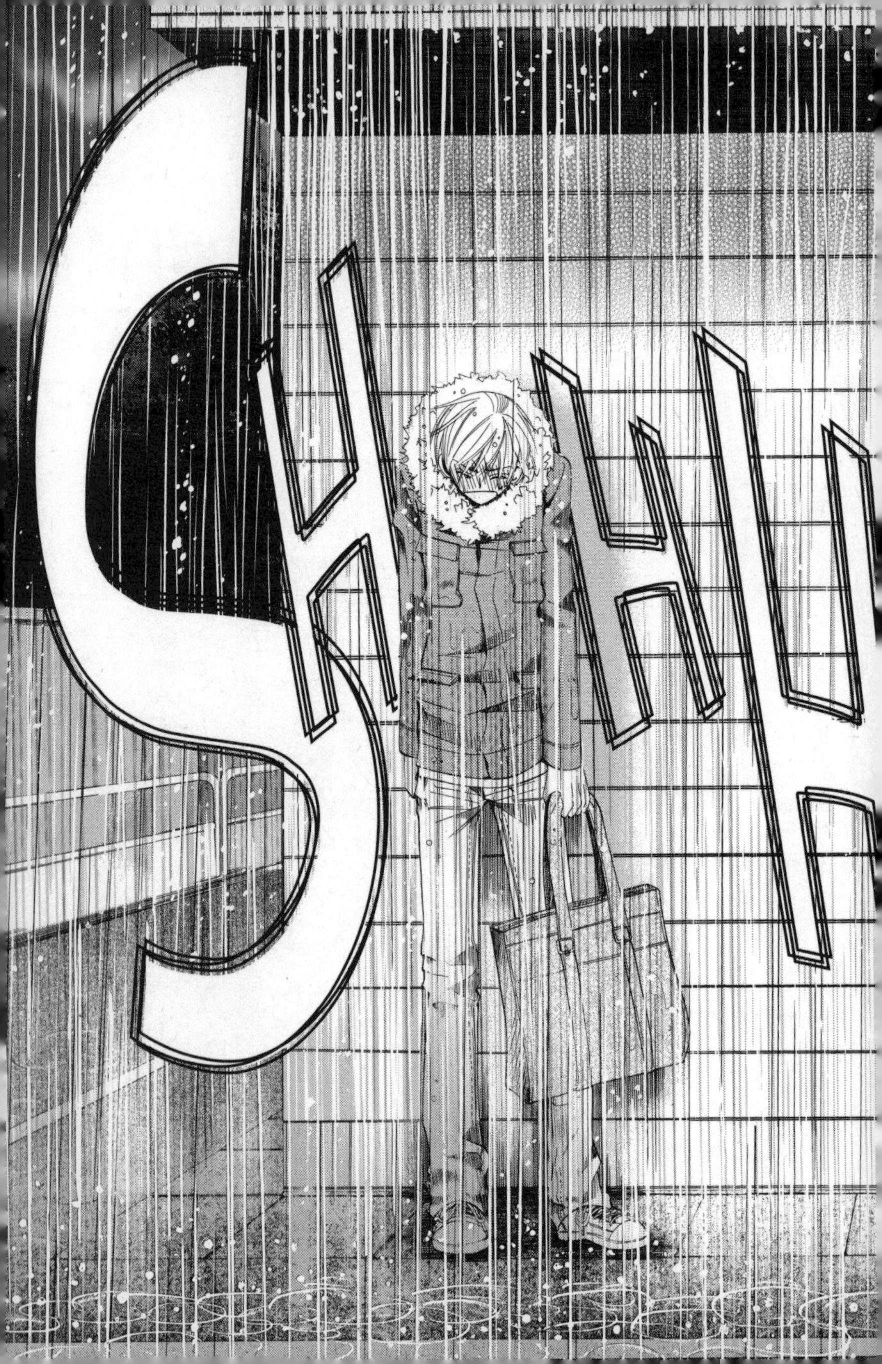
SHHH

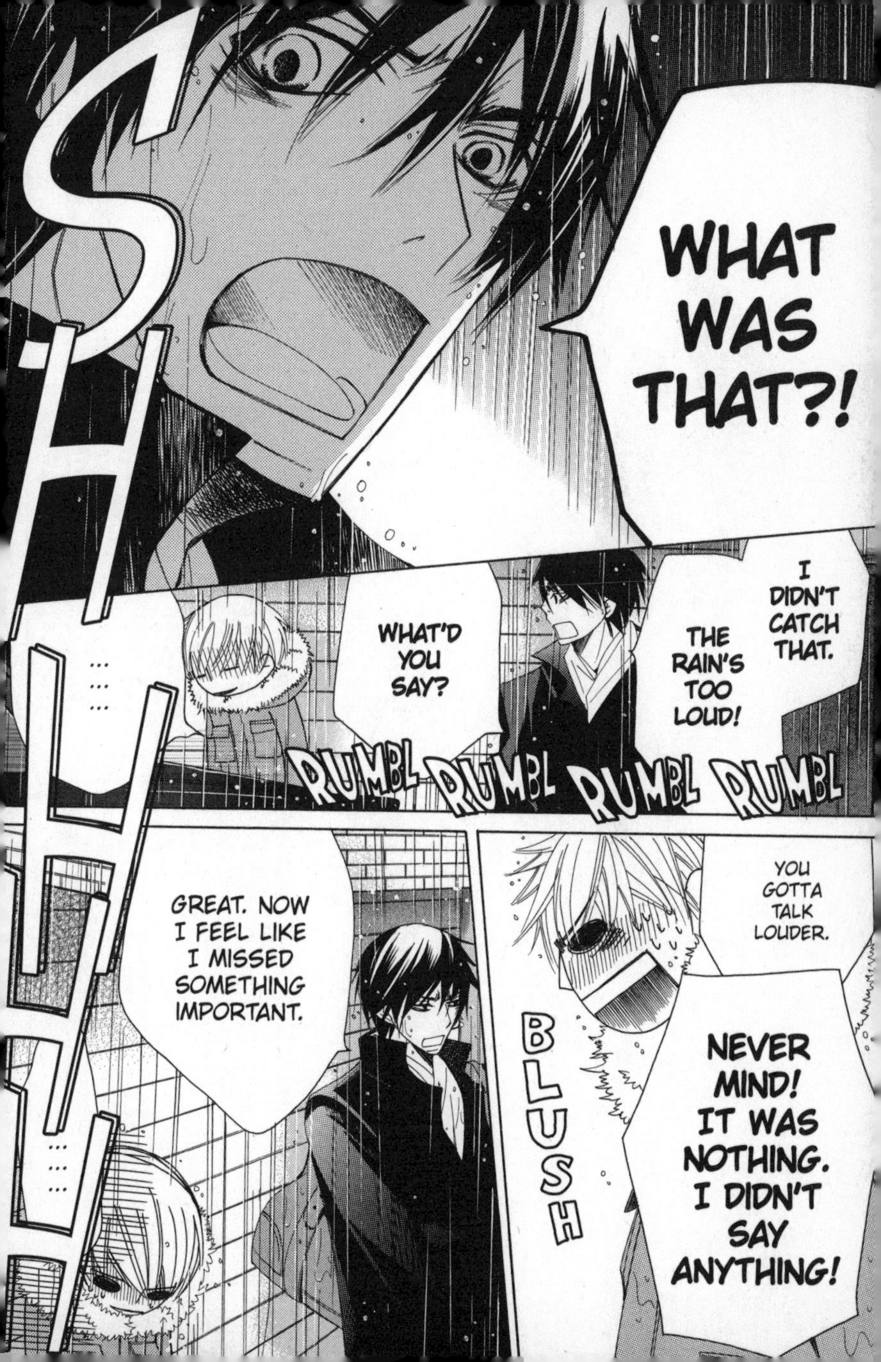
WHAT WAS THAT?!
SHHHH
I DIDN'T CATCH THAT.
THE RAIN'S TOO LOUD!
WHAT'D YOU SAY?
...
...
...
RUMBL RUMBL RUMBL RUMBL
YOU GOTTA TALK LOUDER.
NEVER MIND! IT WAS NOTHING. I DIDN'T SAY ANYTHING!
BLUSH
GREAT. NOW I FEEL LIKE I MISSED SOMETHING IMPORTANT.
...
...
...

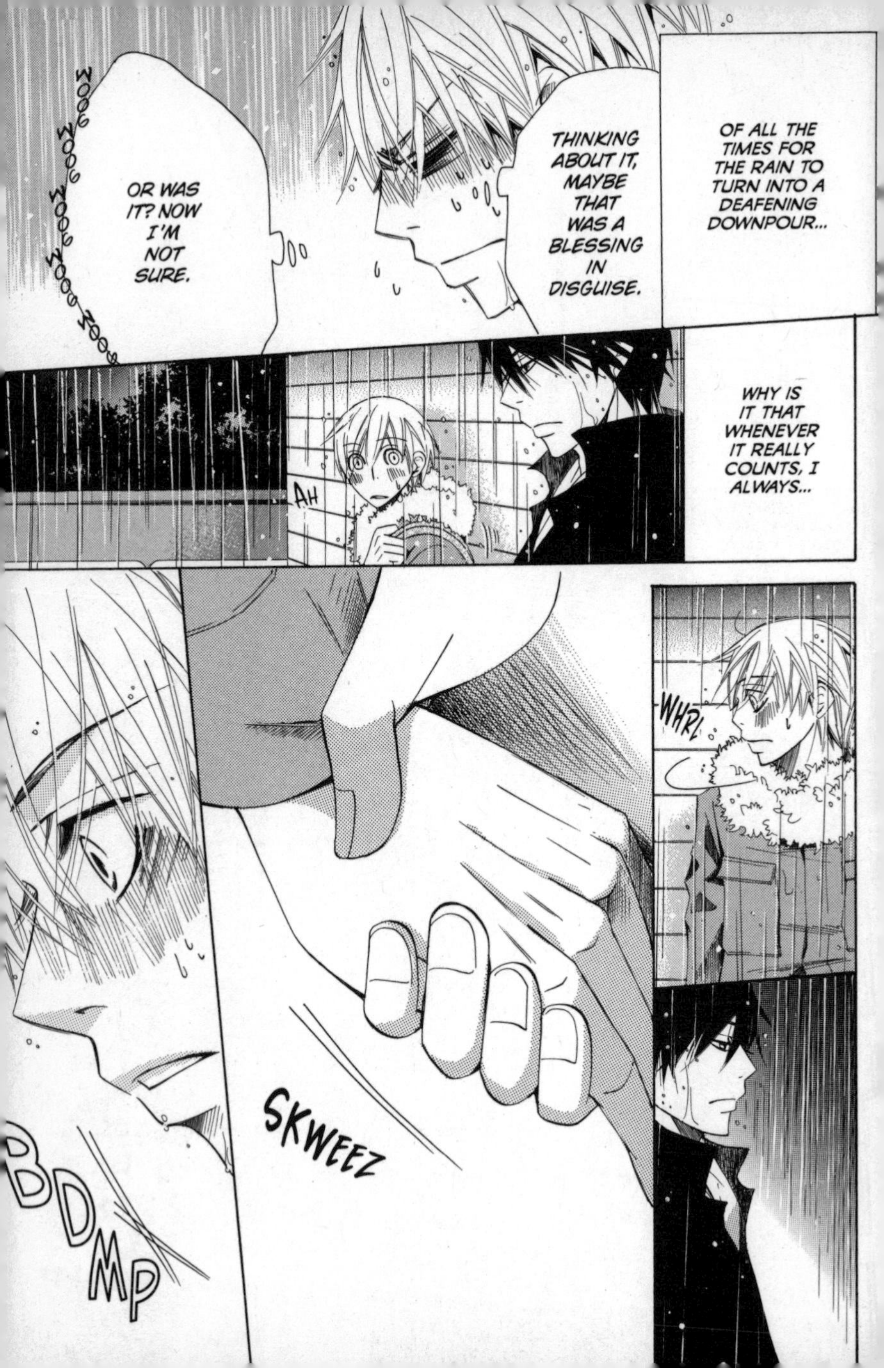
OF ALL THE TIMES FOR THE RAIN TO TURN INTO A DEAFENING DOWNPOUR...
THINKING ABOUT IT, MAYBE THAT WAS A BLESSING IN DISGUISE.
OR WAS IT? NOW I'M NOT SURE.
WHY IS IT THAT WHENEVER IT REALLY COUNTS, I ALWAYS...
AH
WHRL
SKWEEZ
BDMP

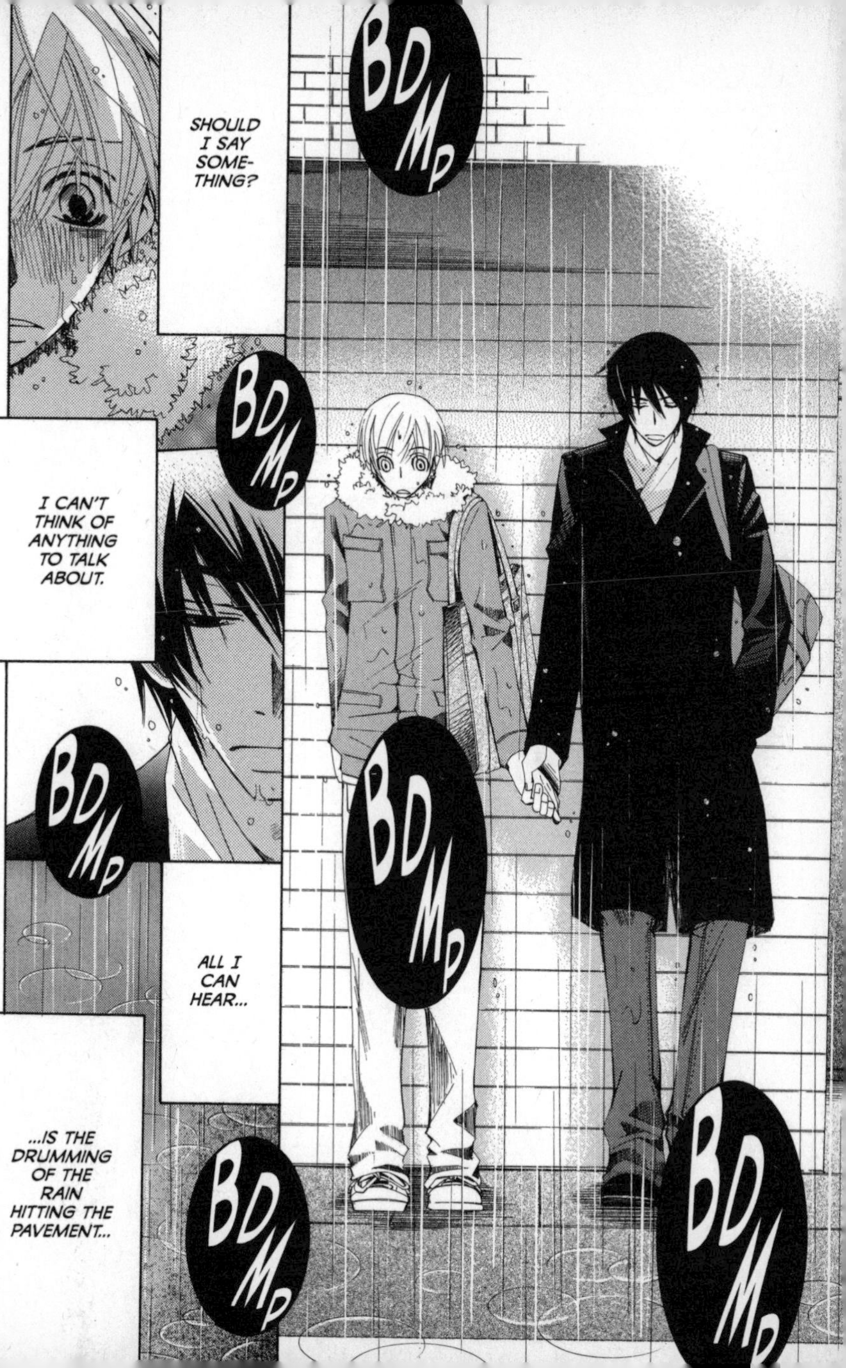
BDMP
BDMP
BDMP
SHOULD I SAY SOME-THING?
BDMP
I CAN'T THINK OF ANYTHING TO TALK ABOUT.
BDMP
ALL I CAN HEAR...
...IS THE DRUMMING OF THE RAIN HITTING THE PAVEMENT...
BDMP

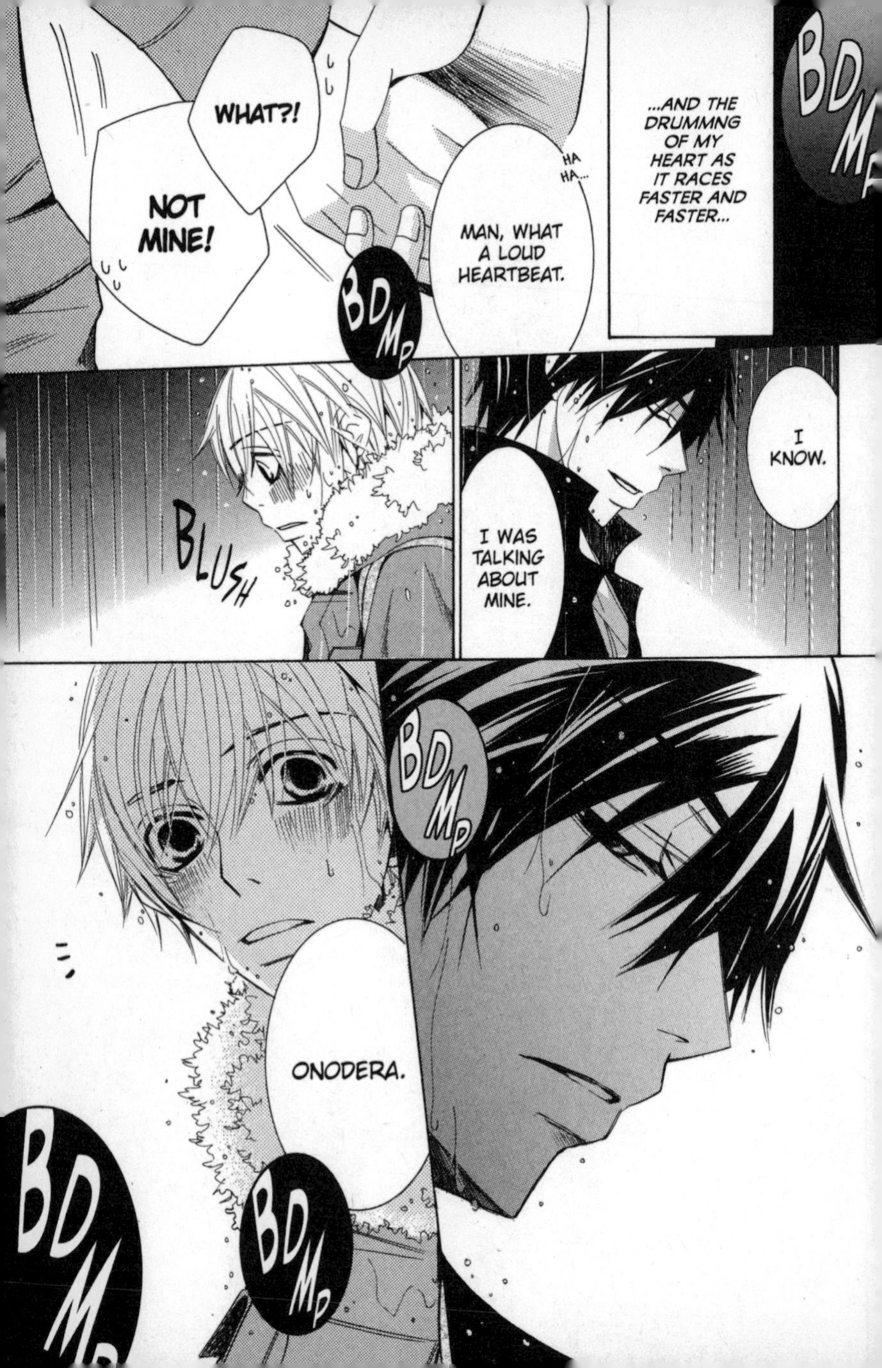
BDMP
...AND THE DRUMMNG OF MY HEART AS IT RACES FASTER AND FASTER...
HA HA...
MAN, WHAT A LOUD HEARTBEAT.
WHAT?!
BDMP
NOT MINE!
I KNOW.
I WAS TALKING ABOUT MINE.
BLUSH
BDMP
ONODERA.
BDMP
BDMP

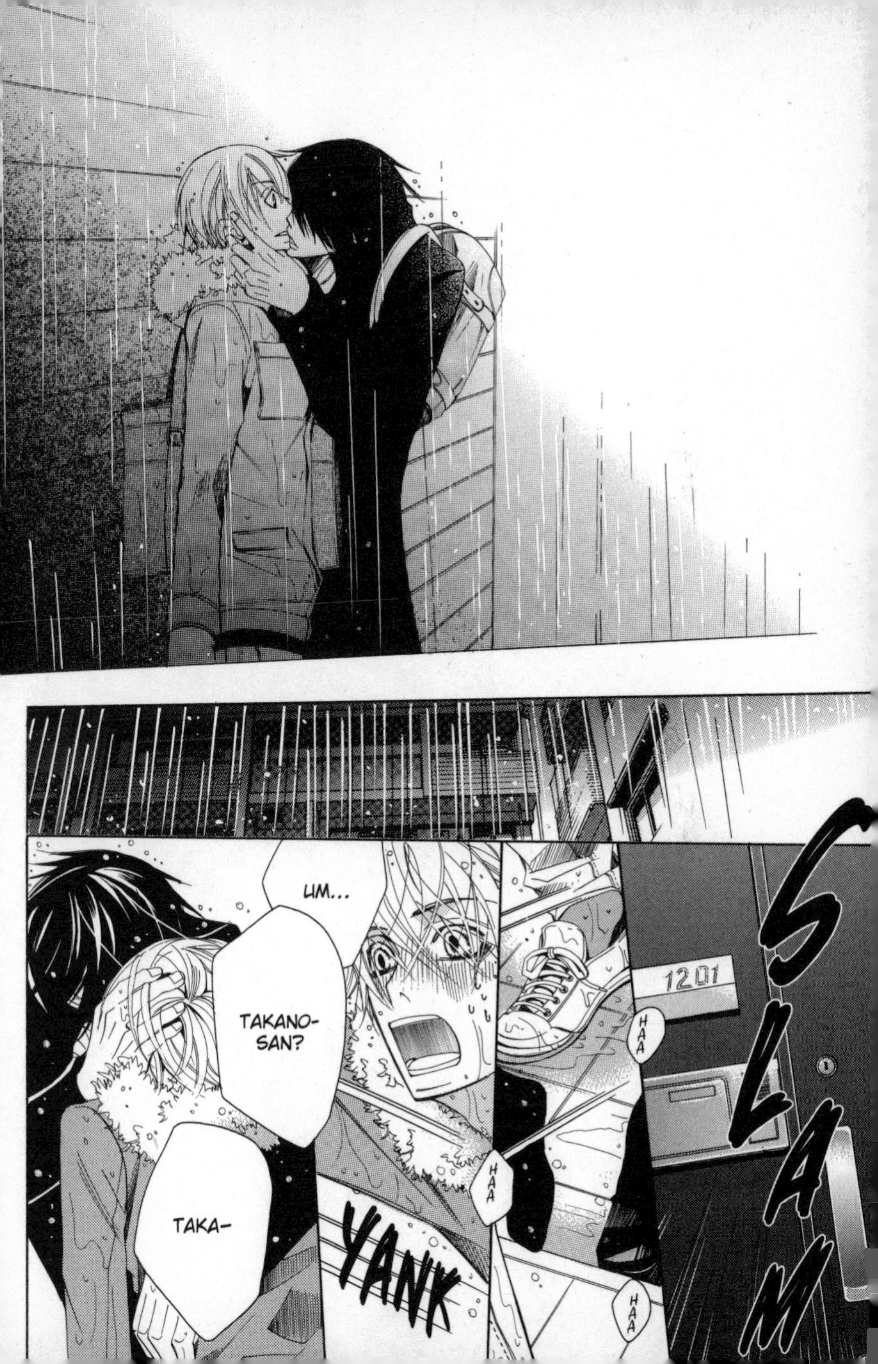
SLAM
1201
HAA
HAA
HAA
YANK
UM...
TAKANO-SAN?
TAKA-

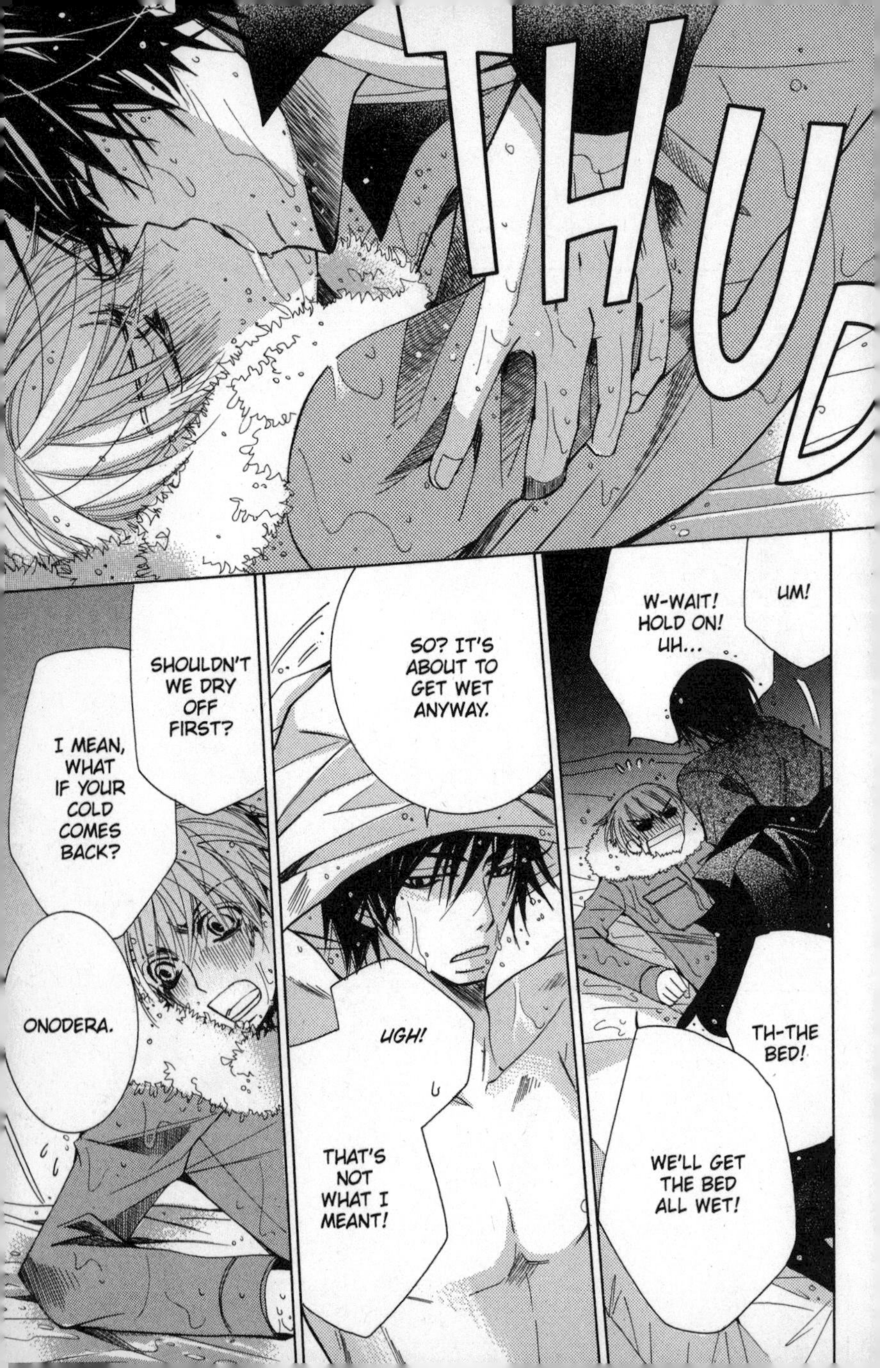
THUD
UM!
W-WAIT! HOLD ON! UH...
TH-THE BED!
WE'LL GET THE BED ALL WET!
SO? IT'S ABOUT TO GET WET ANYWAY.
UGH!
THAT'S NOT WHAT I MEANT!
SHOULDN'T WE DRY OFF FIRST?
I MEAN, WHAT IF YOUR COLD COMES BACK?
ONODERA.

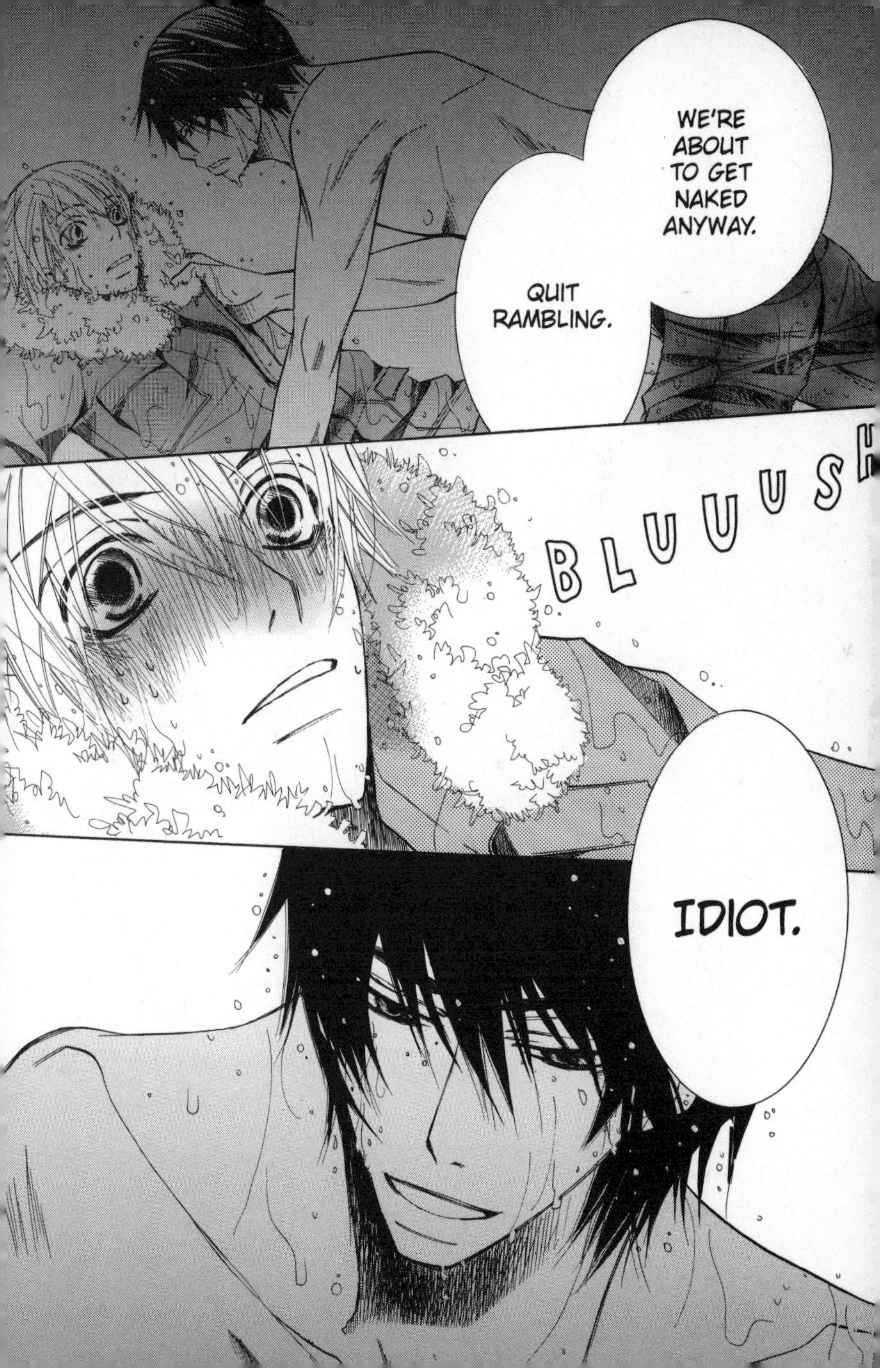
WE'RE ABOUT TO GET NAKED ANYWAY.
QUIT RAMBLING.
BLUUUSH
IDIOT.

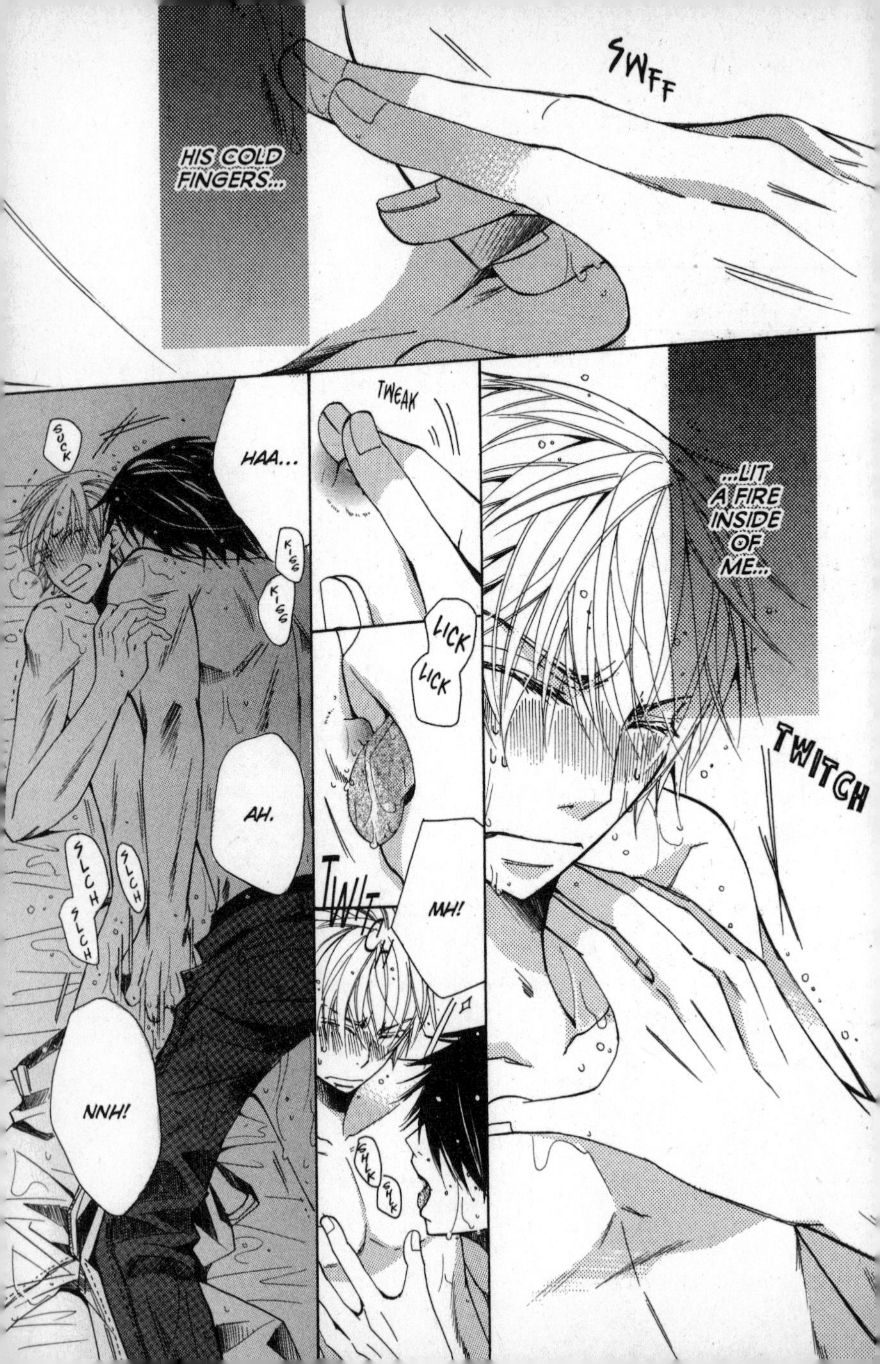
SWFF
HIS COLD FINGERS...
...LIT A FIRE INSIDE OF ME...
TWITCH
TWEAK
LICK LICK
MH!
TWITCH
SHLK SHLK
HAA...
SUCK
KISS KISS
AH.
SLCH SLCH
SLCH SLCH
NNH!

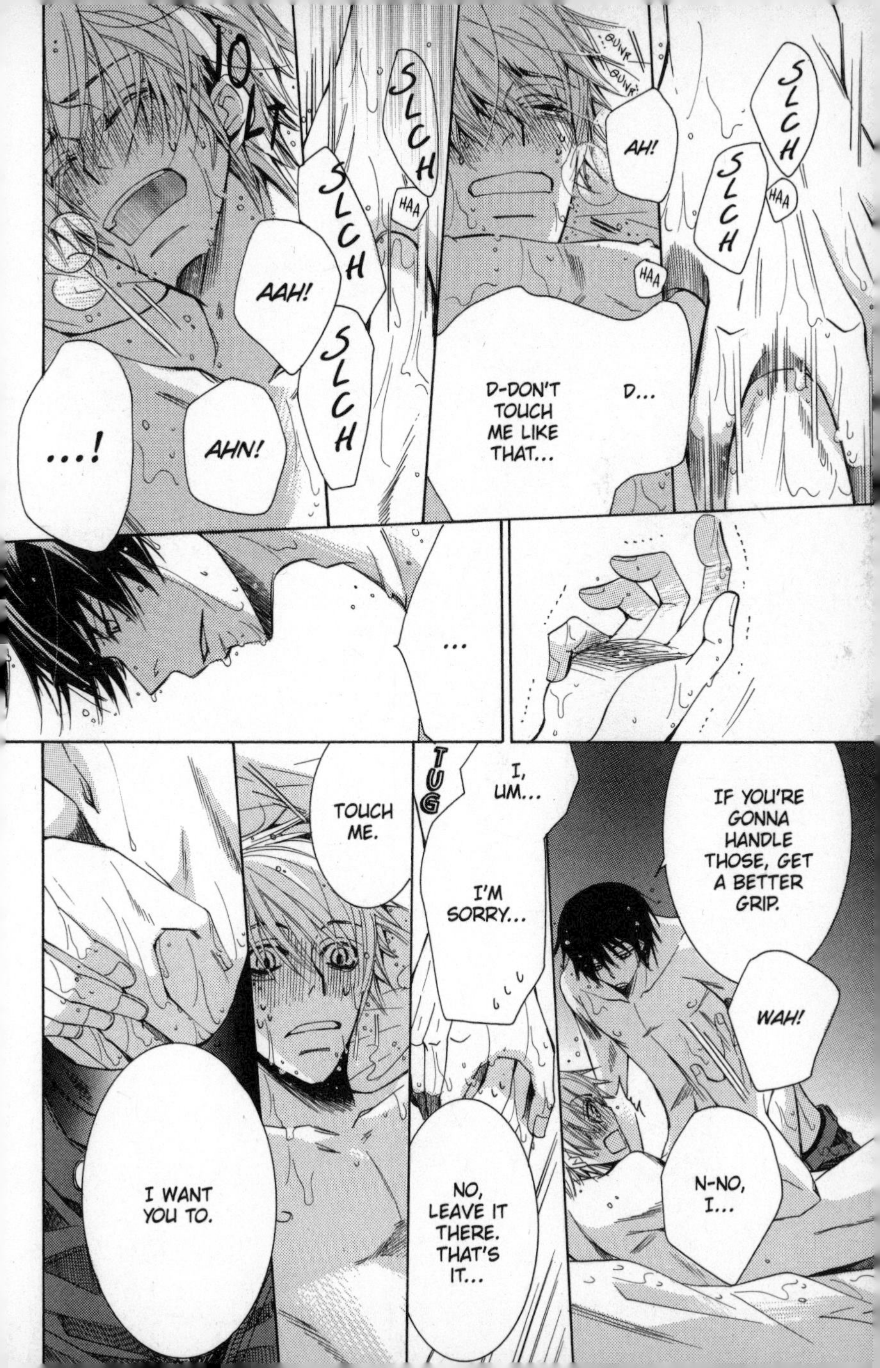
SLCH
SLCH
HAA
AH!
HAA
D...
D-DON'T TOUCH ME LIKE THAT...
SLCH
HAA
JOLT
SLCH
AAH!
SLCH
AHN!
...!
....
...
IF YOU'RE GONNA HANDLE THOSE, GET A BETTER GRIP.
WAH!
N-NO, I...
I, UM...
TUG
I'M SORRY...
NO, LEAVE IT THERE. THAT'S IT...
TOUCH ME.
I WANT YOU TO.

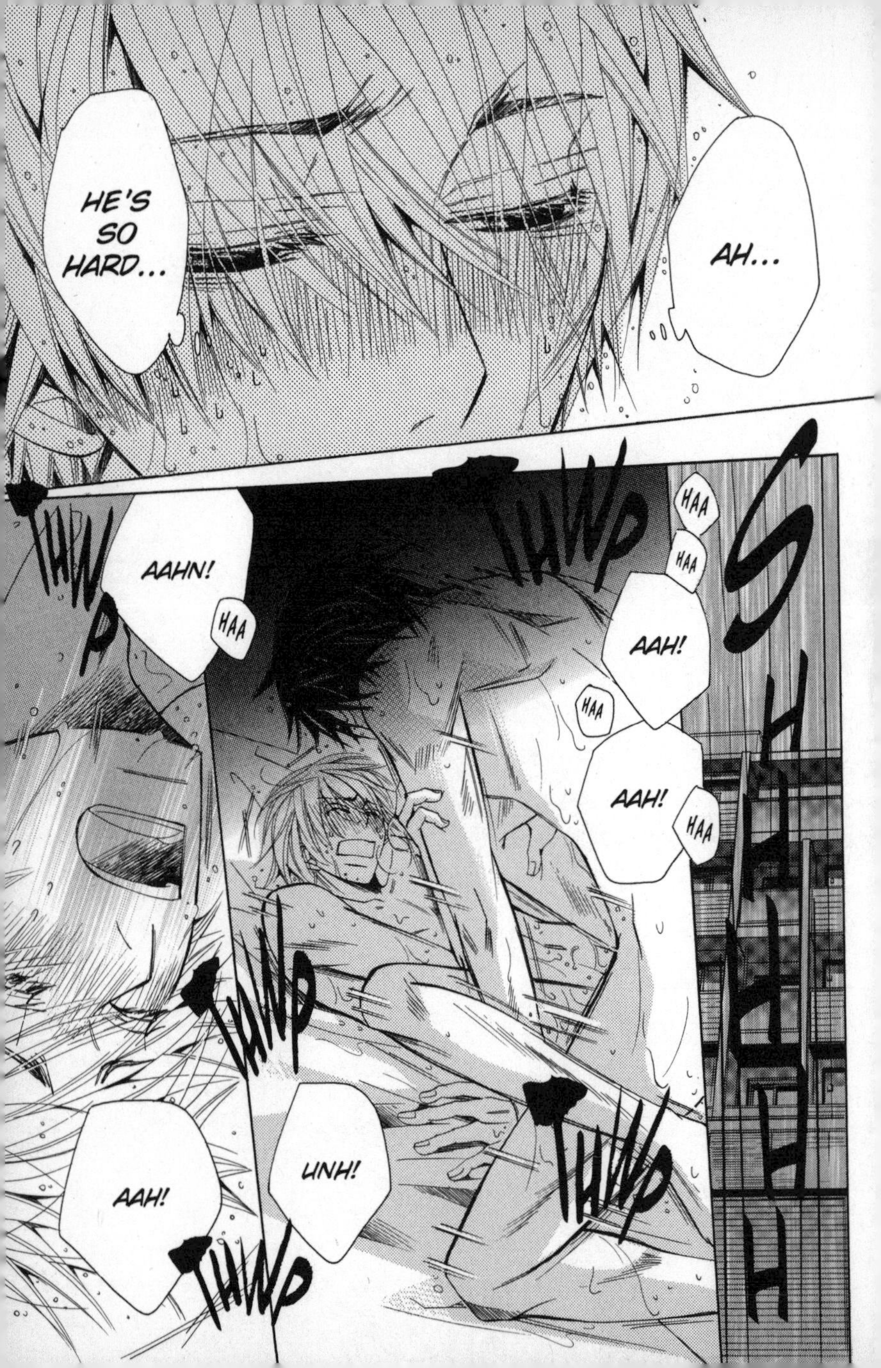
AH...
HE'S SO HARD...
SHHHHHH
THWP
HAA
HAA
AAH!
HAA
AAH!
HAA
THWP
UNH!
AAHN!
HAA
THWP
THWP
AAH!
THWP

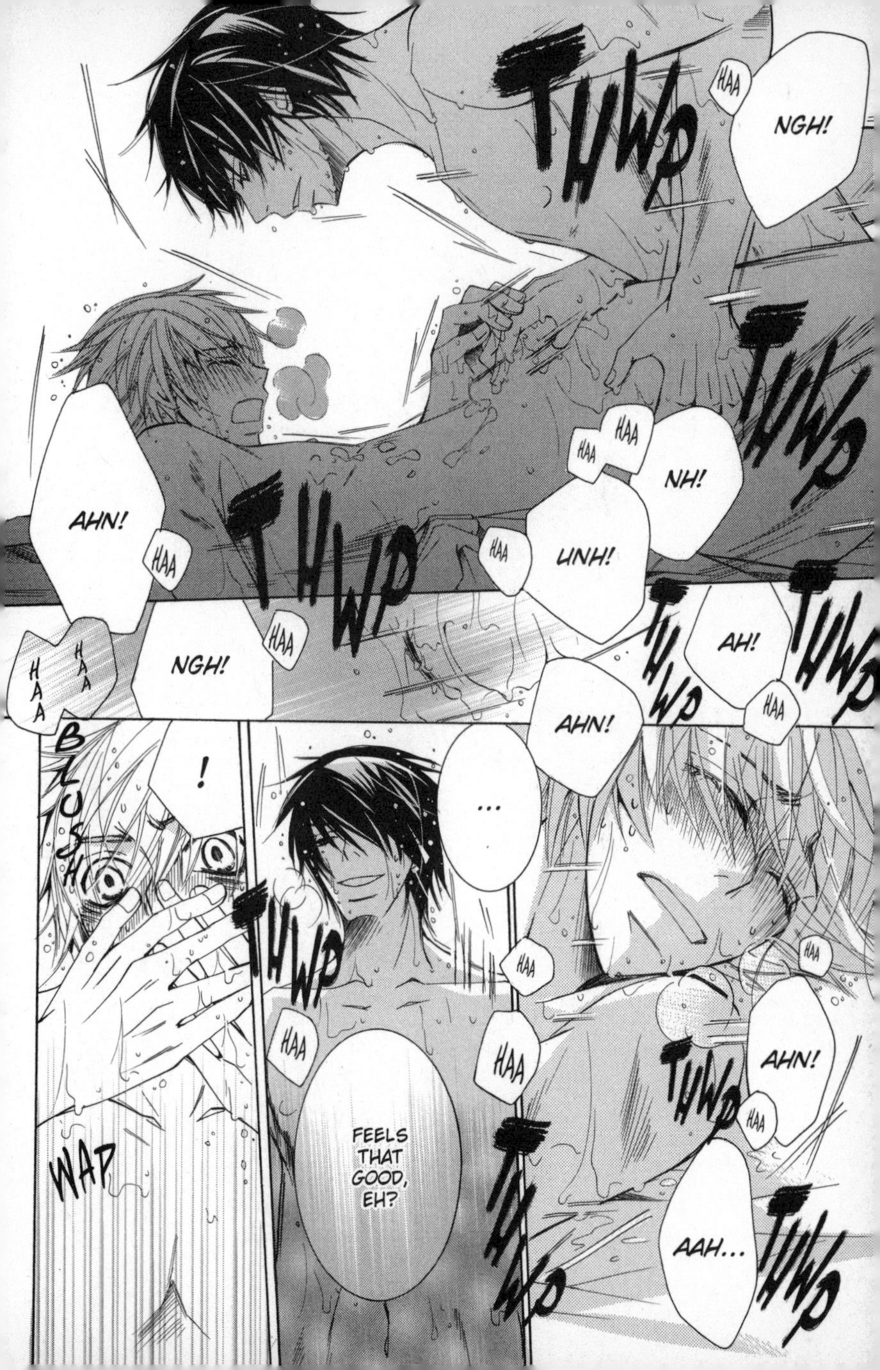
HAA
NGH!
THWP
THWP
HAA HAA
NH!
HAA
UNH!
THWP
AHN!
HAA
THWP
THWP
AH!
HAA
AHN!
HAA
NGH!
HAA HAA HAA
HAA
AHN!
THWP
HAA
AAH...
THWP
...
THWP
HAA
HAA
HAA
FEELS THAT GOOD, EH?
THWP
!
BLUSH
WAP

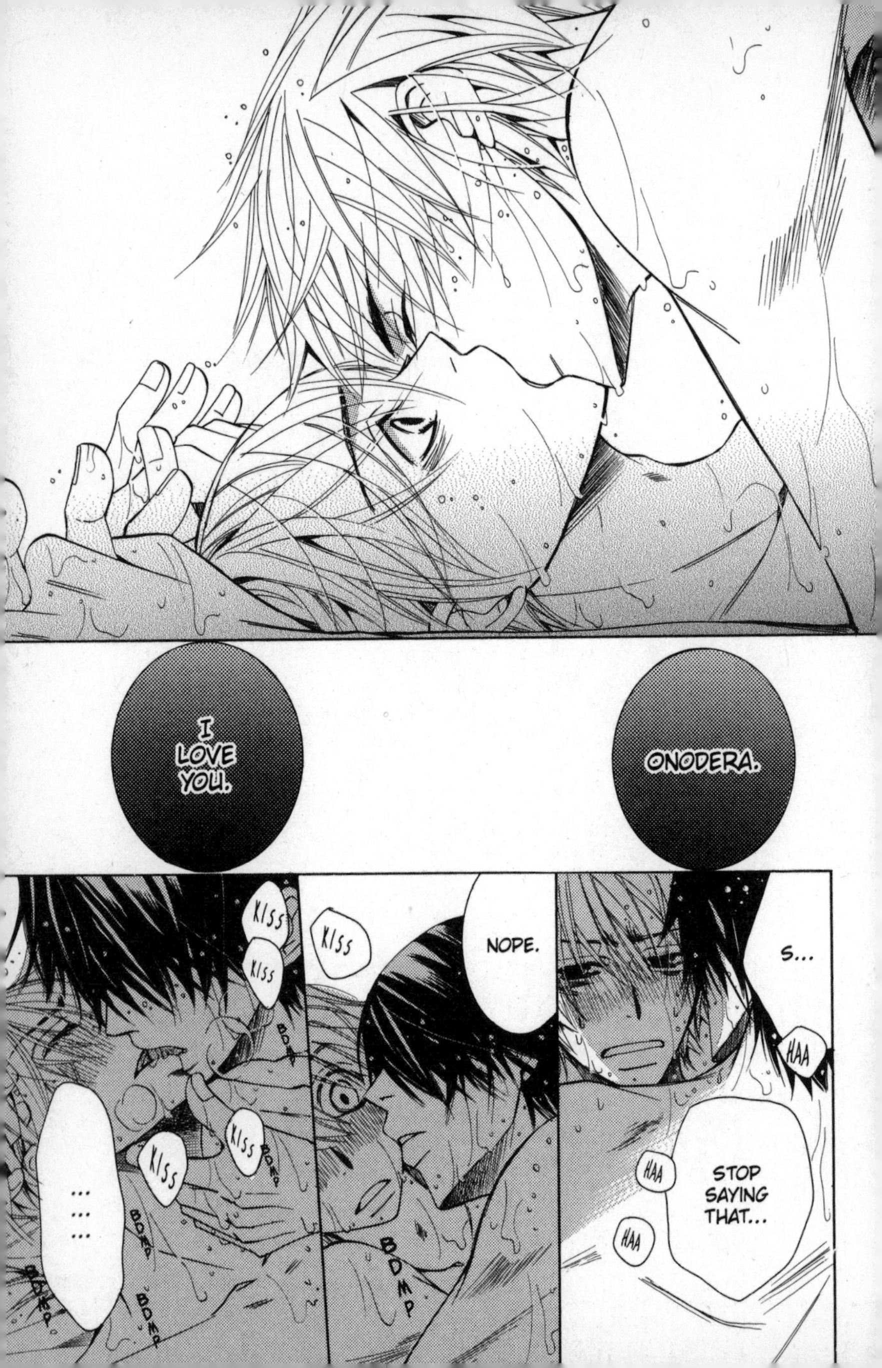
ONODERA.
I LOVE YOU.
S...
HAA
STOP SAYING THAT...
HAA
HAA
NOPE.
KISS
KISS
KISS
BDMP
KISS
KISS
BDMP
BDMP
... ...
BDMP
BDMP
BDMP

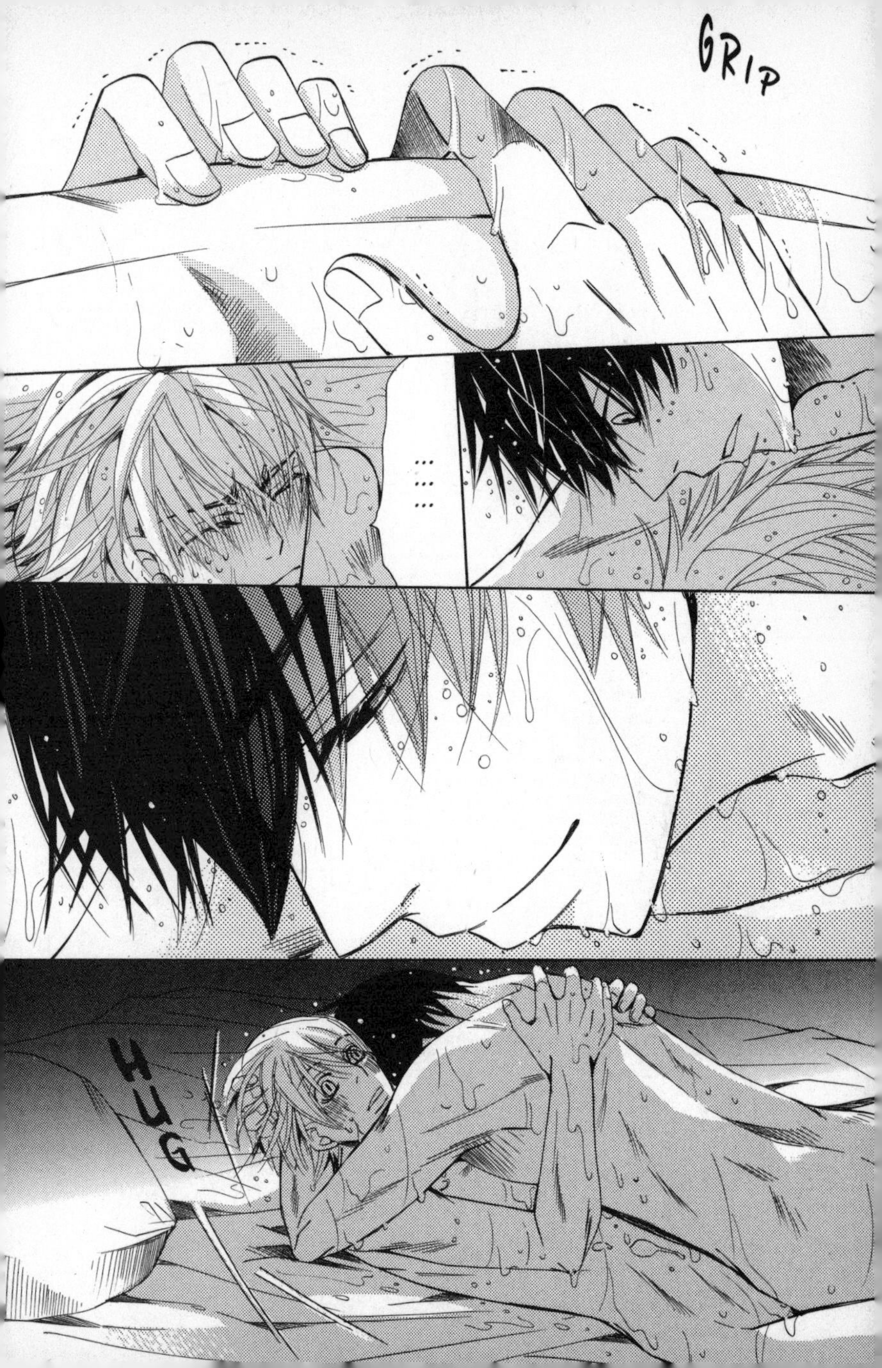
GRIP
...
HUG

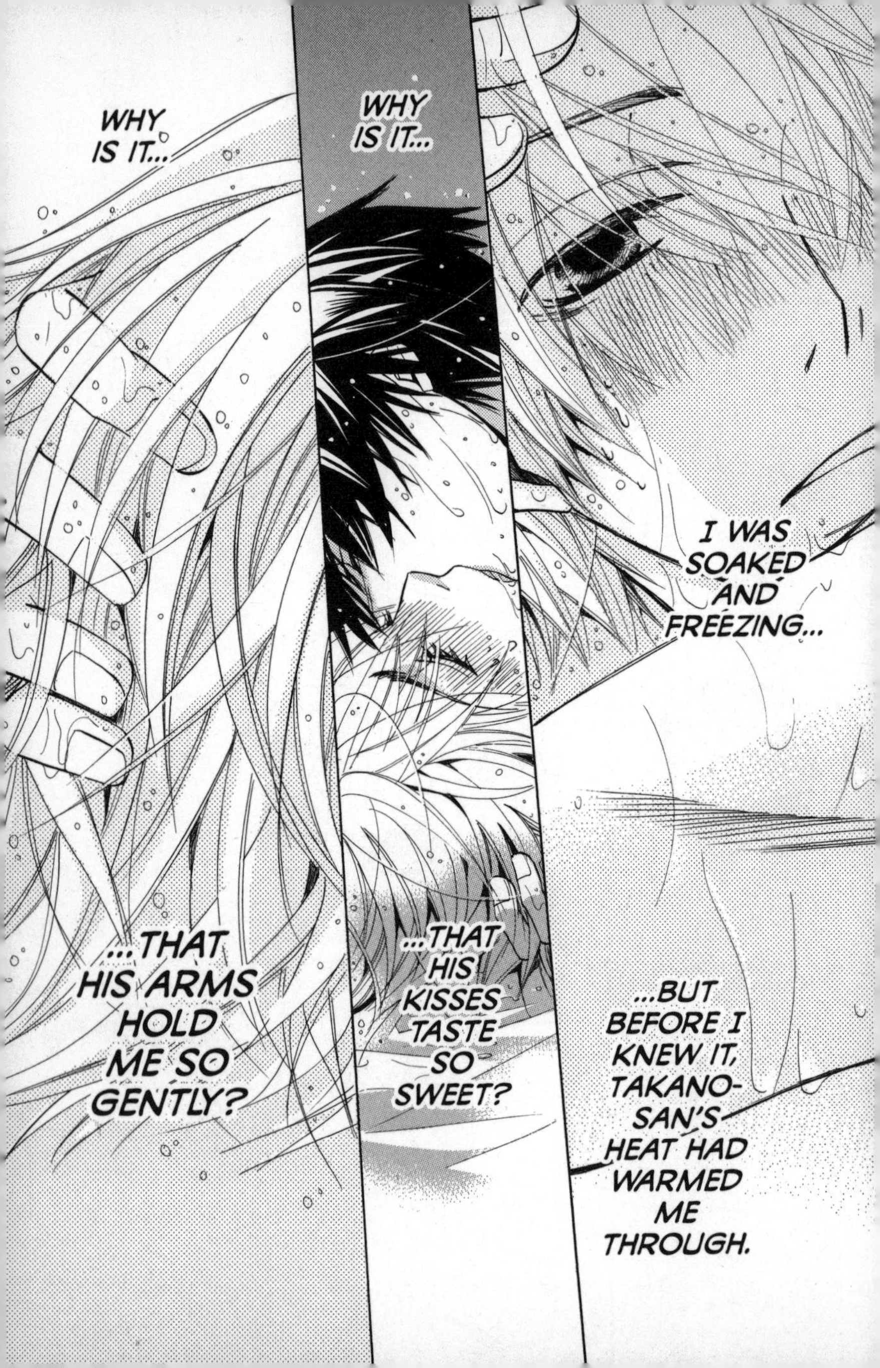
I WAS SOAKED AND FREEZING...
...BUT BEFORE I KNEW IT, TAKANO-SAN'S HEAT HAD WARMED ME THROUGH.
WHY IS IT...
...THAT HIS KISSES TASTE SO SWEET?
WHY IS IT...
...THAT HIS ARMS HOLD ME SO GENTLY?

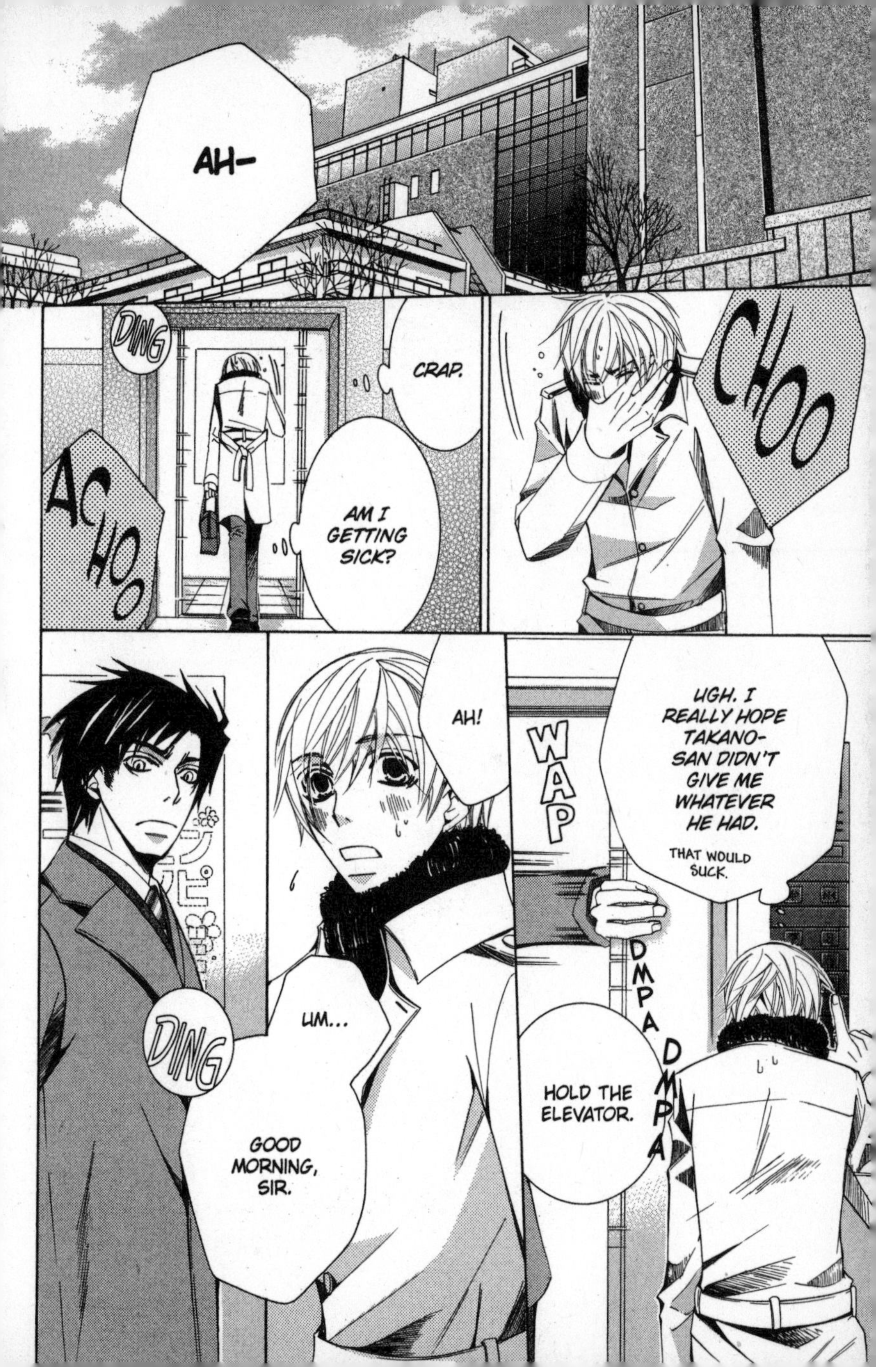
AH-
CHOO
CRAP.
DING
AM I GETTING SICK?
ACHOO
UGH. I REALLY HOPE TAKANO-SAN DIDN'T GIVE ME WHATEVER HE HAD.
THAT WOULD SUCK.
WAP
DMPA DMPA
HOLD THE ELEVATOR.
AH!
UM...
GOOD MORNING, SIR.
DING

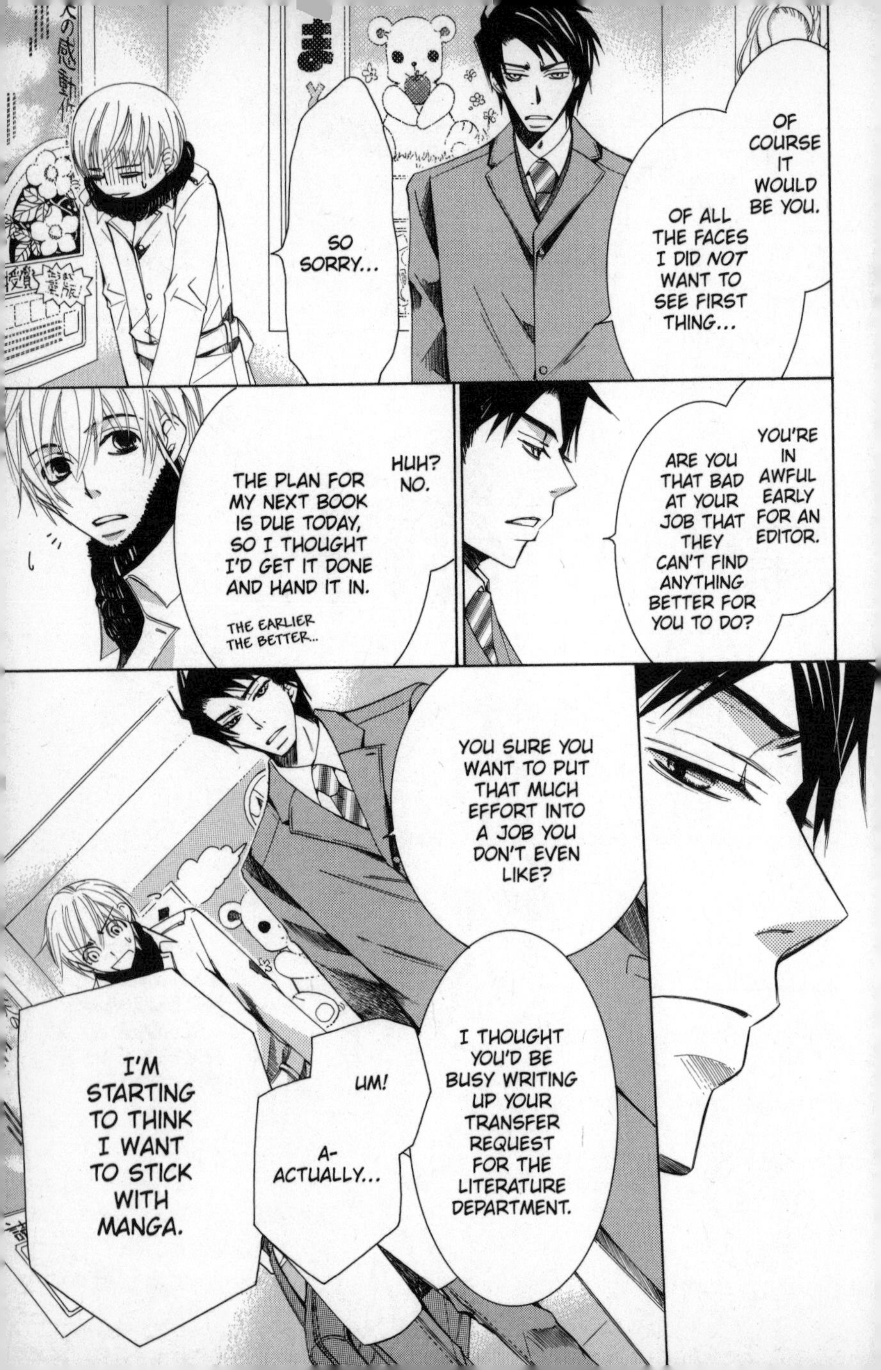
OF COURSE IT WOULD BE YOU.
OF ALL THE FACES I DID *NOT* WANT TO SEE FIRST THING...
SO SORRY...
YOU'RE IN AWFUL EARLY FOR AN EDITOR.
ARE YOU THAT BAD AT YOUR JOB THAT THEY CAN'T FIND ANYTHING BETTER FOR YOU TO DO?
HUH? NO.
THE PLAN FOR MY NEXT BOOK IS DUE TODAY, SO I THOUGHT I'D GET IT DONE AND HAND IT IN.
THE EARLIER THE BETTER...
YOU SURE YOU WANT TO PUT THAT MUCH EFFORT INTO A JOB YOU DON'T EVEN LIKE?
I THOUGHT YOU'D BE BUSY WRITING UP YOUR TRANSFER REQUEST FOR THE LITERATURE DEPARTMENT.
UM!
A- ACTUALLY...
I'M STARTING TO THINK I WANT TO STICK WITH MANGA.

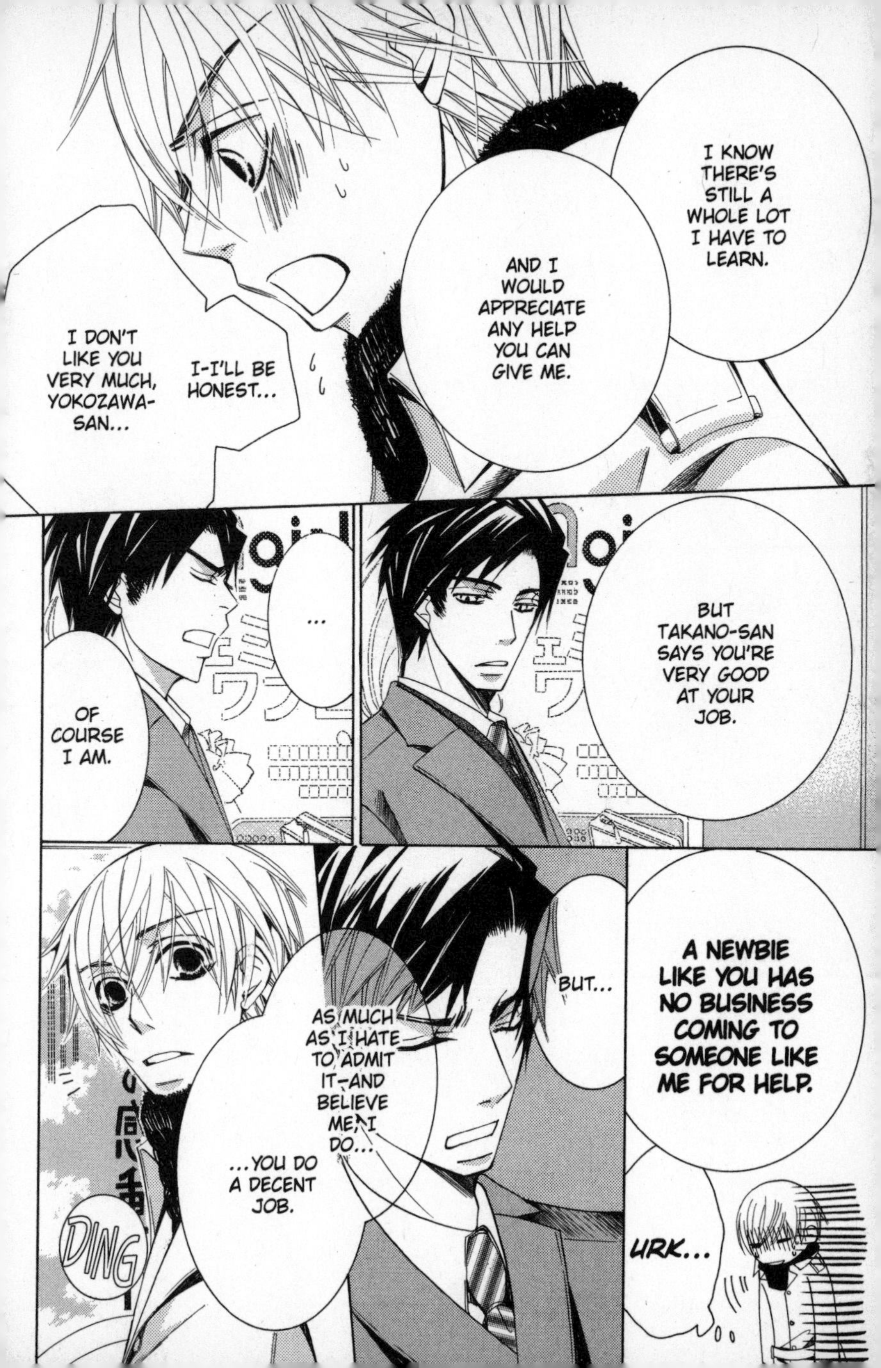
I KNOW THERE'S STILL A WHOLE LOT I HAVE TO LEARN.
AND I WOULD APPRECIATE ANY HELP YOU CAN GIVE ME.
I-I'LL BE HONEST...
I DON'T LIKE YOU VERY MUCH, YOKOZAWA-SAN...
BUT TAKANO-SAN SAYS YOU'RE VERY GOOD AT YOUR JOB.
...
OF COURSE I AM.
A NEWBIE LIKE YOU HAS NO BUSINESS COMING TO SOMEONE LIKE ME FOR HELP.
URK...
BUT...
AS MUCH AS I HATE TO ADMIT IT—AND BELIEVE ME, I DO...
...YOU DO A DECENT JOB.
DING

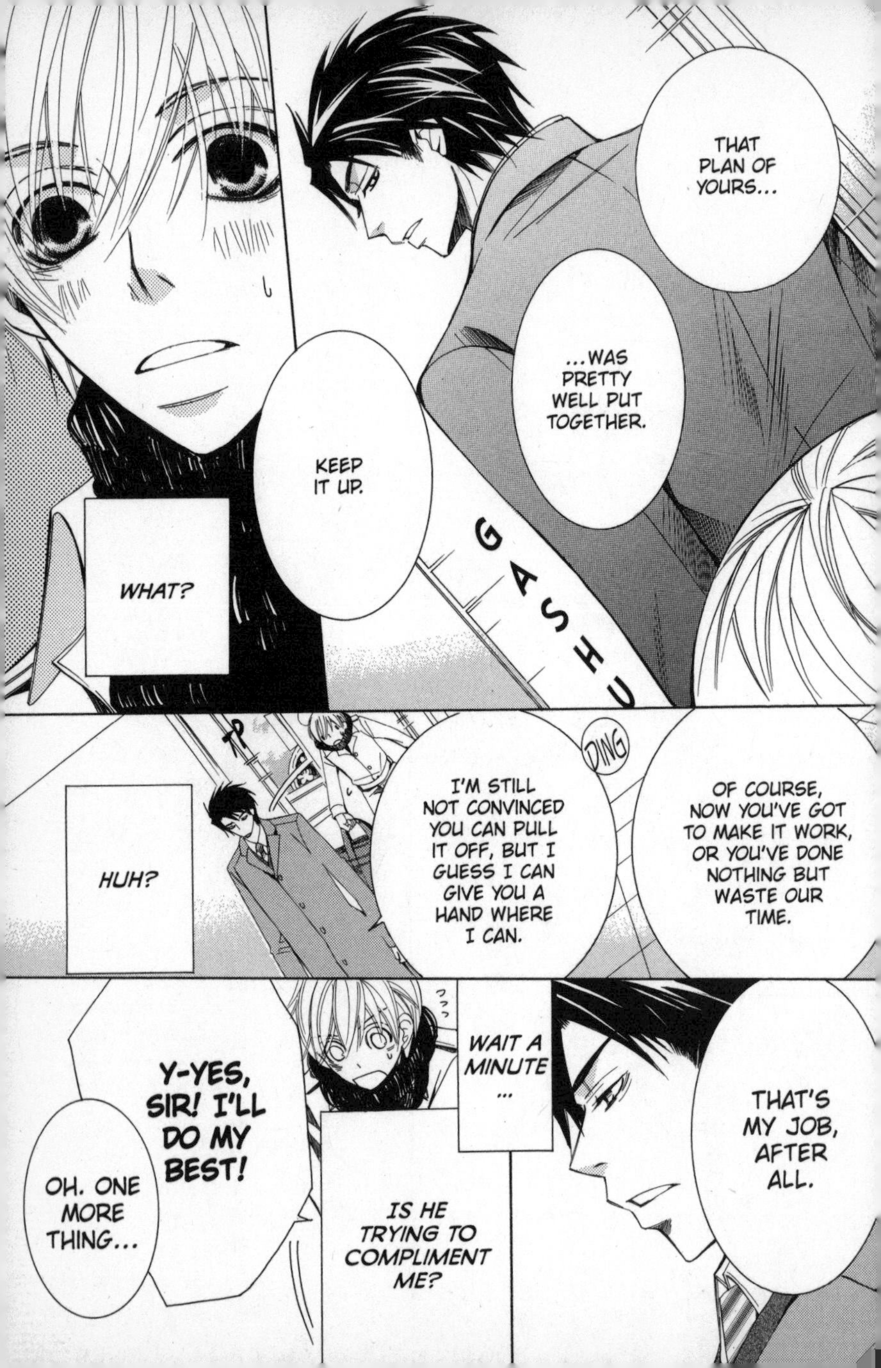
THAT PLAN OF YOURS...
...WAS PRETTY WELL PUT TOGETHER.
KEEP IT UP.
GASHU
WHAT?
OF COURSE, NOW YOU'VE GOT TO MAKE IT WORK, OR YOU'VE DONE NOTHING BUT WASTE OUR TIME.
DING
I'M STILL NOT CONVINCED YOU CAN PULL IT OFF, BUT I GUESS I CAN GIVE YOU A HAND WHERE I CAN.
TP
HUH?
THAT'S MY JOB, AFTER ALL.
WAIT A MINUTE ...
IS HE TRYING TO COMPLIMENT ME?
Y-YES, SIR! I'LL DO MY BEST!
OH. ONE MORE THING...

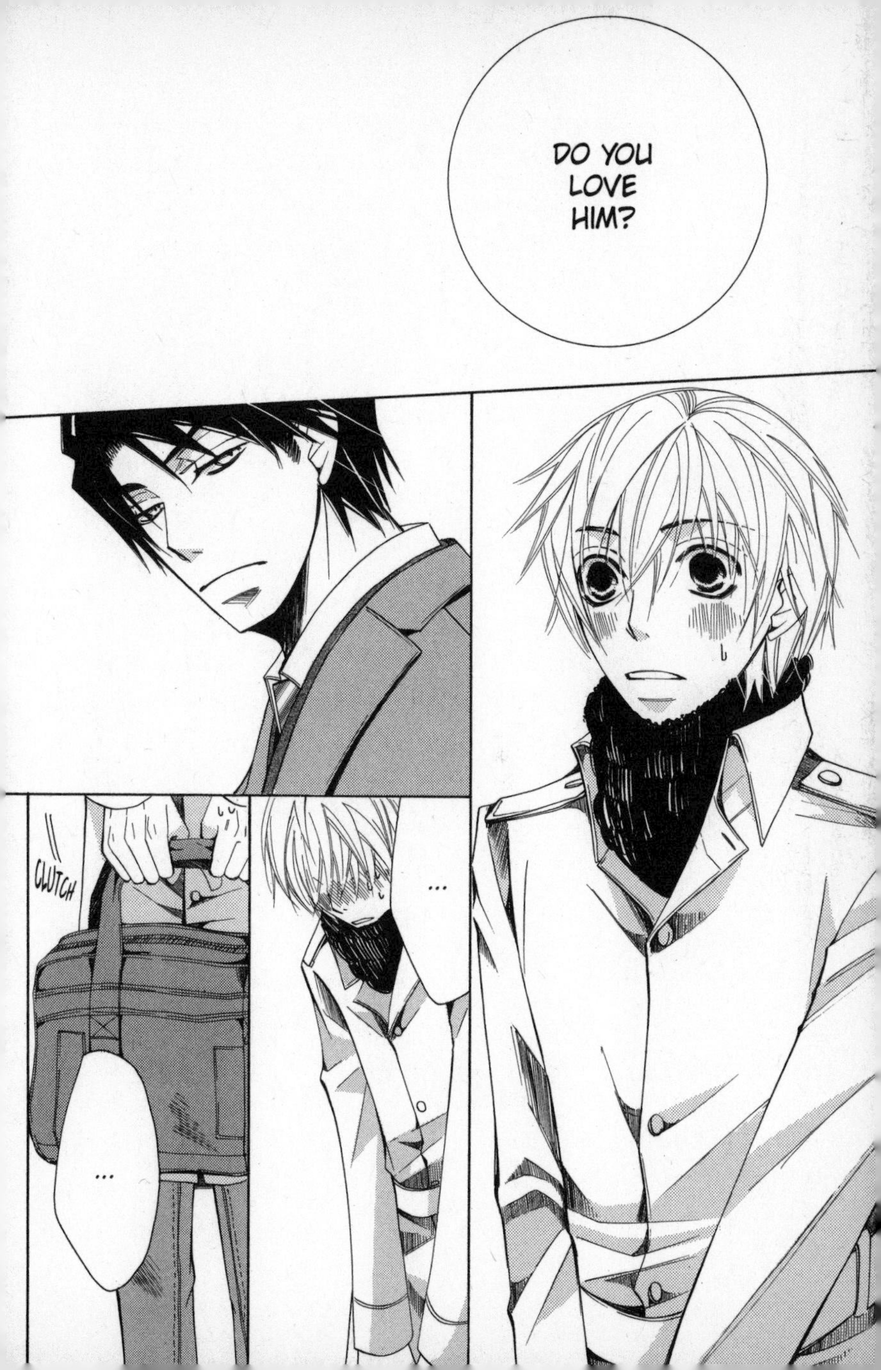
DO YOU
LOVE
HIM?
...
CLUTCH
...

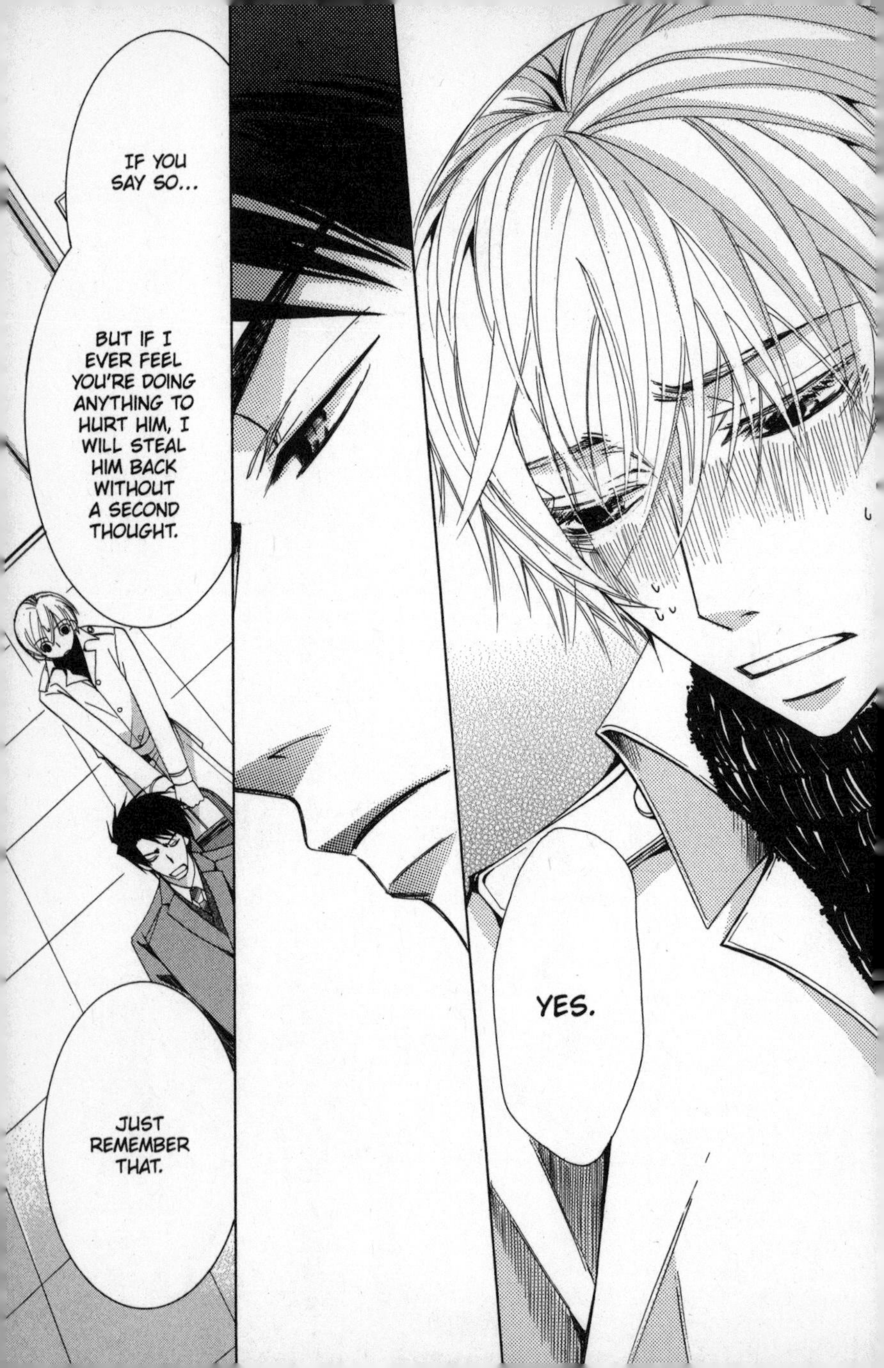
YES.
IF YOU SAY SO...
BUT IF I EVER FEEL YOU'RE DOING ANYTHING TO HURT HIM, I WILL STEAL HIM BACK WITHOUT A SECOND THOUGHT.
JUST REMEMBER THAT.

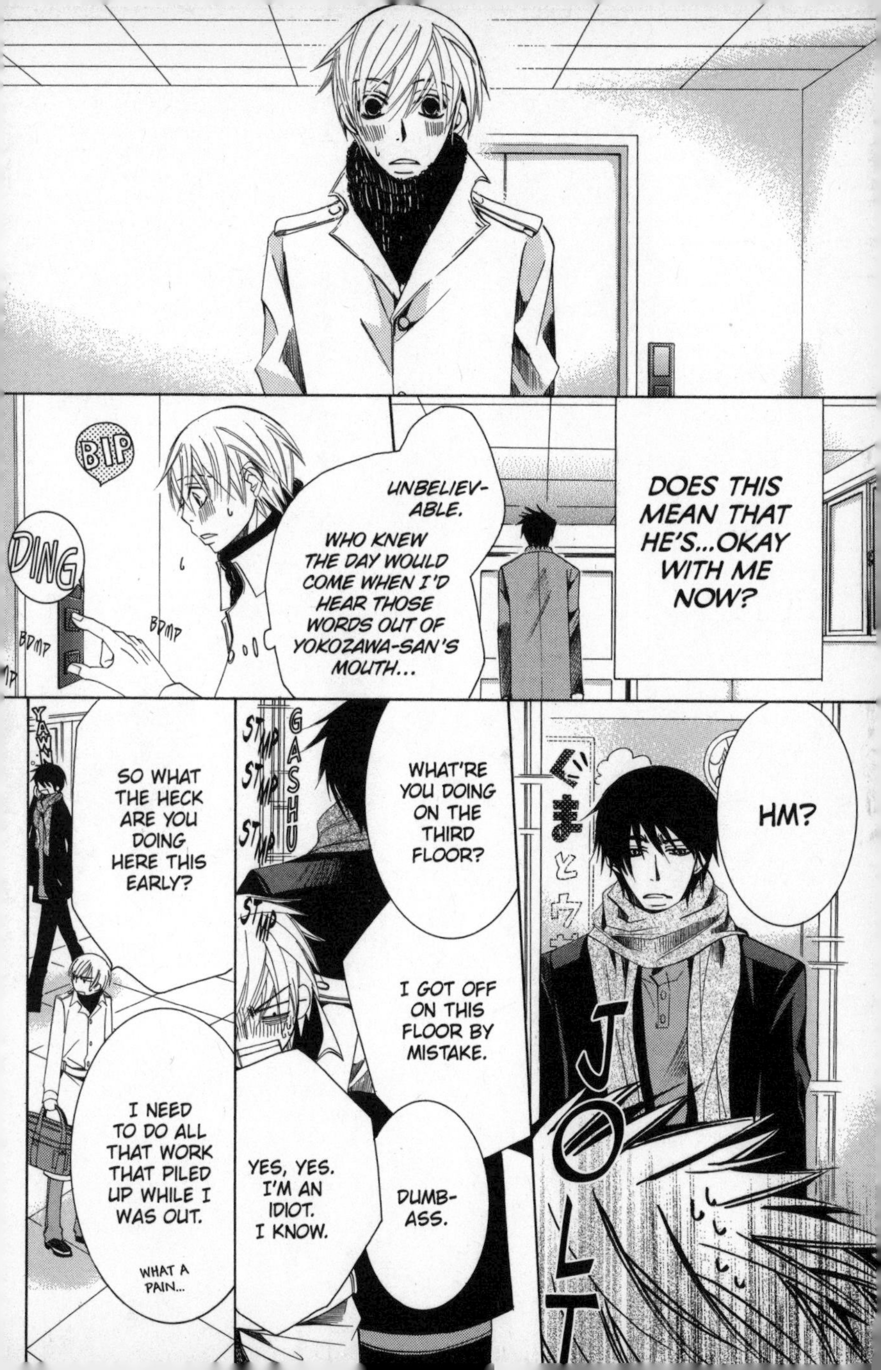
DOES THIS MEAN THAT HE'S...OKAY WITH ME NOW?
UNBELIEV-ABLE.
WHO KNEW THE DAY WOULD COME WHEN I'D HEAR THOSE WORDS OUT OF YOKOZAWA-SAN'S MOUTH...
BIP
DING
BDMP
BDMP
HM?
JOLT
GASHU
STMP STMP STMP STMP
WHAT'RE YOU DOING ON THE THIRD FLOOR?
I GOT OFF ON THIS FLOOR BY MISTAKE.
DUMB-ASS.
YES, YES. I'M AN IDIOT. I KNOW.
YAWN
SO WHAT THE HECK ARE YOU DOING HERE THIS EARLY?
I NEED TO DO ALL THAT WORK THAT PILED UP WHILE I WAS OUT.
WHAT A PAIN...

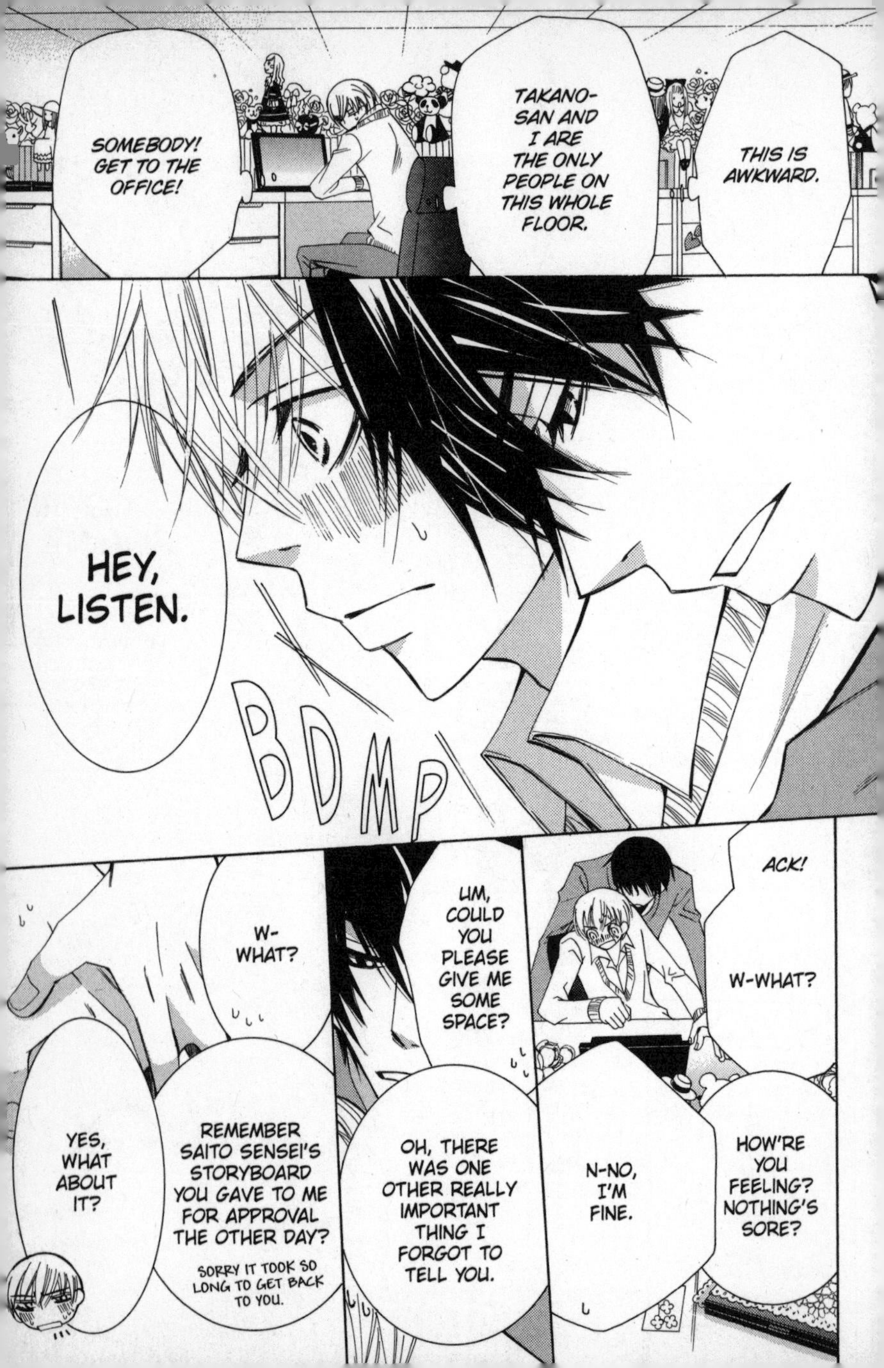
THIS IS AWKWARD.
TAKANO-SAN AND I ARE THE ONLY PEOPLE ON THIS WHOLE FLOOR.
SOMEBODY! GET TO THE OFFICE!
HEY, LISTEN.
BDMP
ACK!
W-WHAT?
HOW'RE YOU FEELING? NOTHING'S SORE?
N-NO, I'M FINE.
UM, COULD YOU PLEASE GIVE ME SOME SPACE?
OH, THERE WAS ONE OTHER REALLY IMPORTANT THING I FORGOT TO TELL YOU.
W-WHAT?
REMEMBER SAITO SENSEI'S STORYBOARD YOU GAVE TO ME FOR APPROVAL THE OTHER DAY?
SORRY IT TOOK SO LONG TO GET BACK TO YOU.
YES, WHAT ABOUT IT?

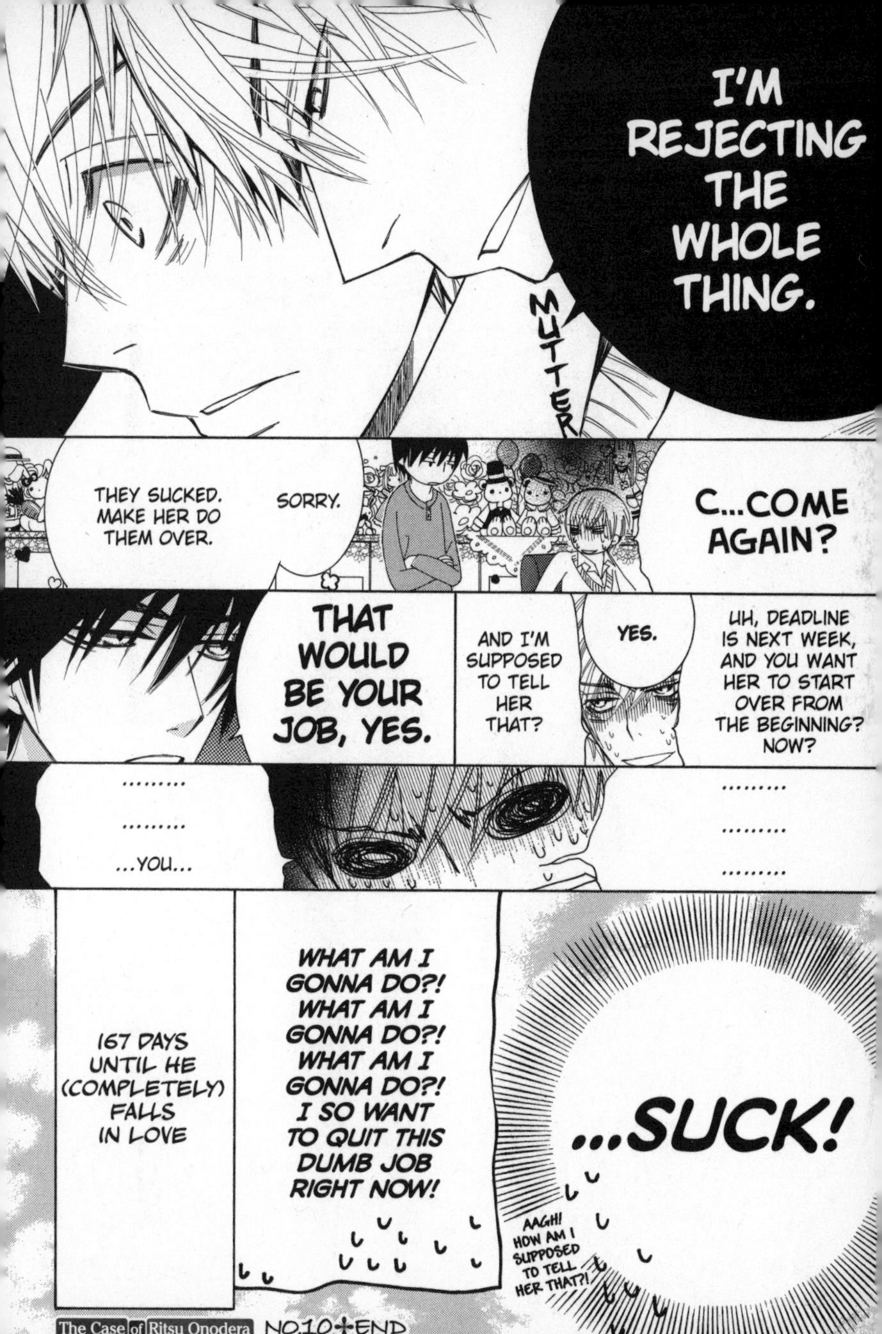
I'M REJECTING THE WHOLE THING.
MUTTER
C...COME AGAIN?
SORRY.
THEY SUCKED. MAKE HER DO THEM OVER.
UH, DEADLINE IS NEXT WEEK, AND YOU WANT HER TO START OVER FROM THE BEGINNING? NOW?
YES.
AND I'M SUPPOSED TO TELL HER THAT?
THAT WOULD BE YOUR JOB, YES.
....
....
....
....
....
...YOU...
...SUCK!
AAGH! HOW AM I SUPPOSED TO TELL HER THAT?!
WHAT AM I GONNA DO?! WHAT AM I GONNA DO?! WHAT AM I GONNA DO?! I SO WANT TO QUIT THIS DUMB JOB RIGHT NOW!
167 DAYS UNTIL HE (COMPLETELY) FALLS IN LOVE

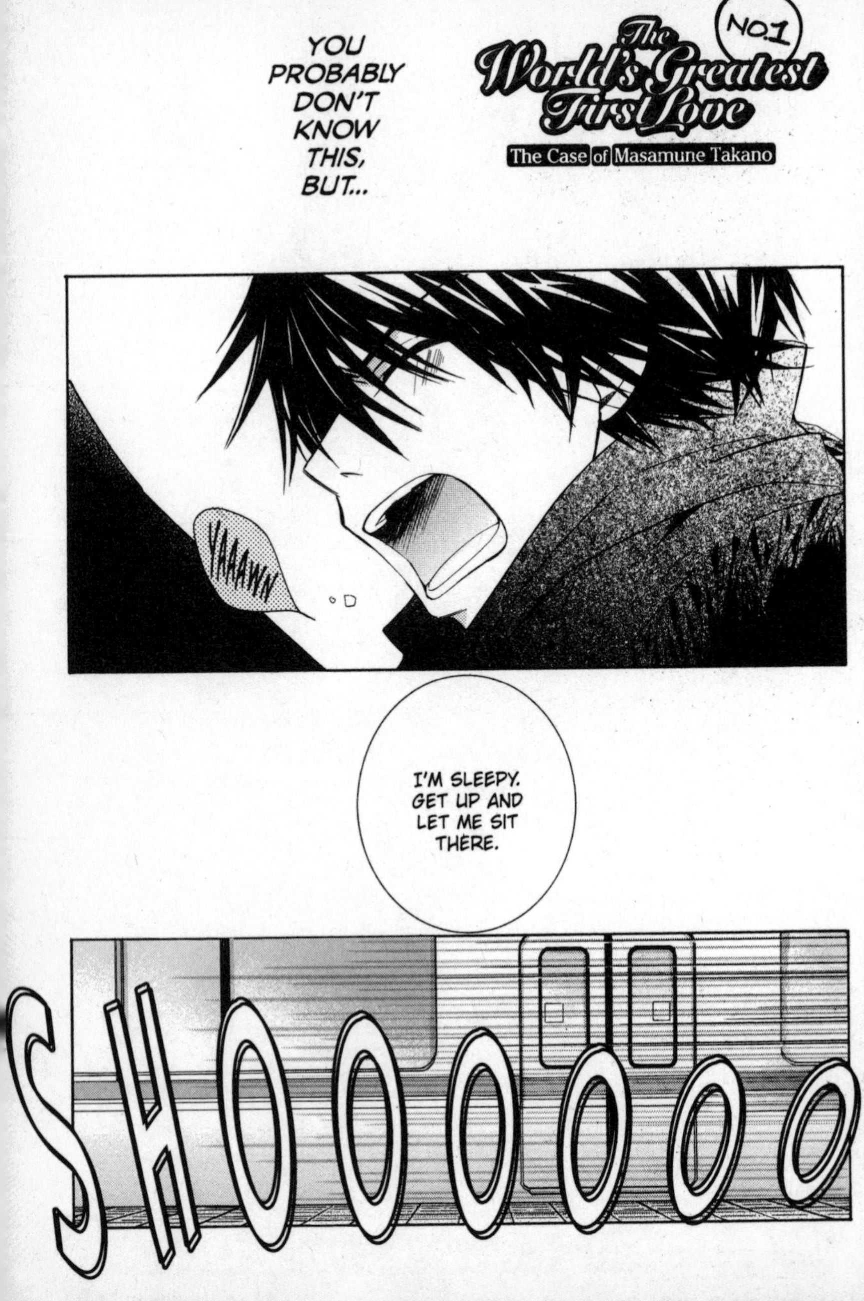
The World's Greatest First Love
NO.1
The Case of Masamune Takano
YOU PROBABLY DON'T KNOW THIS, BUT...
YAAAWN
I'M SLEEPY. GET UP AND LET ME SIT THERE.
SHOOOOOOO

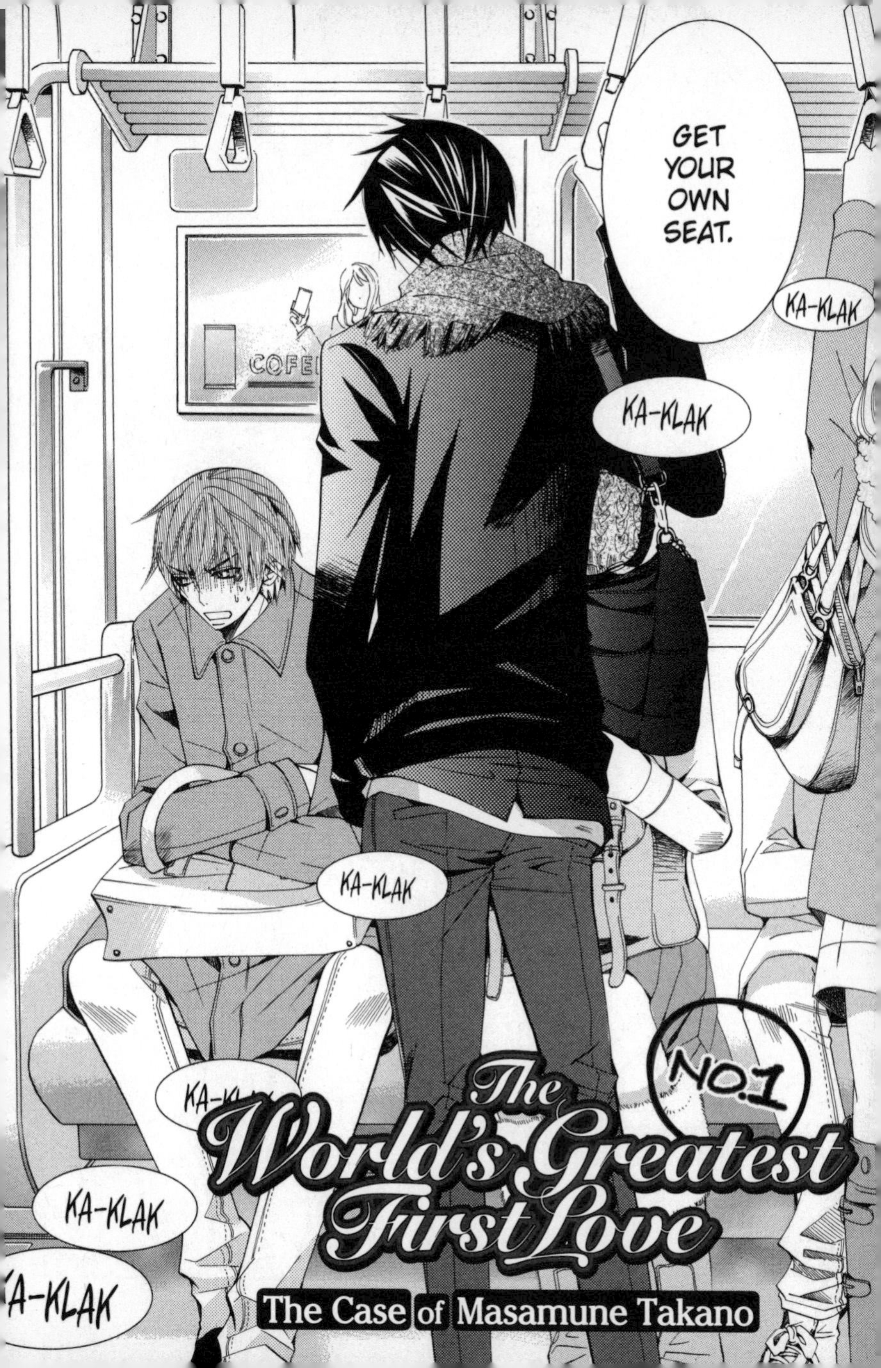
GET YOUR OWN SEAT.
KA-KLAK
KA-KLAK
KA-KLAK
KA-KLAK
NO.1
The World's Greatest First Love
The Case of Masamune Takano

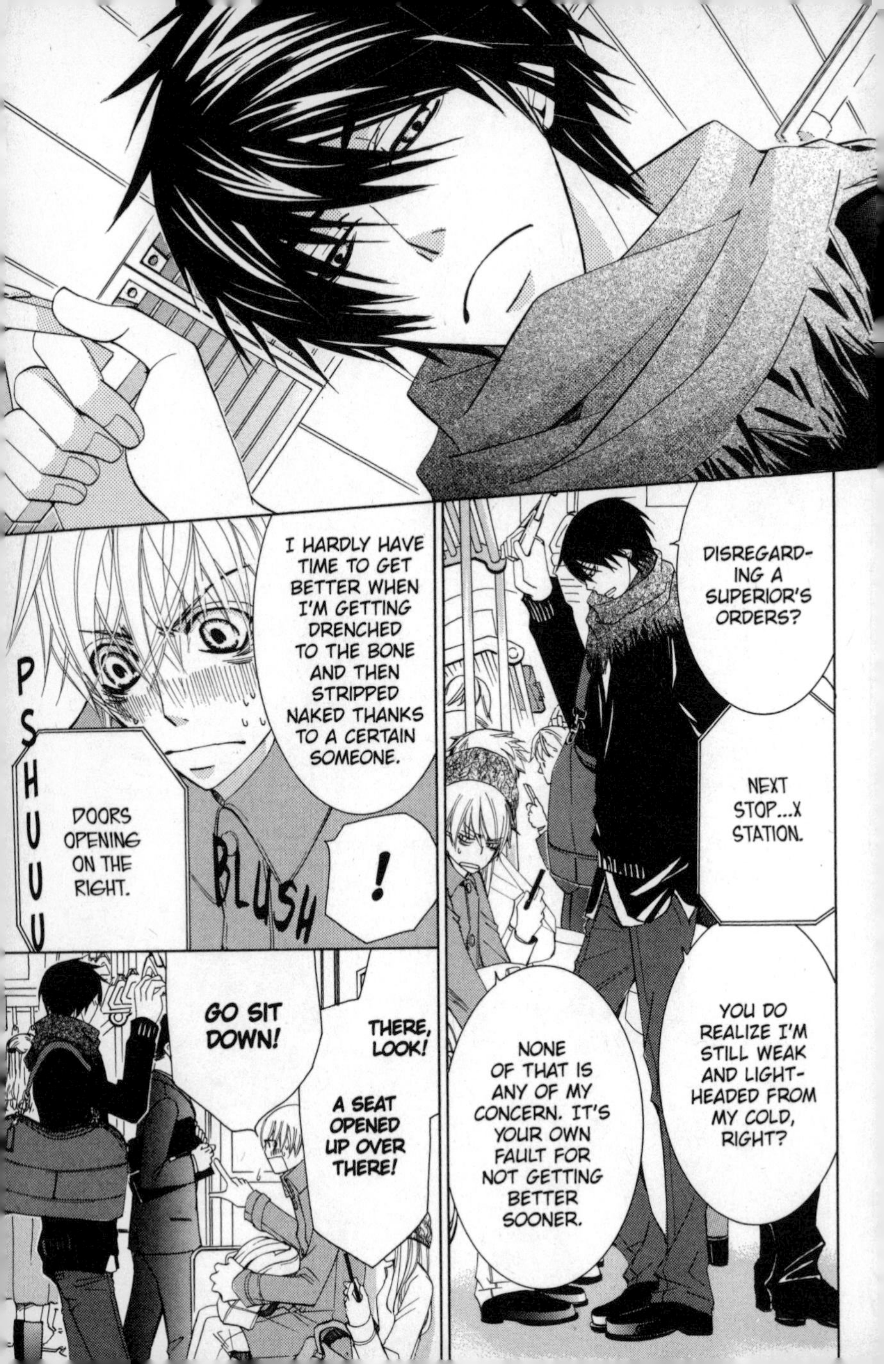
DISREGARD-
ING A
SUPERIOR'S
ORDERS?
NEXT STOP...X STATION.
YOU DO REALIZE I'M STILL WEAK AND LIGHT-HEADED FROM MY COLD, RIGHT?
NONE OF THAT IS ANY OF MY CONCERN. IT'S YOUR OWN FAULT FOR NOT GETTING BETTER SOONER.
I HARDLY HAVE TIME TO GET BETTER WHEN I'M GETTING DRENCHED TO THE BONE AND THEN STRIPPED NAKED THANKS TO A CERTAIN SOMEONE.
!
BLUSH
DOORS OPENING ON THE RIGHT.
PSHUUU
THERE, LOOK!
A SEAT OPENED UP OVER THERE!
GO SIT DOWN!

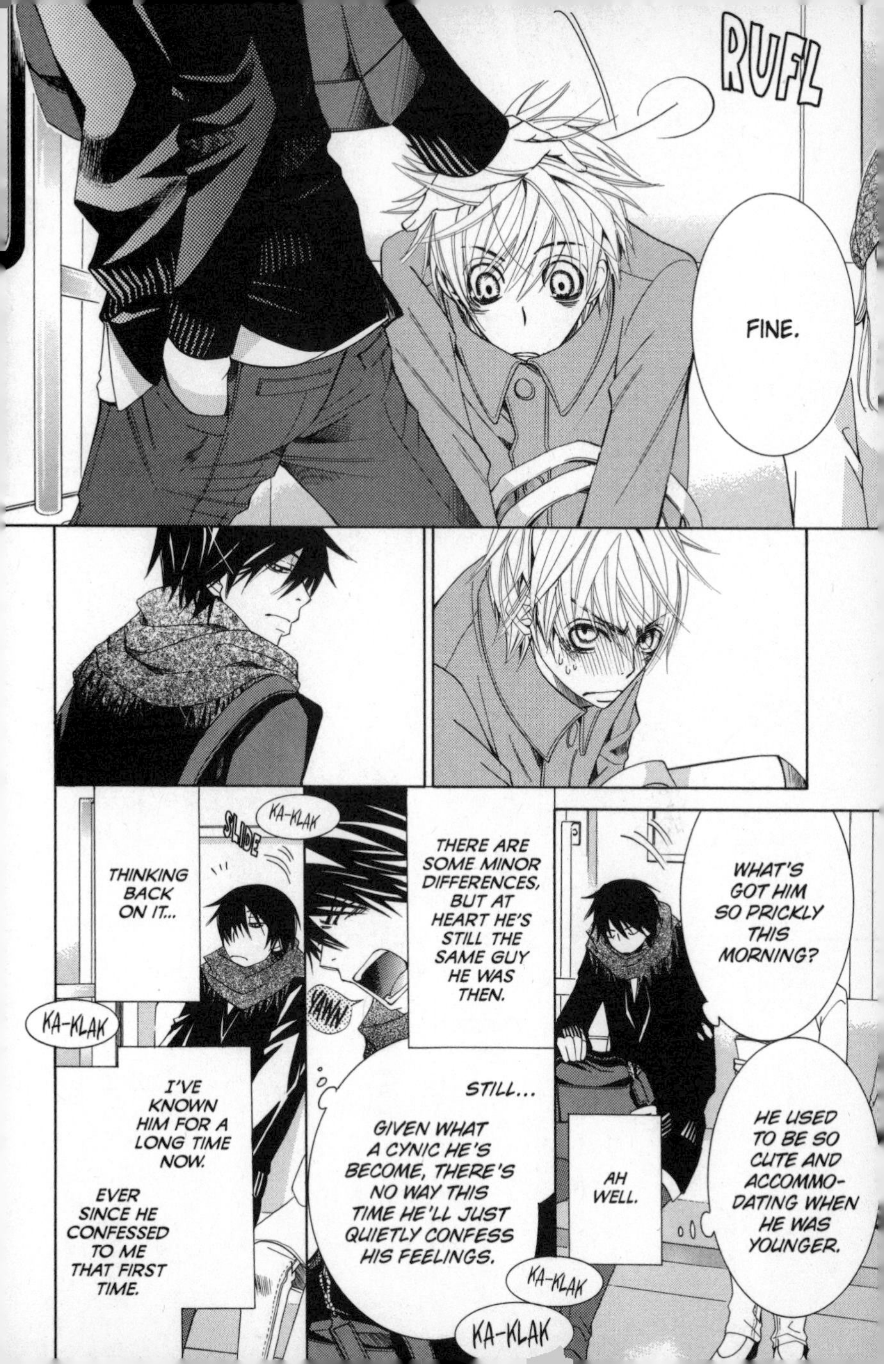
RUFL
FINE.
WHAT'S GOT HIM SO PRICKLY THIS MORNING?
HE USED TO BE SO CUTE AND ACCOMMODATING WHEN HE WAS YOUNGER.
AH WELL.
THERE ARE SOME MINOR DIFFERENCES, BUT AT HEART HE'S STILL THE SAME GUY HE WAS THEN.
YAWN
STILL...
GIVEN WHAT A CYNIC HE'S BECOME, THERE'S NO WAY THIS TIME HE'LL JUST QUIETLY CONFESS HIS FEELINGS.
KA-KLAK
KA-KLAK
KA-KLAK
SLIDE
THINKING BACK ON IT...
KA-KLAK
I'VE KNOWN HIM FOR A LONG TIME NOW.
EVER SINCE HE CONFESSED TO ME THAT FIRST TIME.

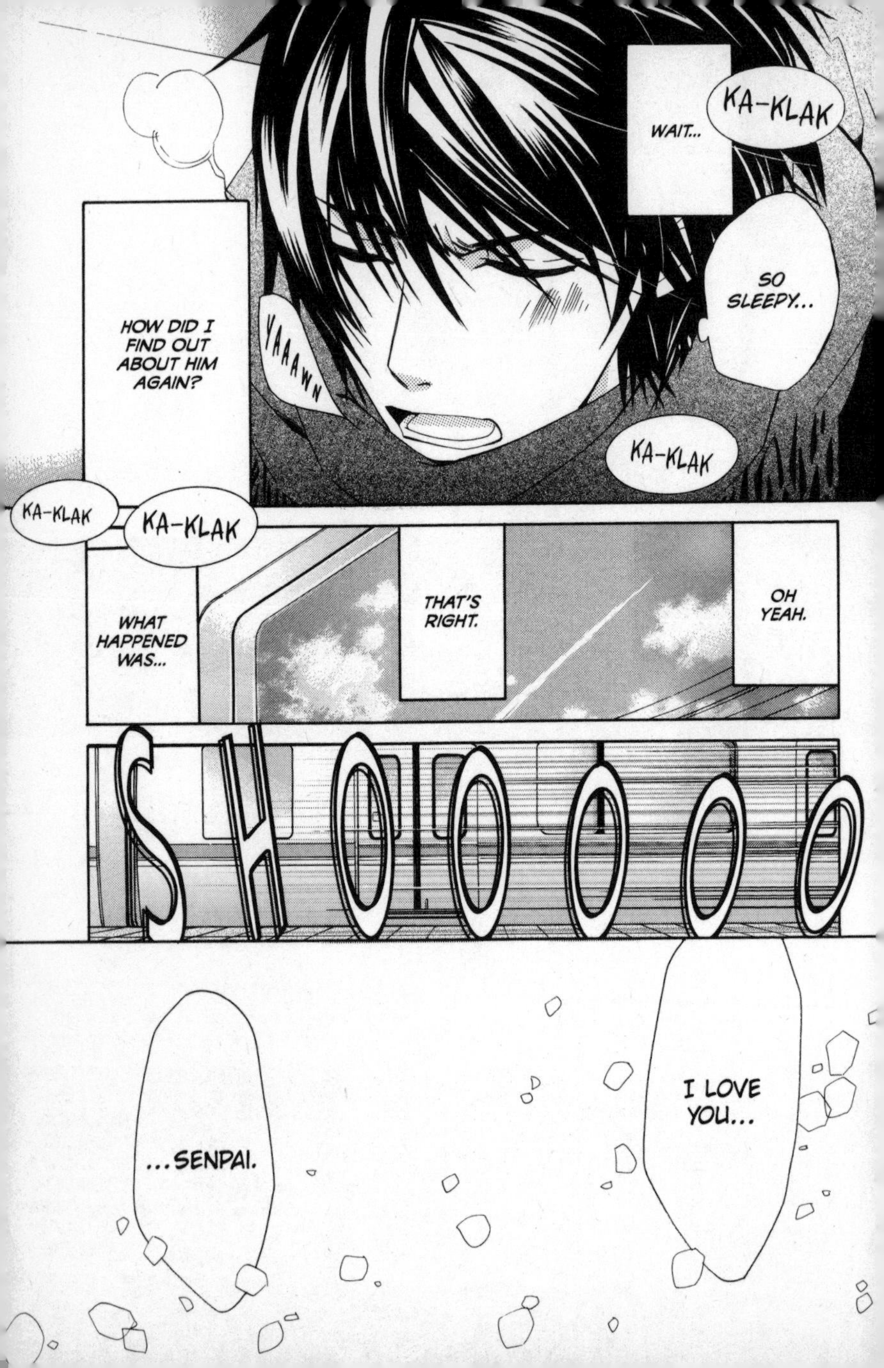
KA-KLAK
WAIT...
SO SLEEPY...
YAAAAWN
KA-KLAK
HOW DID I FIND OUT ABOUT HIM AGAIN?
KA-KLAK
KA-KLAK
OH YEAH.
THAT'S RIGHT.
WHAT HAPPENED WAS...
SHOOOOO
I LOVE YOU...
...SENPAI.

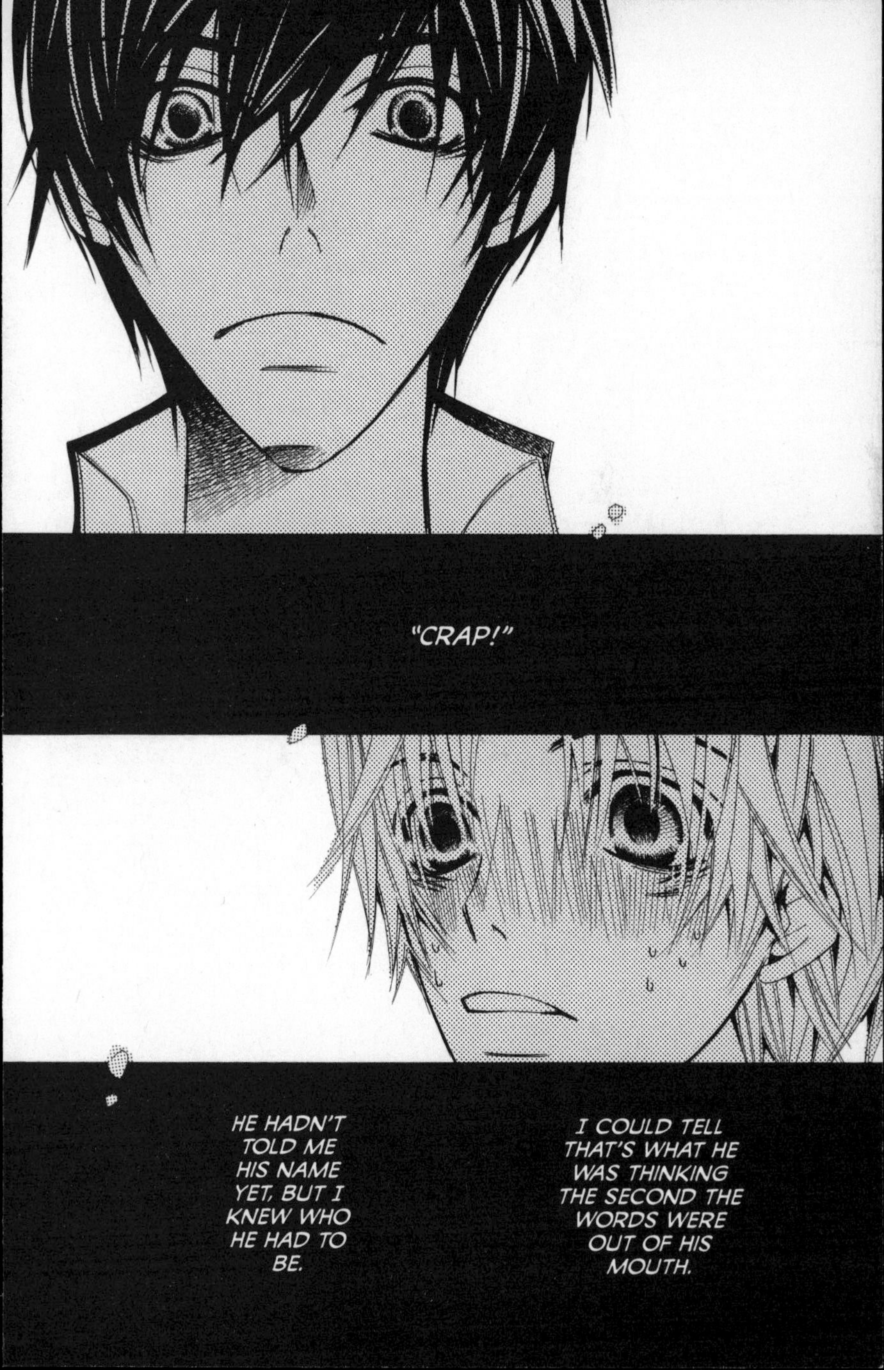
"CRAP!"
I COULD TELL THAT'S WHAT HE WAS THINKING THE SECOND THE WORDS WERE OUT OF HIS MOUTH.
HE HADN'T TOLD ME HIS NAME YET, BUT I KNEW WHO HE HAD TO BE.

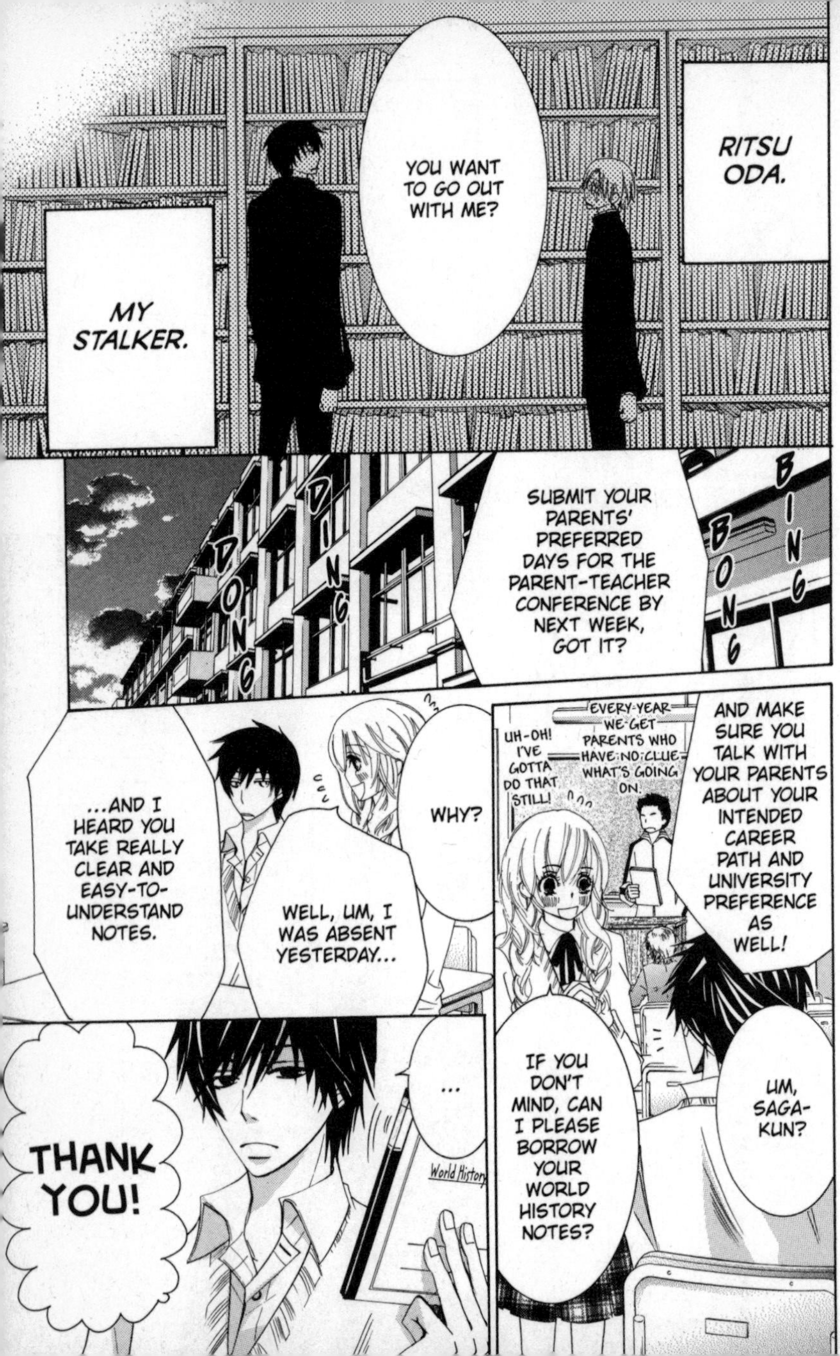
RITSU ODA.
YOU WANT TO GO OUT WITH ME?
MY STALKER.
BING BONG
SUBMIT YOUR PARENTS' PREFERRED DAYS FOR THE PARENT-TEACHER CONFERENCE BY NEXT WEEK, GOT IT?
DING DONG
AND MAKE SURE YOU TALK WITH YOUR PARENTS ABOUT YOUR INTENDED CAREER PATH AND UNIVERSITY PREFERENCE AS WELL!
EVERY YEAR WE GET PARENTS WHO HAVE NO CLUE WHAT'S GOING ON.
UH-OH! I'VE GOTTA DO THAT STILL!
WHY?
WELL, UM, I WAS ABSENT YESTERDAY...
...AND I HEARD YOU TAKE REALLY CLEAR AND EASY-TO-UNDERSTAND NOTES.
UM, SAGA-KUN?
IF YOU DON'T MIND, CAN I PLEASE BORROW YOUR WORLD HISTORY NOTES?
...
World History
THANK YOU!

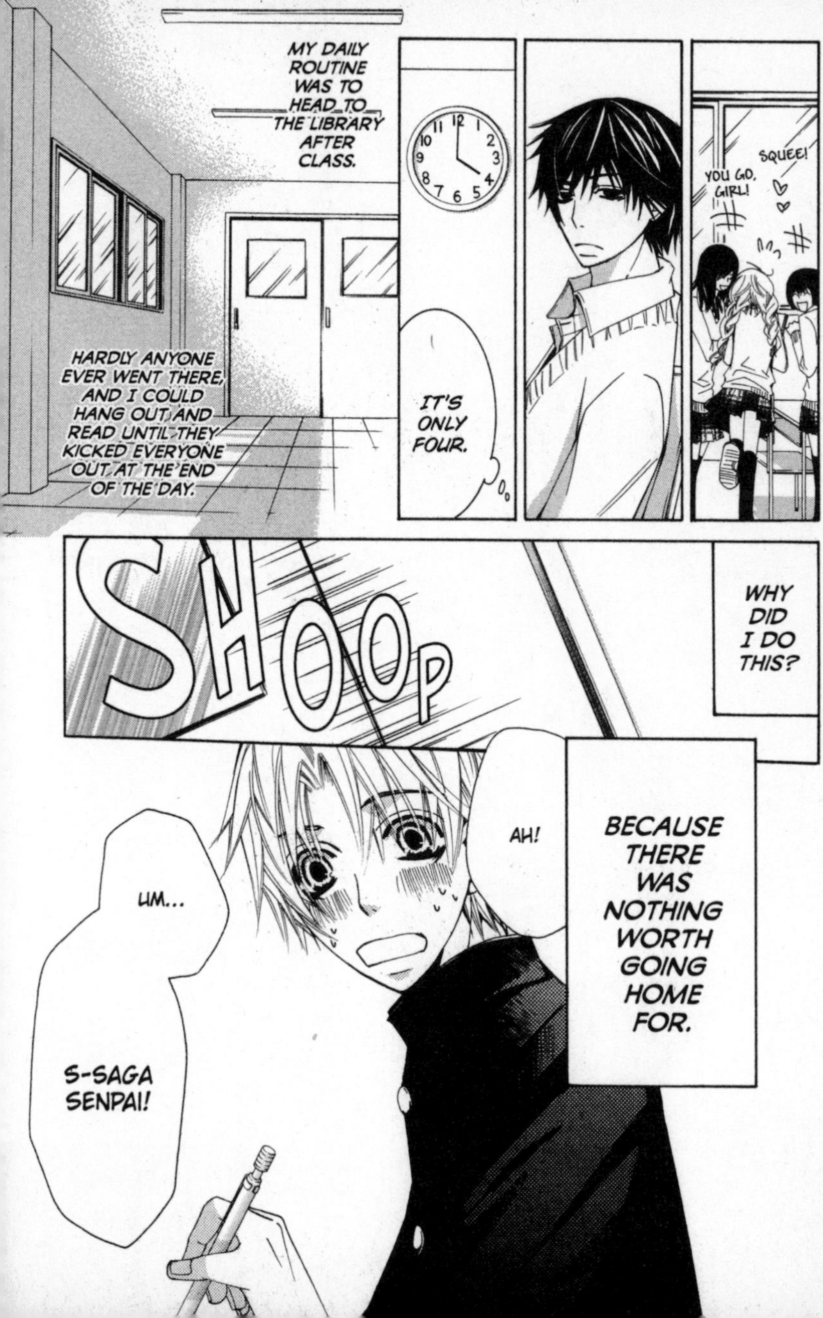

SQUEE!
YOU GO, GIRL!
IT'S ONLY FOUR.
MY DAILY ROUTINE WAS TO HEAD TO THE LIBRARY AFTER CLASS.
HARDLY ANYONE EVER WENT THERE, AND I COULD HANG OUT AND READ UNTIL THEY KICKED EVERYONE OUT AT THE END OF THE DAY.
WHY DID I DO THIS?
SHOOP
BECAUSE THERE WAS NOTHING WORTH GOING HOME FOR.
AH!
UM...
S-SAGA SENPAI!

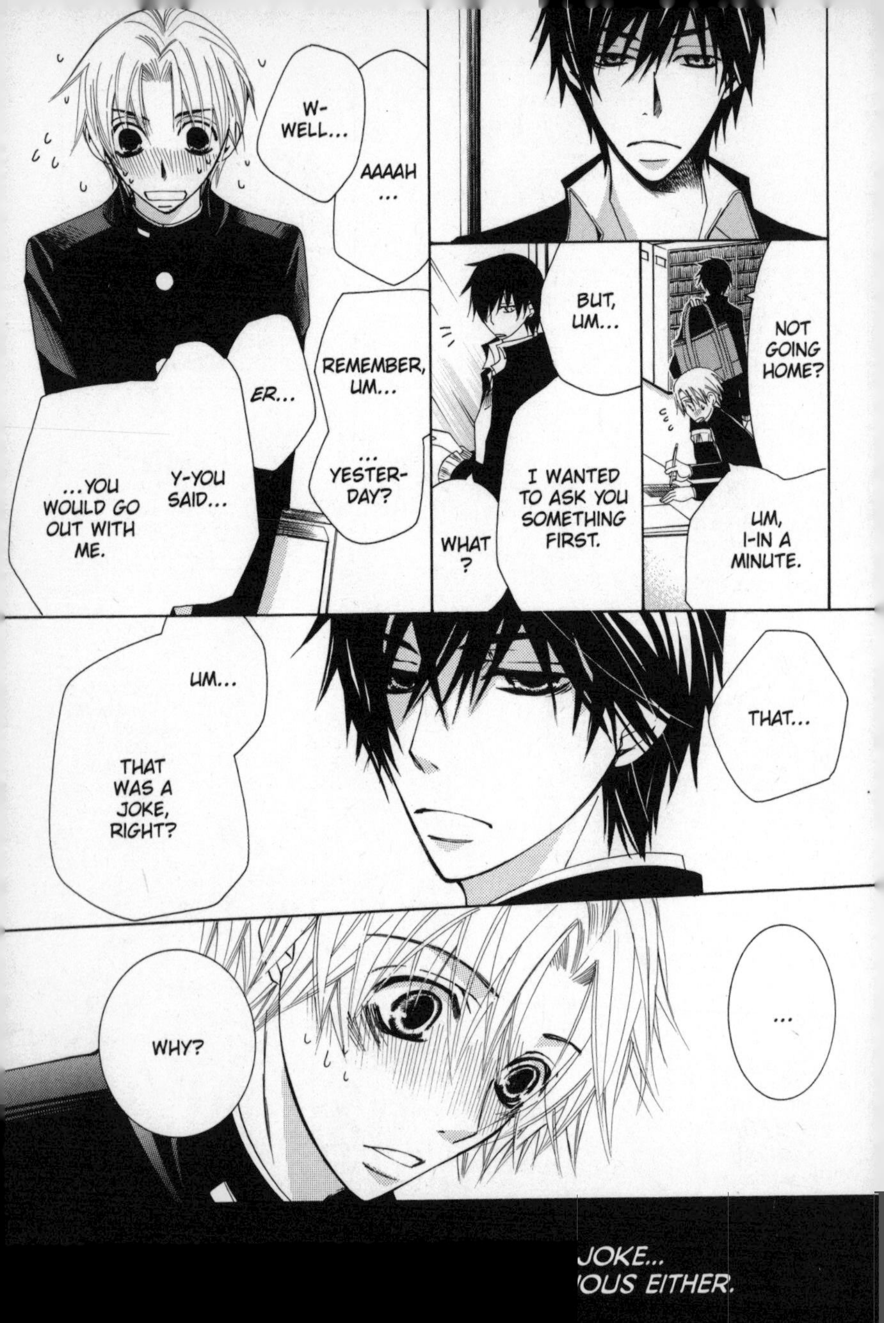
NOT GOING HOME?
UM, I-IN A MINUTE.
BUT, UM...
I WANTED TO ASK YOU SOMETHING FIRST.
WHAT?
W-WELL...
AAAAH...
REMEMBER, UM...
...YESTER-DAY?
ER...
Y-YOU SAID...
...YOU WOULD GO OUT WITH ME.
THAT...
UM...
THAT WAS A JOKE, RIGHT?
...
WHY?
JOKE...
OUS EITHER.

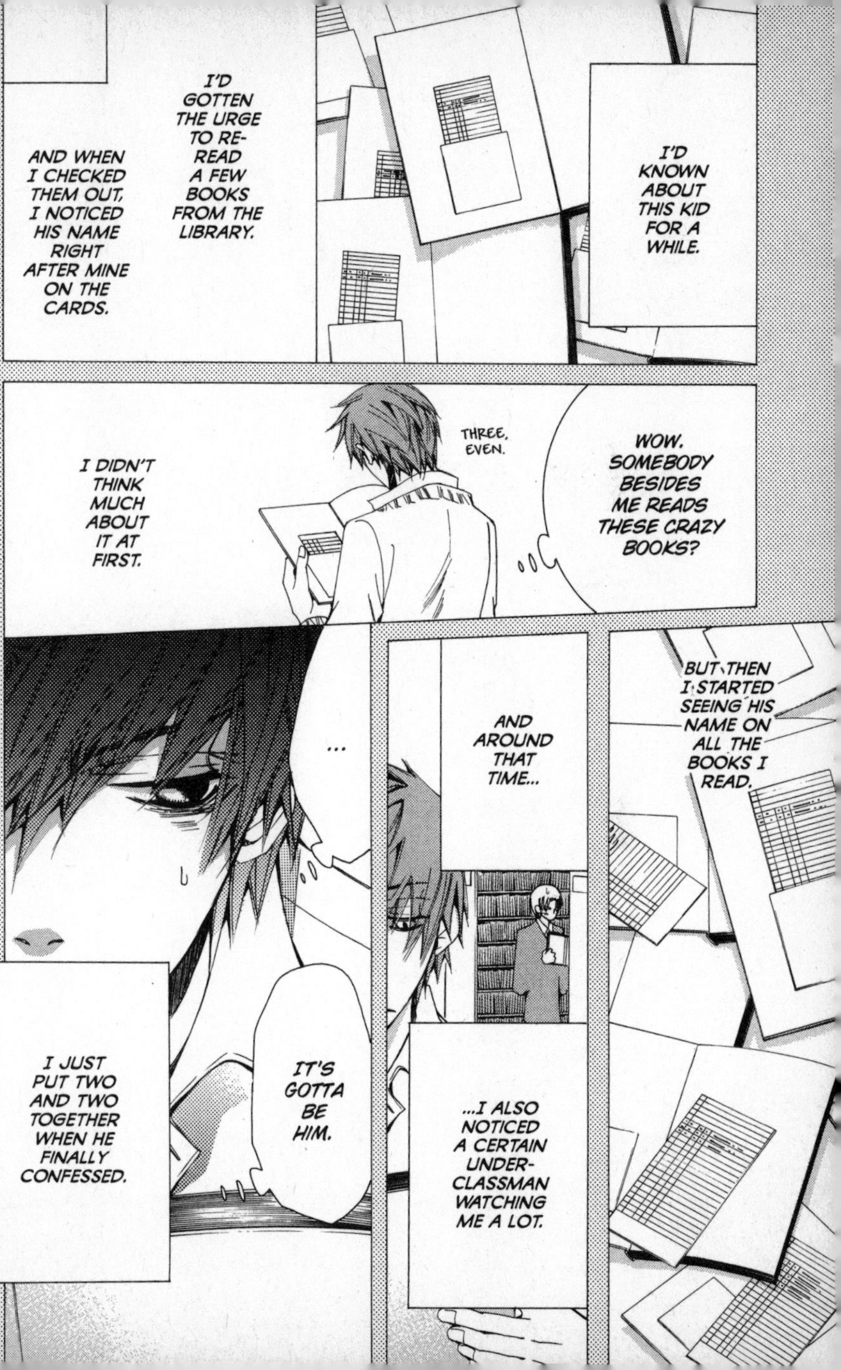
I'D KNOWN ABOUT THIS KID FOR A WHILE.
I'D GOTTEN THE URGE TO RE-READ A FEW BOOKS FROM THE LIBRARY.
AND WHEN I CHECKED THEM OUT, I NOTICED HIS NAME RIGHT AFTER MINE ON THE CARDS.
WOW. SOMEBODY BESIDES ME READS THESE CRAZY BOOKS?
THREE, EVEN.
I DIDN'T THINK MUCH ABOUT IT AT FIRST.
BUT THEN I STARTED SEEING HIS NAME ON ALL THE BOOKS I READ.
AND AROUND THAT TIME...
...I ALSO NOTICED A CERTAIN UNDER-CLASSMAN WATCHING ME A LOT.
...
IT'S GOTTA BE HIM.
I JUST PUT TWO AND TWO TOGETHER WHEN HE FINALLY CONFESSED.

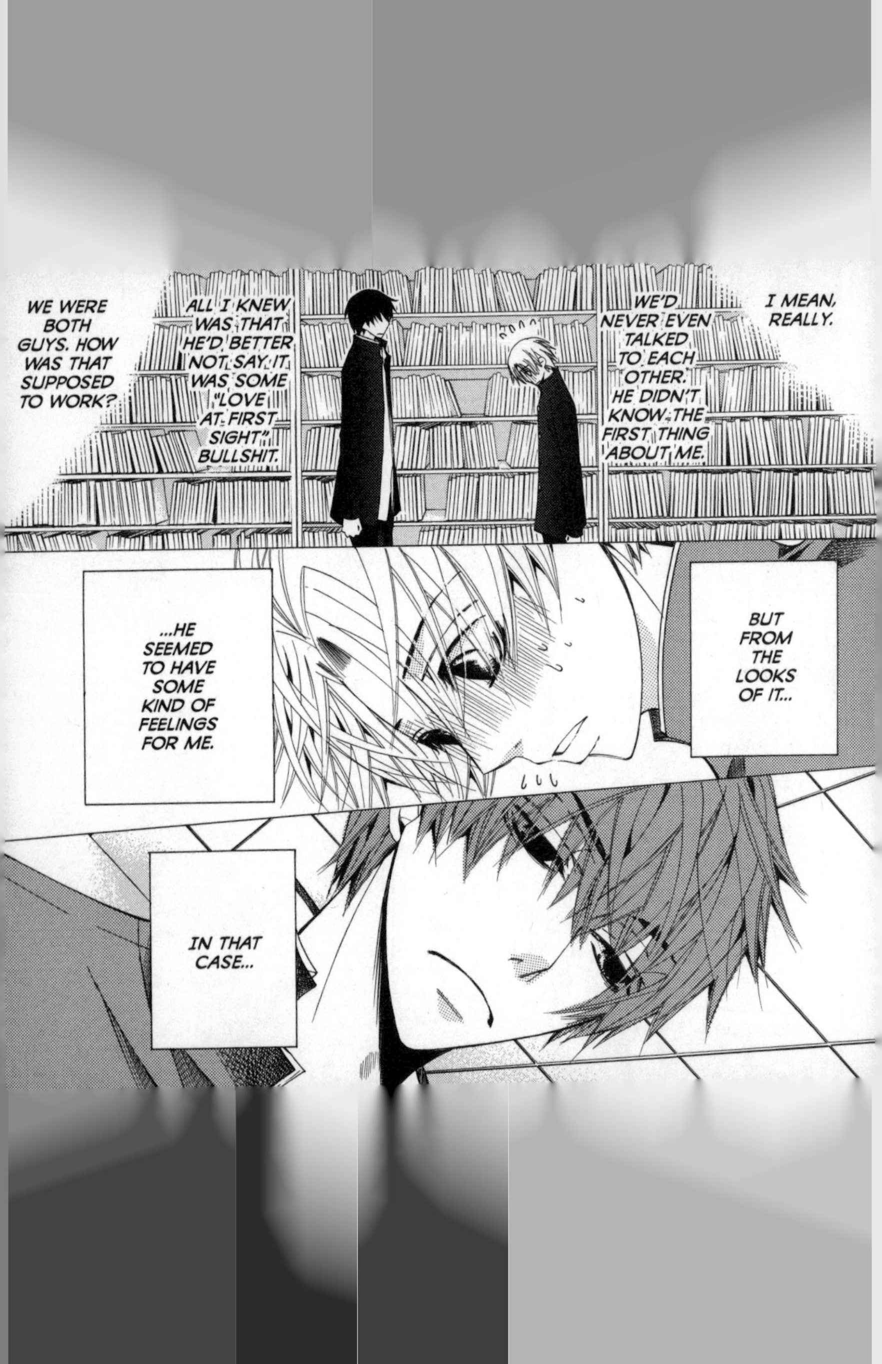
I MEAN, REALLY.
WE'D NEVER EVEN TALKED TO EACH OTHER. HE DIDN'T KNOW THE FIRST THING ABOUT ME.
ALL I KNEW WAS THAT HE'D BETTER NOT SAY IT WAS SOME "LOVE AT FIRST SIGHT" BULLSHIT.
WE WERE BOTH GUYS. HOW WAS THAT SUPPOSED TO WORK?
BUT FROM THE LOOKS OF IT...
...HE SEEMED TO HAVE SOME KIND OF FEELINGS FOR ME.
IN THAT CASE...

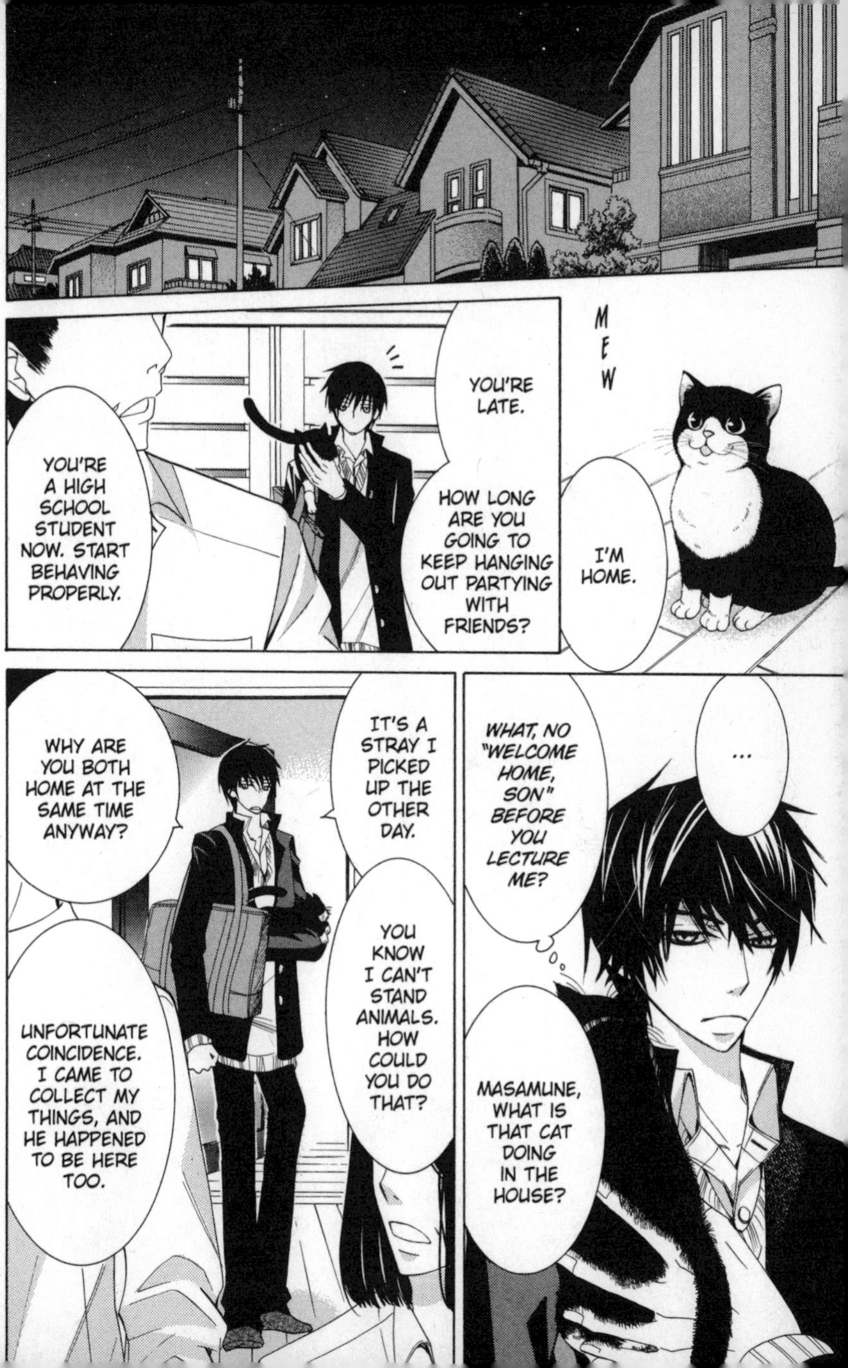
MEW
I'M HOME.
YOU'RE LATE.
HOW LONG ARE YOU GOING TO KEEP HANGING OUT PARTYING WITH FRIENDS?
YOU'RE A HIGH SCHOOL STUDENT NOW. START BEHAVING PROPERLY.
...
WHAT, NO "WELCOME HOME, SON" BEFORE YOU LECTURE ME?
MASAMUNE, WHAT IS THAT CAT DOING IN THE HOUSE?
IT'S A STRAY I PICKED UP THE OTHER DAY.
WHY ARE YOU BOTH HOME AT THE SAME TIME ANYWAY?
YOU KNOW I CAN'T STAND ANIMALS. HOW COULD YOU DO THAT?
UNFORTUNATE COINCIDENCE. I CAME TO COLLECT MY THINGS, AND HE HAPPENED TO BE HERE TOO.

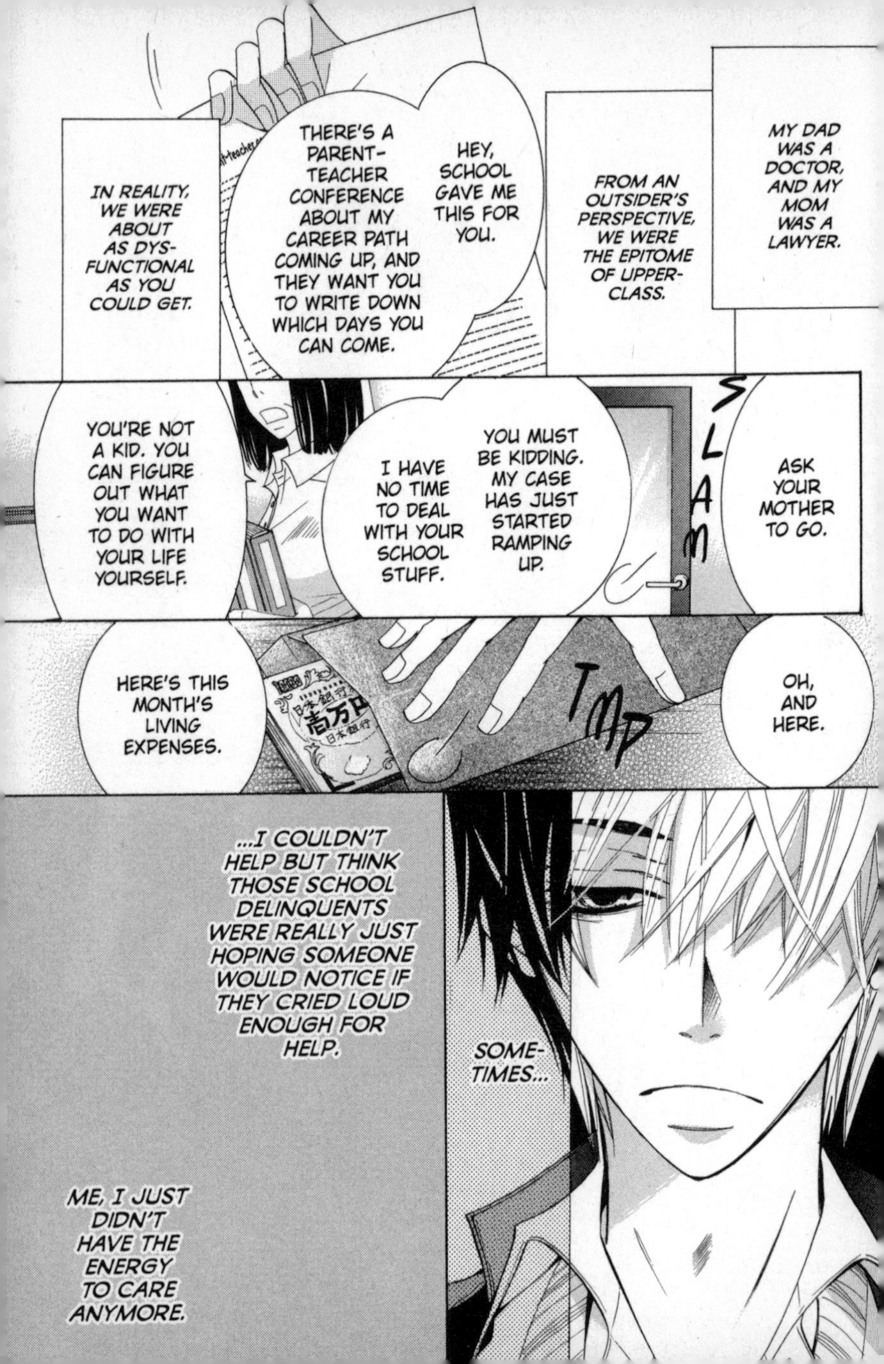
MY DAD WAS A DOCTOR, AND MY MOM WAS A LAWYER.
FROM AN OUTSIDER'S PERSPECTIVE, WE WERE THE EPITOME OF UPPER-CLASS.
HEY, SCHOOL GAVE ME THIS FOR YOU.
THERE'S A PARENT-TEACHER CONFERENCE ABOUT MY CAREER PATH COMING UP, AND THEY WANT YOU TO WRITE DOWN WHICH DAYS YOU CAN COME.
IN REALITY, WE WERE ABOUT AS DYS-FUNCTIONAL AS YOU COULD GET.
ASK YOUR MOTHER TO GO.
SLAM
YOU MUST BE KIDDING. MY CASE HAS JUST STARTED RAMPING UP.
I HAVE NO TIME TO DEAL WITH YOUR SCHOOL STUFF.
YOU'RE NOT A KID. YOU CAN FIGURE OUT WHAT YOU WANT TO DO WITH YOUR LIFE YOURSELF.
OH, AND HERE.
TMP
HERE'S THIS MONTH'S LIVING EXPENSES.
SOME-TIMES...
...I COULDN'T HELP BUT THINK THOSE SCHOOL DELINQUENTS WERE REALLY JUST HOPING SOMEONE WOULD NOTICE IF THEY CRIED LOUD ENOUGH FOR HELP.
ME, I JUST DIDN'T HAVE THE ENERGY TO CARE ANYMORE.

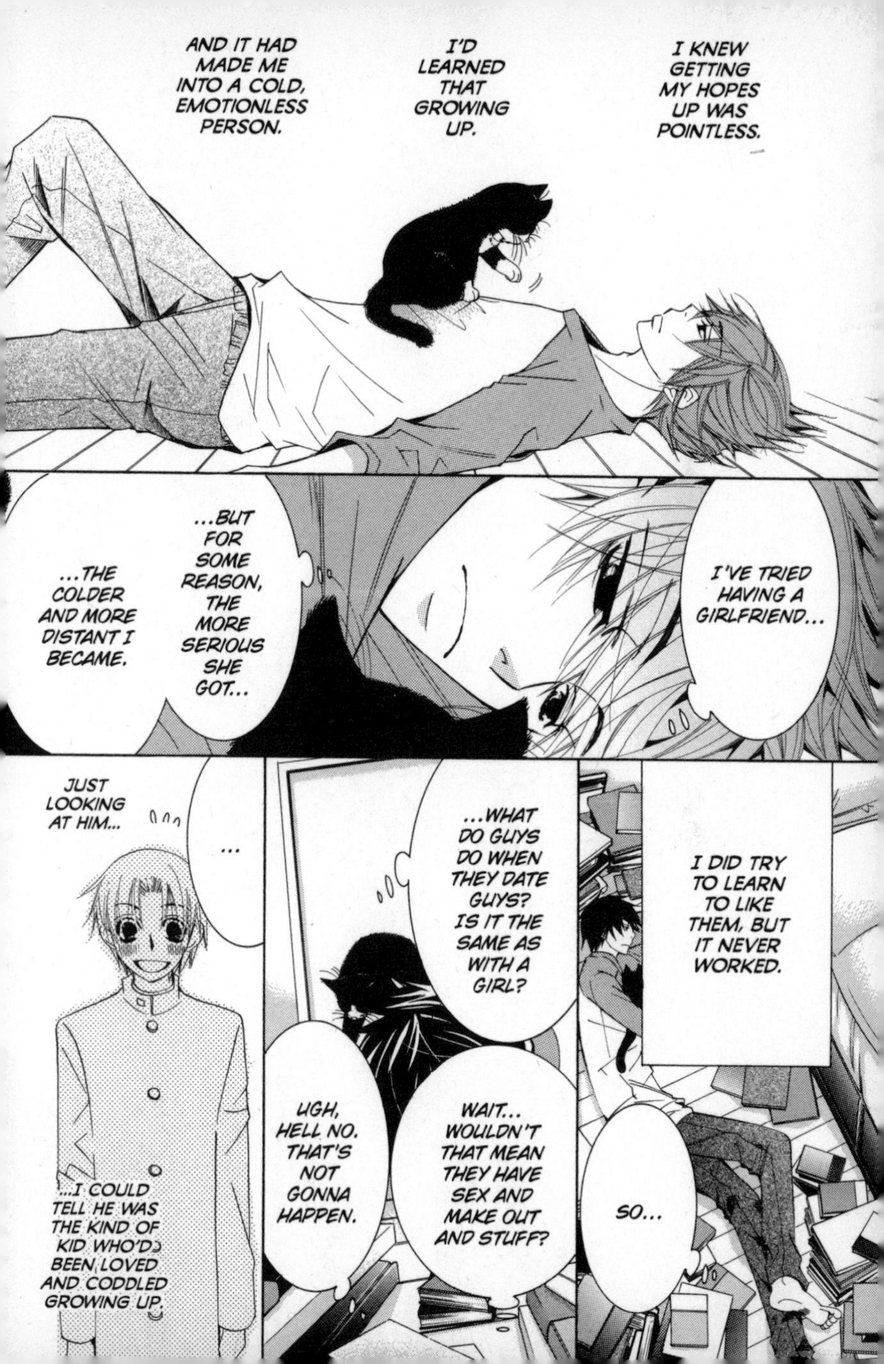
I KNEW GETTING MY HOPES UP WAS POINTLESS.
I'D LEARNED THAT GROWING UP.
AND IT HAD MADE ME INTO A COLD, EMOTIONLESS PERSON.
I'VE TRIED HAVING A GIRLFRIEND...
...BUT FOR SOME REASON, THE MORE SERIOUS SHE GOT...
...THE COLDER AND MORE DISTANT I BECAME.
I DID TRY TO LEARN TO LIKE THEM, BUT IT NEVER WORKED.
SO...
...WHAT DO GUYS DO WHEN THEY DATE GUYS? IS IT THE SAME AS WITH A GIRL?
WAIT... WOULDN'T THAT MEAN THEY HAVE SEX AND MAKE OUT AND STUFF?
UGH, HELL NO. THAT'S NOT GONNA HAPPEN.
...
JUST LOOKING AT HIM...
...I COULD TELL HE WAS THE KIND OF KID WHO'D BEEN LOVED AND CODDLED GROWING UP.

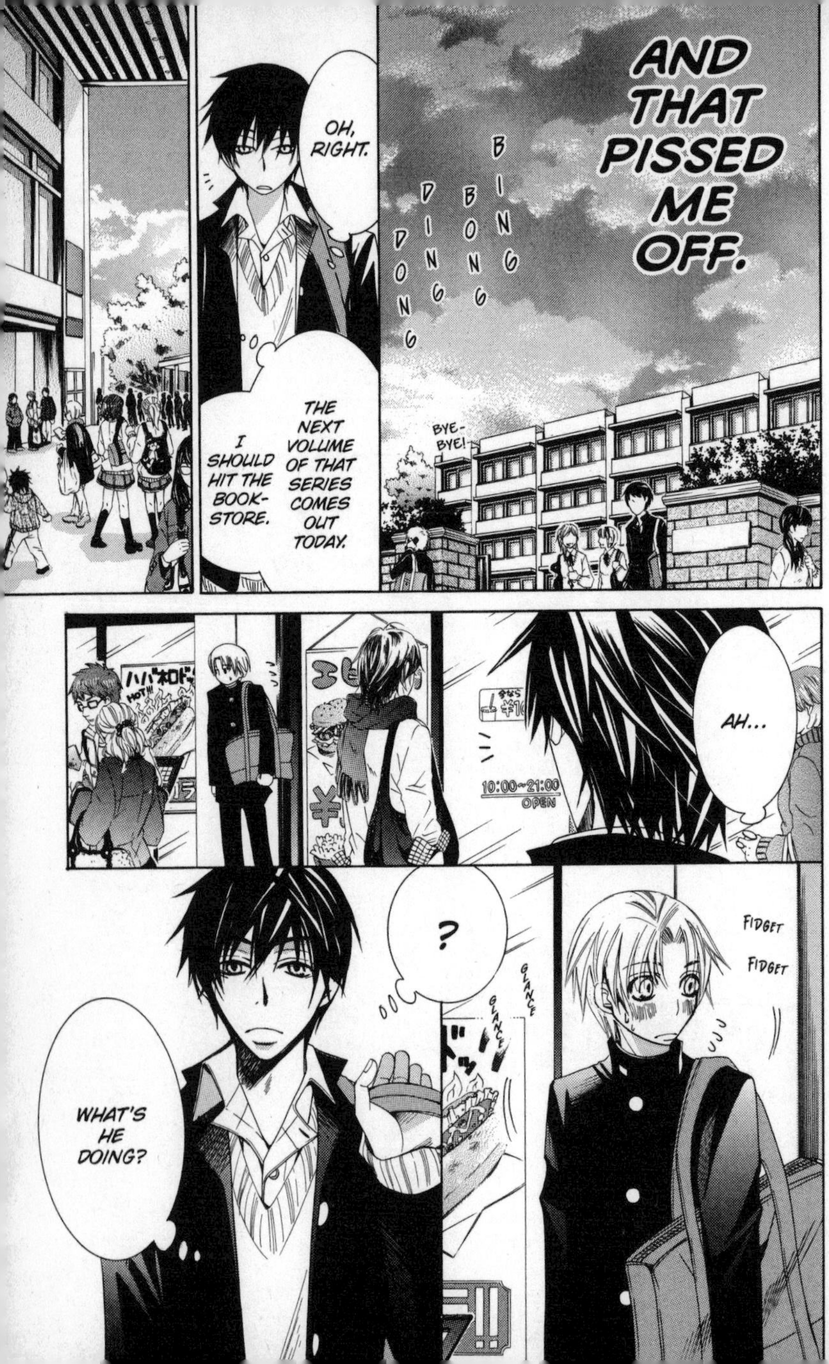
AND THAT PISSED ME OFF.
BING BONG
DING DONG
BYE-BYE!
OH, RIGHT.
THE NEXT VOLUME OF THAT SERIES COMES OUT TODAY.
I SHOULD HIT THE BOOK-STORE.
AH...
10:00~21:00 OPEN
HOT!!
FIDGET
FIDGET
?
GLANCE
GLANCE
WHAT'S HE DOING?

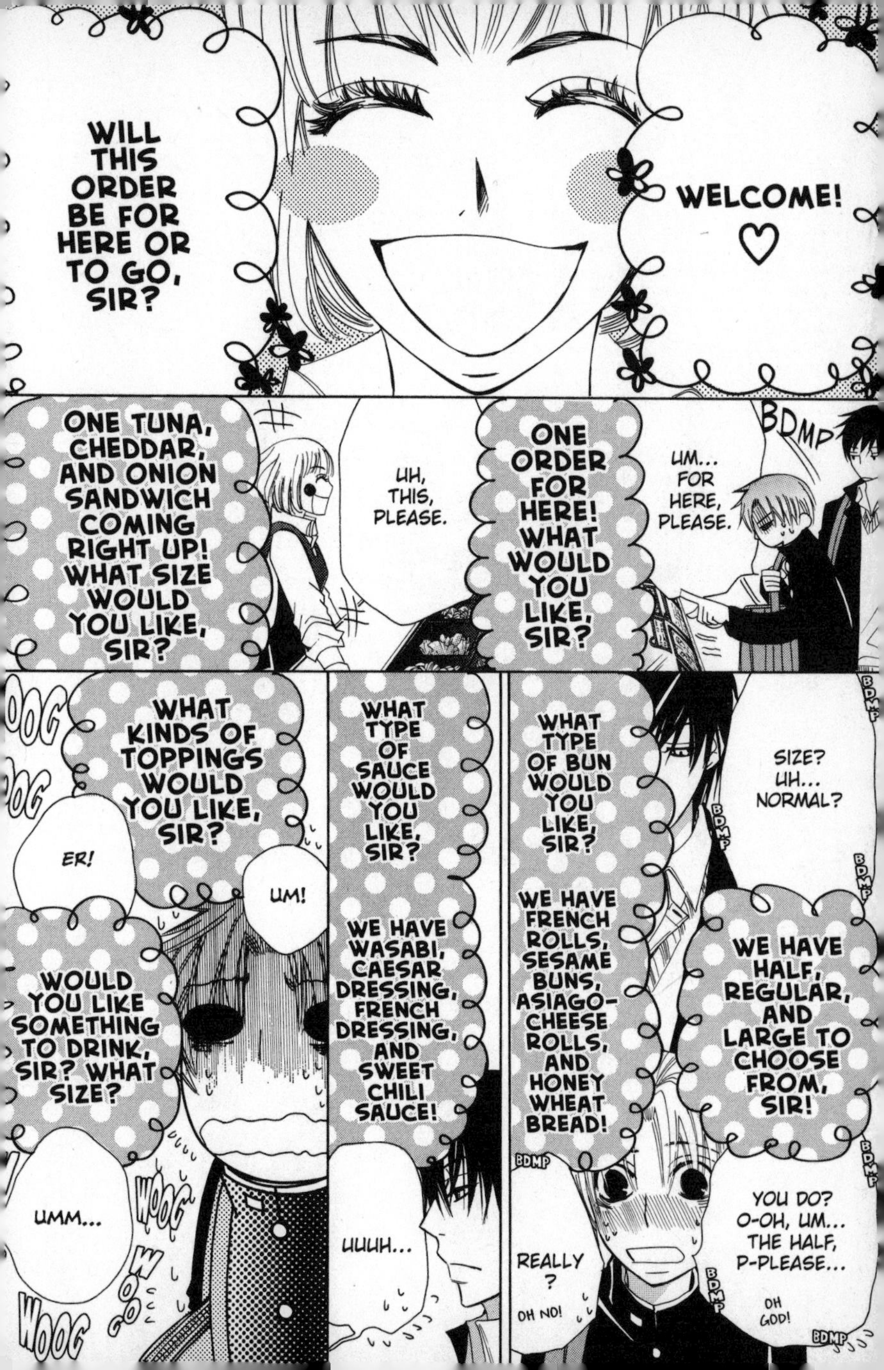
WELCOME! ♡
WILL THIS ORDER BE FOR HERE OR TO GO, SIR?
BDMP
UM... FOR HERE, PLEASE.
ONE ORDER FOR HERE! WHAT WOULD YOU LIKE, SIR?
UH, THIS, PLEASE.
ONE TUNA, CHEDDAR, AND ONION SANDWICH COMING RIGHT UP! WHAT SIZE WOULD YOU LIKE, SIR?
SIZE? UH... NORMAL?
BDMP
WE HAVE HALF, REGULAR, AND LARGE TO CHOOSE FROM, SIR!
YOU DO? O-OH, UM... THE HALF, P-PLEASE...
OH GOD!
BDMP
WHAT TYPE OF BUN WOULD YOU LIKE, SIR?
BDMP
WE HAVE FRENCH ROLLS, SESAME BUNS, ASIAGO-CHEESE ROLLS, AND HONEY WHEAT BREAD!
REALLY ?
OH NO!
BDMP
WHAT TYPE OF SAUCE WOULD YOU LIKE, SIR?
WE HAVE WASABI, CAESAR DRESSING, FRENCH DRESSING, AND SWEET CHILI SAUCE!
UUUH...
WOOG
WOOG
WHAT KINDS OF TOPPINGS WOULD YOU LIKE, SIR?
UM!
ER!
WOULD YOU LIKE SOMETHING TO DRINK, SIR? WHAT SIZE?
UMM...
WOOG
WOOOO
WOOG

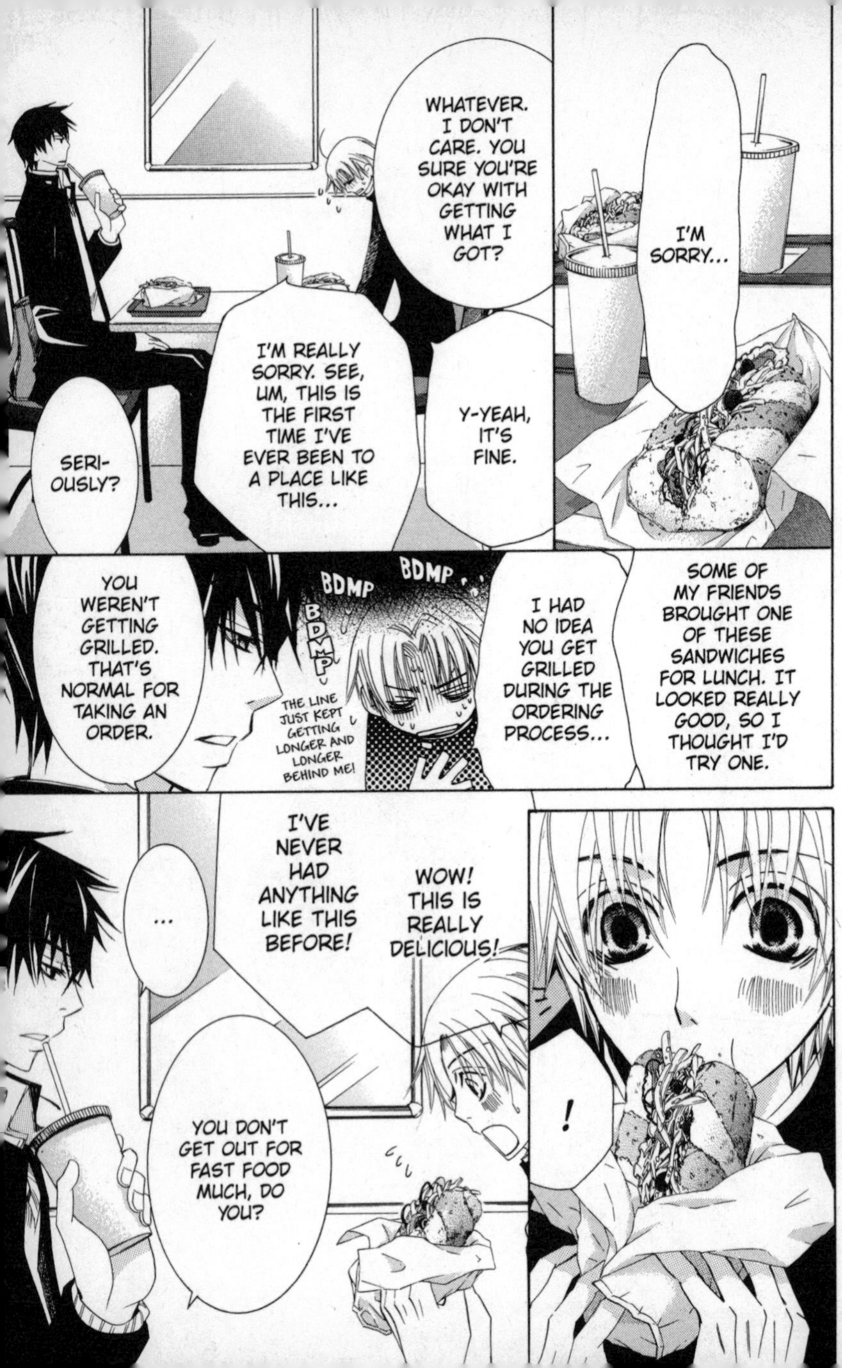
I'M SORRY...
WHATEVER. I DON'T CARE. YOU SURE YOU'RE OKAY WITH GETTING WHAT I GOT?
Y-YEAH, IT'S FINE.
I'M REALLY SORRY. SEE, UM, THIS IS THE FIRST TIME I'VE EVER BEEN TO A PLACE LIKE THIS...
SERI-OUSLY?
SOME OF MY FRIENDS BROUGHT ONE OF THESE SANDWICHES FOR LUNCH. IT LOOKED REALLY GOOD, SO I THOUGHT I'D TRY ONE.
I HAD NO IDEA YOU GET GRILLED DURING THE ORDERING PROCESS...
BDMP
BDMP
BDMP
THE LINE JUST KEPT GETTING LONGER AND LONGER BEHIND ME!
YOU WEREN'T GETTING GRILLED. THAT'S NORMAL FOR TAKING AN ORDER.
!
WOW! THIS IS REALLY DELICIOUS!
I'VE NEVER HAD ANYTHING LIKE THIS BEFORE!
...
YOU DON'T GET OUT FOR FAST FOOD MUCH, DO YOU?

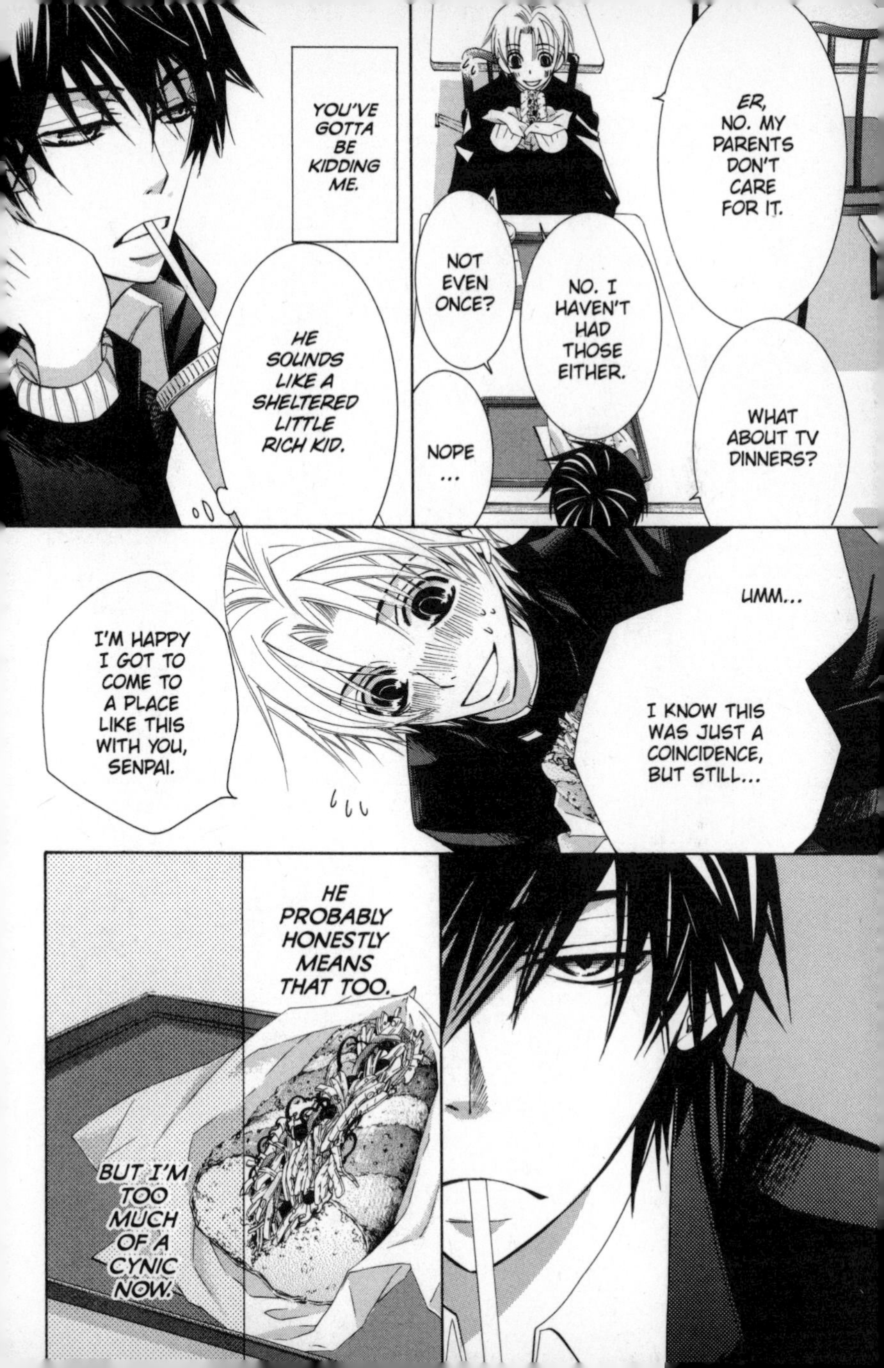
ER, NO. MY PARENTS DON'T CARE FOR IT.
WHAT ABOUT TV DINNERS?
NO. I HAVEN'T HAD THOSE EITHER.
NOT EVEN ONCE?
NOPE ...
YOU'VE GOTTA BE KIDDING ME.
HE SOUNDS LIKE A SHELTERED LITTLE RICH KID.
UMM...
I KNOW THIS WAS JUST A COINCIDENCE, BUT STILL...
I'M HAPPY I GOT TO COME TO A PLACE LIKE THIS WITH YOU, SENPAI.
HE PROBABLY HONESTLY MEANS THAT TOO.
BUT I'M TOO MUCH OF A CYNIC NOW.

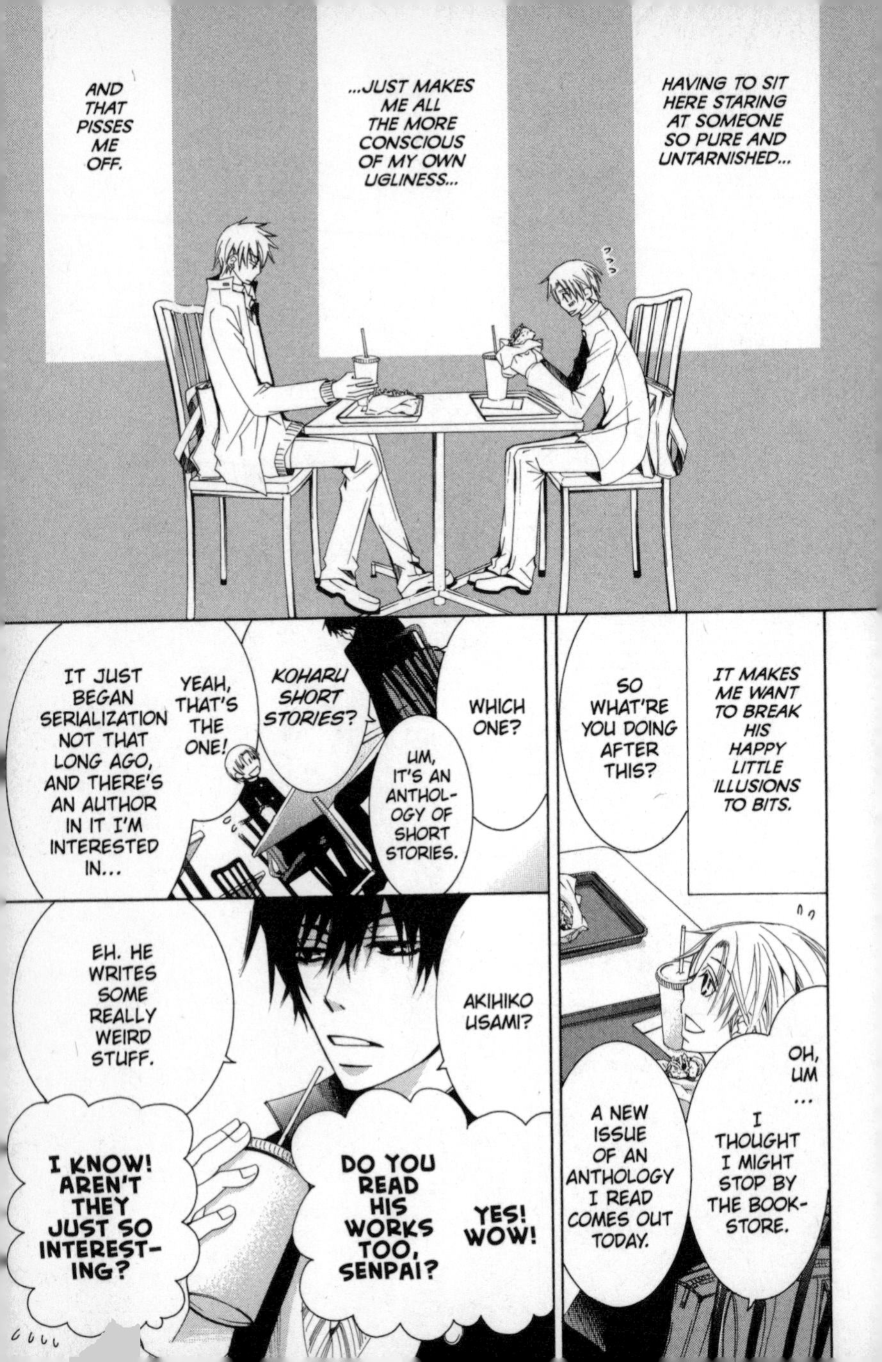
HAVING TO SIT HERE STARING AT SOMEONE SO PURE AND UNTARNISHED...
...JUST MAKES ME ALL THE MORE CONSCIOUS OF MY OWN UGLINESS...
AND THAT PISSES ME OFF.
IT MAKES ME WANT TO BREAK HIS HAPPY LITTLE ILLUSIONS TO BITS.
SO WHAT'RE YOU DOING AFTER THIS?
OH, UM ... I THOUGHT I MIGHT STOP BY THE BOOK-STORE.
A NEW ISSUE OF AN ANTHOLOGY I READ COMES OUT TODAY.
WHICH ONE?
UM, IT'S AN ANTHOL-OGY OF SHORT STORIES.
KOHARU SHORT STORIES?
YEAH, THAT'S THE ONE!
IT JUST BEGAN SERIALIZATION NOT THAT LONG AGO, AND THERE'S AN AUTHOR IN IT I'M INTERESTED IN...
AKIHIKO USAMI?
YES! WOW!
DO YOU READ HIS WORKS TOO, SENPAI?
EH. HE WRITES SOME REALLY WEIRD STUFF.
I KNOW! AREN'T THEY JUST SO INTEREST-ING?

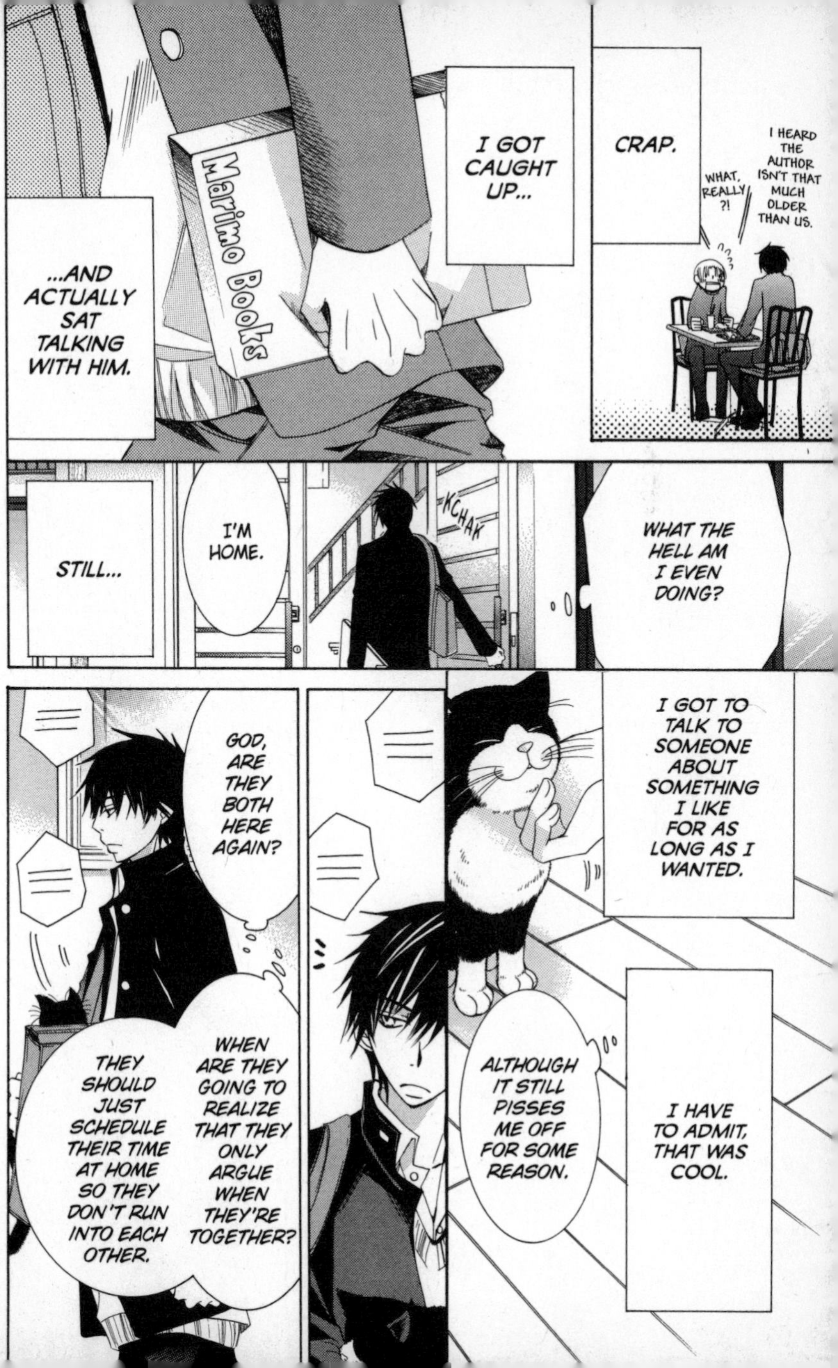
CRAP.
I HEARD THE AUTHOR ISN'T THAT MUCH OLDER THAN US.
WHAT, REALLY?!
I GOT CAUGHT UP...
...AND ACTUALLY SAT TALKING WITH HIM.
Marimo Books
WHAT THE HELL AM I EVEN DOING?
KCHAK
I'M HOME.
STILL...
I GOT TO TALK TO SOMEONE ABOUT SOMETHING I LIKE FOR AS LONG AS I WANTED.
I HAVE TO ADMIT, THAT WAS COOL.
ALTHOUGH IT STILL PISSES ME OFF FOR SOME REASON.
GOD, ARE THEY BOTH HERE AGAIN?
WHEN ARE THEY GOING TO REALIZE THAT THEY ONLY ARGUE WHEN THEY'RE TOGETHER?
THEY SHOULD JUST SCHEDULE THEIR TIME AT HOME SO THEY DON'T RUN INTO EACH OTHER.

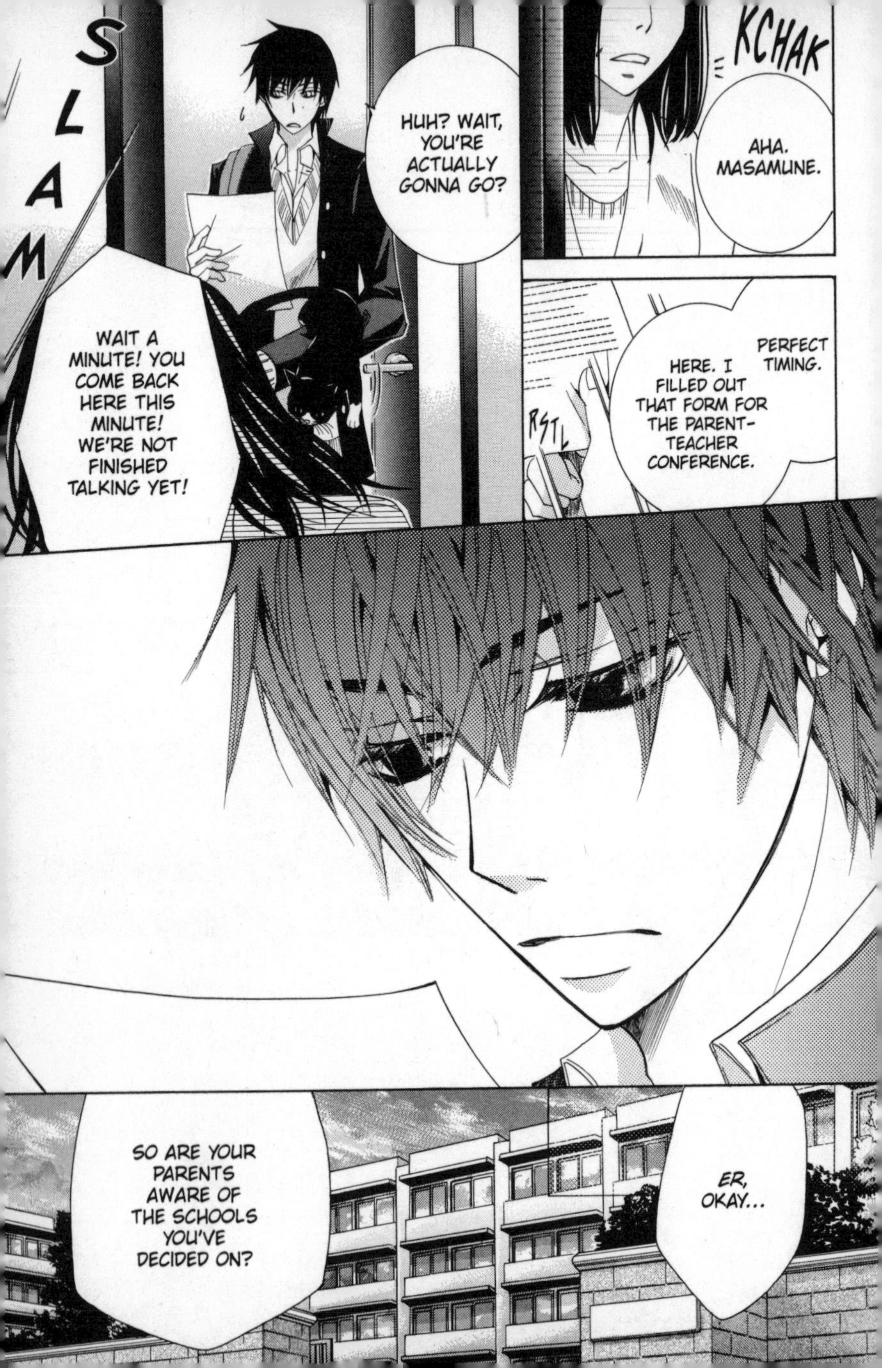
KCHAK
AHA. MASAMUNE.
RSTL
PERFECT TIMING.
HERE. I FILLED OUT THAT FORM FOR THE PARENT-TEACHER CONFERENCE.
HUH? WAIT, YOU'RE ACTUALLY GONNA GO?
SLAM
WAIT A MINUTE! YOU COME BACK HERE THIS MINUTE! WE'RE NOT FINISHED TALKING YET!
ER, OKAY...
SO ARE YOUR PARENTS AWARE OF THE SCHOOLS YOU'VE DECIDED ON?

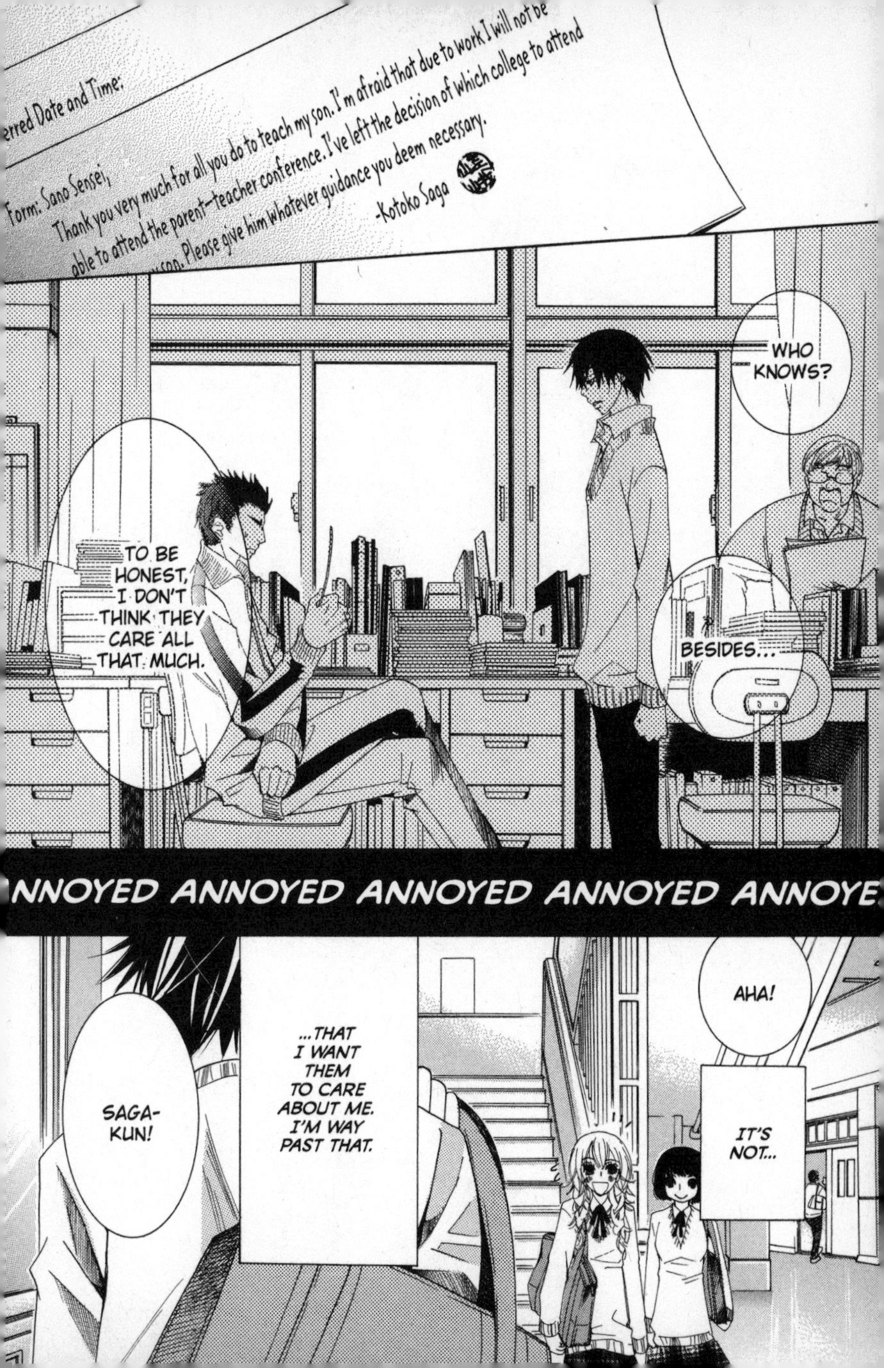
erred Date and Time:
Form: Sano Sensei,
Thank you very much for all you do to teach my son. I'm afraid that due to work I will not be
able to attend the parent-teacher conference. I've left the decision of which college to attend
son. Please give him whatever guidance you deem necessary.
-Kotoko Saga
WHO KNOWS?
TO BE HONEST, I DON'T THINK THEY CARE ALL THAT MUCH.
BESIDES...
NNOYED ANNOYED ANNOYED ANNOYED ANNOYE
AHA!
IT'S NOT...
...THAT I WANT THEM TO CARE ABOUT ME. I'M WAY PAST THAT.
SAGA-KUN!

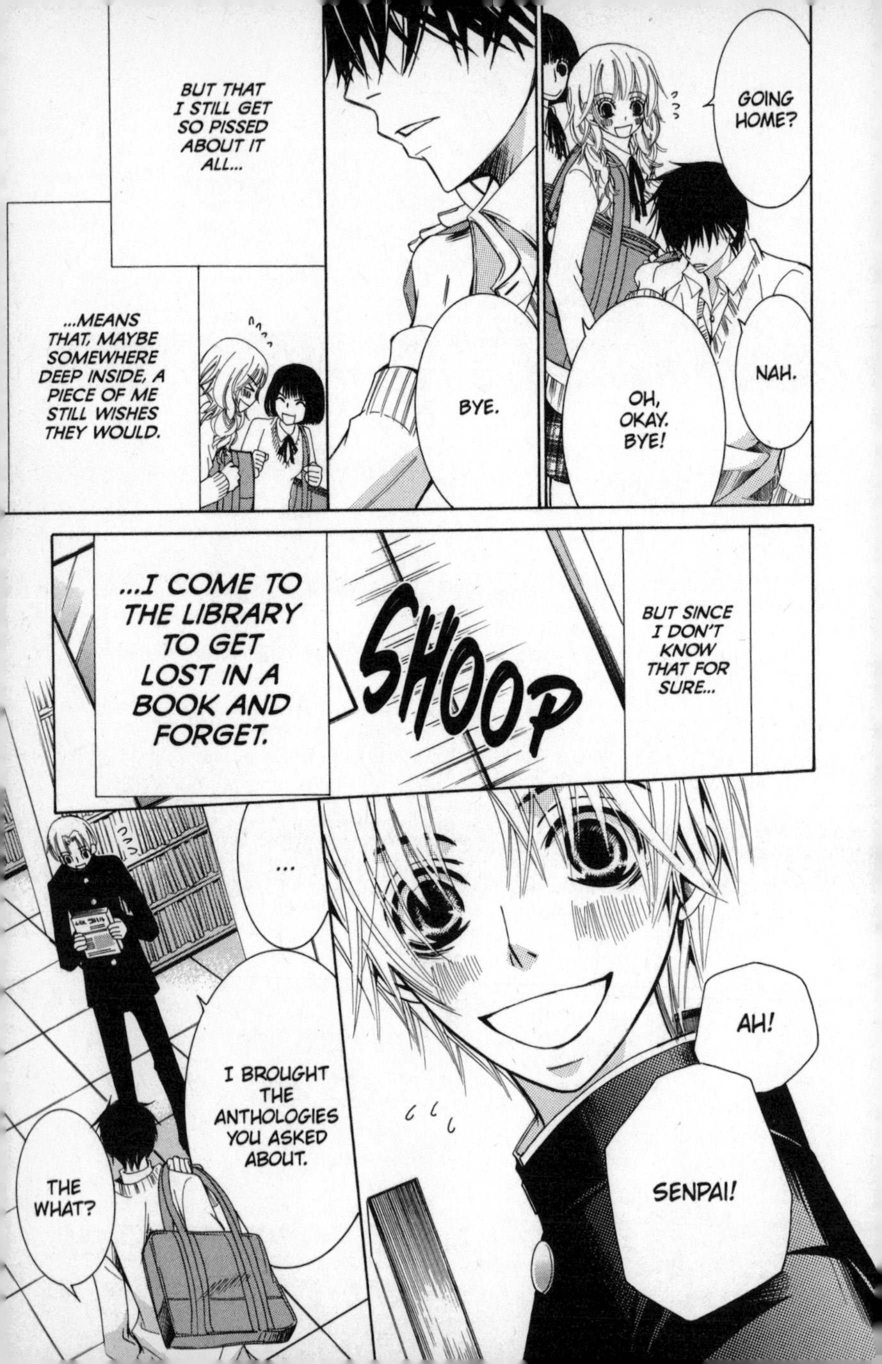
GOING HOME?
NAH.
OH, OKAY. BYE!
BYE.
BUT THAT I STILL GET SO PISSED ABOUT IT ALL...
...MEANS THAT, MAYBE SOMEWHERE DEEP INSIDE, A PIECE OF ME STILL WISHES THEY WOULD.
BUT SINCE I DON'T KNOW THAT FOR SURE...
SHOOP
...I COME TO THE LIBRARY TO GET LOST IN A BOOK AND FORGET.
AH!
SENPAI!
...
I BROUGHT THE ANTHOLOGIES YOU ASKED ABOUT.
THE WHAT?

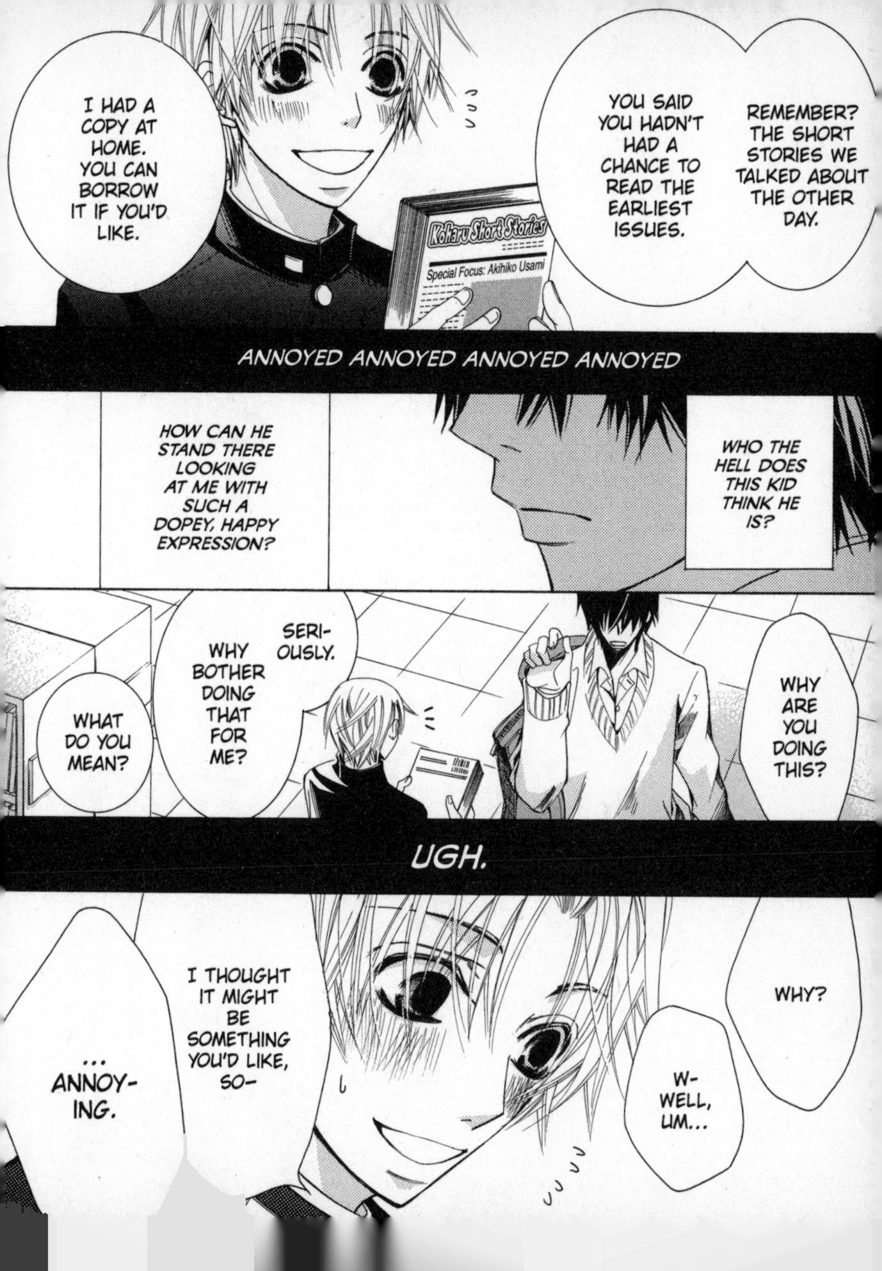
REMEMBER? THE SHORT STORIES WE TALKED ABOUT THE OTHER DAY.
YOU SAID YOU HADN'T HAD A CHANCE TO READ THE EARLIEST ISSUES.
Koharu Short Stories
Special Focus: Akihiko Usami
I HAD A COPY AT HOME. YOU CAN BORROW IT IF YOU'D LIKE.
ANNOYED ANNOYED ANNOYED ANNOYED
WHO THE HELL DOES THIS KID THINK HE IS?
HOW CAN HE STAND THERE LOOKING AT ME WITH SUCH A DOPEY, HAPPY EXPRESSION?
WHY ARE YOU DOING THIS?
SERI-OUSLY.
WHY BOTHER DOING THAT FOR ME?
WHAT DO YOU MEAN?
UGH.
WHY?
W-WELL, UM...
I THOUGHT IT MIGHT BE SOMETHING YOU'D LIKE, SO-
...ANNOY-ING.

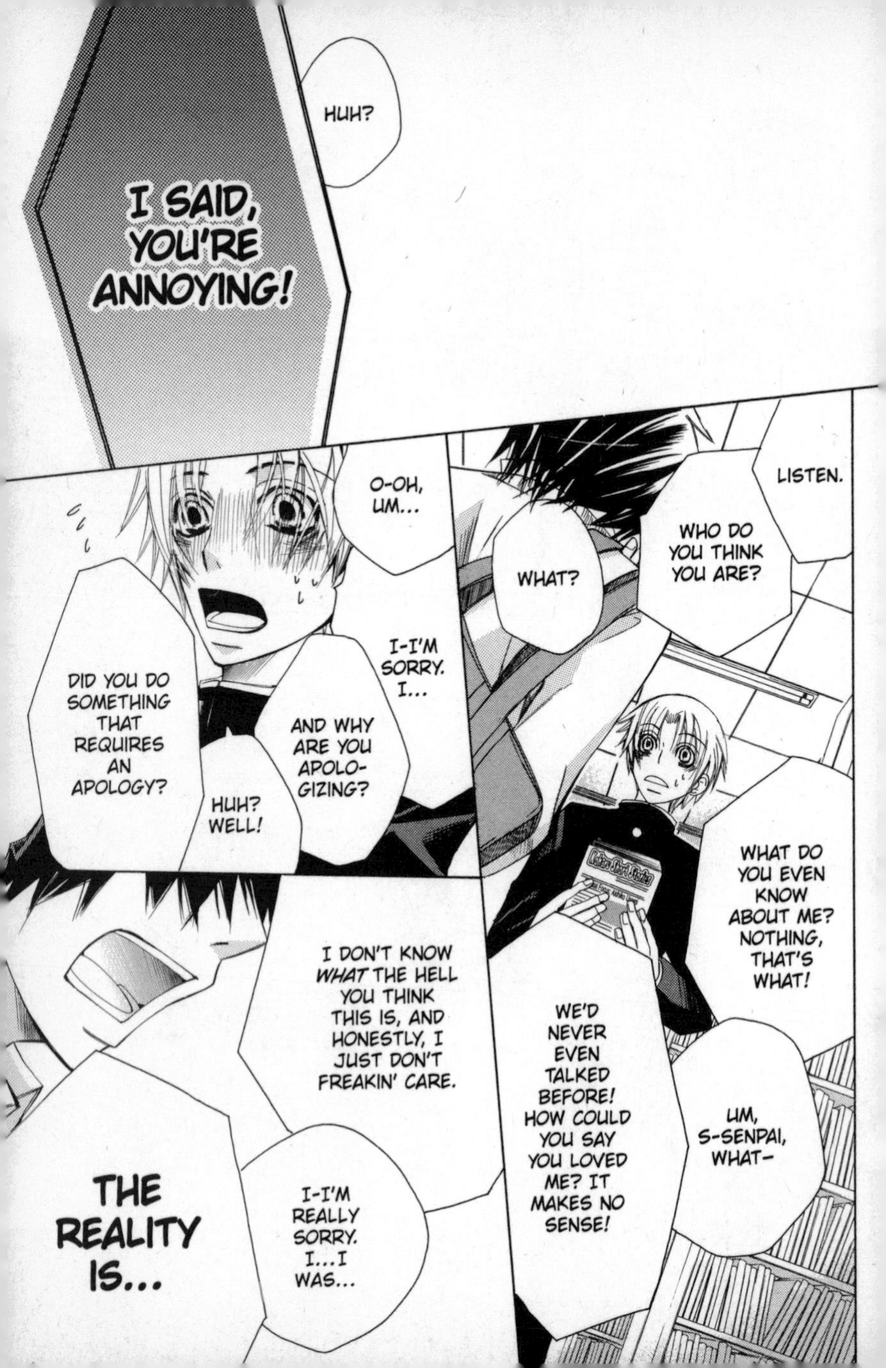
HUH?
I SAID, YOU'RE ANNOYING!
LISTEN.
WHO DO YOU THINK YOU ARE?
WHAT?
WHAT DO YOU EVEN KNOW ABOUT ME? NOTHING, THAT'S WHAT!
UM, S-SENPAI, WHAT-
WE'D NEVER EVEN TALKED BEFORE! HOW COULD YOU SAY YOU LOVED ME? IT MAKES NO SENSE!
O-OH, UM...
I-I'M SORRY. I...
AND WHY ARE YOU APOLOGIZING?
DID YOU DO SOMETHING THAT REQUIRES AN APOLOGY?
HUH? WELL!
I DON'T KNOW *WHAT* THE HELL YOU THINK THIS IS, AND HONESTLY, I JUST DON'T FREAKIN' CARE.
I-I'M REALLY SORRY. I...I WAS...
THE REALITY IS...

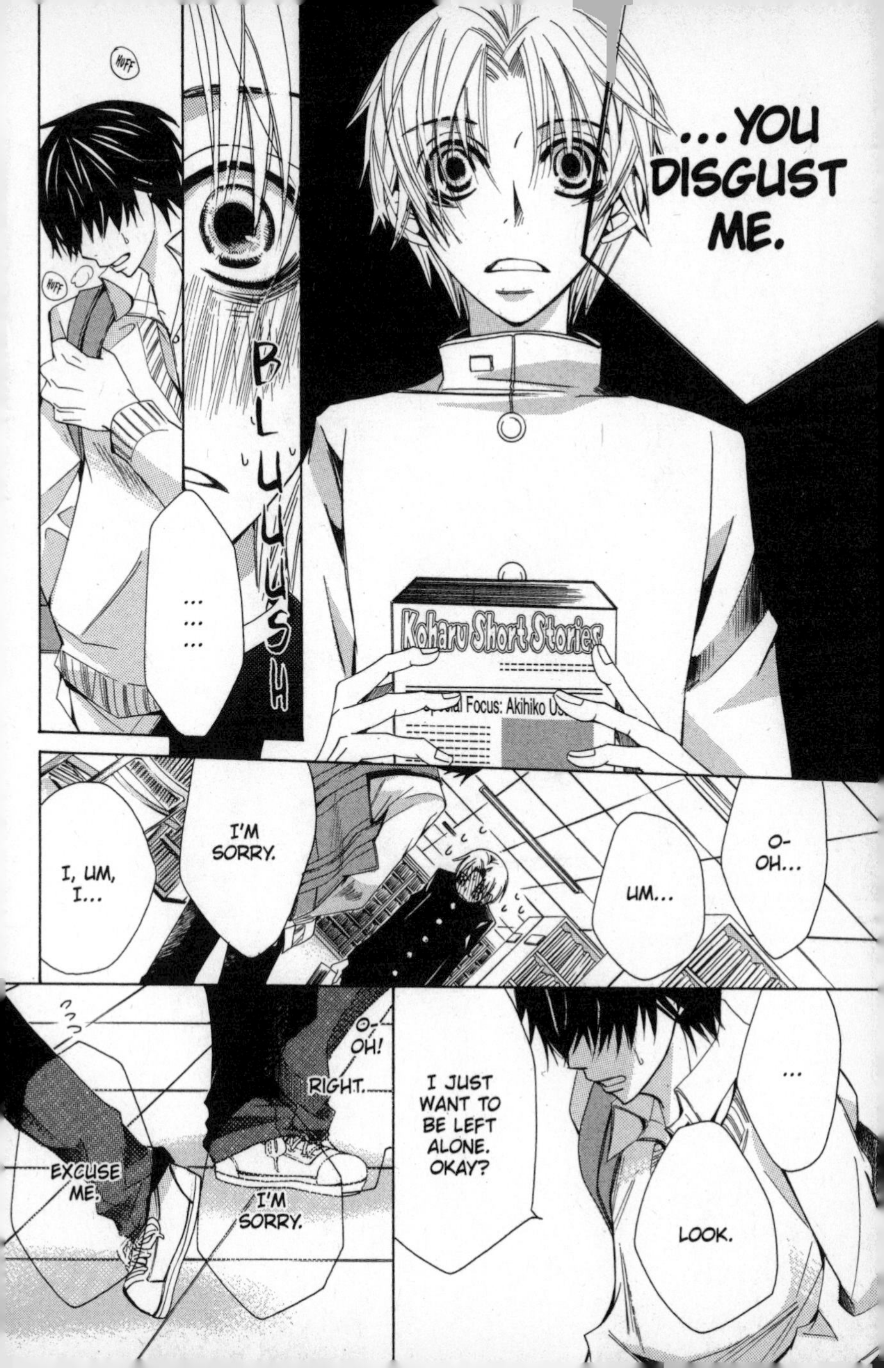
...YOU DISGUST ME.
Koharu Short Stories
BLUUUSH
...
...
...
HUFF
HUFF
O- OH...
UM...
I'M SORRY.
I, UM, I...
...
LOOK.
I JUST WANT TO BE LEFT ALONE. OKAY?
O- OH!
RIGHT.
I'M SORRY.
EXCUSE ME.

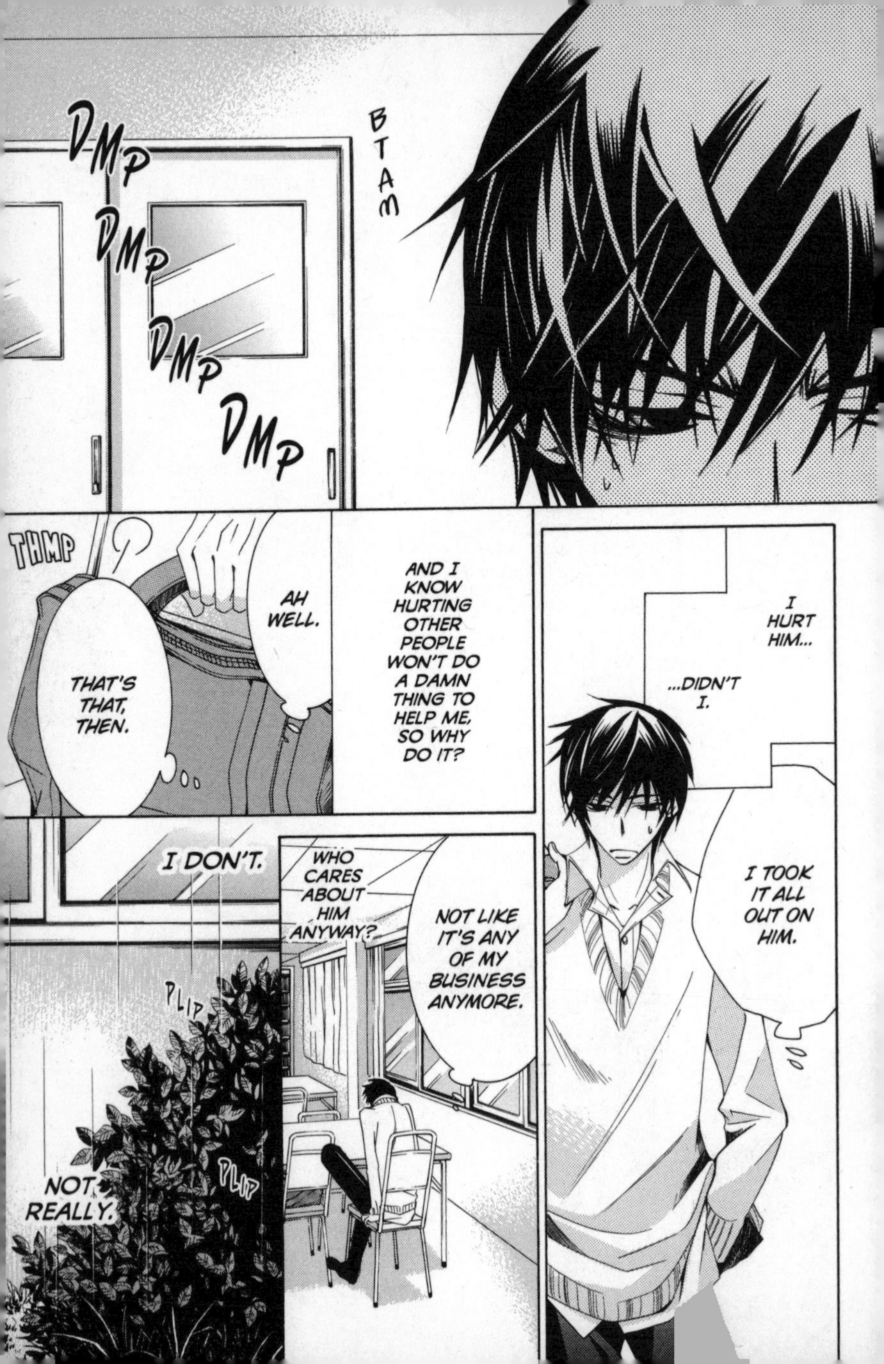
BTAM
DMP
DMP
DMP
DMP
I HURT HIM...
...DIDN'T I.
I TOOK IT ALL OUT ON HIM.
AND I KNOW HURTING OTHER PEOPLE WON'T DO A DAMN THING TO HELP ME, SO WHY DO IT?
THMP
AH WELL.
THAT'S THAT, THEN.
NOT LIKE IT'S ANY OF MY BUSINESS ANYMORE.
WHO CARES ABOUT HIM ANYWAY?
I DON'T.
PLIP
PLIP
NOT REALLY.

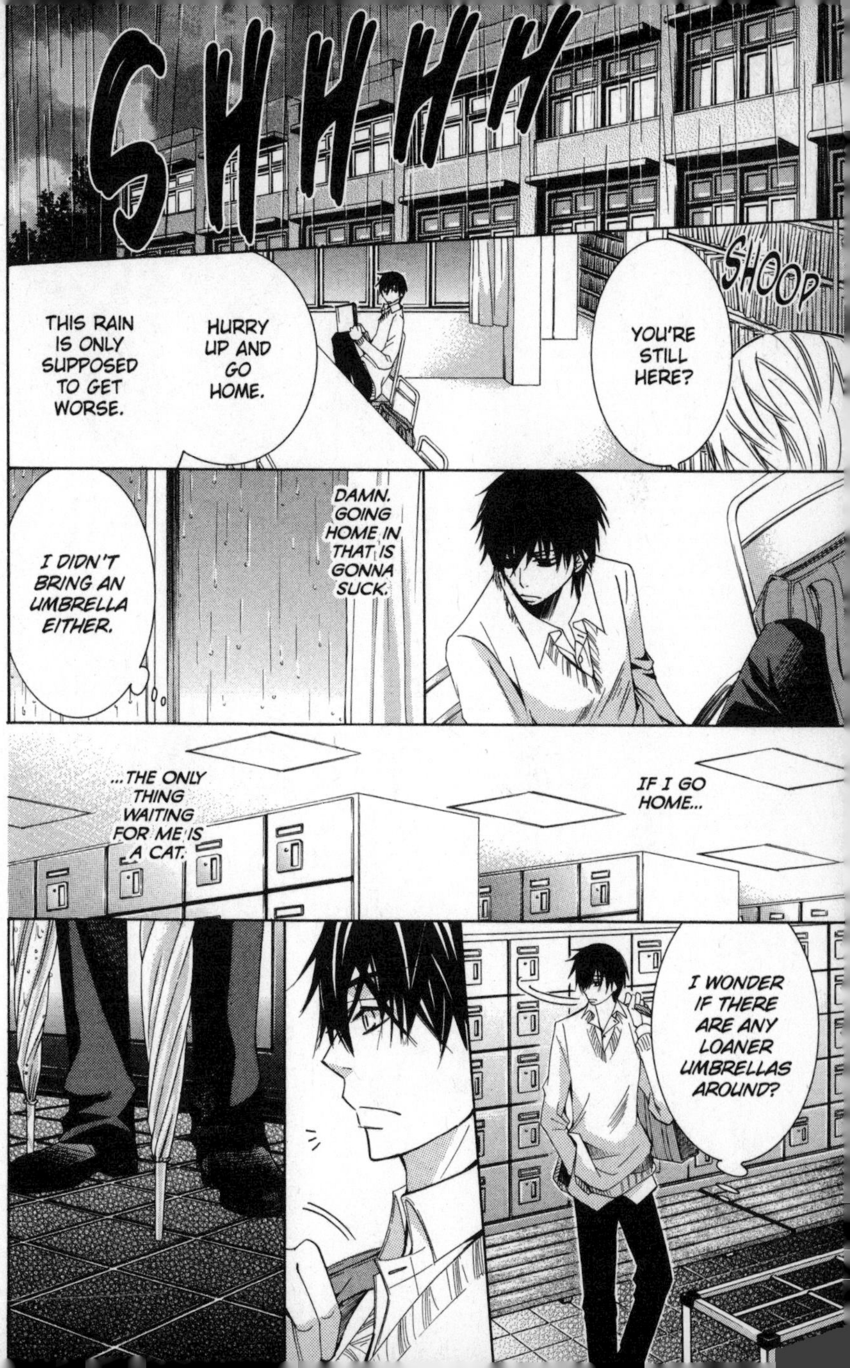
SHHHH
SHOOP
YOU'RE STILL HERE?
HURRY UP AND GO HOME.
THIS RAIN IS ONLY SUPPOSED TO GET WORSE.
DAMN. GOING HOME IN THAT IS GONNA SUCK.
I DIDN'T BRING AN UMBRELLA EITHER.
IF I GO HOME...
...THE ONLY THING WAITING FOR ME IS A CAT.
I WONDER IF THERE ARE ANY LONER UMBRELLAS AROUND?

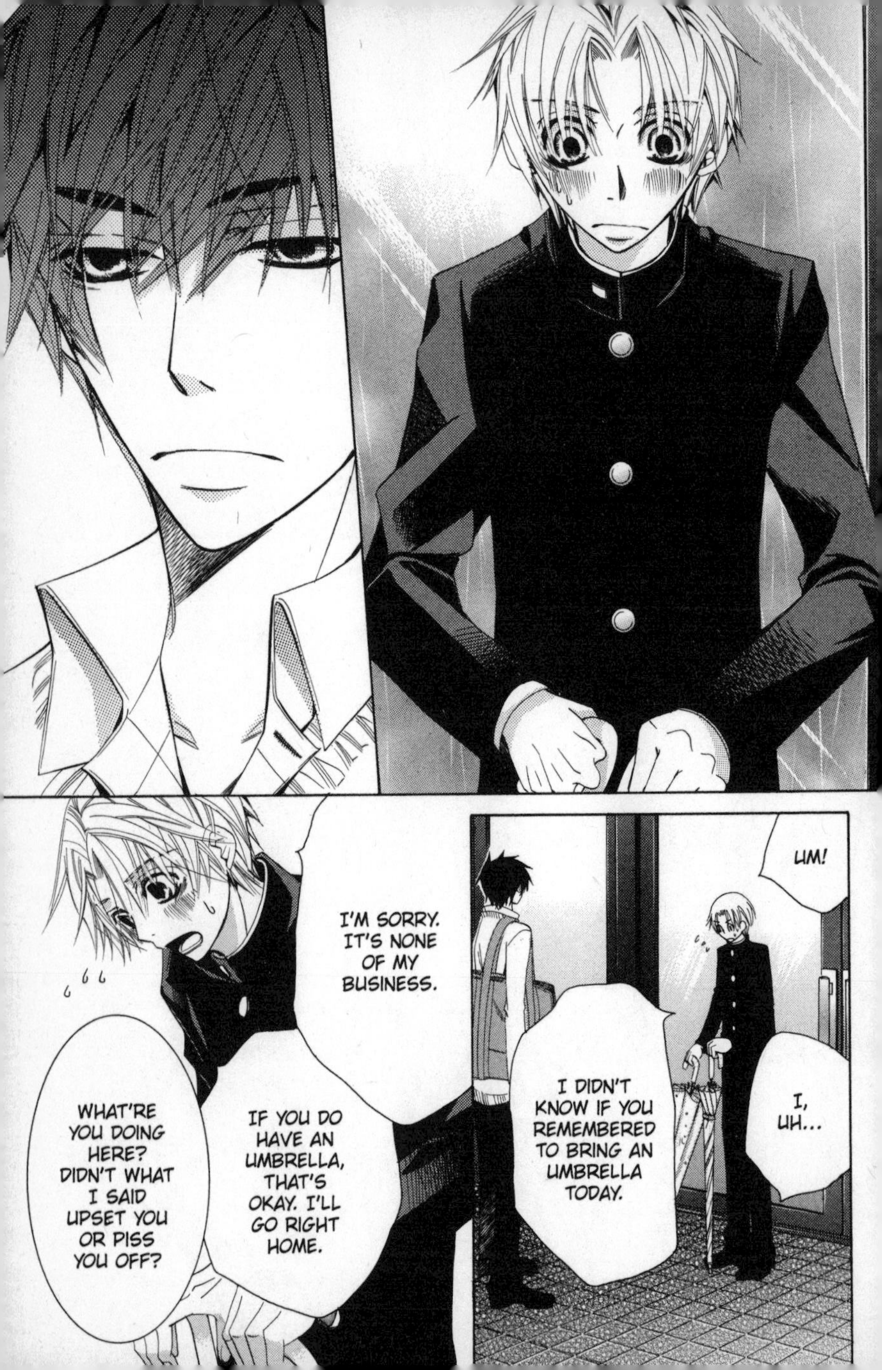
UM!
I, UH...
I DIDN'T KNOW IF YOU REMEMBERED TO BRING AN UMBRELLA TODAY.
I'M SORRY. IT'S NONE OF MY BUSINESS.
IF YOU DO HAVE AN UMBRELLA, THAT'S OKAY. I'LL GO RIGHT HOME.
WHAT'RE YOU DOING HERE? DIDN'T WHAT I SAID UPSET YOU OR PISS YOU OFF?

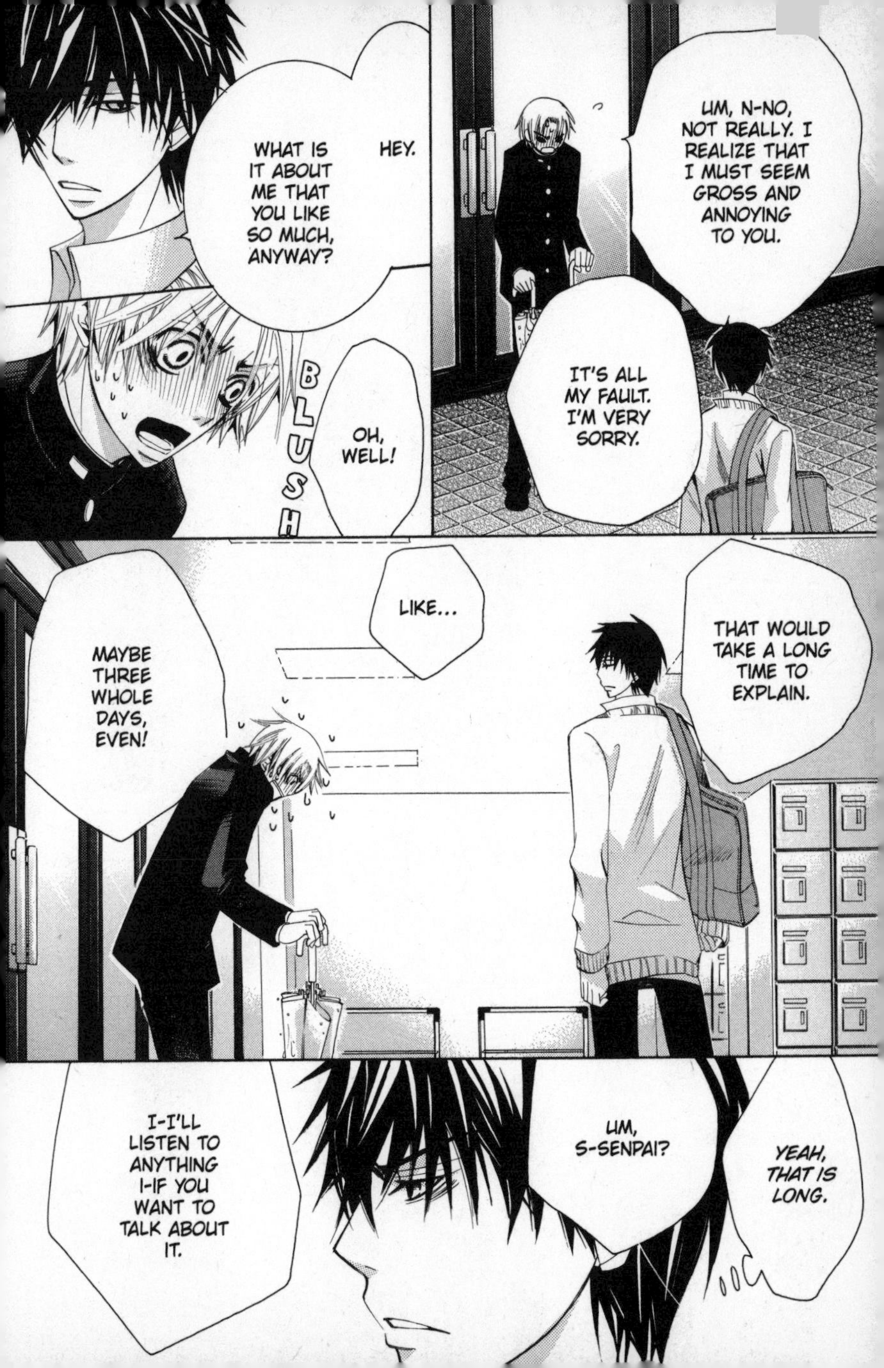
UM, N-NO, NOT REALLY. I REALIZE THAT I MUST SEEM GROSS AND ANNOYING TO YOU.
IT'S ALL MY FAULT. I'M VERY SORRY.
HEY.
WHAT IS IT ABOUT ME THAT YOU LIKE SO MUCH, ANYWAY?
BLUSH
OH, WELL!
THAT WOULD TAKE A LONG TIME TO EXPLAIN.
LIKE...
MAYBE THREE WHOLE DAYS, EVEN!
YEAH, THAT IS LONG.
UM, S-SENPAI?
I-I'LL LISTEN TO ANYTHING I-IF YOU WANT TO TALK ABOUT IT.

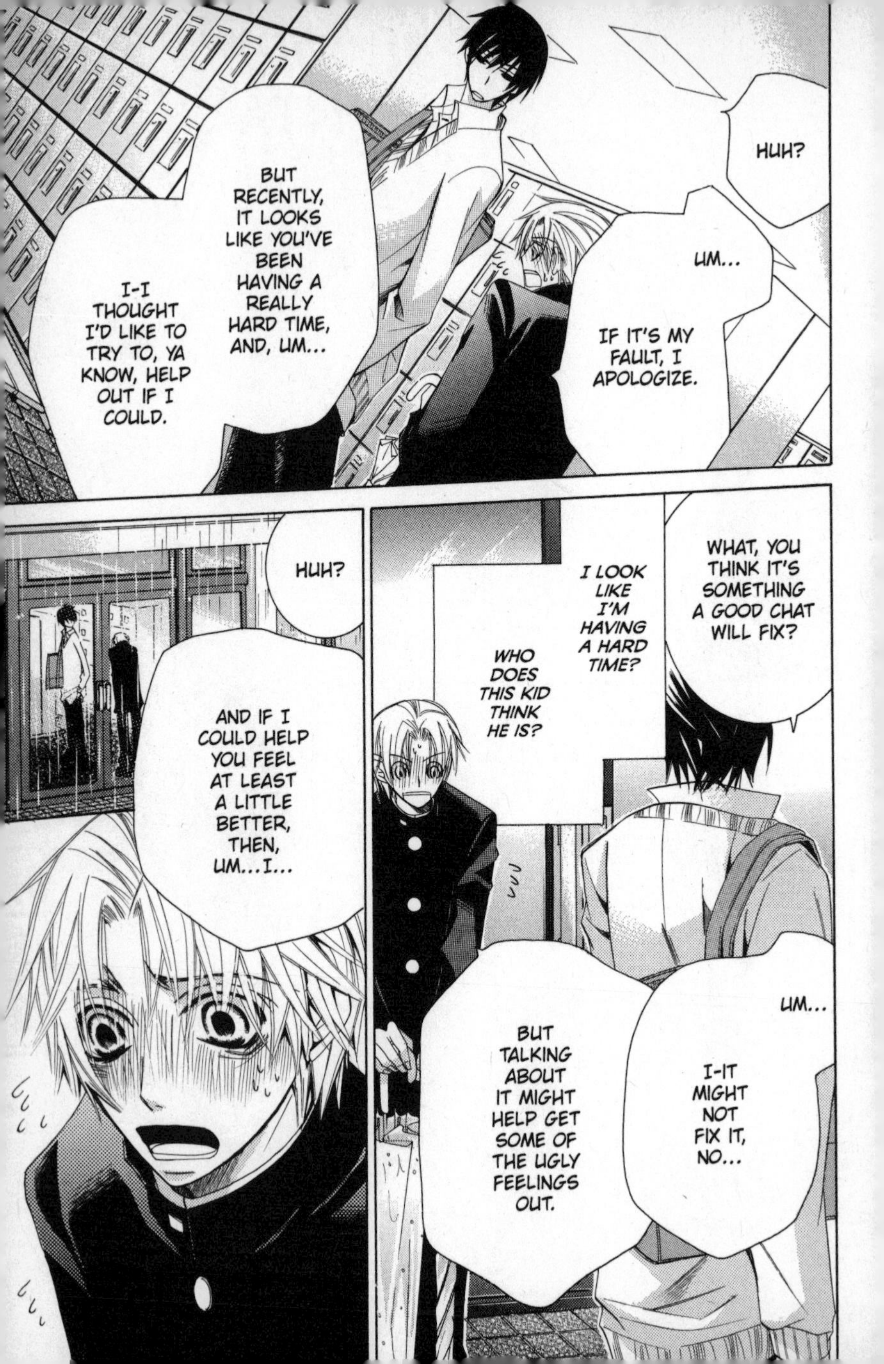
HUH?
UM...
IF IT'S MY FAULT, I APOLOGIZE.
BUT RECENTLY, IT LOOKS LIKE YOU'VE BEEN HAVING A REALLY HARD TIME, AND, UM...
I-I THOUGHT I'D LIKE TO TRY TO, YA KNOW, HELP OUT IF I COULD.
WHAT, YOU THINK IT'S SOMETHING A GOOD CHAT WILL FIX?
I LOOK LIKE I'M HAVING A HARD TIME?
WHO DOES THIS KID THINK HE IS?
UM...
I-IT MIGHT NOT FIX IT, NO...
BUT TALKING ABOUT IT MIGHT HELP GET SOME OF THE UGLY FEELINGS OUT.
HUH?
AND IF I COULD HELP YOU FEEL AT LEAST A LITTLE BETTER, THEN, UM...I...

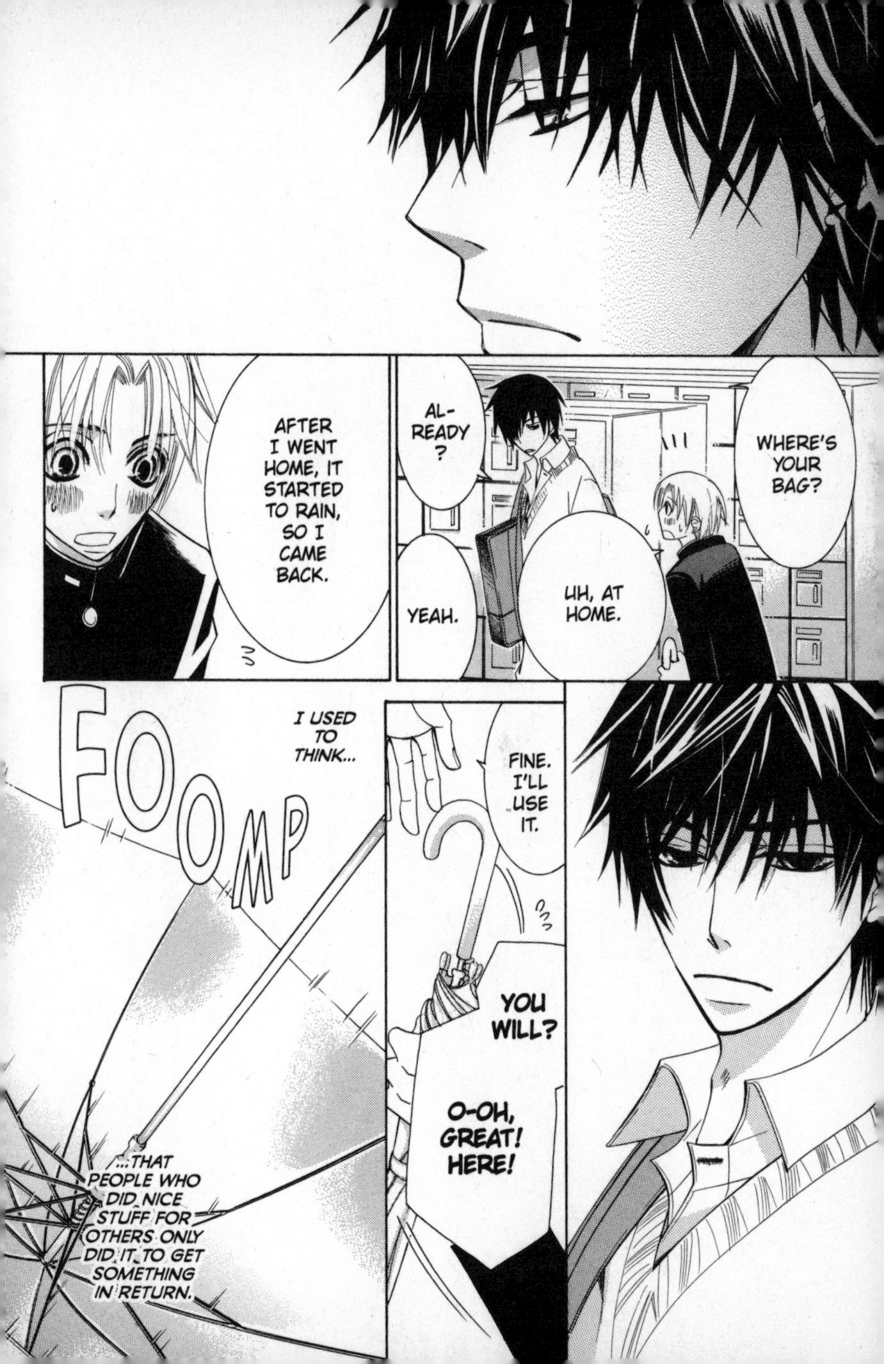
WHERE'S YOUR BAG?
UH, AT HOME.
AL-READY?
YEAH.
AFTER I WENT HOME, IT STARTED TO RAIN, SO I CAME BACK.
FINE. I'LL USE IT.
YOU WILL?
O-OH, GREAT! HERE!
I USED TO THINK...
FOOMP
...THAT PEOPLE WHO DID NICE STUFF FOR OTHERS ONLY DID IT TO GET SOMETHING IN RETURN.

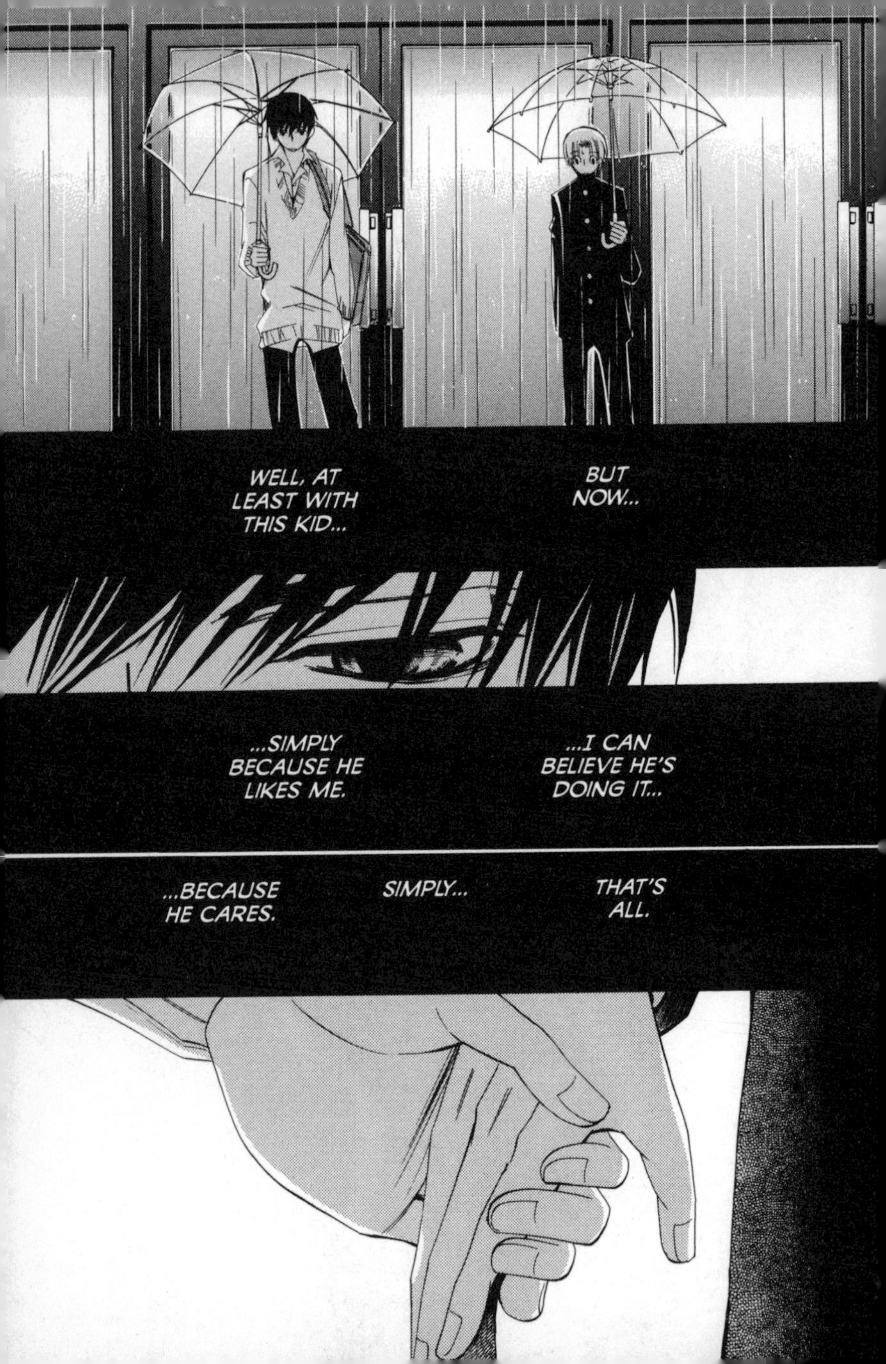
BUT NOW...
WELL, AT LEAST WITH THIS KID...
...I CAN BELIEVE HE'S DOING IT...
...SIMPLY BECAUSE HE LIKES ME.
THAT'S ALL.
SIMPLY...
...BECAUSE HE CARES.

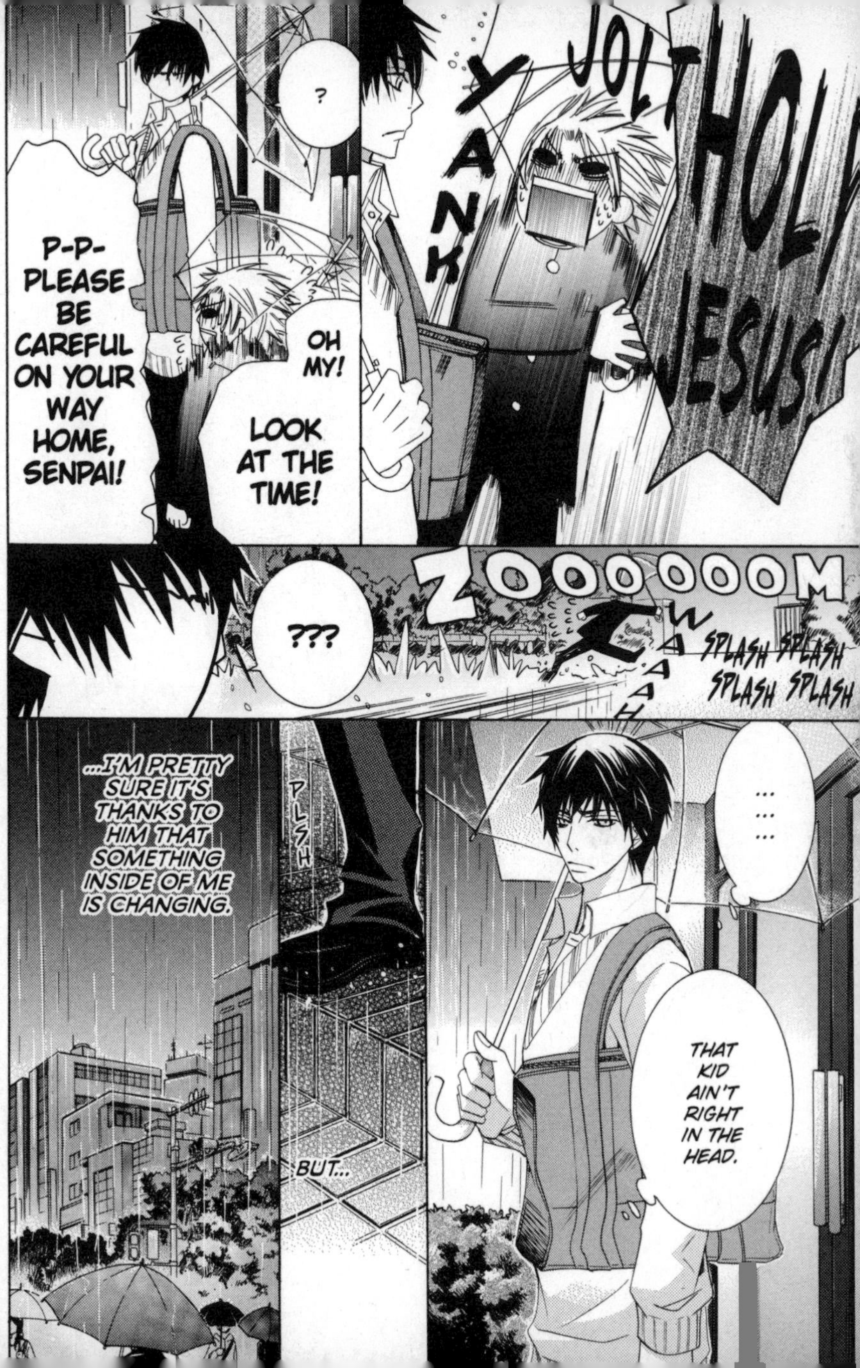
JOLT
HOLY JESUS!
YANK
?
OH MY!
LOOK AT THE TIME!
P-P-PLEASE BE CAREFUL ON YOUR WAY HOME, SENPAI!
ZOOOOOOM
WAAAH
SPLASH SPLASH SPLASH SPLASH
???
......
THAT KID AIN'T RIGHT IN THE HEAD.
PLSH
BUT...
...I'M PRETTY SURE IT'S THANKS TO HIM THAT SOMETHING INSIDE OF ME IS CHANGING.

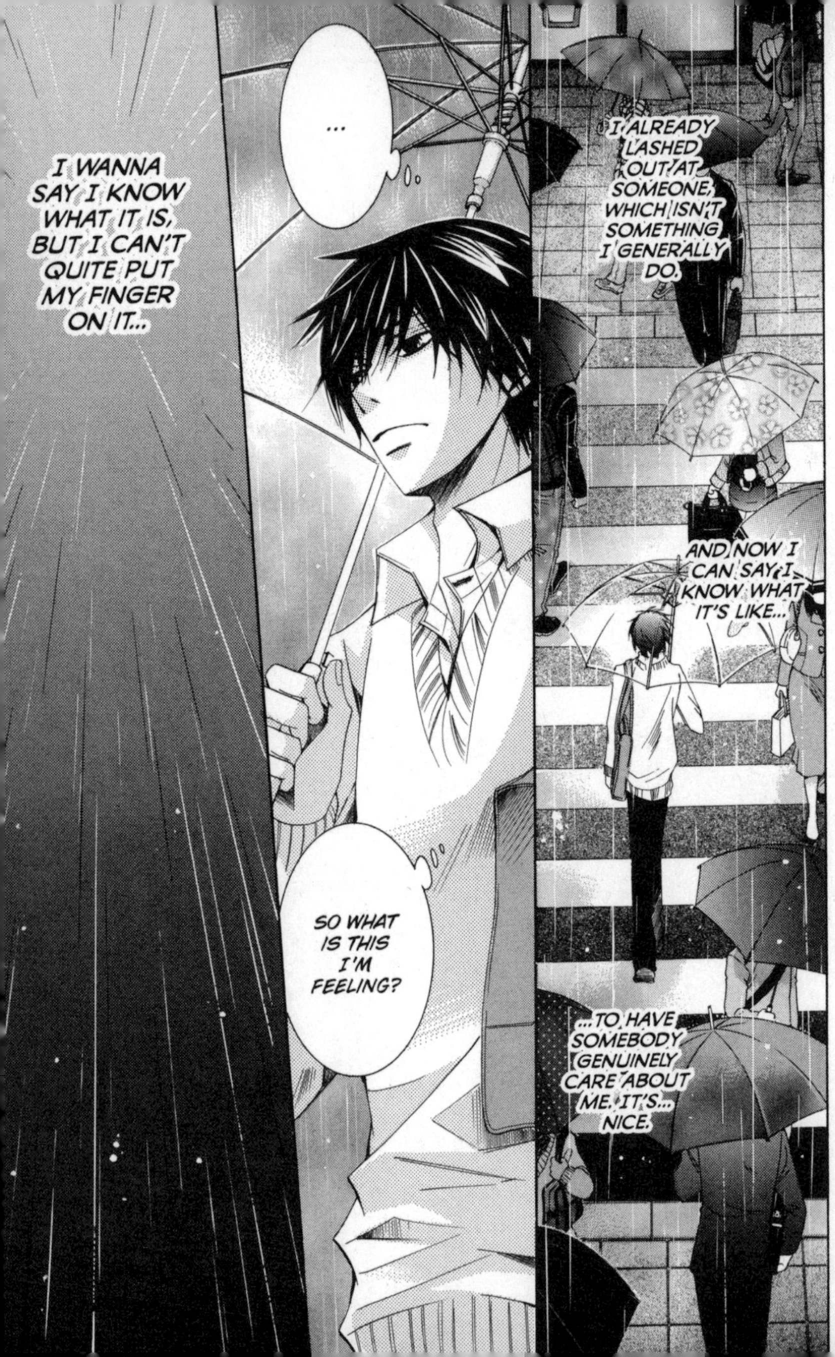
I ALREADY LASHED OUT AT SOMEONE, WHICH ISN'T SOMETHING I GENERALLY DO.
AND NOW I CAN SAY I KNOW WHAT IT'S LIKE...
...TO HAVE SOMEBODY GENUINELY CARE ABOUT ME. IT'S... NICE.
...
SO WHAT IS THIS I'M FEELING?
I WANNA SAY I KNOW WHAT IT IS, BUT I CAN'T QUITE PUT MY FINGER ON IT...

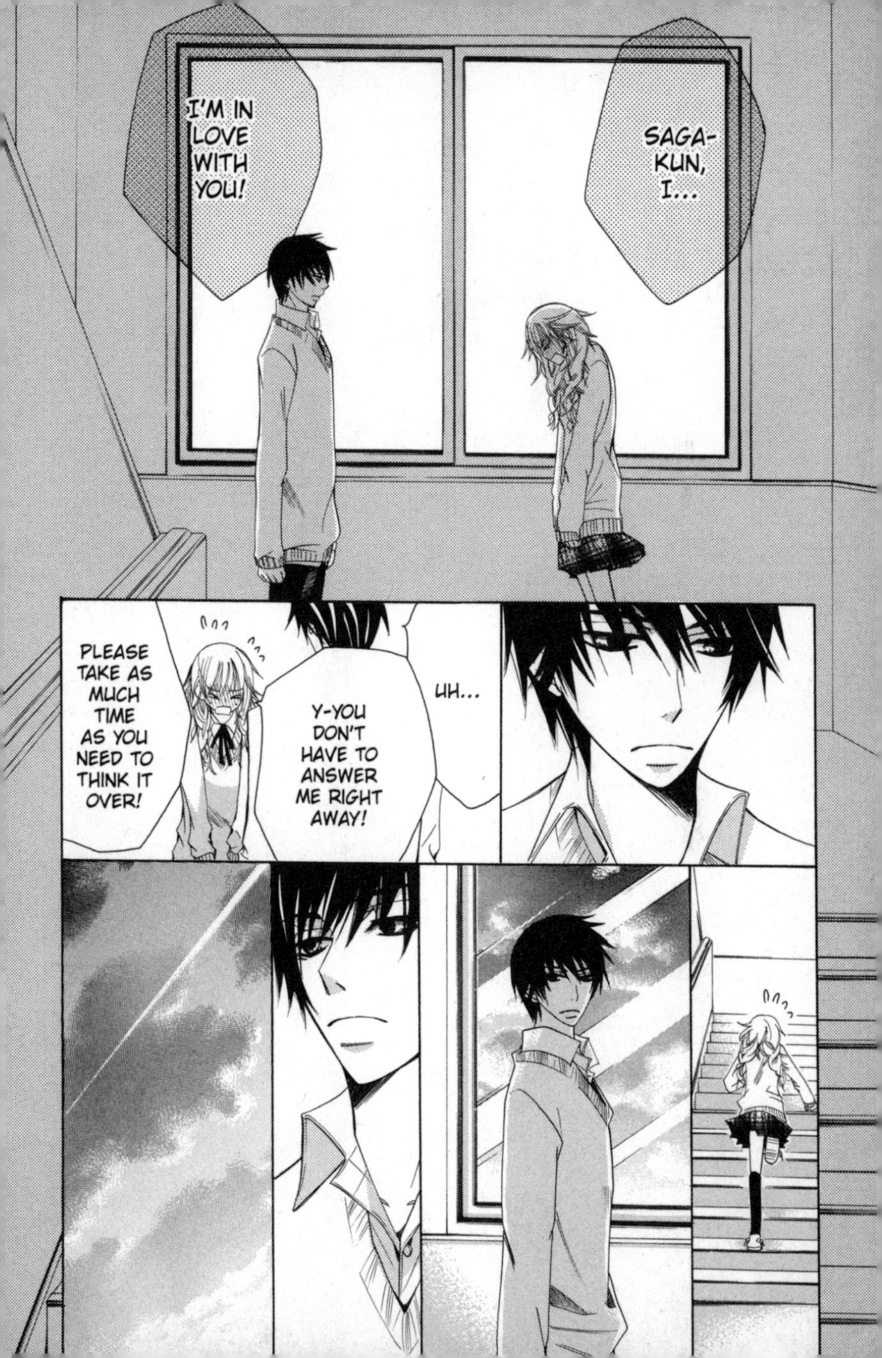
SAGA-KUN, I...
I'M IN LOVE WITH YOU!
UH...
Y-YOU DON'T HAVE TO ANSWER ME RIGHT AWAY!
PLEASE TAKE AS MUCH TIME AS YOU NEED TO THINK IT OVER!

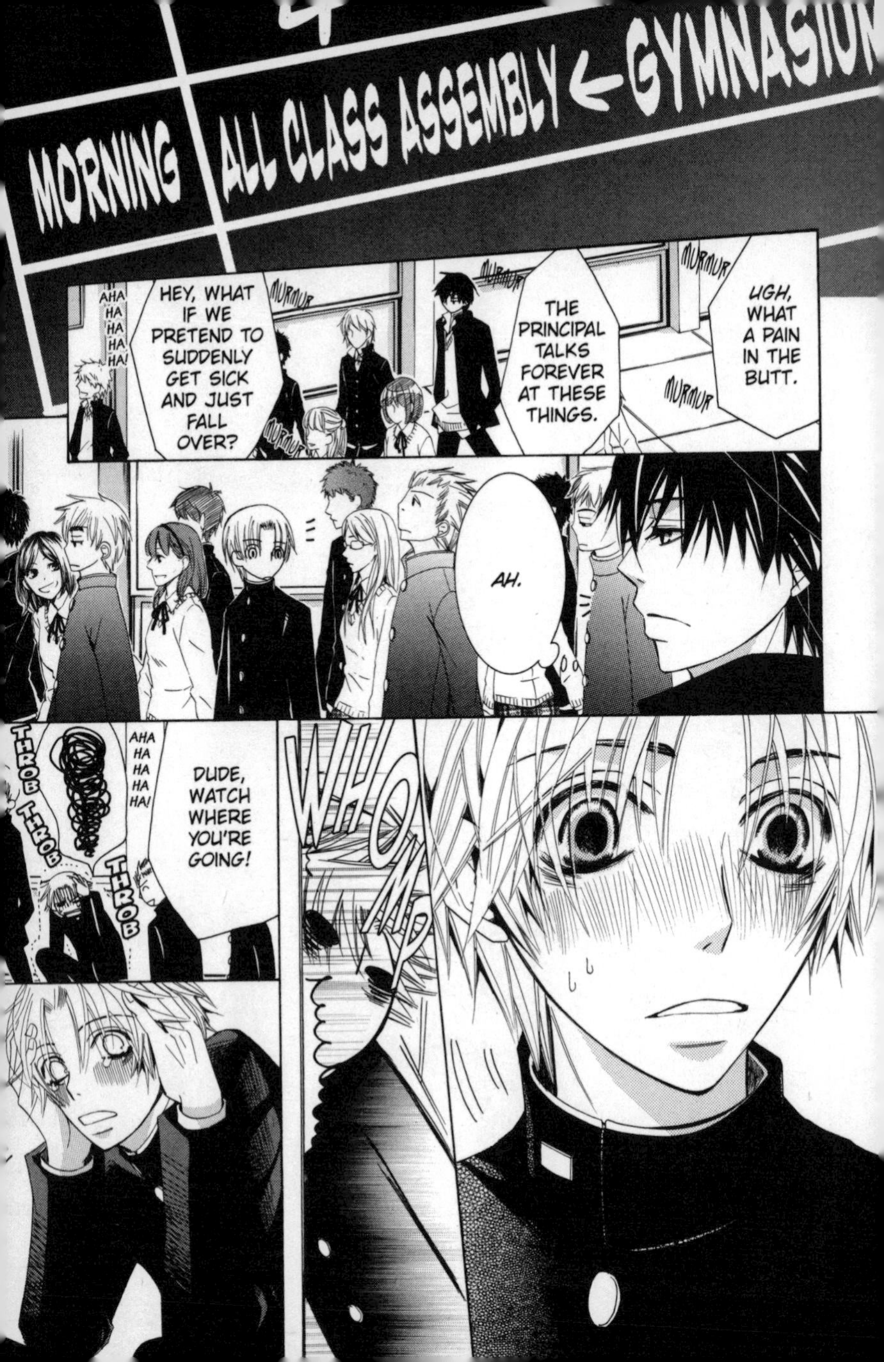
MORNING
ALL CLASS ASSEMBLY ← GYMNASIU
MURMUR
UGH, WHAT A PAIN IN THE BUTT.
MURMUR
MURMUR
THE PRINCIPAL TALKS FOREVER AT THESE THINGS.
MURMUR
HEY, WHAT IF WE PRETEND TO SUDDENLY GET SICK AND JUST FALL OVER?
MURMUR
AHA HA HA HA HA!
AH.
WHOMP
DUDE, WATCH WHERE YOU'RE GOING!
AHA HA HA HA HA!
THROB
THROB THROB

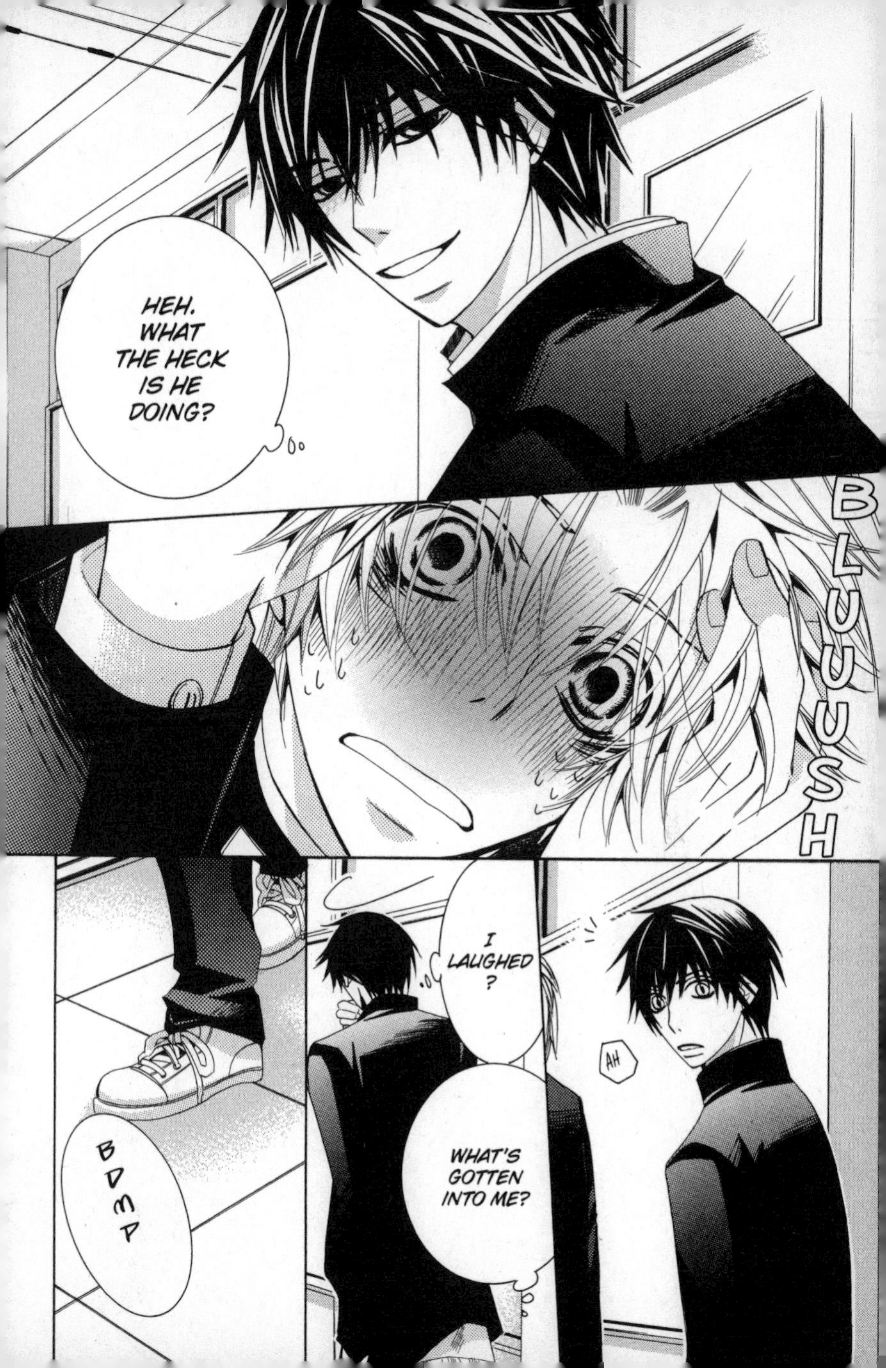
HEH. WHAT THE HECK IS HE DOING?
BLUUUSH
AH
I LAUGHED?
WHAT'S GOTTEN INTO ME?
BDMP

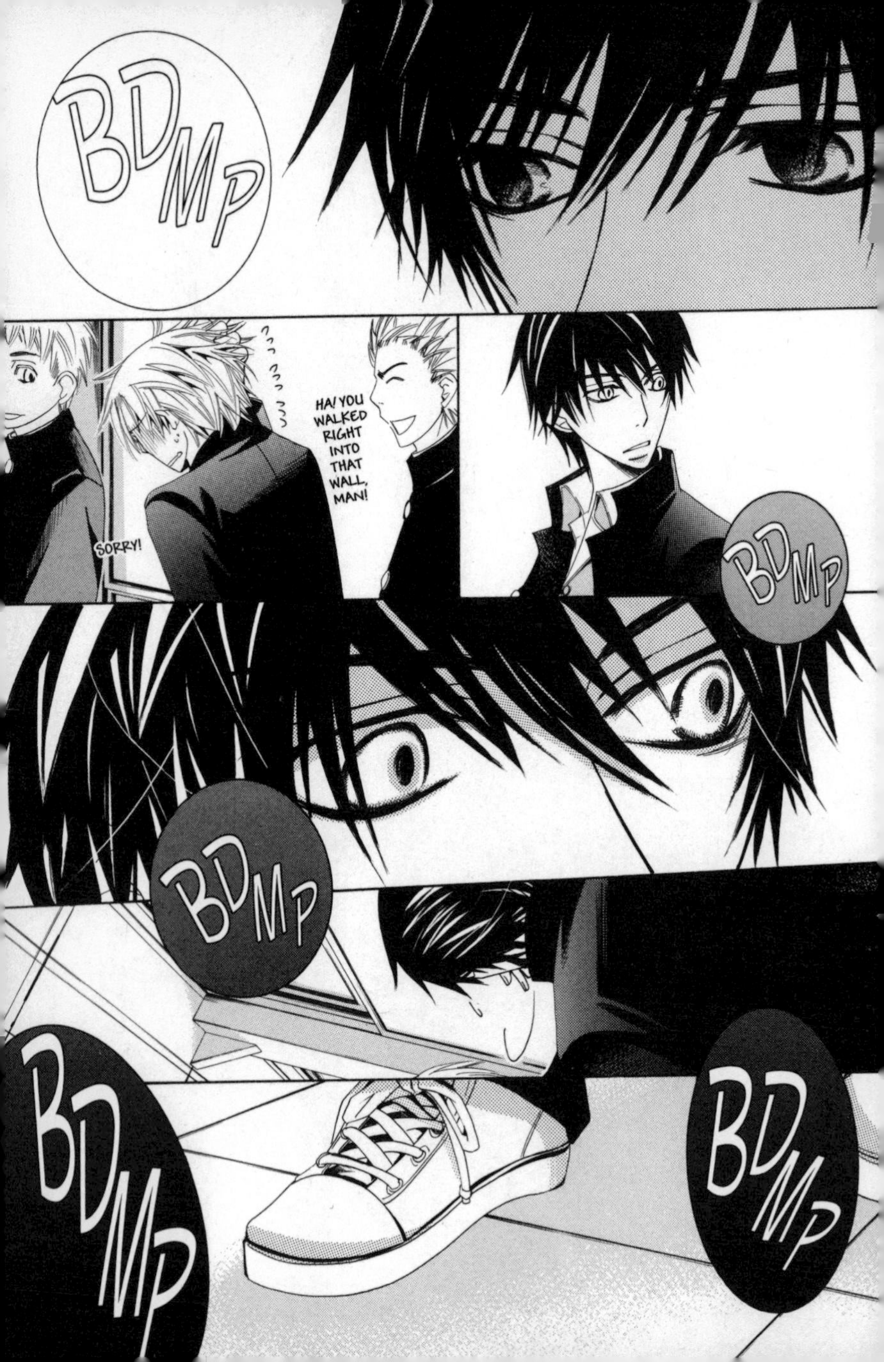
BDMP
BDMP
HA! YOU WALKED RIGHT INTO THAT WALL, MAN!
SORRY!
BDMP
BDMP
BDMP

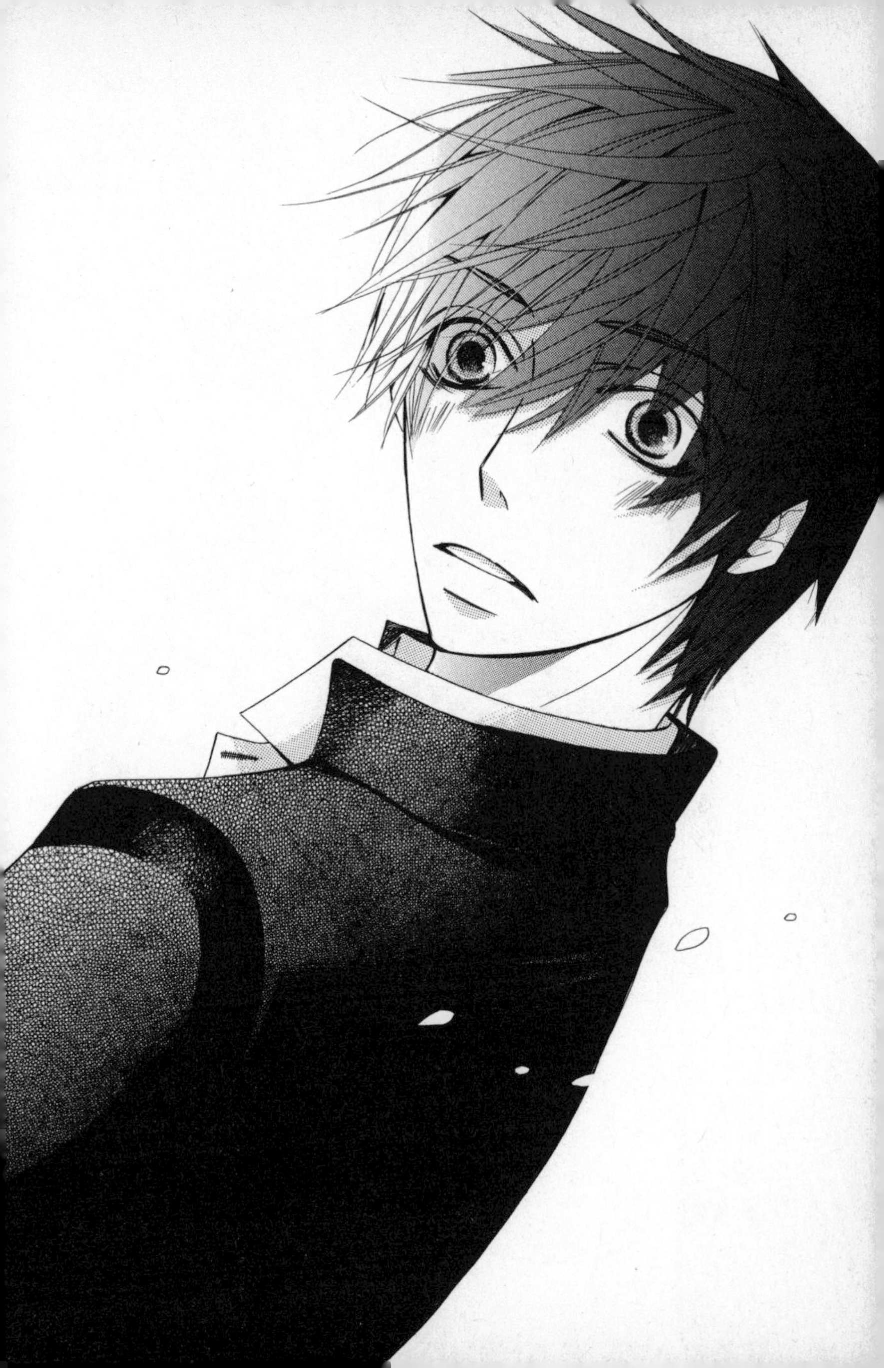

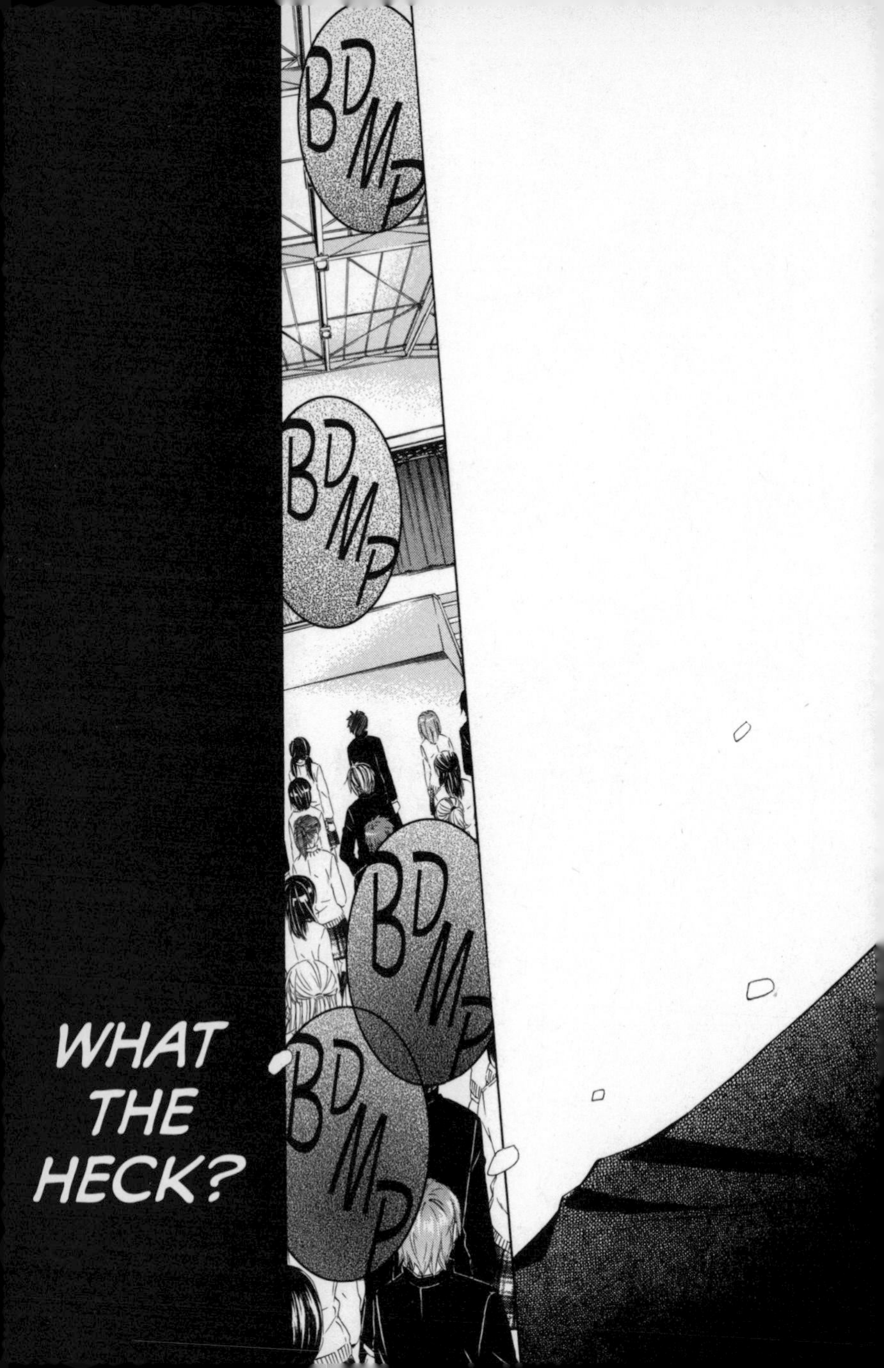
BDMP
BDMP
BDMP
BDMP
WHAT THE HECK?

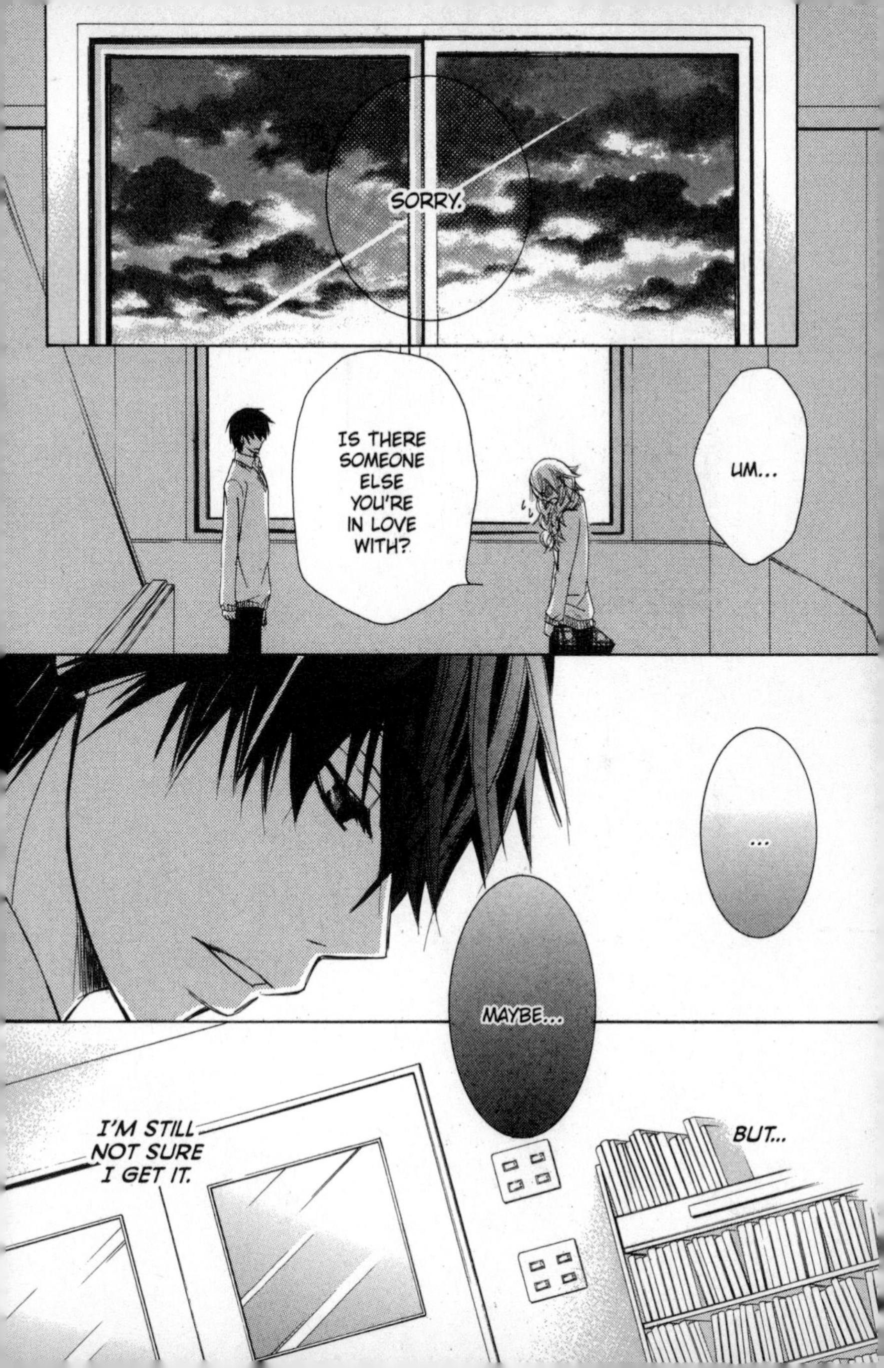
SORRY.
UM...
IS THERE SOMEONE ELSE YOU'RE IN LOVE WITH?
...
MAYBE...
BUT...
I'M STILL NOT SURE I GET IT.

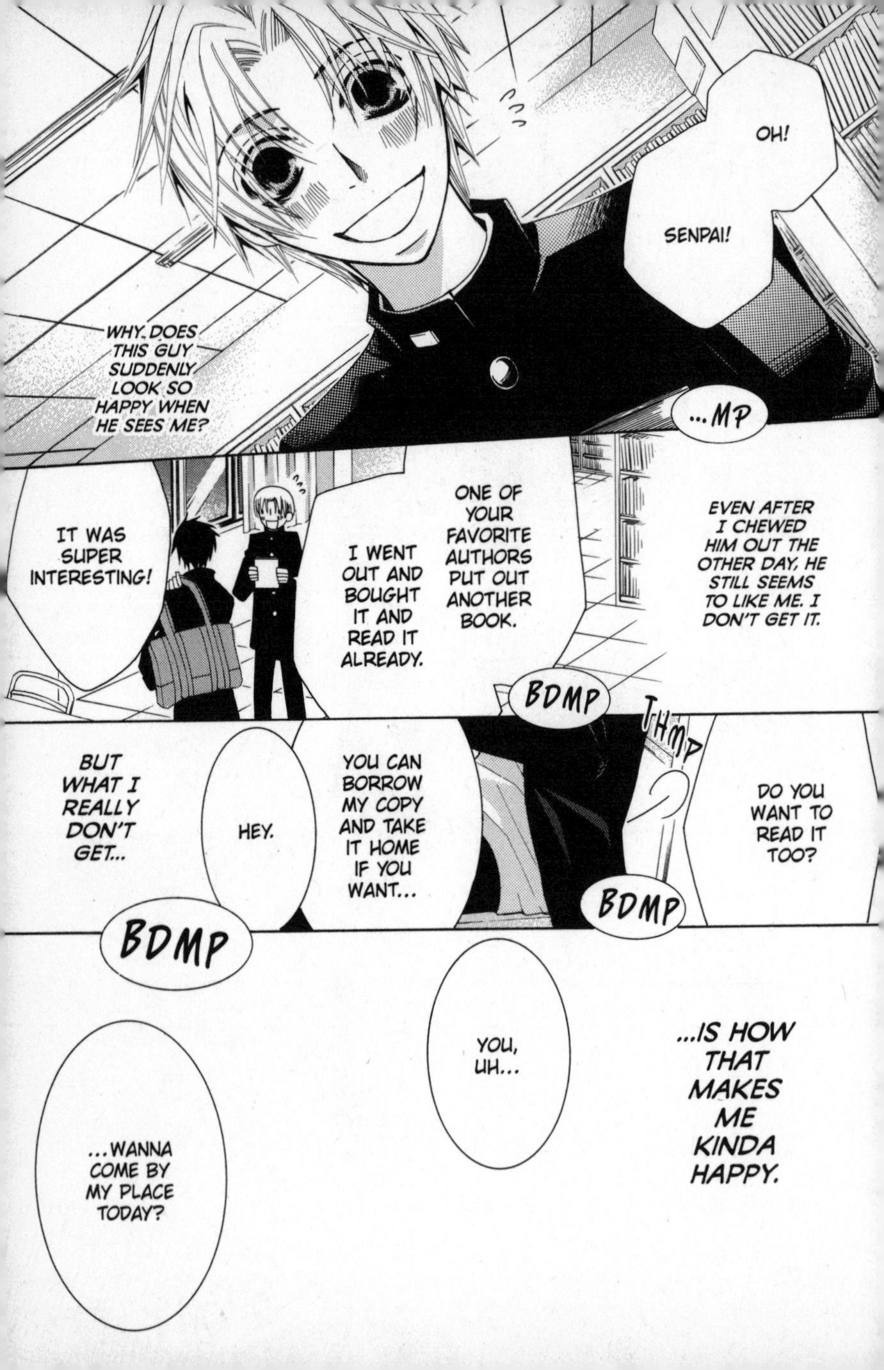
OH!
SENPAI!
...MP
WHY DOES THIS GUY SUDDENLY LOOK SO HAPPY WHEN HE SEES ME?
EVEN AFTER I CHEWED HIM OUT THE OTHER DAY, HE STILL SEEMS TO LIKE ME. I DON'T GET IT.
BDMP
ONE OF YOUR FAVORITE AUTHORS PUT OUT ANOTHER BOOK.
I WENT OUT AND BOUGHT IT AND READ IT ALREADY.
IT WAS SUPER INTERESTING!
DO YOU WANT TO READ IT TOO?
THMP
BDMP
YOU CAN BORROW MY COPY AND TAKE IT HOME IF YOU WANT...
HEY.
BUT WHAT I REALLY DON'T GET...
BDMP
...IS HOW THAT MAKES ME KINDA HAPPY.
YOU, UH...
...WANNA COME BY MY PLACE TODAY?

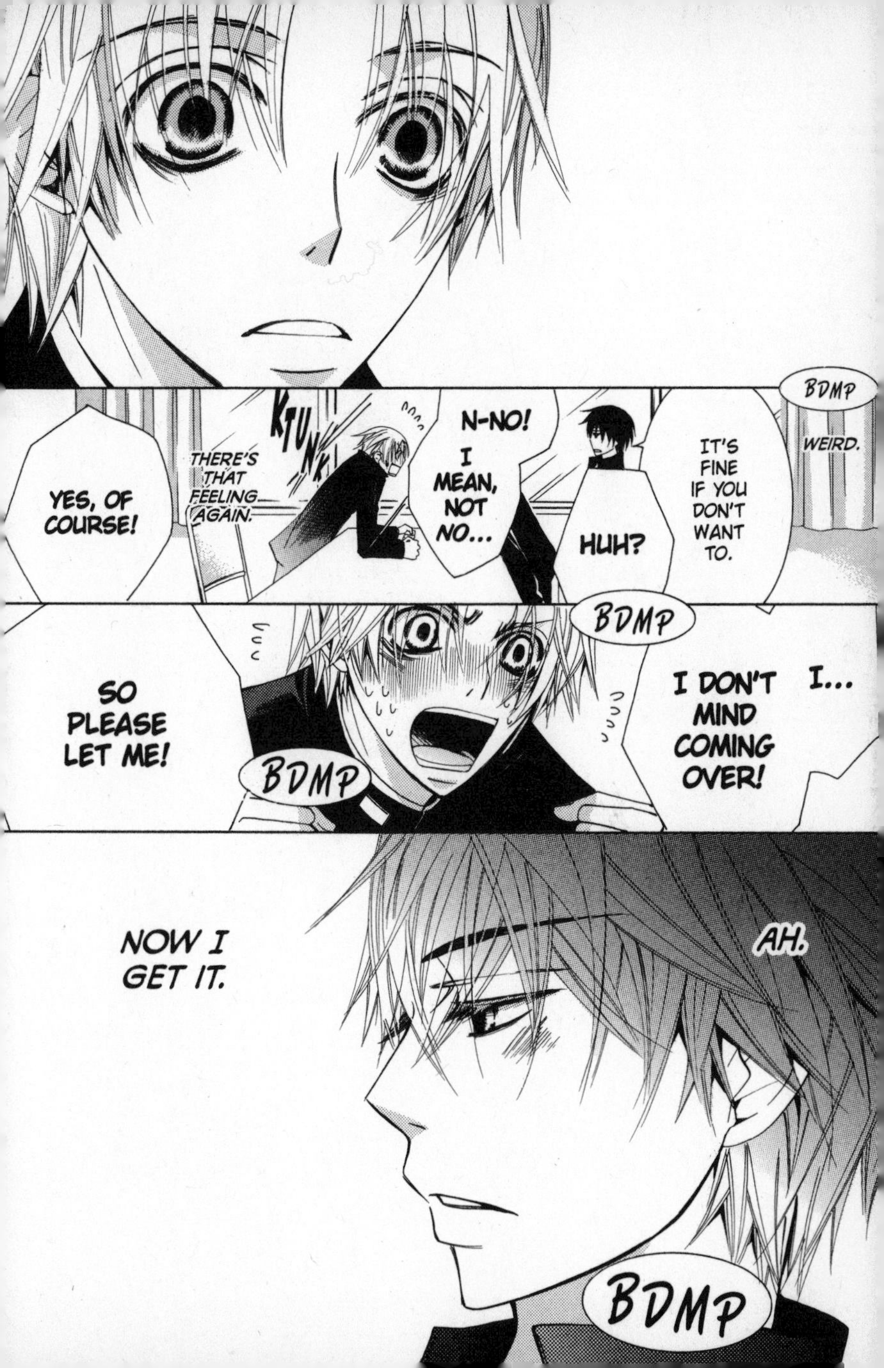
BDMP
WEIRD.
IT'S FINE IF YOU DON'T WANT TO.
HUH?
N-NO!
I MEAN, NOT NO...
KTUNK
THERE'S THAT FEELING AGAIN.
YES, OF COURSE!
I...
I DON'T MIND COMING OVER!
BDMP
BDMP
SO PLEASE LET ME!
AH.
NOW I GET IT.
BDMP

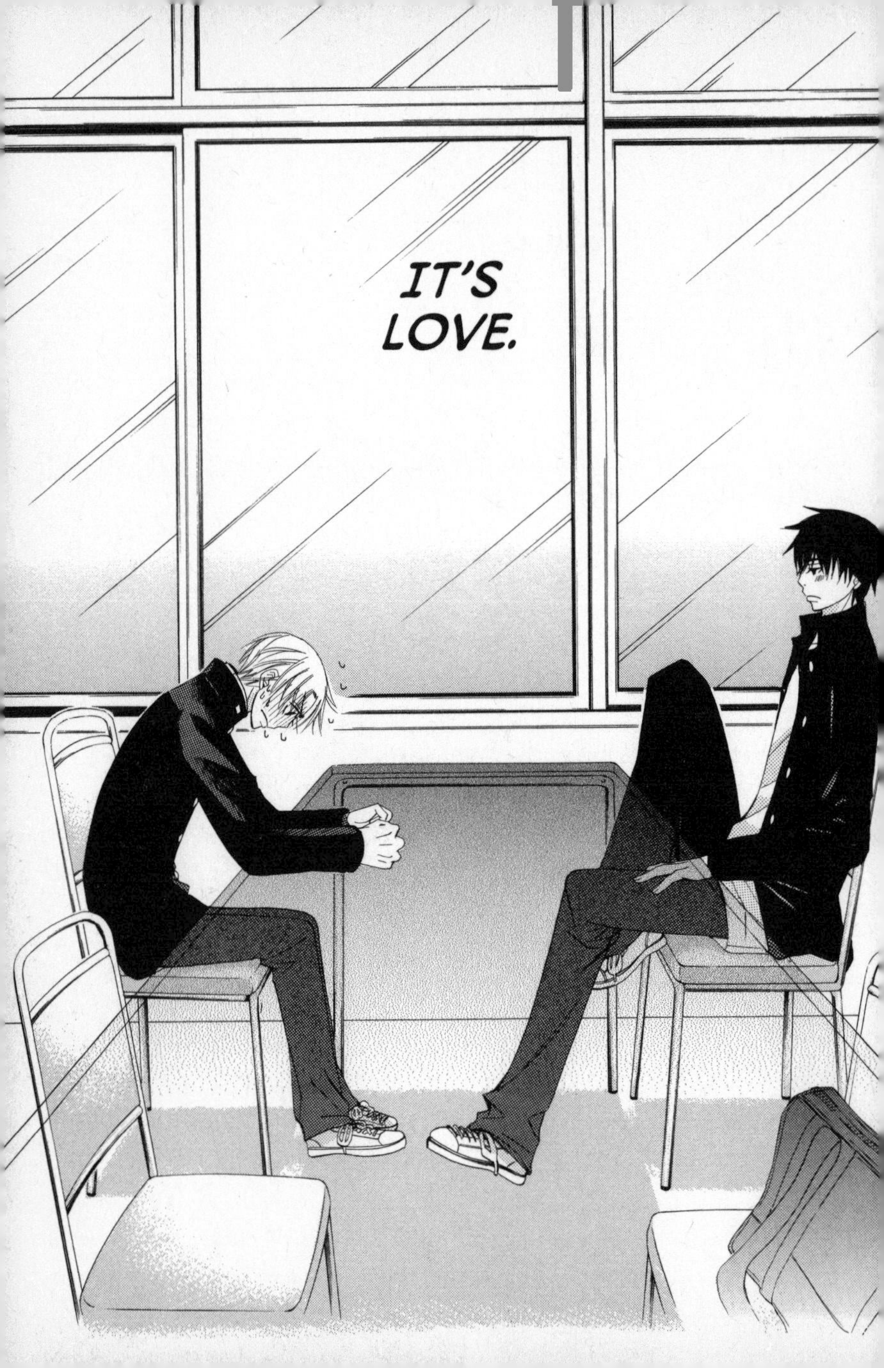
IT'S LOVE.

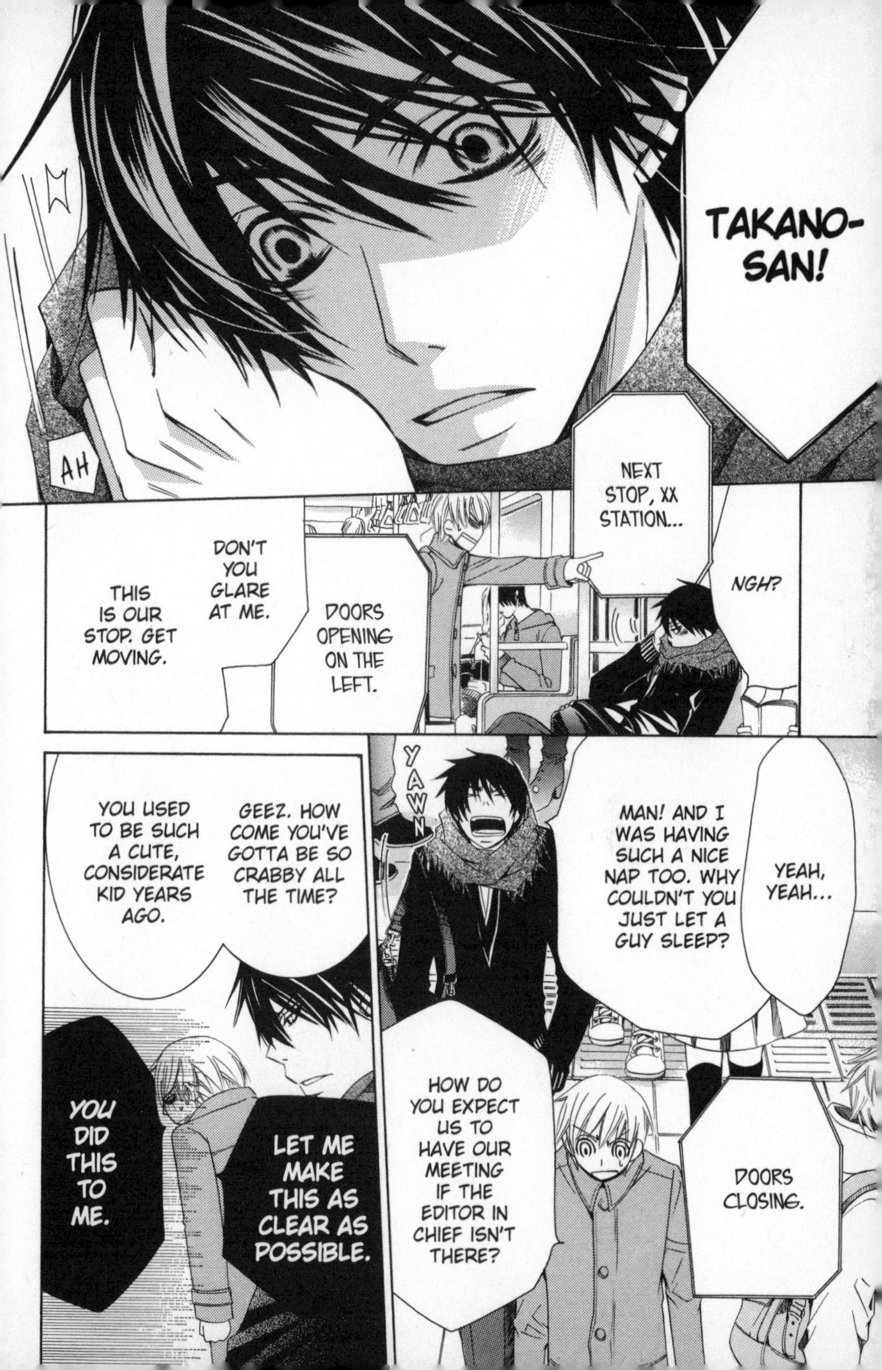
TAKANO-SAN!
AH
NEXT STOP, XX STATION...
NGH?
DOORS OPENING ON THE LEFT.
DON'T YOU GLARE AT ME.
THIS IS OUR STOP. GET MOVING.
YEAH, YEAH...
MAN! AND I WAS HAVING SUCH A NICE NAP TOO. WHY COULDN'T YOU JUST LET A GUY SLEEP?
YAWN
GEEZ. HOW COME YOU'VE GOTTA BE SO CRABBY ALL THE TIME?
YOU USED TO BE SUCH A CUTE, CONSIDERATE KID YEARS AGO.
DOORS CLOSING.
HOW DO YOU EXPECT US TO HAVE OUR MEETING IF THE EDITOR IN CHIEF ISN'T THERE?
LET ME MAKE THIS AS CLEAR AS POSSIBLE.
YOU DID THIS TO ME.

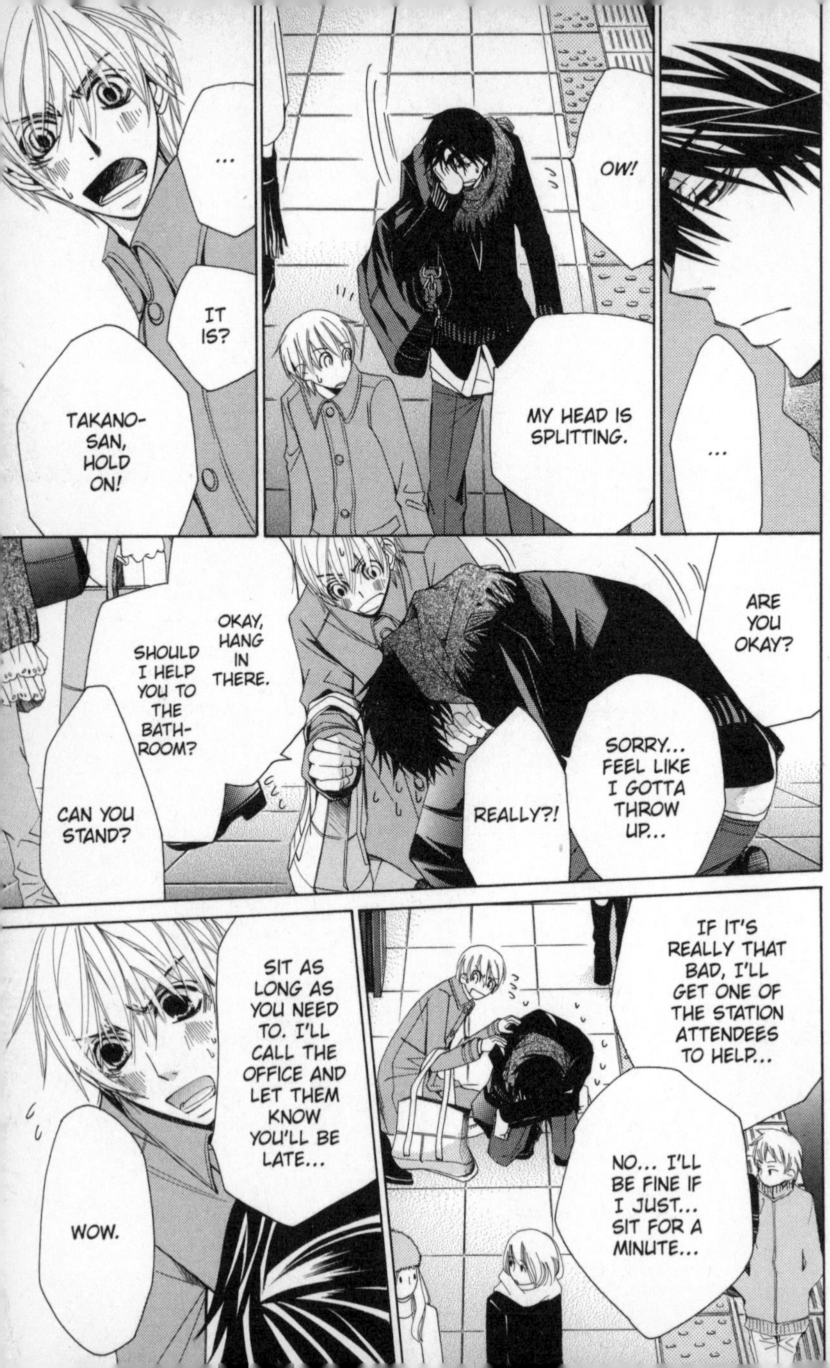
...
OW!
MY HEAD IS SPLITTING.
...
IT IS?
TAKANO-SAN, HOLD ON!
ARE YOU OKAY?
SORRY... FEEL LIKE I GOTTA THROW UP...
REALLY?!
OKAY, HANG IN THERE.
SHOULD I HELP YOU TO THE BATH-ROOM?
CAN YOU STAND?
IF IT'S REALLY THAT BAD, I'LL GET ONE OF THE STATION ATTENDEES TO HELP...
NO... I'LL BE FINE IF I JUST... SIT FOR A MINUTE...
SIT AS LONG AS YOU NEED TO. I'LL CALL THE OFFICE AND LET THEM KNOW YOU'LL BE LATE...
WOW.

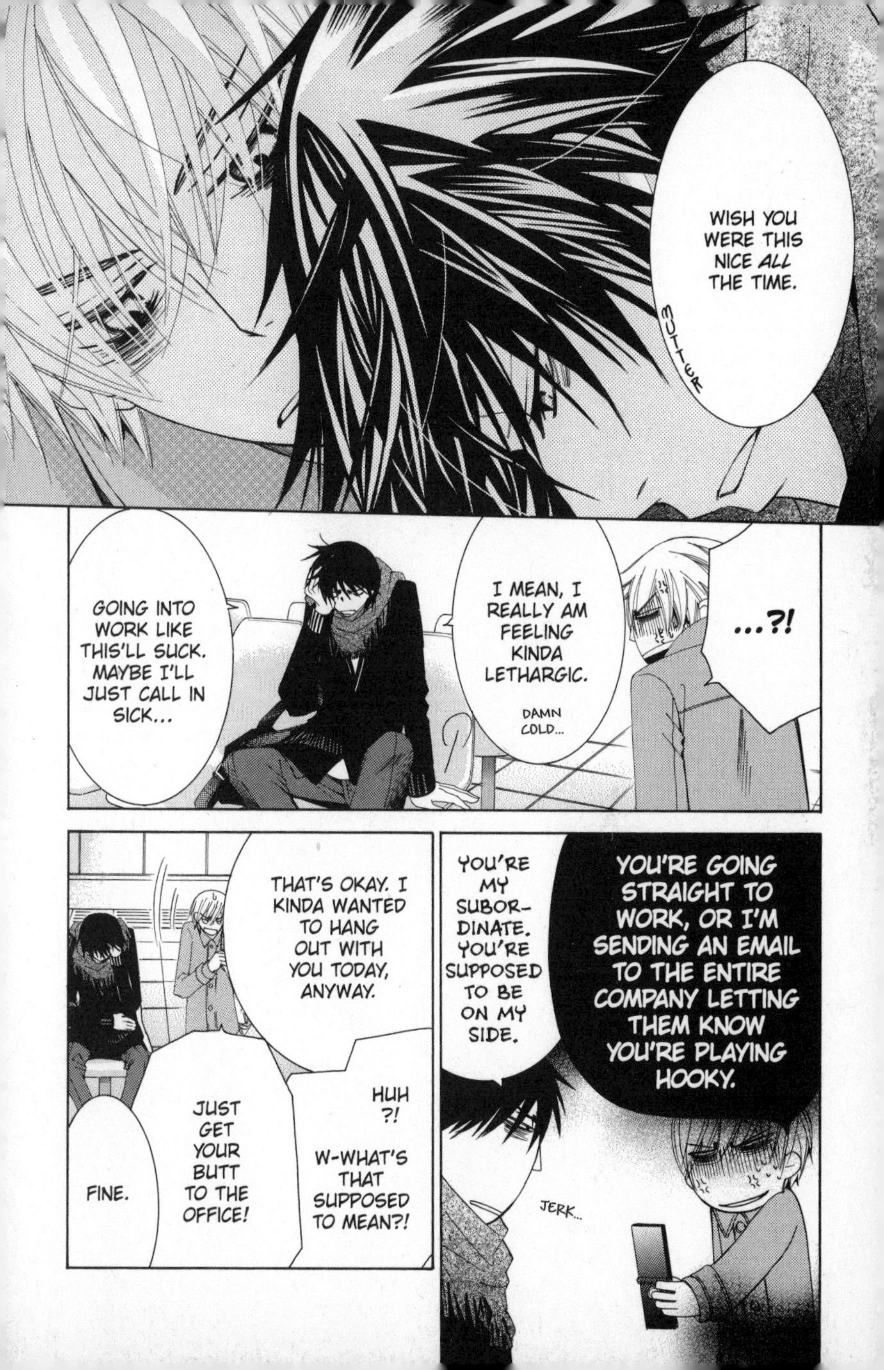
WISH YOU WERE THIS NICE *ALL* THE TIME.
MUTTER
...?!
I MEAN, I REALLY AM FEELING KINDA LETHARGIC.
DAMN COLD...
GOING INTO WORK LIKE THIS'LL SUCK. MAYBE I'LL JUST CALL IN SICK...
YOU'RE GOING STRAIGHT TO WORK, OR I'M SENDING AN EMAIL TO THE ENTIRE COMPANY LETTING THEM KNOW YOU'RE PLAYING HOOKY.
YOU'RE MY SUBOR-DINATE. YOU'RE SUPPOSED TO BE ON MY SIDE.
JERK...
THAT'S OKAY. I KINDA WANTED TO HANG OUT WITH YOU TODAY, ANYWAY.
HUH ?!
W-WHAT'S THAT SUPPOSED TO MEAN?!
JUST GET YOUR BUTT TO THE OFFICE!
FINE.

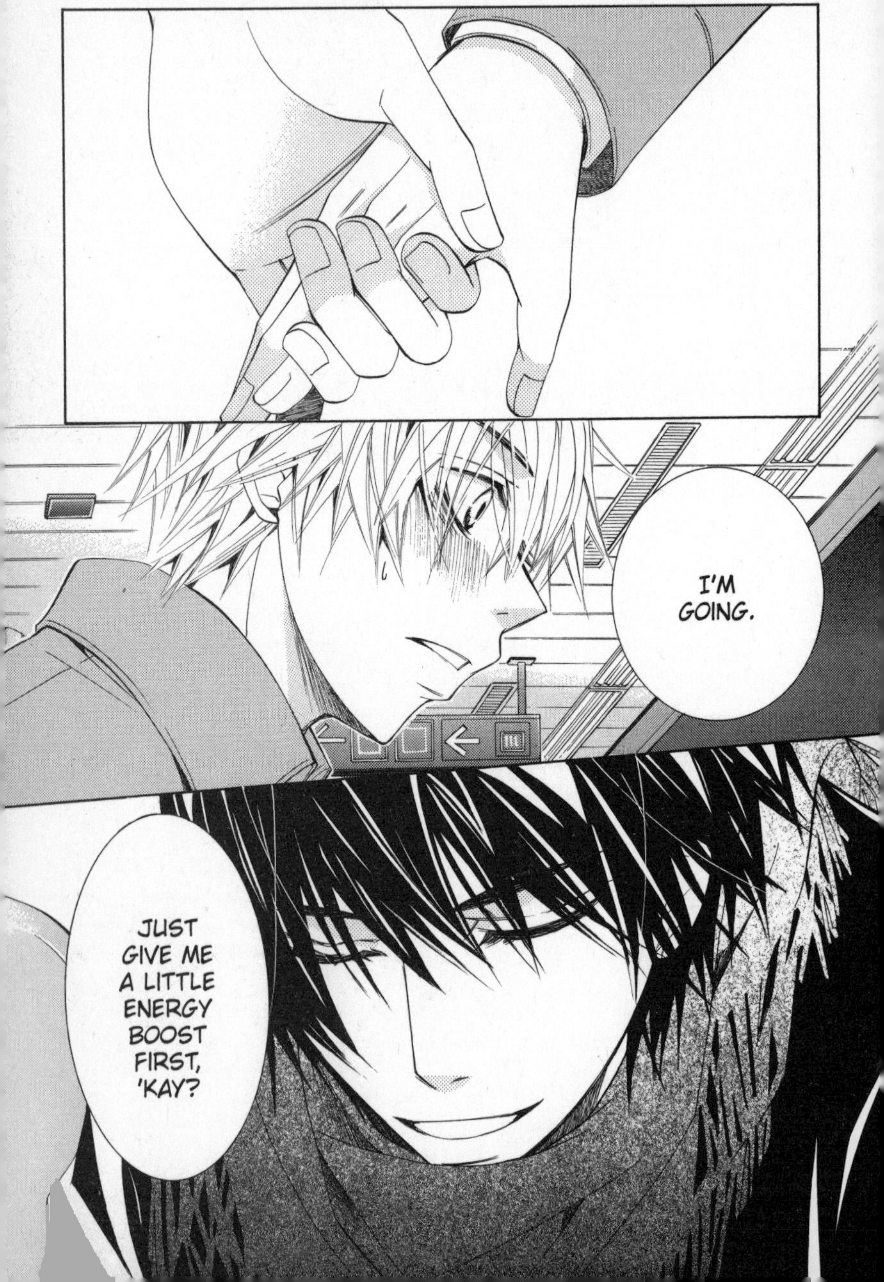
I'M GOING.
JUST GIVE ME A LITTLE ENERGY BOOST FIRST, 'KAY?

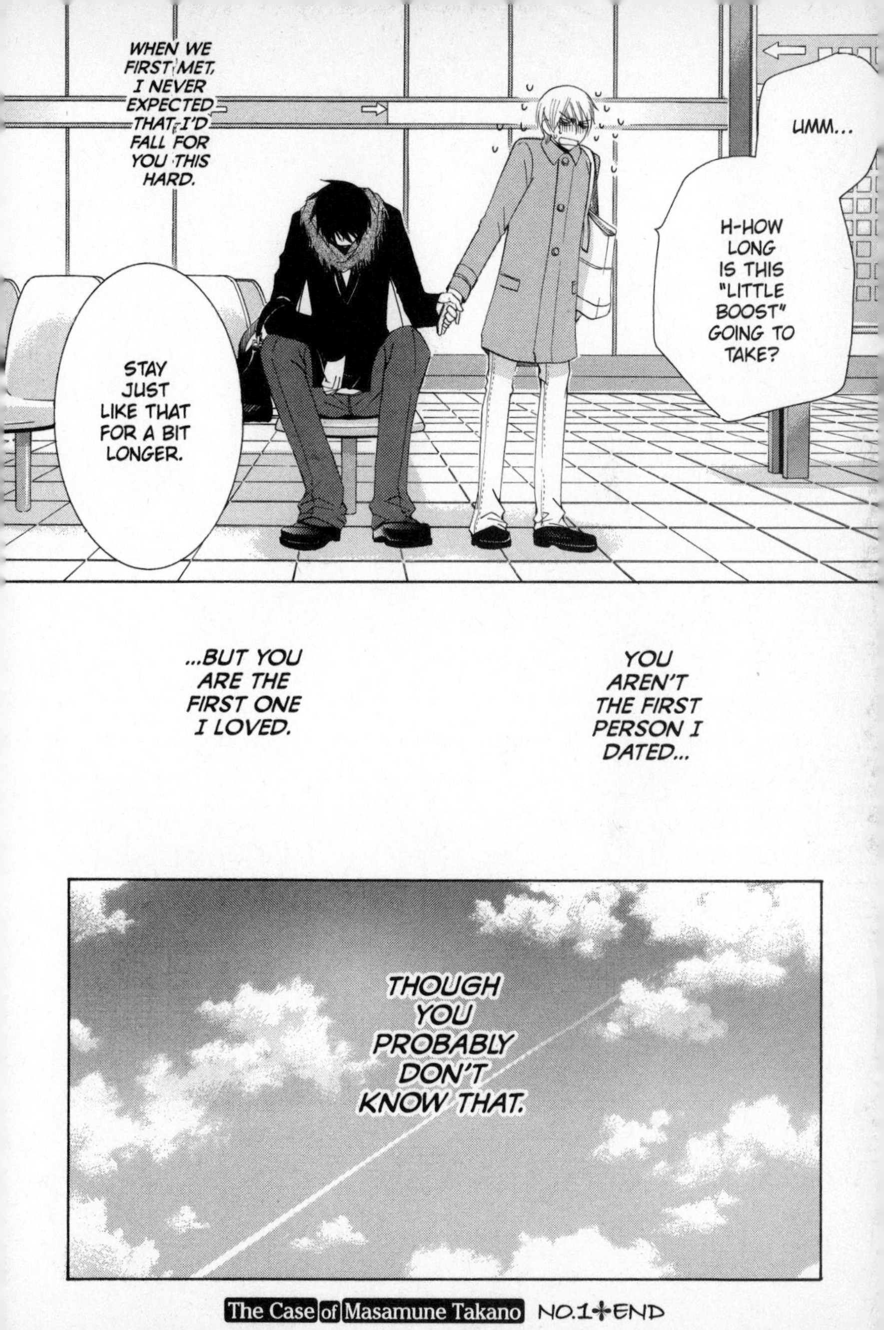
UMM...
WHEN WE FIRST MET, I NEVER EXPECTED THAT I'D FALL FOR YOU THIS HARD.
H-HOW LONG IS THIS "LITTLE BOOST" GOING TO TAKE?
STAY JUST LIKE THAT FOR A BIT LONGER.
YOU AREN'T THE FIRST PERSON I DATED...
...BUT YOU ARE THE FIRST ONE I LOVED.
THOUGH YOU PROBABLY DON'T KNOW THAT.

The Case of Masamune Takano NO.1 ✣ END

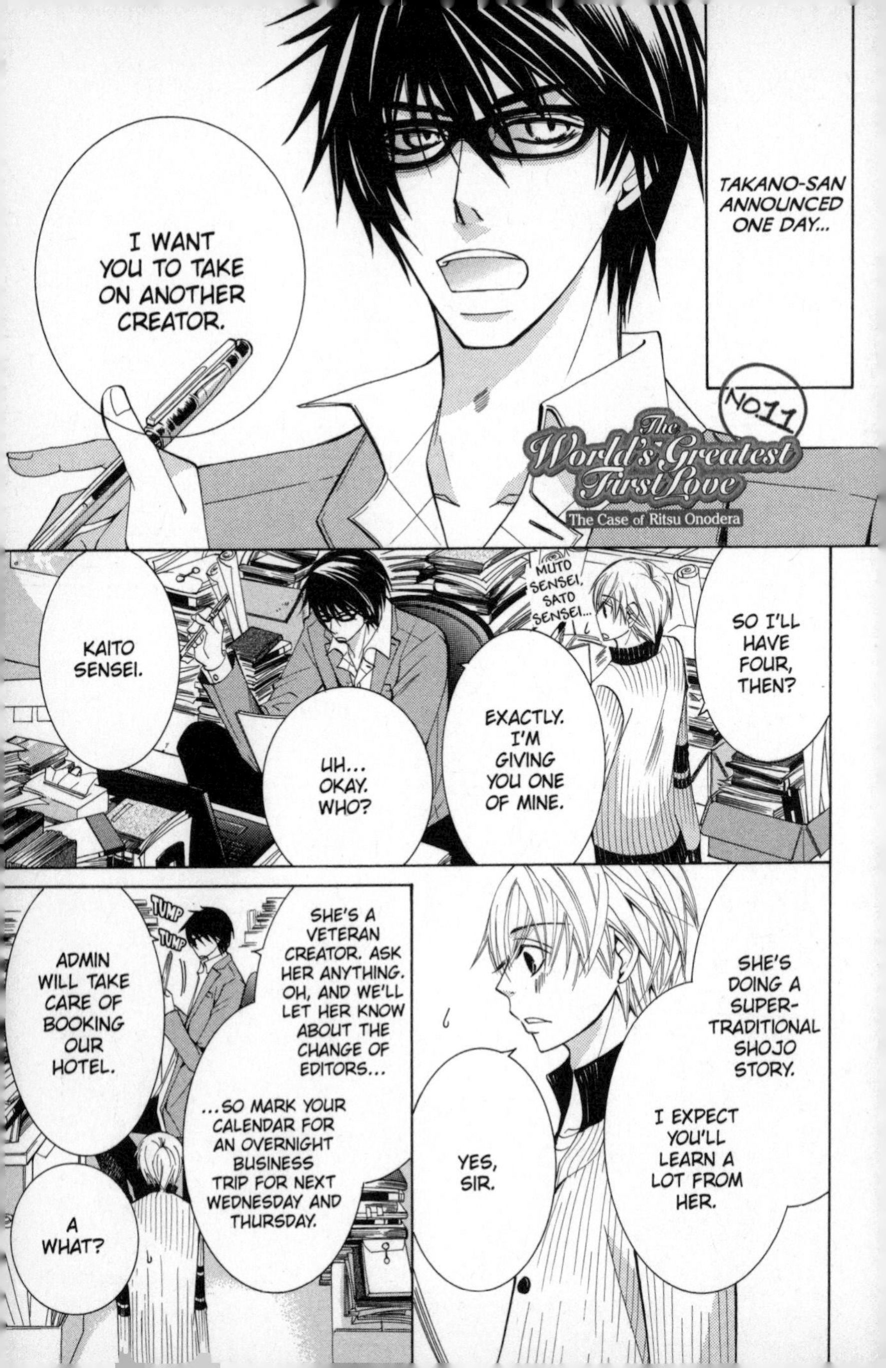
TAKANO-SAN ANNOUNCED ONE DAY...
NO.11
The World's Greatest First Love
The Case of Ritsu Onodera
I WANT YOU TO TAKE ON ANOTHER CREATOR.
SO I'LL HAVE FOUR, THEN?
MUTO SENSEI, SATO SENSEI...
EXACTLY. I'M GIVING YOU ONE OF MINE.
UH... OKAY. WHO?
KAITO SENSEI.
SHE'S DOING A SUPER-TRADITIONAL SHOJO STORY.
I EXPECT YOU'LL LEARN A LOT FROM HER.
YES, SIR.
SHE'S A VETERAN CREATOR. ASK HER ANYTHING. OH, AND WE'LL LET HER KNOW ABOUT THE CHANGE OF EDITORS...
TUMP
TUMP
...SO MARK YOUR CALENDAR FOR AN OVERNIGHT BUSINESS TRIP FOR NEXT WEDNESDAY AND THURSDAY.
ADMIN WILL TAKE CARE OF BOOKING OUR HOTEL.
A WHAT?

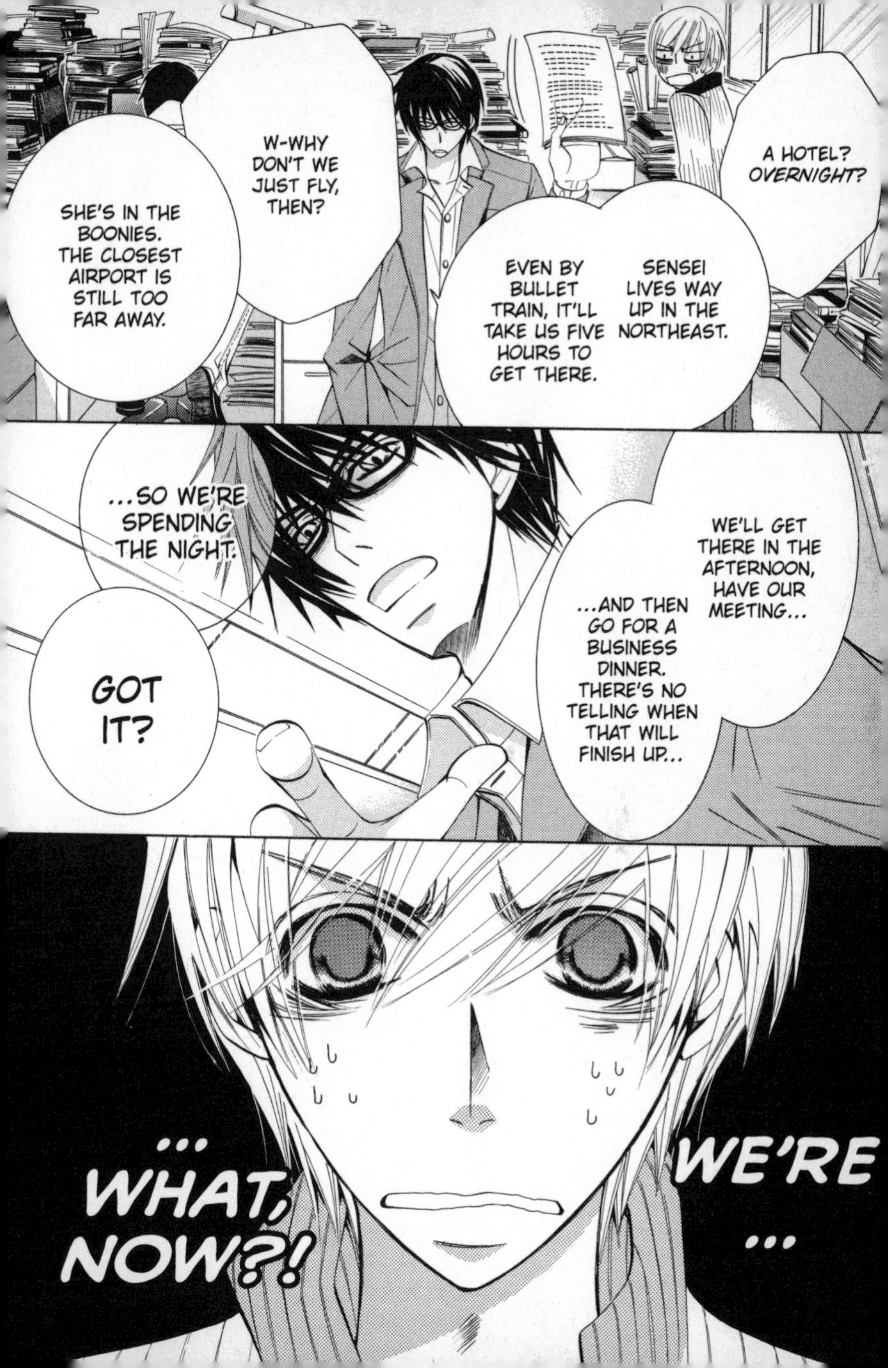
A HOTEL? OVERNIGHT?
SENSEI LIVES WAY UP IN THE NORTHEAST.
EVEN BY BULLET TRAIN, IT'LL TAKE US FIVE HOURS TO GET THERE.
W-WHY DON'T WE JUST FLY, THEN?
SHE'S IN THE BOONIES. THE CLOSEST AIRPORT IS STILL TOO FAR AWAY.
WE'LL GET THERE IN THE AFTERNOON, HAVE OUR MEETING...
...AND THEN GO FOR A BUSINESS DINNER. THERE'S NO TELLING WHEN THAT WILL FINISH UP...
...SO WE'RE SPENDING THE NIGHT.
GOT IT?
WE'RE...
...WHAT, NOW?!

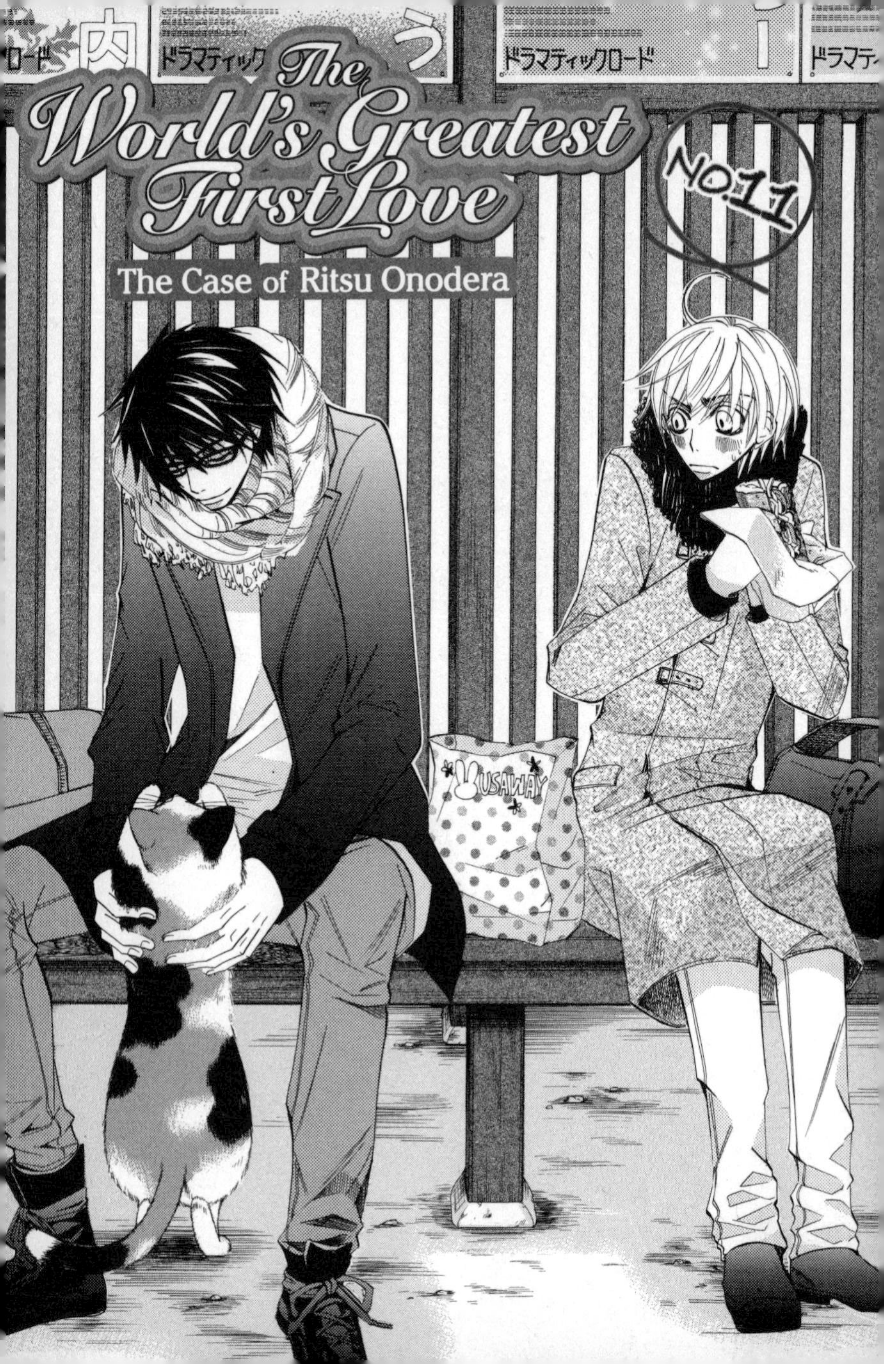
ロード
肉
ドラマティック
う
ドラマティックロード
ドラマティ
The World's Greatest First Love
NO.11
The Case of Ritsu Onodera
USAWAY

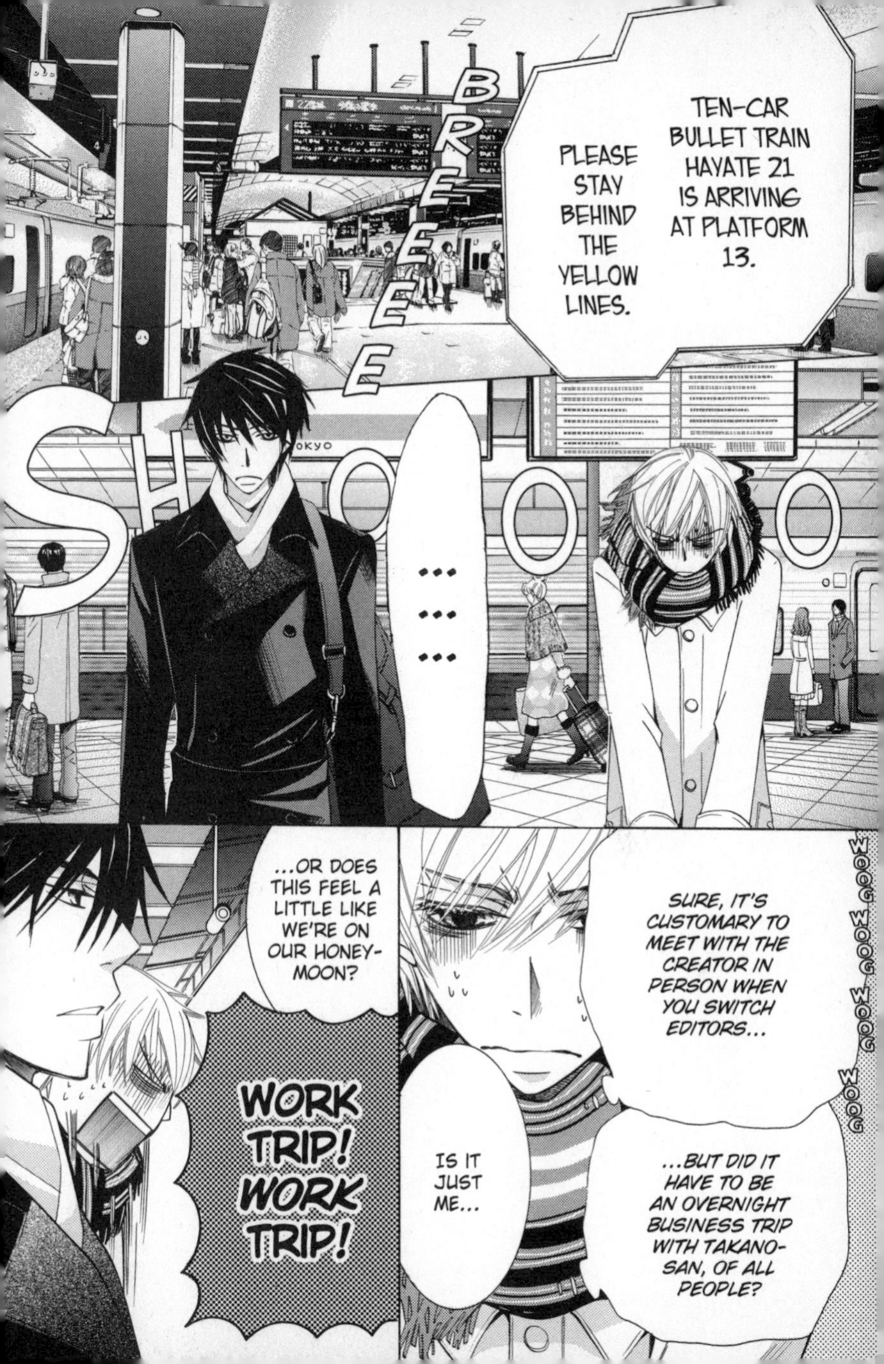

BREEEEEE
TEN-CAR BULLET TRAIN HAYATE 21 IS ARRIVING AT PLATFORM 13.
PLEASE STAY BEHIND THE YELLOW LINES.
OKYO
SHOOOO
... ...
WOOG WOOG WOOG WOOG
SURE, IT'S CUSTOMARY TO MEET WITH THE CREATOR IN PERSON WHEN YOU SWITCH EDITORS...
...BUT DID IT HAVE TO BE AN OVERNIGHT BUSINESS TRIP WITH TAKANO-SAN, OF ALL PEOPLE?
IS IT JUST ME...
...OR DOES THIS FEEL A LITTLE LIKE WE'RE ON OUR HONEY-MOON?
WORK TRIP! WORK TRIP!

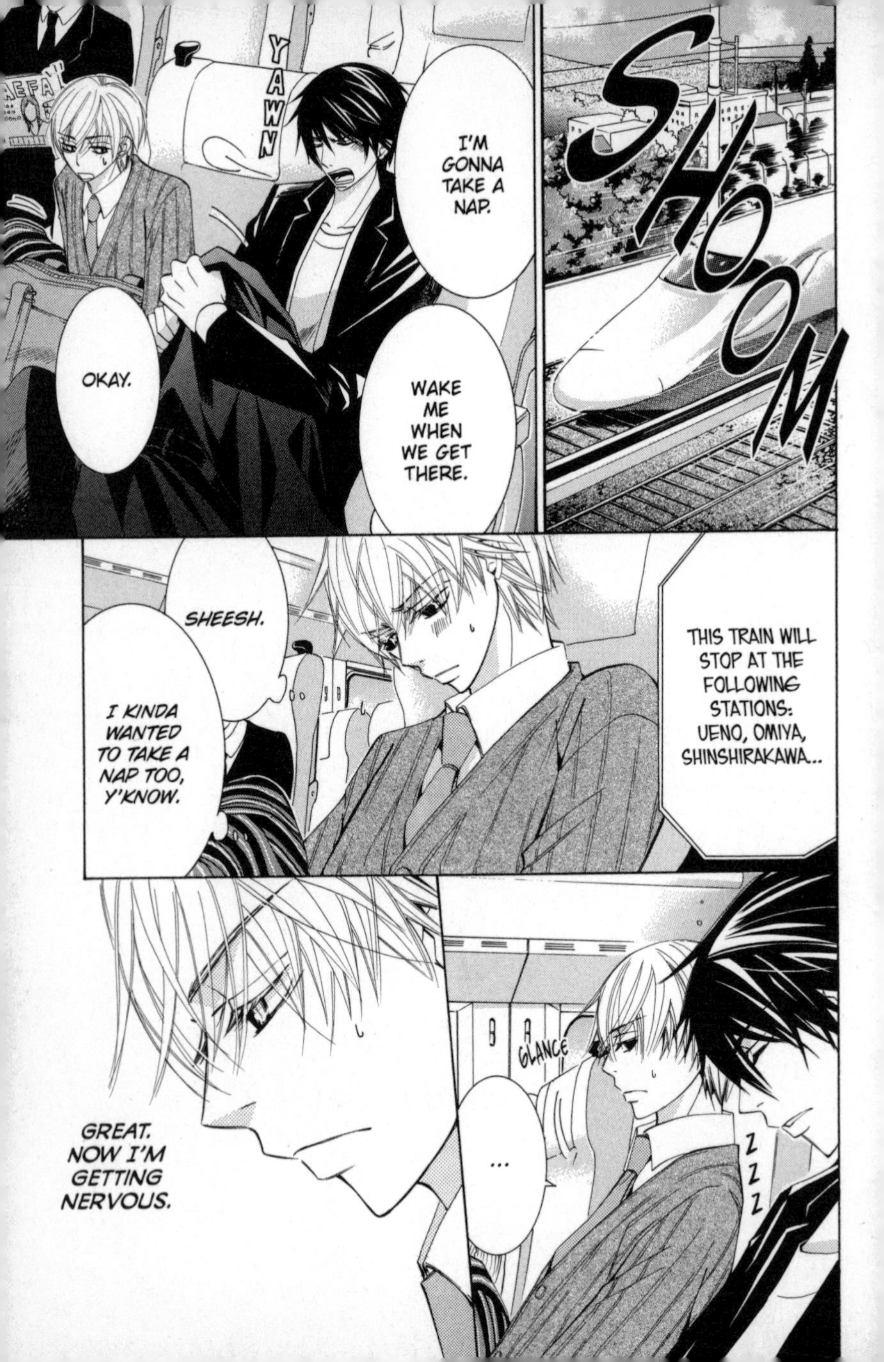
SHOOM
YAWN
I'M GONNA TAKE A NAP.
WAKE ME WHEN WE GET THERE.
OKAY.
THIS TRAIN WILL STOP AT THE FOLLOWING STATIONS: UENO, OMIYA, SHINSHIRAKAWA...
SHEESH.
I KINDA WANTED TO TAKE A NAP TOO, Y'KNOW.
GLANCE
...
ZZZ
GREAT. NOW I'M GETTING NERVOUS.

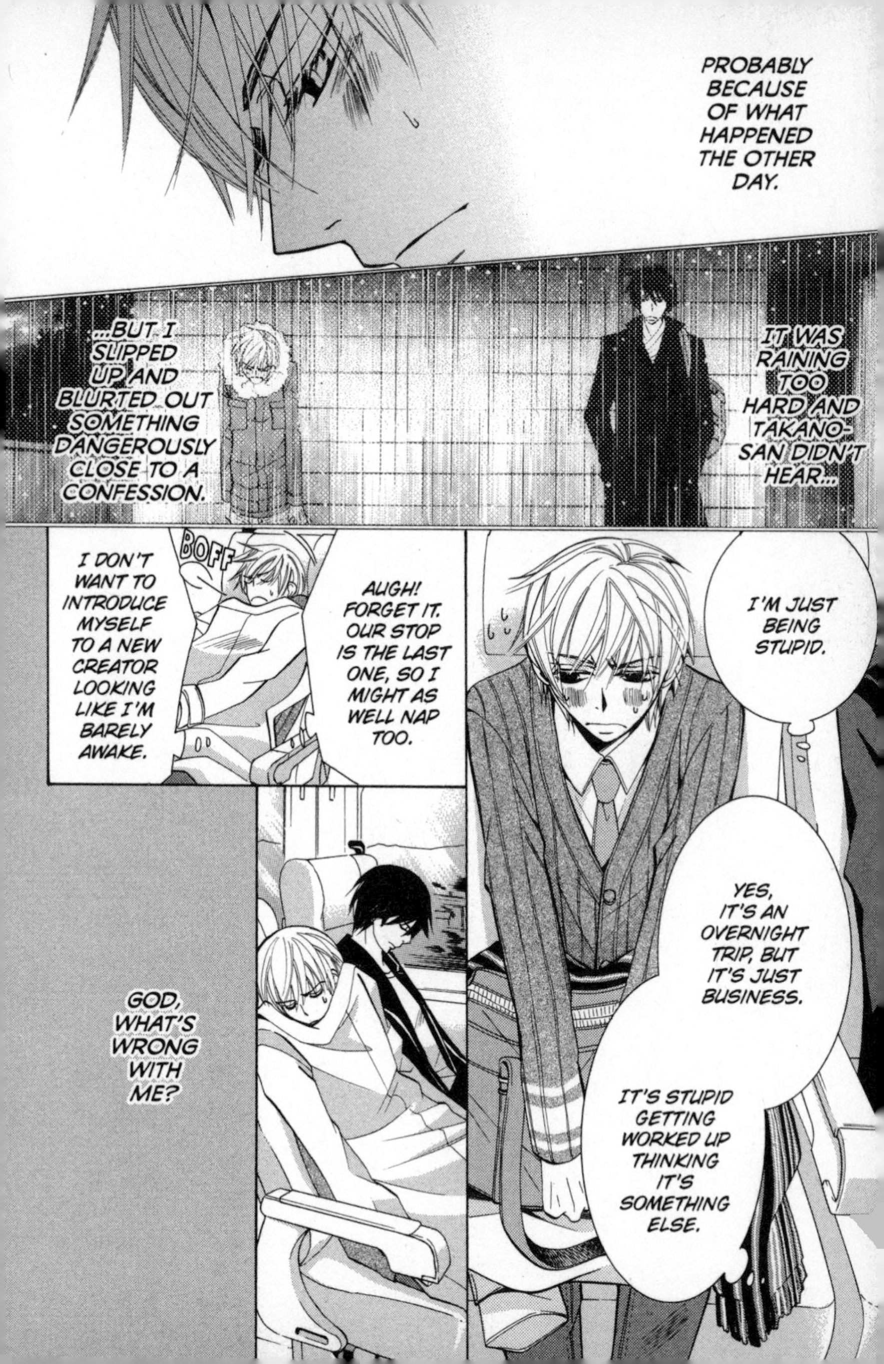
PROBABLY BECAUSE OF WHAT HAPPENED THE OTHER DAY.
IT WAS RAINING TOO HARD AND TAKANO-SAN DIDN'T HEAR...
...BUT I SLIPPED UP AND BLURTED OUT SOMETHING DANGEROUSLY CLOSE TO A CONFESSION.
I'M JUST BEING STUPID.
YES, IT'S AN OVERNIGHT TRIP, BUT IT'S JUST BUSINESS.
IT'S STUPID GETTING WORKED UP THINKING IT'S SOMETHING ELSE.
AUGH! FORGET IT. OUR STOP IS THE LAST ONE, SO I MIGHT AS WELL NAP TOO.
BOFF
I DON'T WANT TO INTRODUCE MYSELF TO A NEW CREATOR LOOKING LIKE I'M BARELY AWAKE.
GOD, WHAT'S WRONG WITH ME?

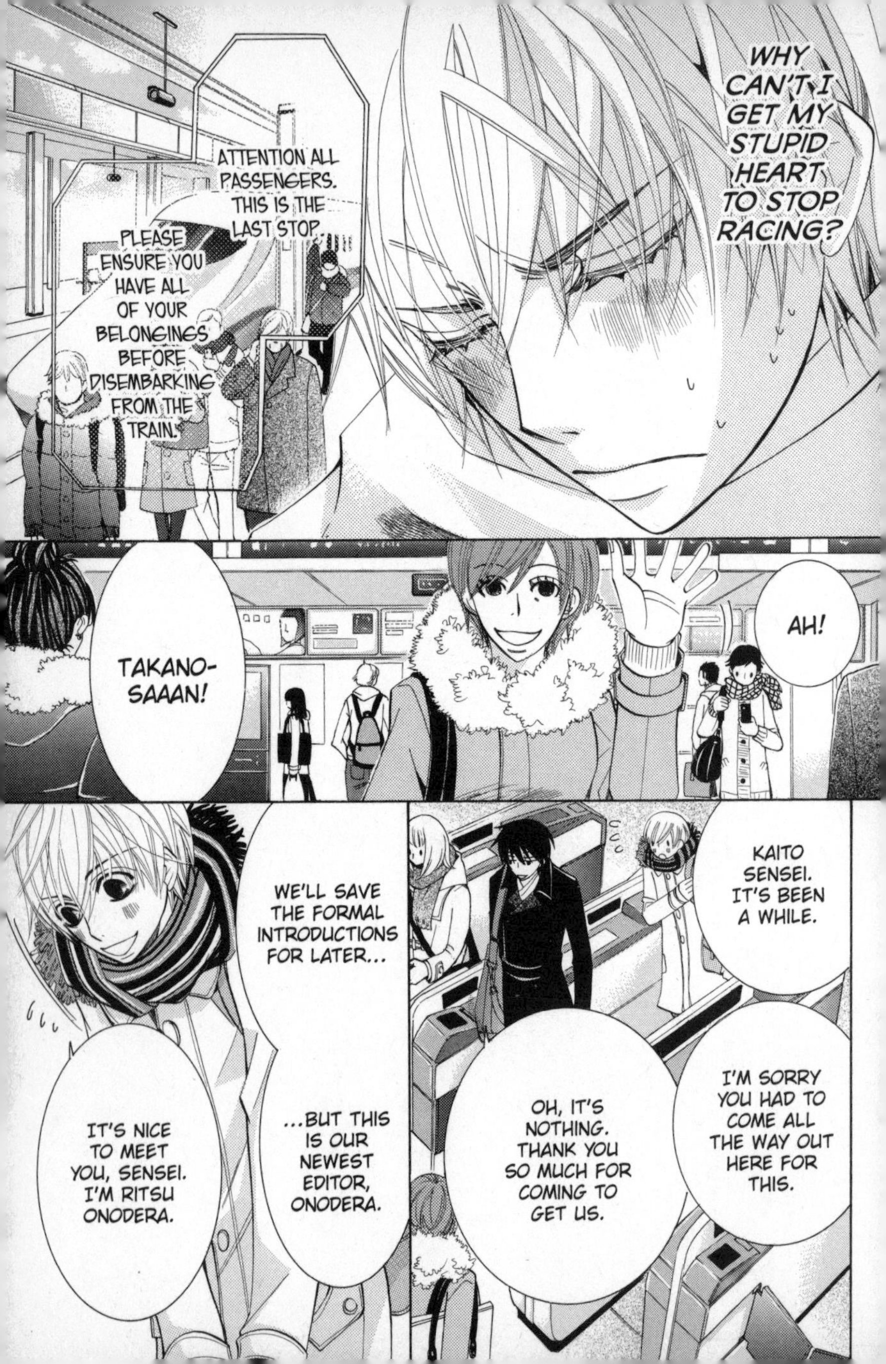
WHY CAN'T I GET MY STUPID HEART TO STOP RACING?
ATTENTION ALL PASSENGERS. THIS IS THE LAST STOP.
PLEASE ENSURE YOU HAVE ALL OF YOUR BELONGINGS BEFORE DISEMBARKING FROM THE TRAIN.
AH!
TAKANO-SAAAN!
KAITO SENSEI. IT'S BEEN A WHILE.
I'M SORRY YOU HAD TO COME ALL THE WAY OUT HERE FOR THIS.
OH, IT'S NOTHING. THANK YOU SO MUCH FOR COMING TO GET US.
WE'LL SAVE THE FORMAL INTRODUCTIONS FOR LATER...
...BUT THIS IS OUR NEWEST EDITOR, ONODERA.
IT'S NICE TO MEET YOU, SENSEI. I'M RITSU ONODERA.

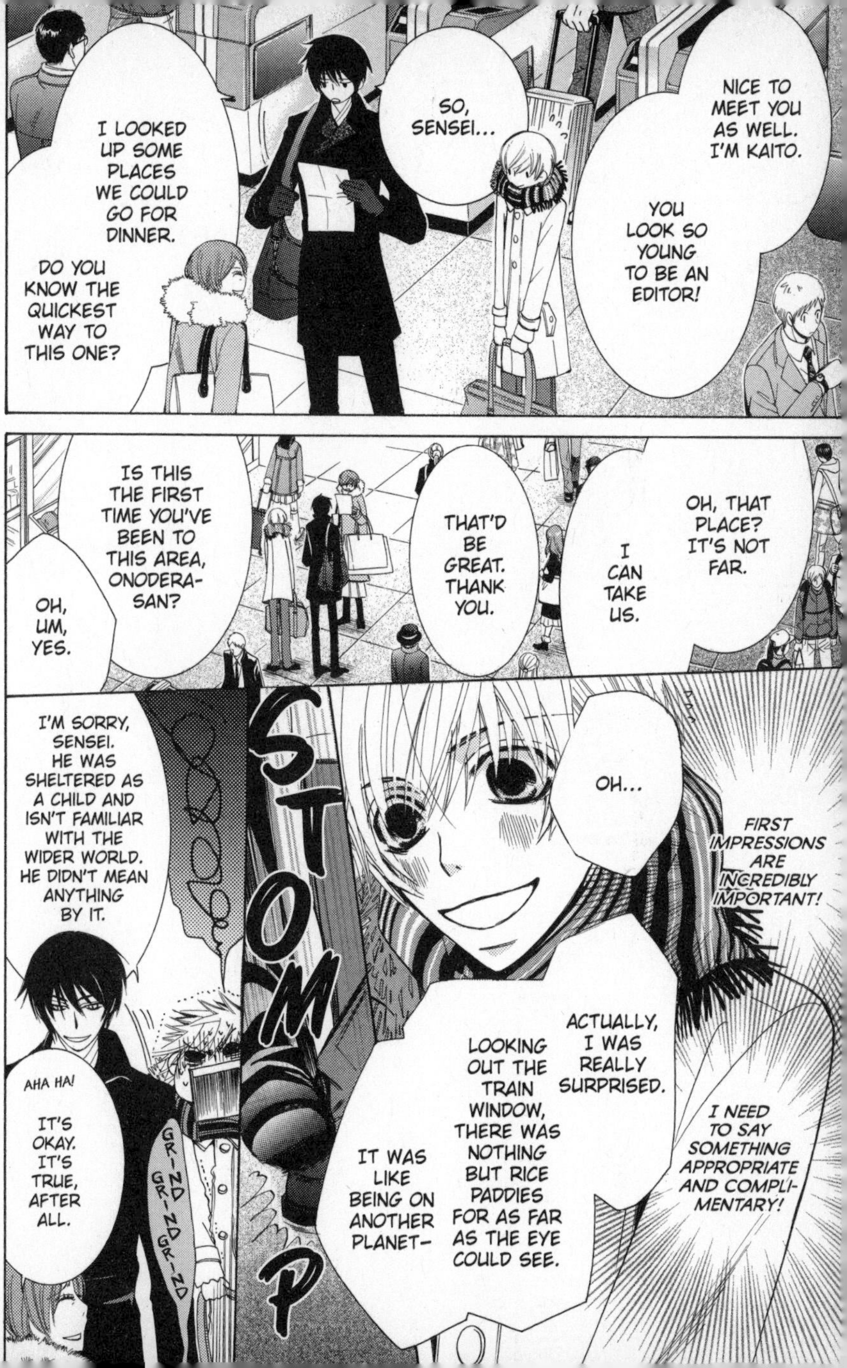
NICE TO MEET YOU AS WELL. I'M KAITO.
YOU LOOK SO YOUNG TO BE AN EDITOR!
SO, SENSEI...
I LOOKED UP SOME PLACES WE COULD GO FOR DINNER.
DO YOU KNOW THE QUICKEST WAY TO THIS ONE?
OH, THAT PLACE? IT'S NOT FAR.
I CAN TAKE US.
THAT'D BE GREAT. THANK YOU.
IS THIS THE FIRST TIME YOU'VE BEEN TO THIS AREA, ONODERA-SAN?
OH, UM, YES.
OH...
FIRST IMPRESSIONS ARE INCREDIBLY IMPORTANT!
I NEED TO SAY SOMETHING APPROPRIATE AND COMPLIMENTARY!
ACTUALLY, I WAS REALLY SURPRISED.
LOOKING OUT THE TRAIN WINDOW, THERE WAS NOTHING BUT RICE PADDIES FOR AS FAR AS THE EYE COULD SEE.
IT WAS LIKE BEING ON ANOTHER PLANET-
STOMP
I'M SORRY, SENSEI. HE WAS SHELTERED AS A CHILD AND ISN'T FAMILIAR WITH THE WIDER WORLD. HE DIDN'T MEAN ANYTHING BY IT.
AHA HA!
IT'S OKAY. IT'S TRUE, AFTER ALL.
GRIND GRIND GRIND

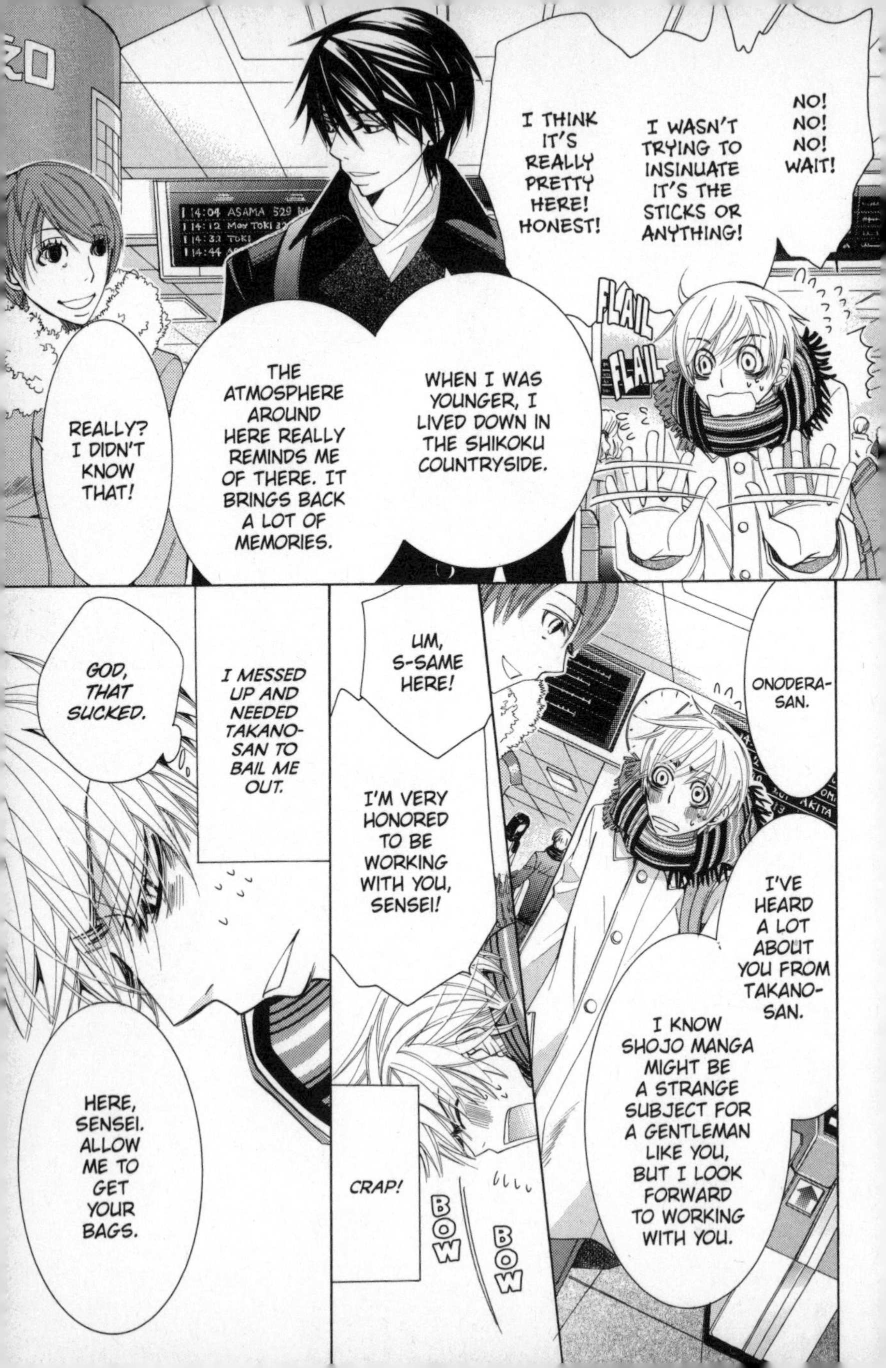
NO! NO! NO! WAIT!
I WASN'T TRYING TO INSINUATE IT'S THE STICKS OR ANYTHING!
I THINK IT'S REALLY PRETTY HERE! HONEST!
FLAIL
FLAIL
WHEN I WAS YOUNGER, I LIVED DOWN IN THE SHIKOKU COUNTRYSIDE.
THE ATMOSPHERE AROUND HERE REALLY REMINDS ME OF THERE. IT BRINGS BACK A LOT OF MEMORIES.
REALLY? I DIDN'T KNOW THAT!
ONODERA-SAN.
I'VE HEARD A LOT ABOUT YOU FROM TAKANO-SAN.
I KNOW SHOJO MANGA MIGHT BE A STRANGE SUBJECT FOR A GENTLEMAN LIKE YOU, BUT I LOOK FORWARD TO WORKING WITH YOU.
UM, S-SAME HERE!
I'M VERY HONORED TO BE WORKING WITH YOU, SENSEI!
BOW
BOW
CRAP!
I MESSED UP AND NEEDED TAKANO-SAN TO BAIL ME OUT.
GOD, THAT SUCKED.
HERE, SENSEI. ALLOW ME TO GET YOUR BAGS.

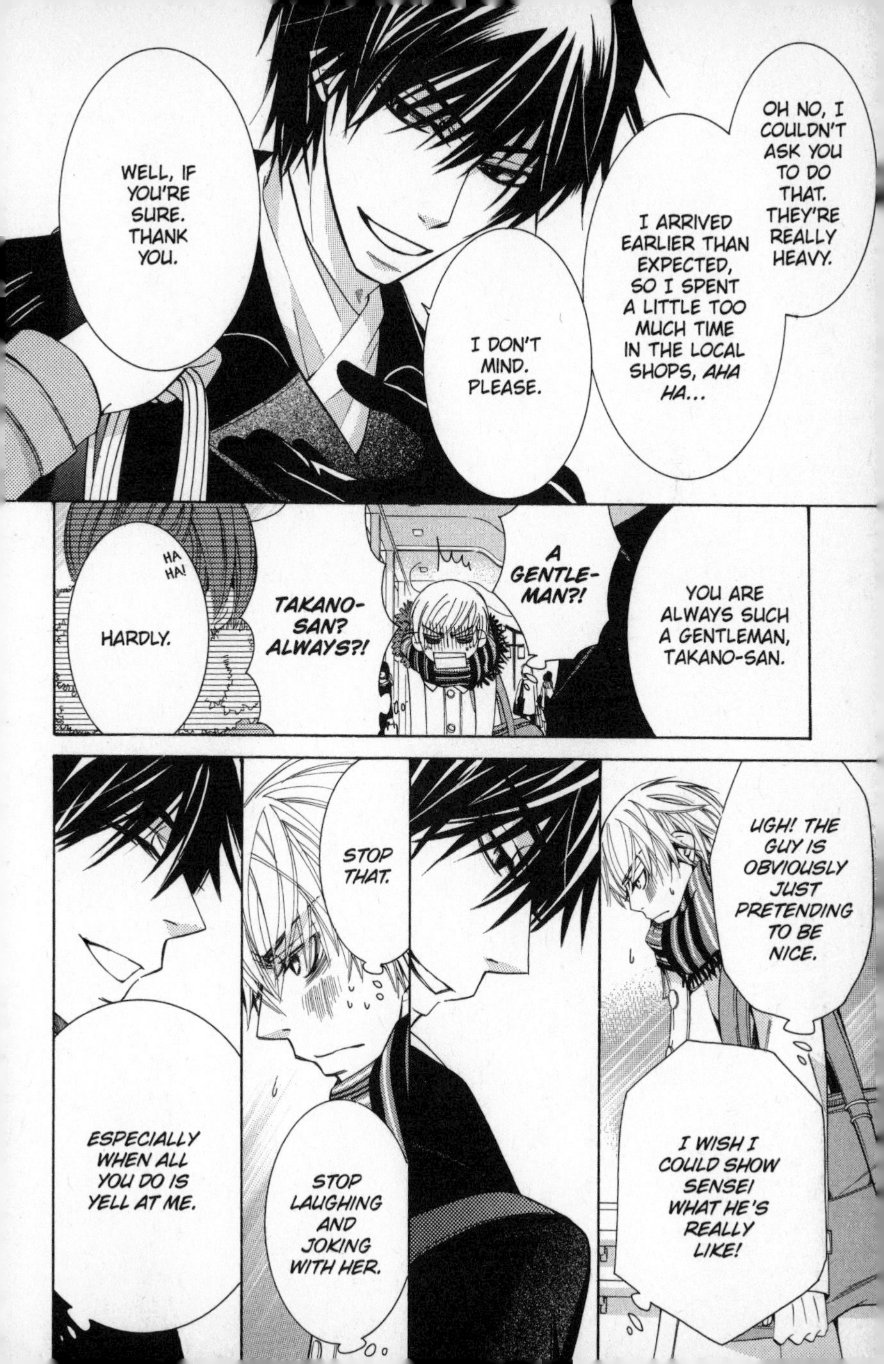
OH NO, I COULDN'T ASK YOU TO DO THAT. THEY'RE REALLY HEAVY.
I ARRIVED EARLIER THAN EXPECTED, SO I SPENT A LITTLE TOO MUCH TIME IN THE LOCAL SHOPS, AHA HA...
I DON'T MIND. PLEASE.
WELL, IF YOU'RE SURE. THANK YOU.
YOU ARE ALWAYS SUCH A GENTLEMAN, TAKANO-SAN.
A GENTLE-MAN?!
TAKANO-SAN? ALWAYS?!
HA HA!
HARDLY.
UGH! THE GUY IS OBVIOUSLY JUST PRETENDING TO BE NICE.
I WISH I COULD SHOW SENSEI WHAT HE'S REALLY LIKE!
STOP THAT.
STOP LAUGHING AND JOKING WITH HER.
ESPECIALLY WHEN ALL YOU DO IS YELL AT ME.

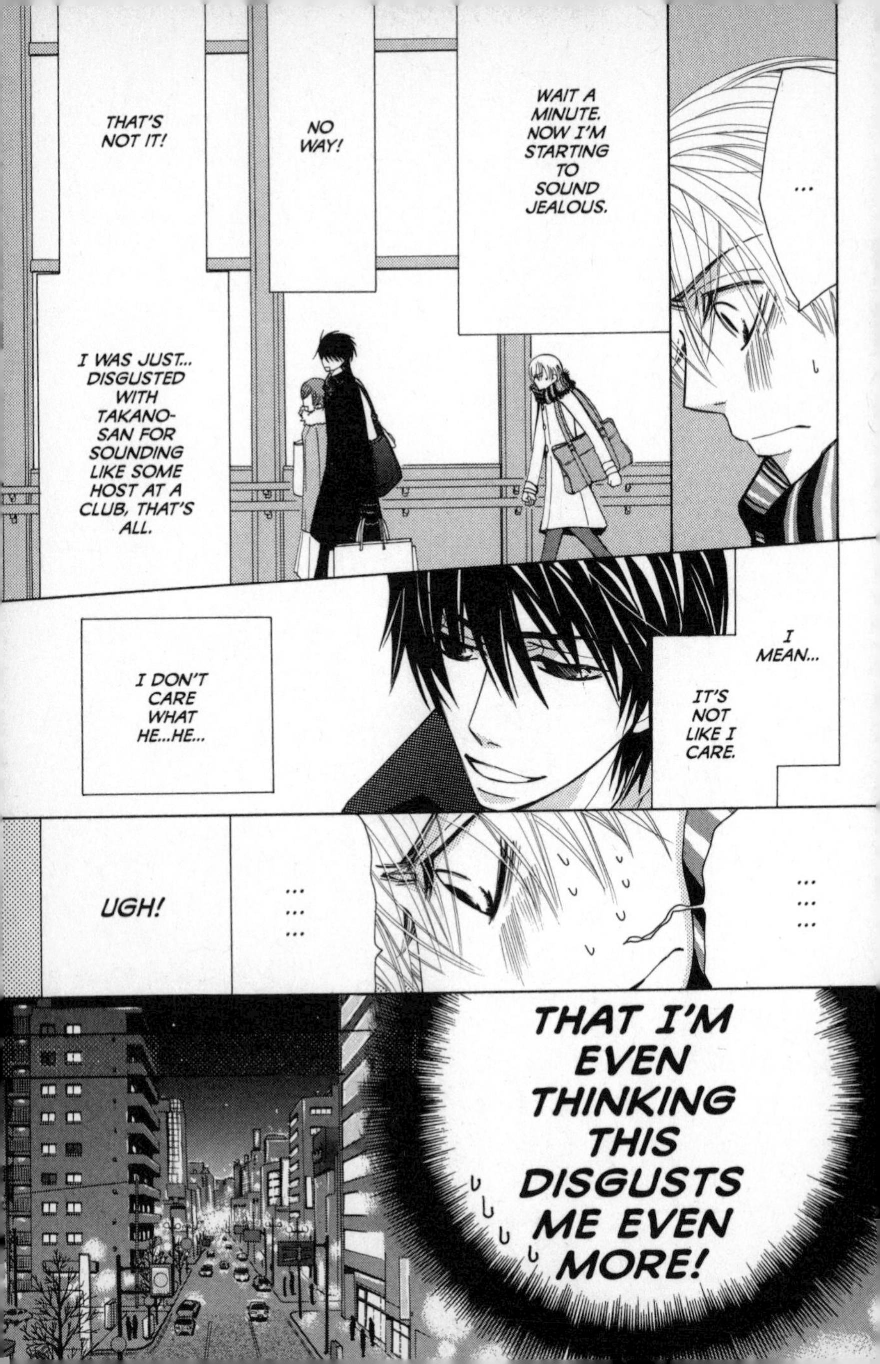
...
WAIT A MINUTE. NOW I'M STARTING TO SOUND JEALOUS.
NO WAY!
THAT'S NOT IT!
I WAS JUST... DISGUSTED WITH TAKANO-SAN FOR SOUNDING LIKE SOME HOST AT A CLUB, THAT'S ALL.
I MEAN...
IT'S NOT LIKE I CARE.
I DON'T CARE WHAT HE...HE...
... ...
... ...
UGH!
THAT I'M EVEN THINKING THIS DISGUSTS ME EVEN MORE!

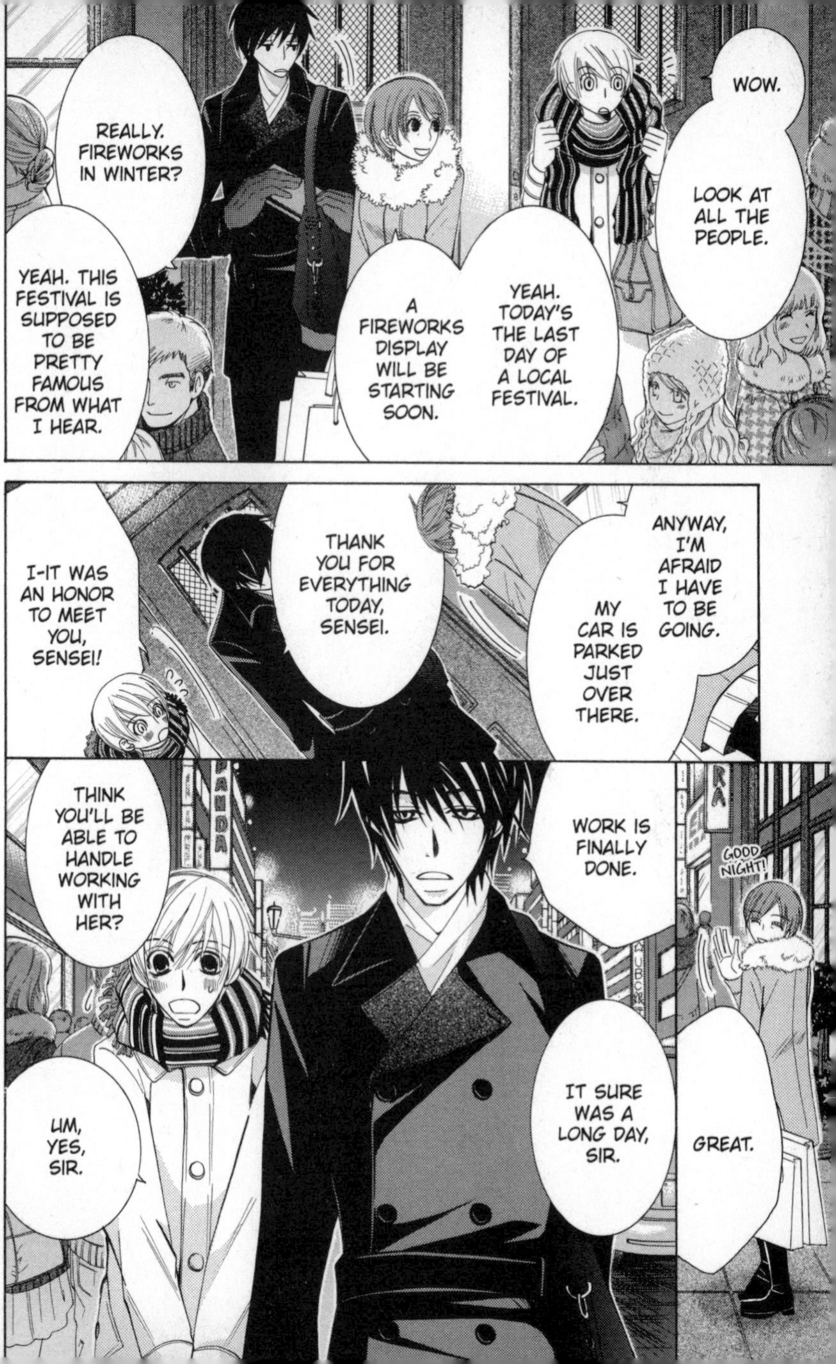
WOW.
LOOK AT ALL THE PEOPLE.
YEAH. TODAY'S THE LAST DAY OF A LOCAL FESTIVAL.
A FIREWORKS DISPLAY WILL BE STARTING SOON.
REALLY. FIREWORKS IN WINTER?
YEAH. THIS FESTIVAL IS SUPPOSED TO BE PRETTY FAMOUS FROM WHAT I HEAR.
ANYWAY, I'M AFRAID I HAVE TO BE GOING.
MY CAR IS PARKED JUST OVER THERE.
THANK YOU FOR EVERYTHING TODAY, SENSEI.
I-IT WAS AN HONOR TO MEET YOU, SENSEI!
GOOD NIGHT!
GREAT.
WORK IS FINALLY DONE.
IT SURE WAS A LONG DAY, SIR.
THINK YOU'LL BE ABLE TO HANDLE WORKING WITH HER?
UM, YES, SIR.

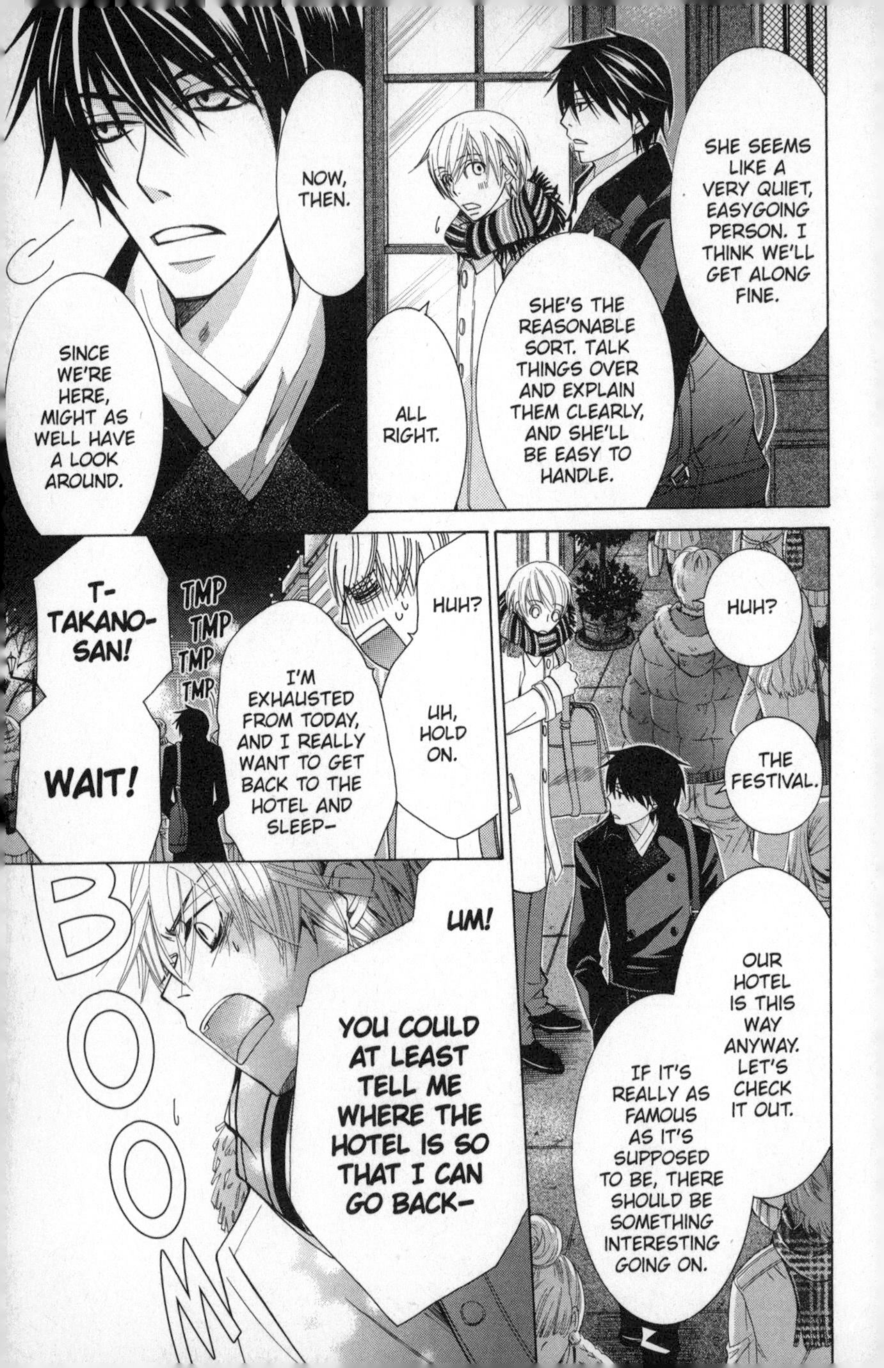

SHE SEEMS LIKE A VERY QUIET, EASYGOING PERSON. I THINK WE'LL GET ALONG FINE.
SHE'S THE REASONABLE SORT. TALK THINGS OVER AND EXPLAIN THEM CLEARLY, AND SHE'LL BE EASY TO HANDLE.
ALL RIGHT.
NOW, THEN.
SINCE WE'RE HERE, MIGHT AS WELL HAVE A LOOK AROUND.
HUH?
THE FESTIVAL.
OUR HOTEL IS THIS WAY ANYWAY. LET'S CHECK IT OUT.
IF IT'S REALLY AS FAMOUS AS IT'S SUPPOSED TO BE, THERE SHOULD BE SOMETHING INTERESTING GOING ON.
HUH?
UH, HOLD ON.
I'M EXHAUSTED FROM TODAY, AND I REALLY WANT TO GET BACK TO THE HOTEL AND SLEEP-
TMP TMP TMP TMP
T-TAKANO-SAN!
WAIT!
UM!
YOU COULD AT LEAST TELL ME WHERE THE HOTEL IS SO THAT I CAN GO BACK-
BOOOM

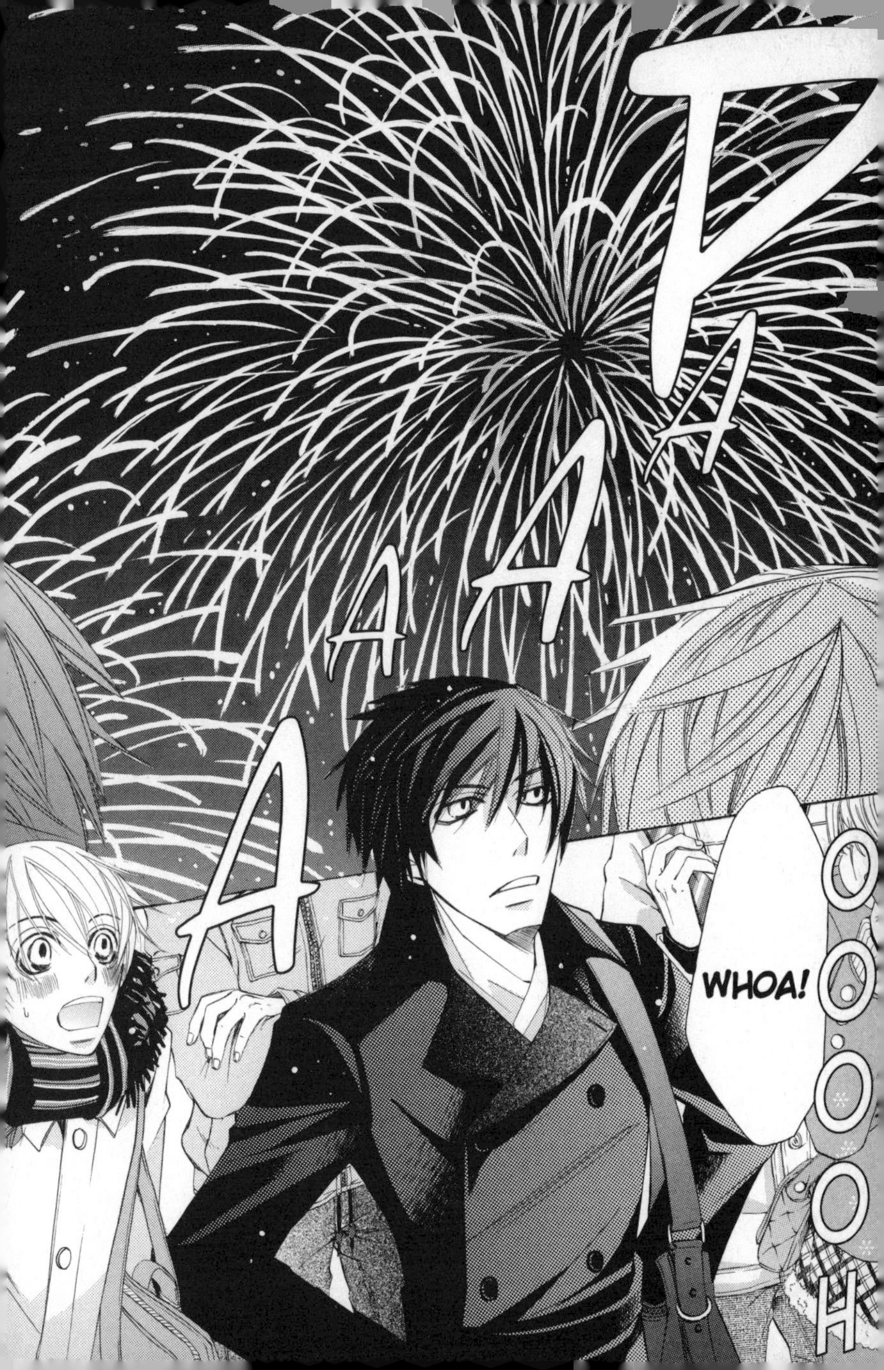
PAAAA
OOOOH
WHOA!

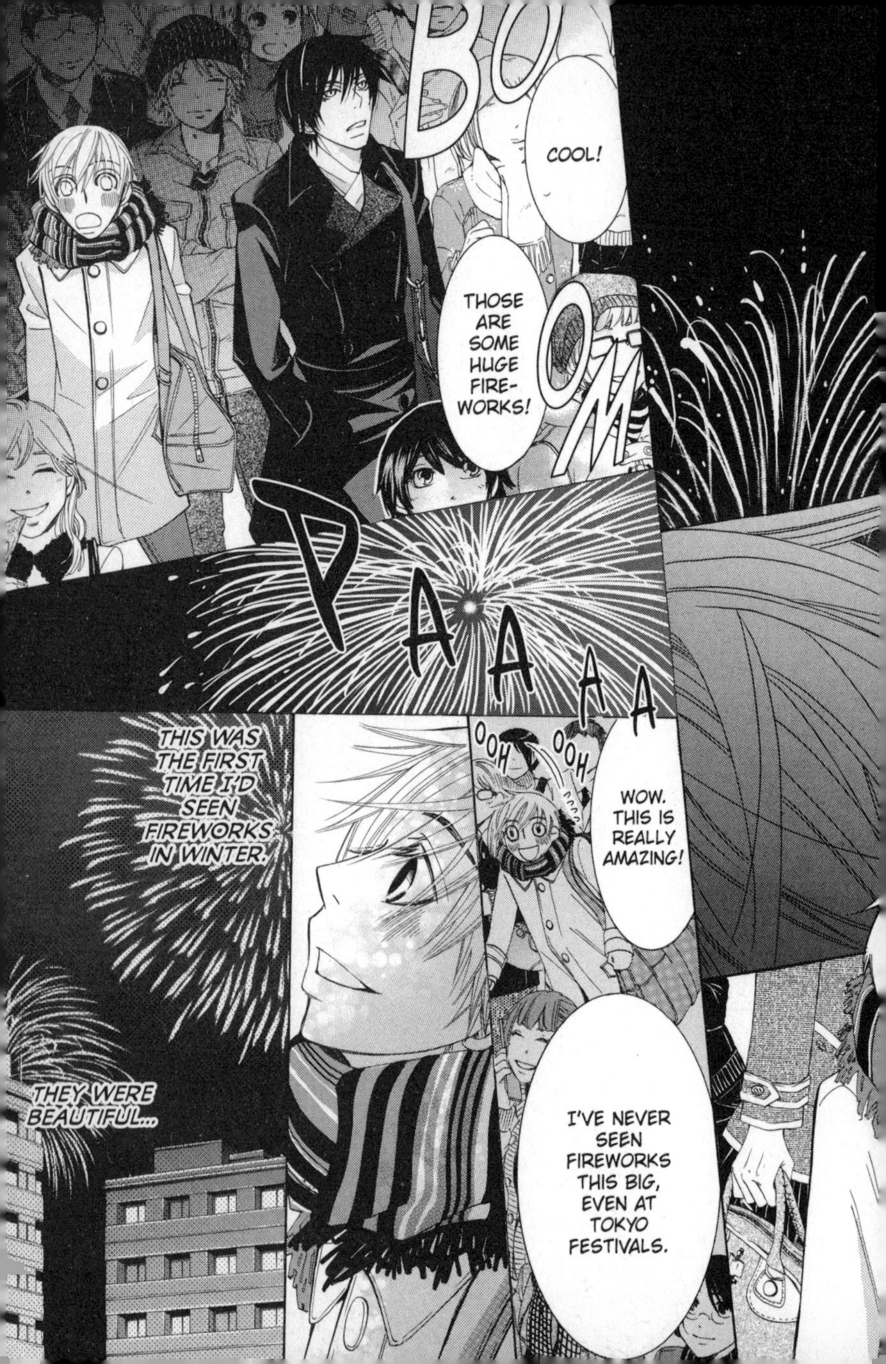
BOOM
COOL!
THOSE ARE SOME HUGE FIRE-WORKS!
PAAAAA
OOH OOH
WOW. THIS IS REALLY AMAZING!
I'VE NEVER SEEN FIREWORKS THIS BIG, EVEN AT TOKYO FESTIVALS.
THIS WAS THE FIRST TIME I'D SEEN FIREWORKS IN WINTER.
THEY WERE BEAUTIFUL...

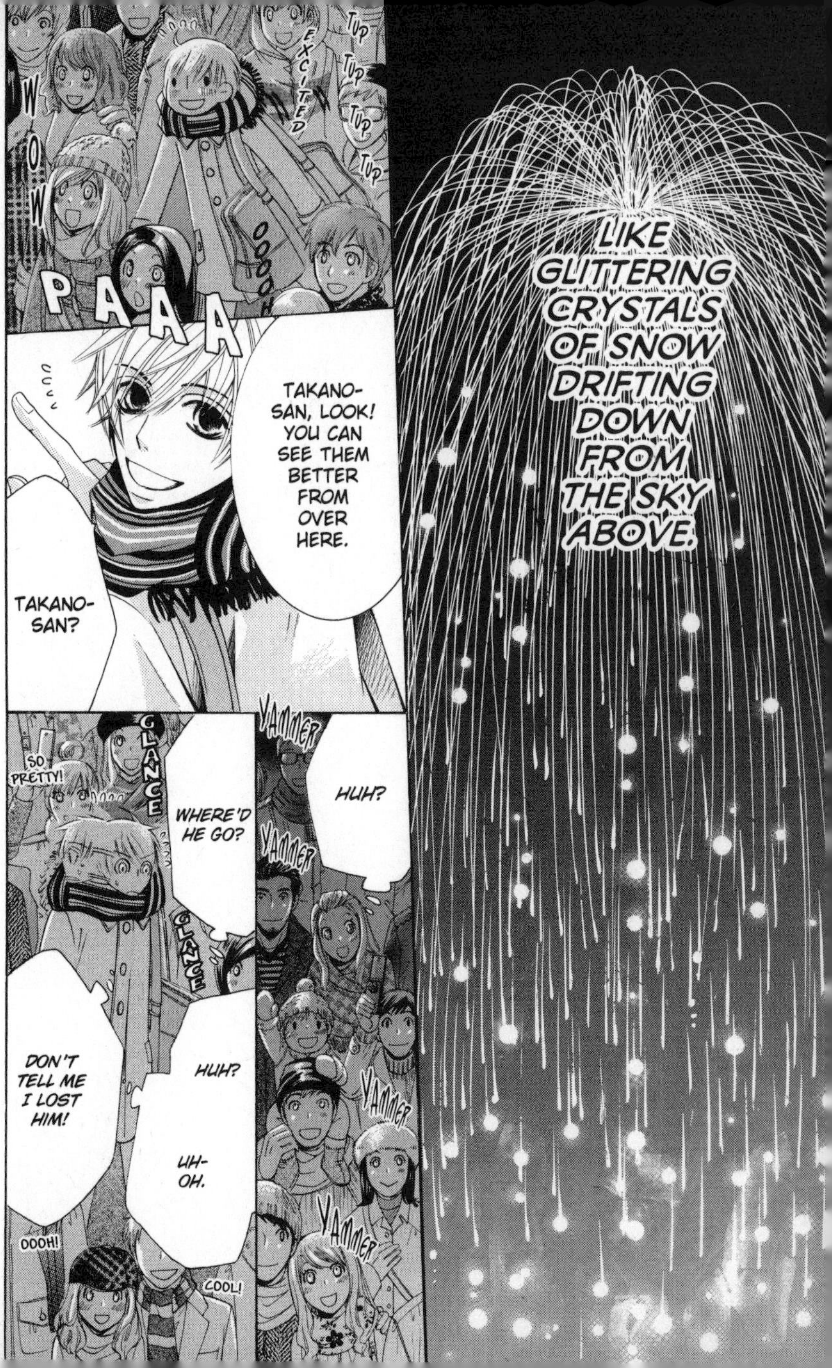

LIKE GLITTERING CRYSTALS OF SNOW DRIFTING DOWN FROM THE SKY ABOVE.
TUP TUP TUP TUP
EXCITED
WOW
PAAA
TAKANO-SAN, LOOK! YOU CAN SEE THEM BETTER FROM OVER HERE.
TAKANO-SAN?
YAMMER
HUH?
YAMMER
YAMMER
YAMMER
GLANCE
SO PRETTY!
WHERE'D HE GO?
GLANCE
HUH?
DON'T TELL ME I LOST HIM!
UH-OH.
OOOH!
COOL!

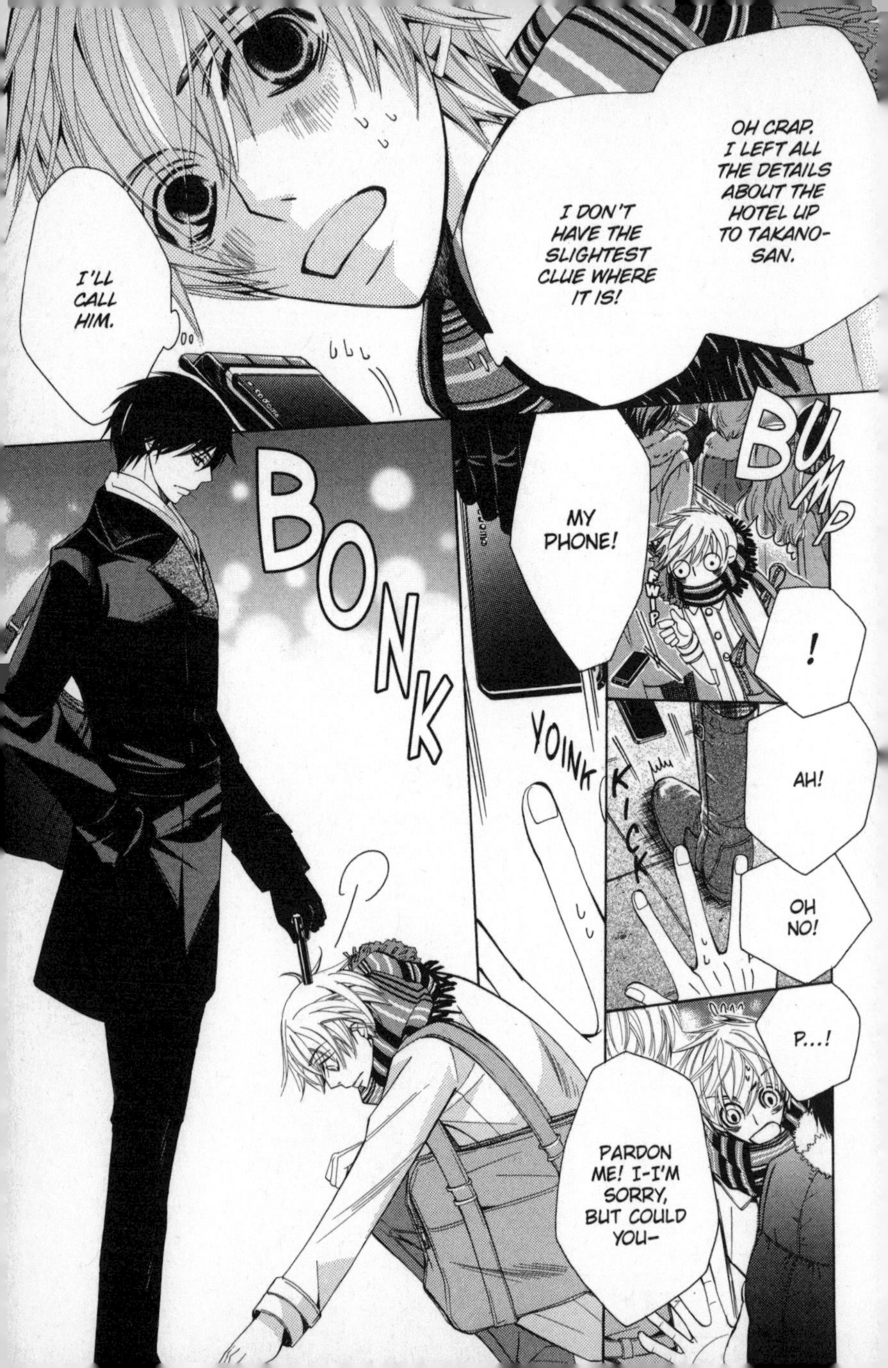
OH CRAP. I LEFT ALL THE DETAILS ABOUT THE HOTEL UP TO TAKANO-SAN.
I DON'T HAVE THE SLIGHTEST CLUE WHERE IT IS!
I'LL CALL HIM.
BUMP
FWIP
!
MY PHONE!
KICK
AH!
OH NO!
P...!
PARDON ME! I-I'M SORRY, BUT COULD YOU-
YOINK
BONK

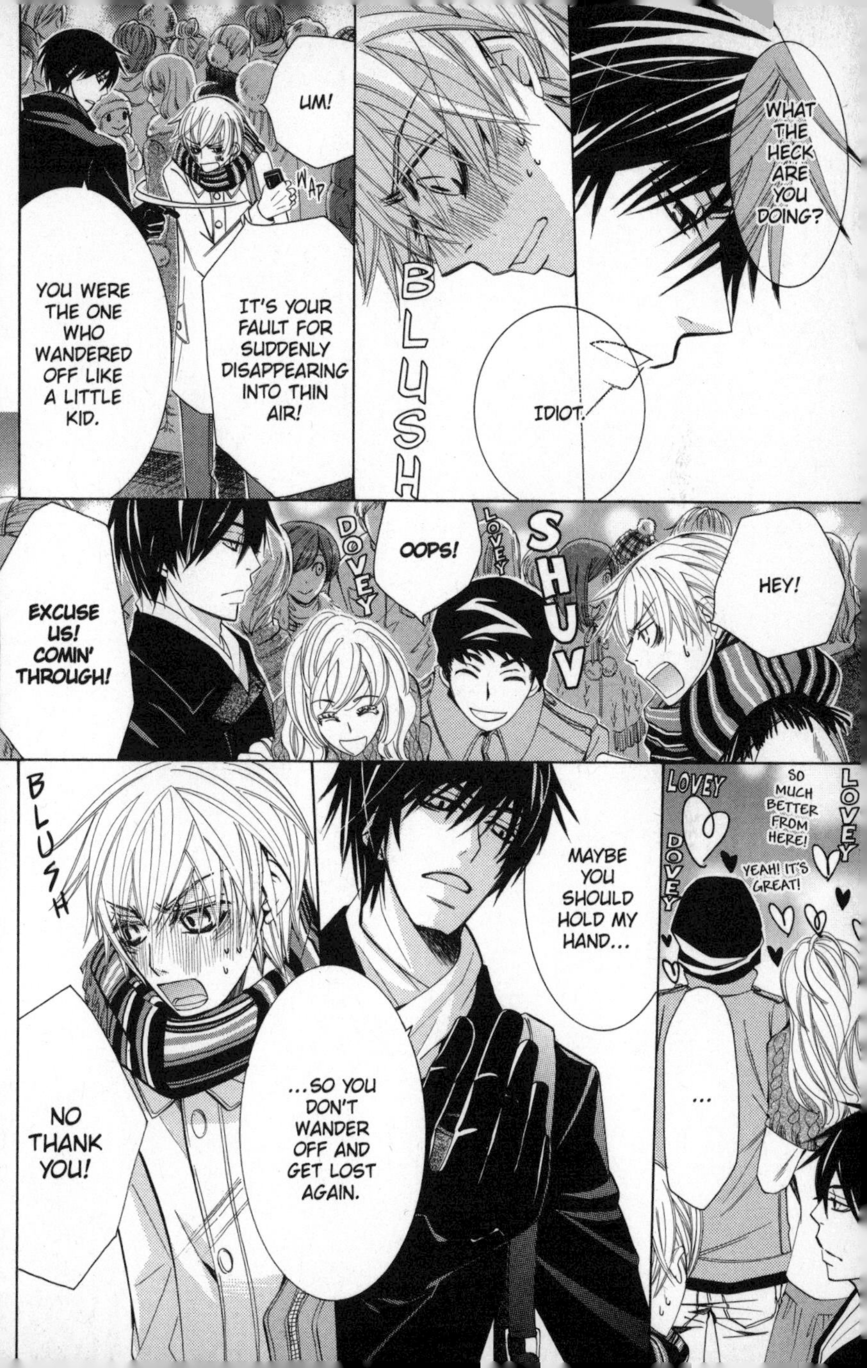
WHAT THE HECK ARE YOU DOING?
IDIOT.
BLUSH
UM!
WAP
IT'S YOUR FAULT FOR SUDDENLY DISAPPEARING INTO THIN AIR!
YOU WERE THE ONE WHO WANDERED OFF LIKE A LITTLE KID.
HEY!
SHUV
LOVEY DOVEY
OOPS!
EXCUSE US! COMIN' THROUGH!
LOVEY
SO MUCH BETTER FROM HERE!
LOVEY DOVEY
YEAH! IT'S GREAT!
...
MAYBE YOU SHOULD HOLD MY HAND...
...SO YOU DON'T WANDER OFF AND GET LOST AGAIN.
BLUSH
NO THANK YOU!

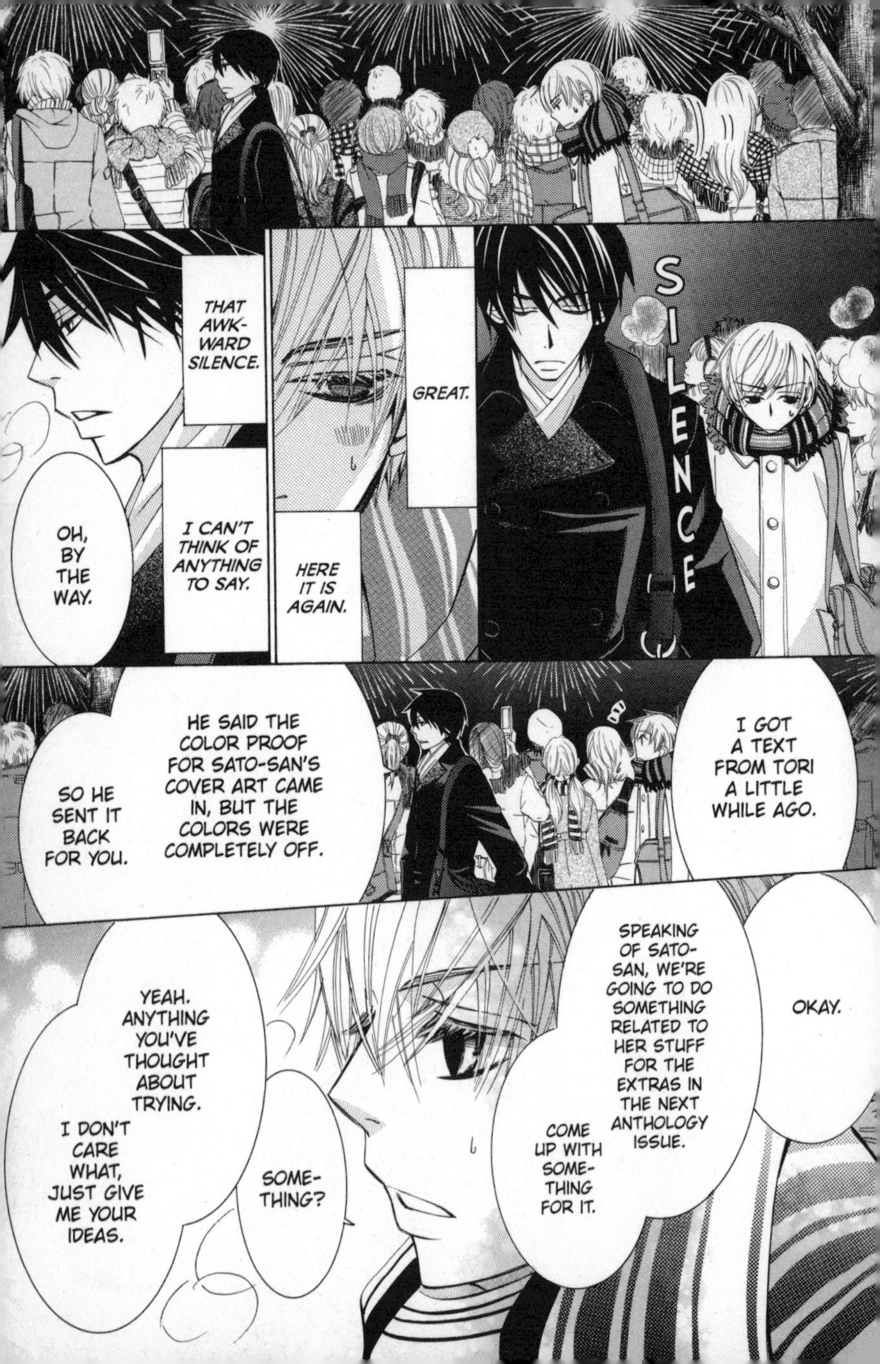
SILENCE
GREAT.
HERE IT IS AGAIN.
THAT AWKWARD SILENCE.
I CAN'T THINK OF ANYTHING TO SAY.
OH, BY THE WAY.
I GOT A TEXT FROM TORI A LITTLE WHILE AGO.
HE SAID THE COLOR PROOF FOR SATO-SAN'S COVER ART CAME IN, BUT THE COLORS WERE COMPLETELY OFF.
SO HE SENT IT BACK FOR YOU.
OKAY.
SPEAKING OF SATO-SAN, WE'RE GOING TO DO SOMETHING RELATED TO HER STUFF FOR THE EXTRAS IN THE NEXT ANTHOLOGY ISSUE.
COME UP WITH SOMETHING FOR IT.
SOMETHING?
YEAH. ANYTHING YOU'VE THOUGHT ABOUT TRYING.
I DON'T CARE WHAT, JUST GIVE ME YOUR IDEAS.

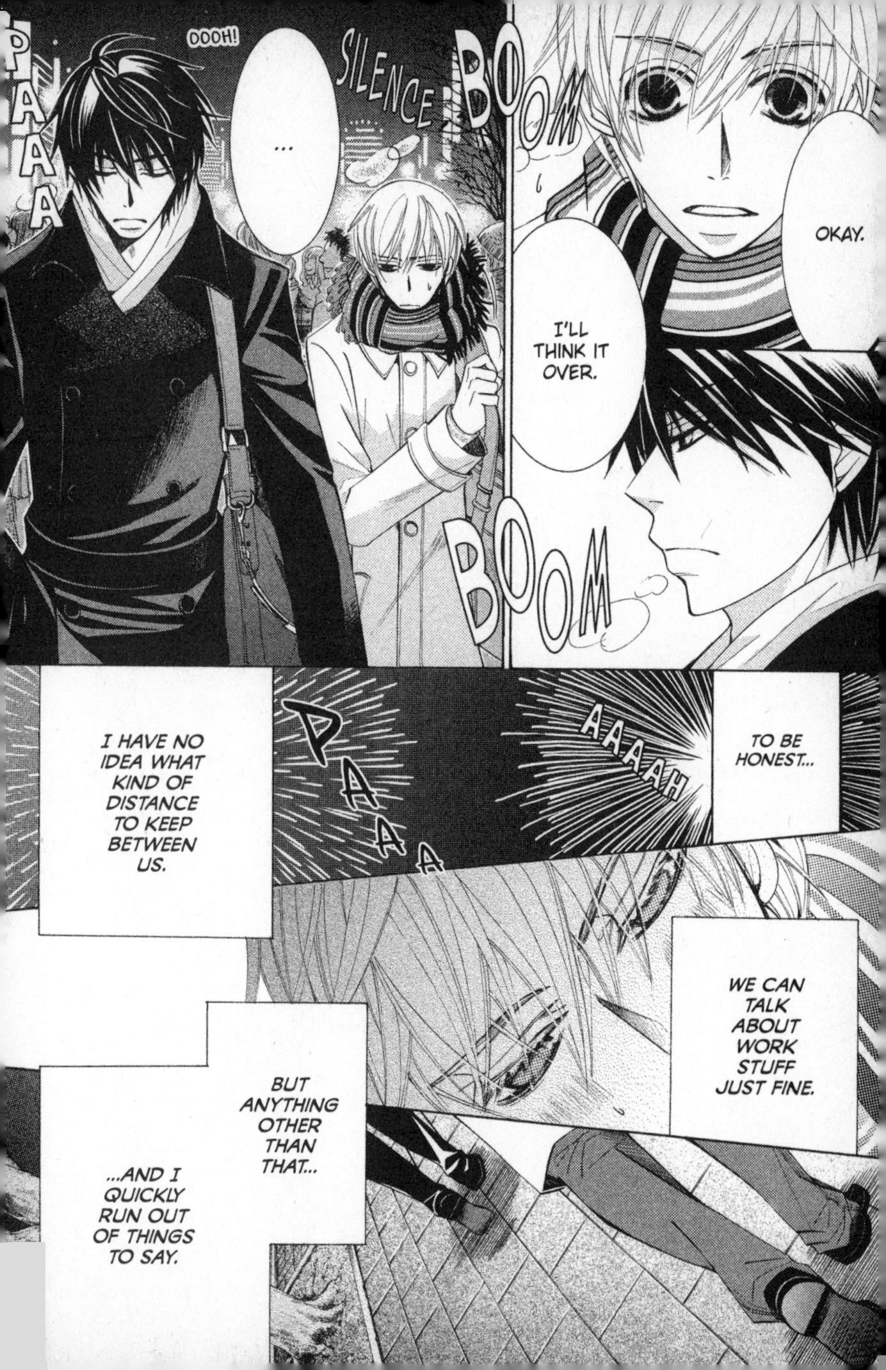
BOOM
OKAY.
I'LL THINK IT OVER.
BOOM
SILENCE
...
OOOH!
PAAAA
TO BE HONEST...
AAAAAH
PAAAA
I HAVE NO IDEA WHAT KIND OF DISTANCE TO KEEP BETWEEN US.
WE CAN TALK ABOUT WORK STUFF JUST FINE.
BUT ANYTHING OTHER THAN THAT...
...AND I QUICKLY RUN OUT OF THINGS TO SAY.

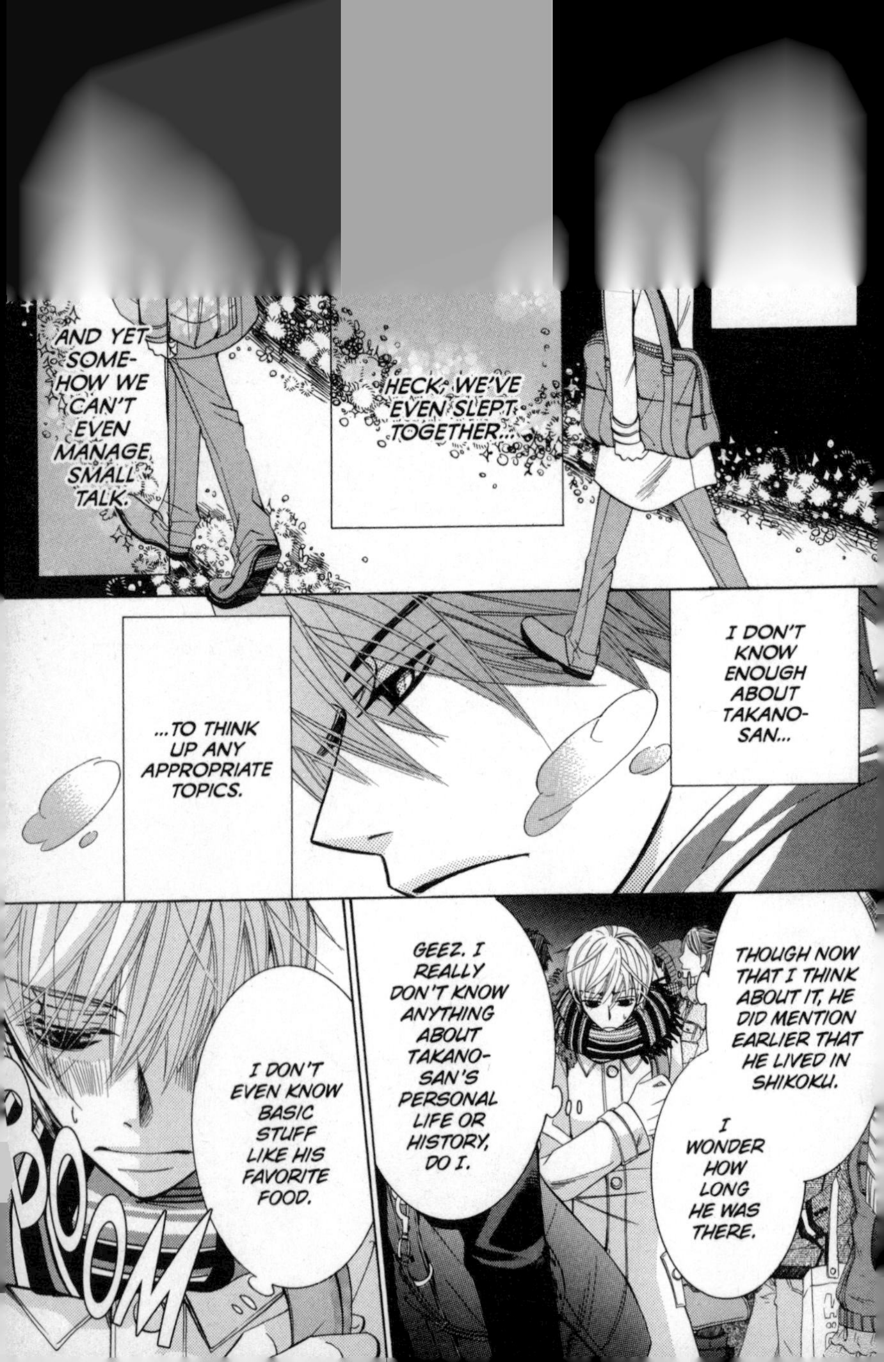
HECK, WE'VE EVEN SLEPT TOGETHER...
AND YET SOME-HOW WE CAN'T EVEN MANAGE SMALL TALK.
I DON'T KNOW ENOUGH ABOUT TAKANO-SAN...
...TO THINK UP ANY APPROPRIATE TOPICS.
THOUGH NOW THAT I THINK ABOUT IT, HE DID MENTION EARLIER THAT HE LIVED IN SHIKOKU.
I WONDER HOW LONG HE WAS THERE.
GEEZ. I REALLY DON'T KNOW ANYTHING ABOUT TAKANO-SAN'S PERSONAL LIFE OR HISTORY, DO I.
I DON'T EVEN KNOW BASIC STUFF LIKE HIS FAVORITE FOOD.
POOM

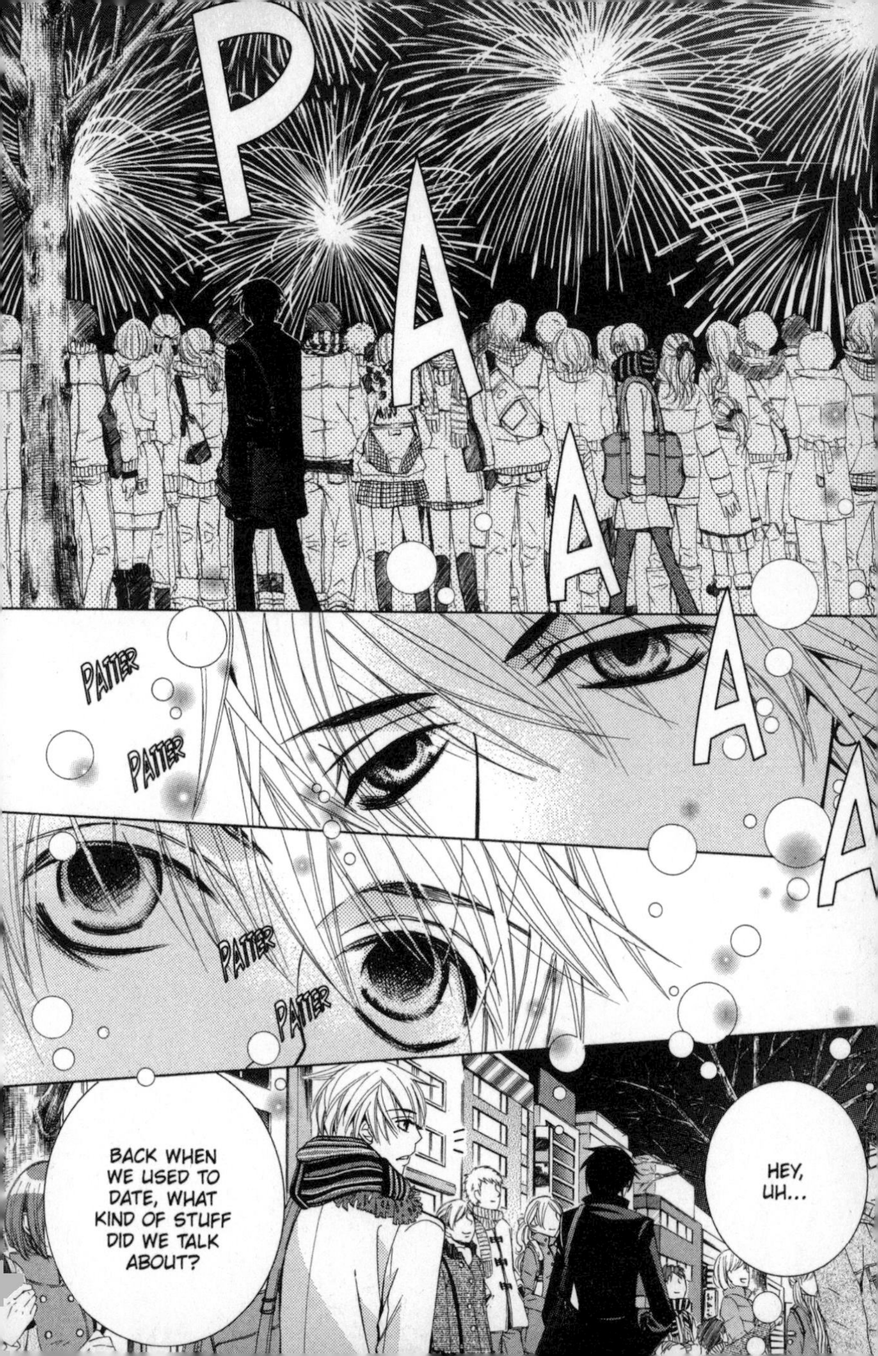
PAAAAA
PATTER
PATTER
PATTER
PATTER
HEY, UH...
BACK WHEN WE USED TO DATE, WHAT KIND OF STUFF DID WE TALK ABOUT?

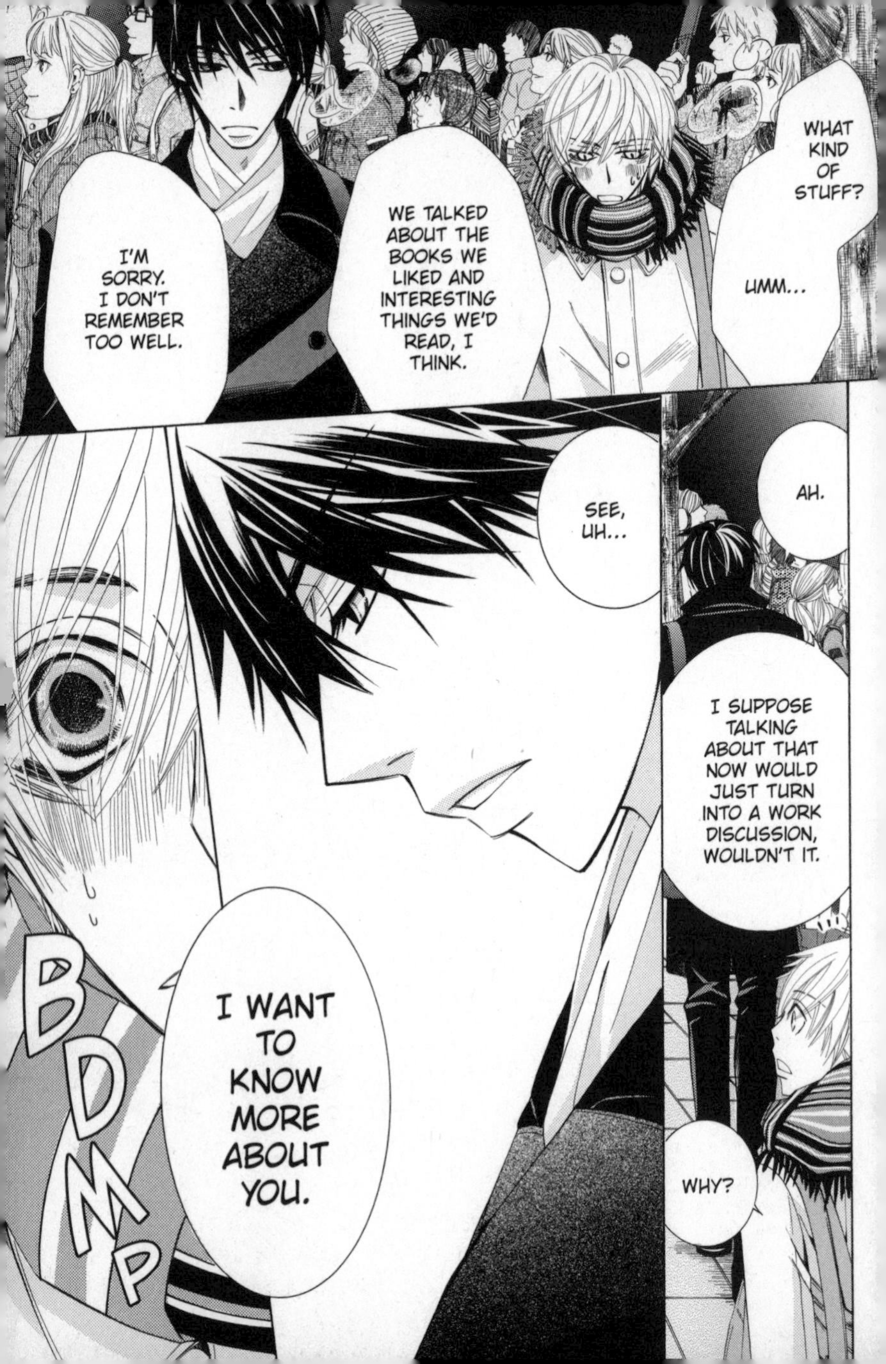
WHAT KIND OF STUFF?
UMM...
WE TALKED ABOUT THE BOOKS WE LIKED AND INTERESTING THINGS WE'D READ, I THINK.
I'M SORRY. I DON'T REMEMBER TOO WELL.
AH.
I SUPPOSE TALKING ABOUT THAT NOW WOULD JUST TURN INTO A WORK DISCUSSION, WOULDN'T IT.
WHY?
SEE, UH...
I WANT TO KNOW MORE ABOUT YOU.
BDMP

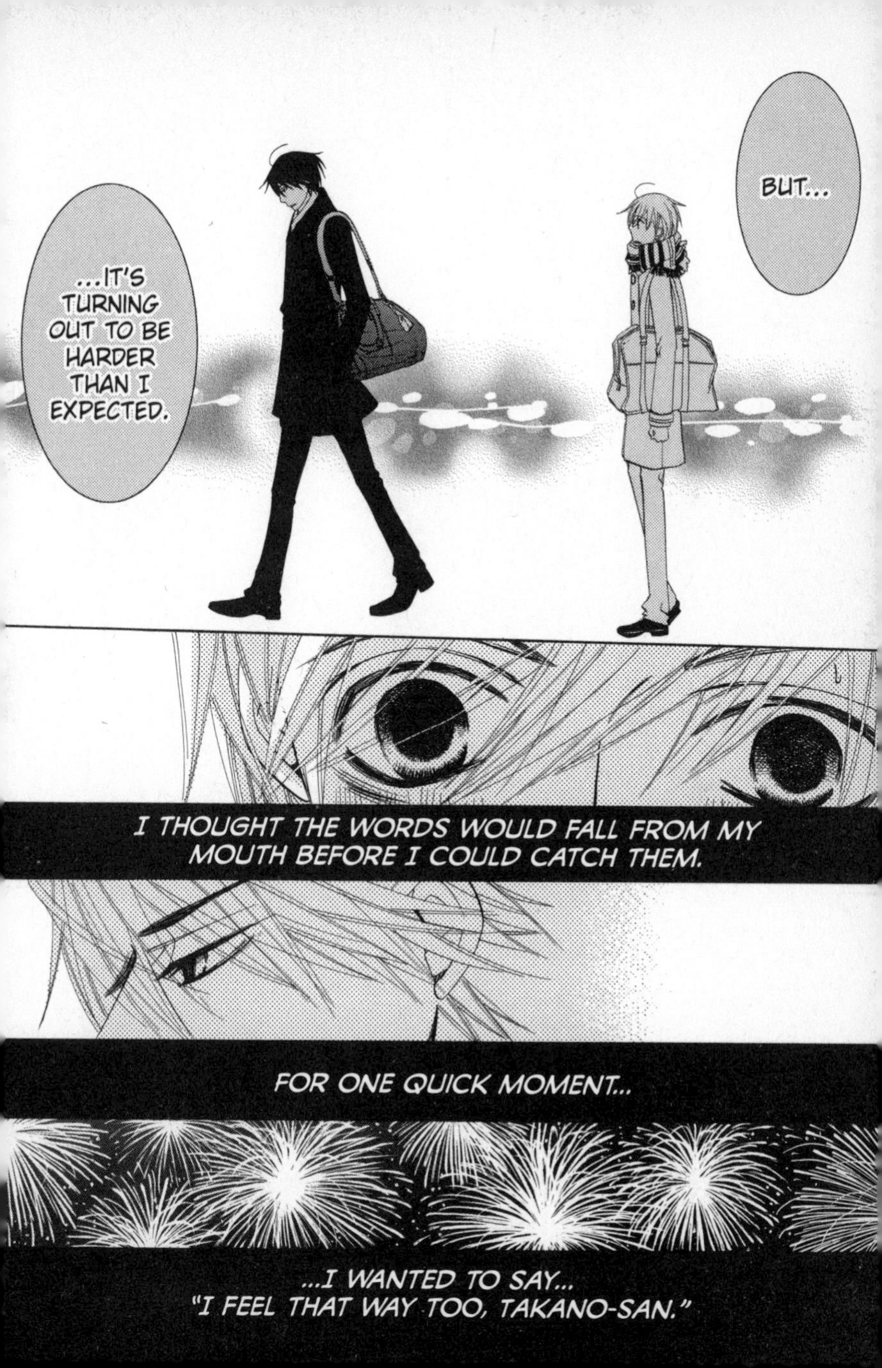
BUT...
...IT'S TURNING OUT TO BE HARDER THAN I EXPECTED.
I THOUGHT THE WORDS WOULD FALL FROM MY MOUTH BEFORE I COULD CATCH THEM.
FOR ONE QUICK MOMENT...
...I WANTED TO SAY... "I FEEL THAT WAY TOO, TAKANO-SAN."

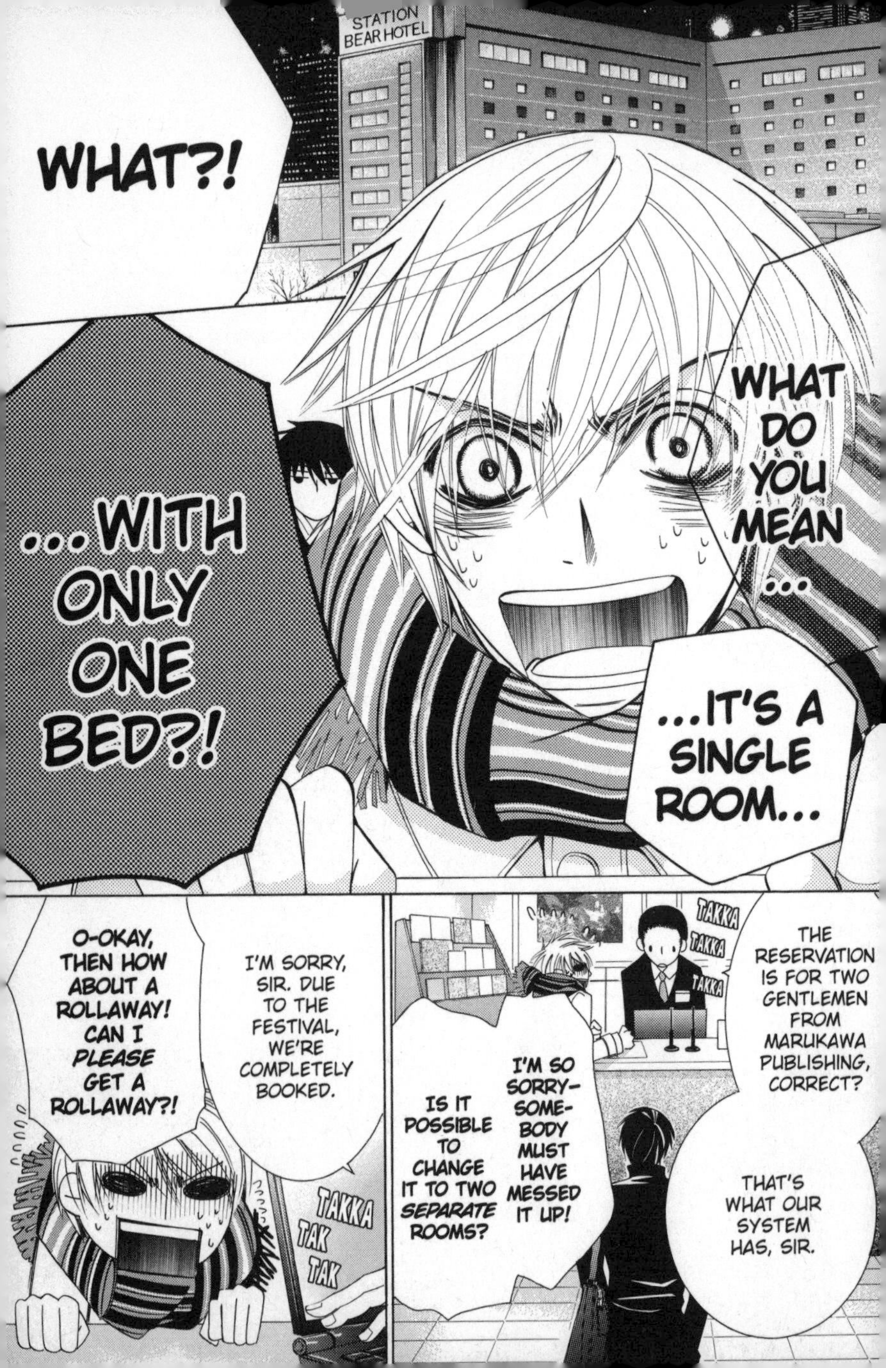
STATION BEAR HOTEL
WHAT?!
WHAT DO YOU MEAN...
...IT'S A SINGLE ROOM...
...WITH ONLY ONE BED?!
THE RESERVATION IS FOR TWO GENTLEMEN FROM MARUKAWA PUBLISHING, CORRECT?
TAKKA TAKKA TAKKA
THAT'S WHAT OUR SYSTEM HAS, SIR.
I'M SO SORRY- SOMEBODY MUST HAVE MESSED IT UP!
IS IT POSSIBLE TO CHANGE IT TO TWO *SEPARATE* ROOMS?
I'M SORRY, SIR. DUE TO THE FESTIVAL, WE'RE COMPLETELY BOOKED.
O-OKAY, THEN HOW ABOUT A ROLLAWAY! CAN I *PLEASE* GET A ROLLAWAY?!
TAKKA TAK TAK

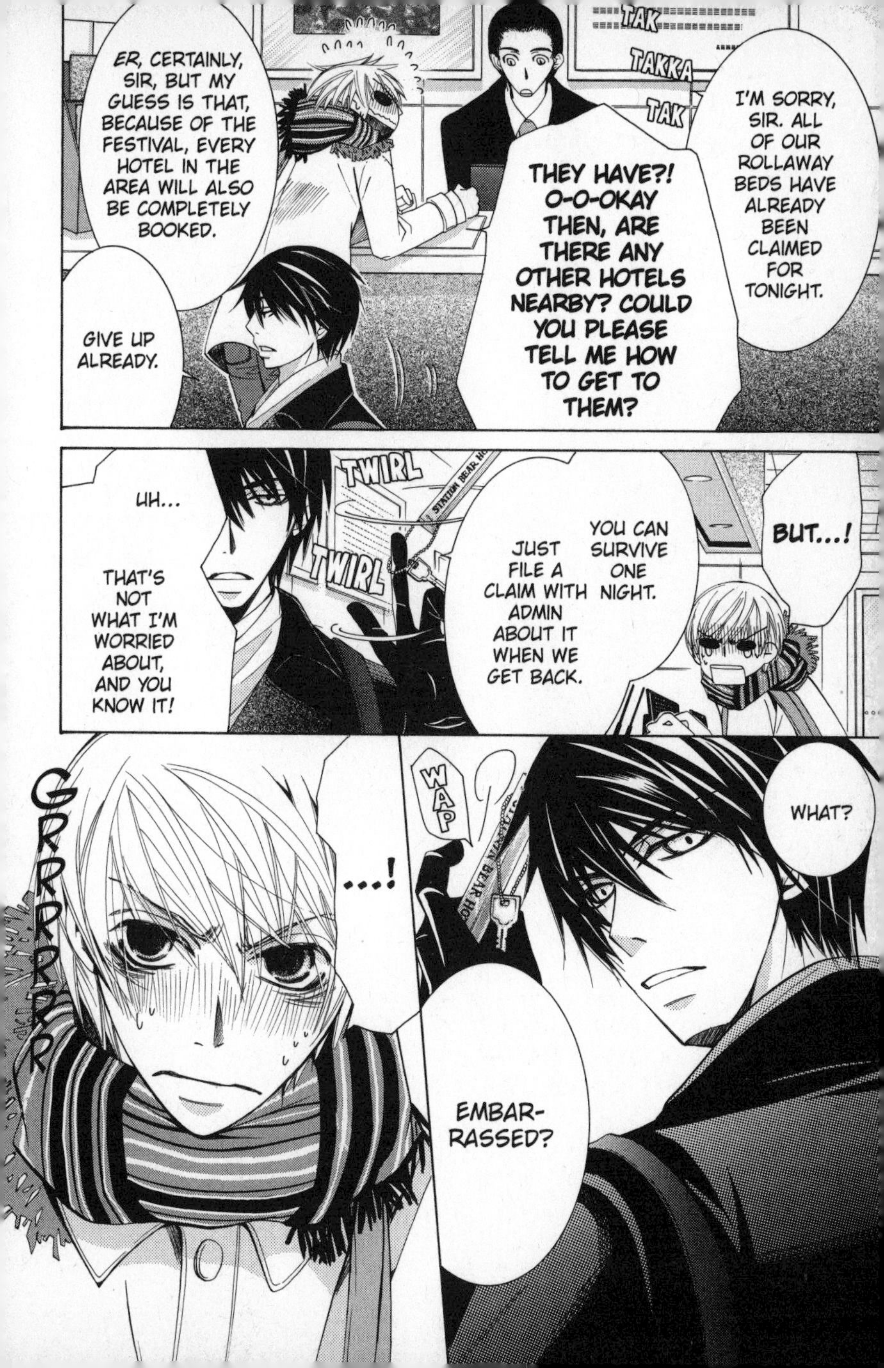
I'M SORRY, SIR. ALL OF OUR ROLLAWAY BEDS HAVE ALREADY BEEN CLAIMED FOR TONIGHT.
TAK
TAKKA
TAK
THEY HAVE?! O-O-OKAY THEN, ARE THERE ANY OTHER HOTELS NEARBY? COULD YOU PLEASE TELL ME HOW TO GET TO THEM?
ER, CERTAINLY, SIR, BUT MY GUESS IS THAT, BECAUSE OF THE FESTIVAL, EVERY HOTEL IN THE AREA WILL ALSO BE COMPLETELY BOOKED.
GIVE UP ALREADY.
BUT...!
YOU CAN SURVIVE ONE NIGHT.
JUST FILE A CLAIM WITH ADMIN ABOUT IT WHEN WE GET BACK.
TWIRL
TWIRL
UH...
THAT'S NOT WHAT I'M WORRIED ABOUT, AND YOU KNOW IT!
WHAT?
WAP
EMBAR-RASSED?
...!
GRRRRRR

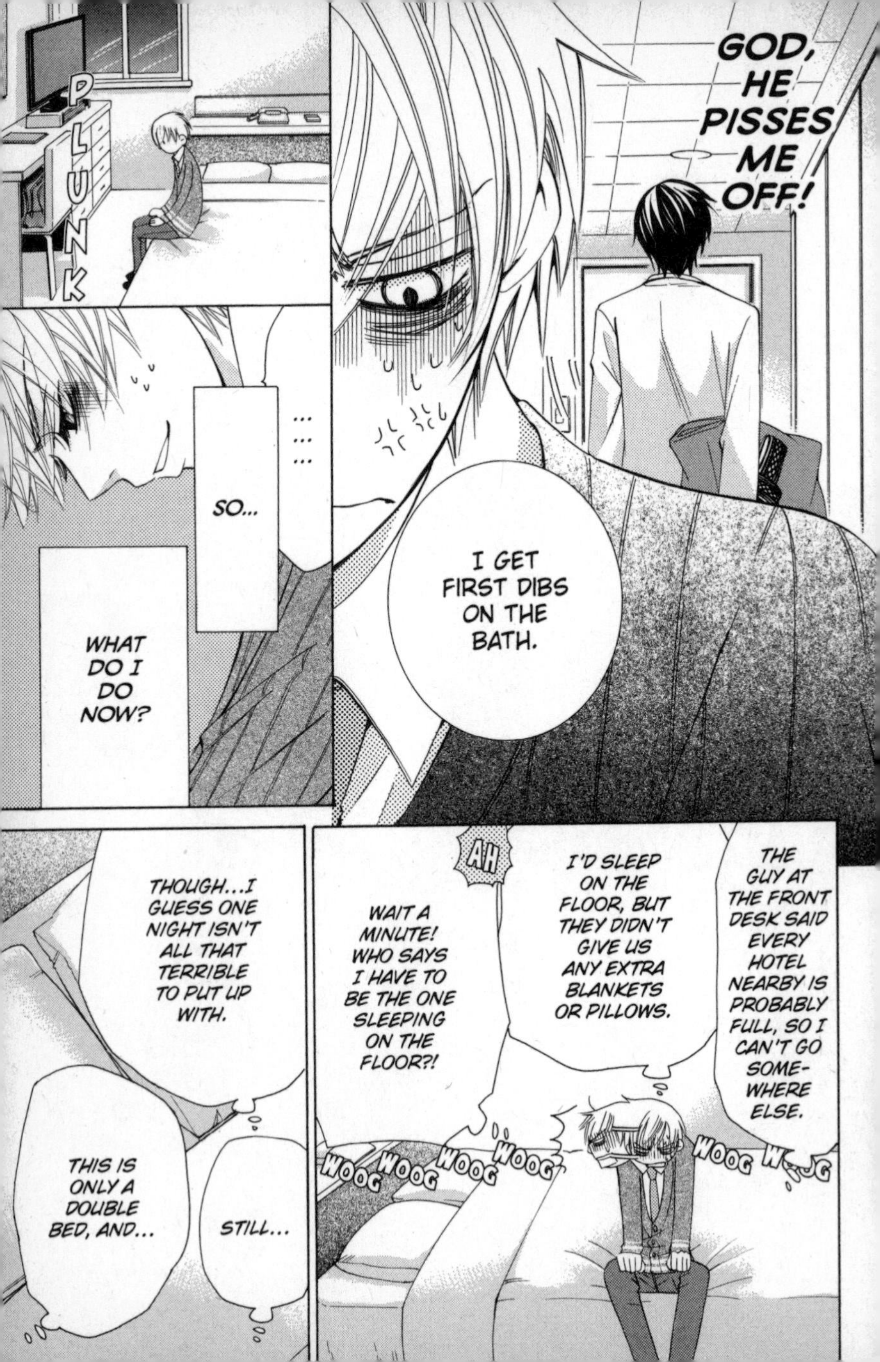
GOD, HE PISSES ME OFF!
I GET FIRST DIBS ON THE BATH.
PLUNK
......
SO...
WHAT DO I DO NOW?
THE GUY AT THE FRONT DESK SAID EVERY HOTEL NEARBY IS PROBABLY FULL, SO I CAN'T GO SOME-WHERE ELSE.
I'D SLEEP ON THE FLOOR, BUT THEY DIDN'T GIVE US ANY EXTRA BLANKETS OR PILLOWS.
AH
WAIT A MINUTE! WHO SAYS I HAVE TO BE THE ONE SLEEPING ON THE FLOOR?!
WOOG
WOOG
WOOG
WOOG
WOOG
THOUGH...I GUESS ONE NIGHT ISN'T ALL THAT TERRIBLE TO PUT UP WITH.
STILL...
THIS IS ONLY A DOUBLE BED, AND...

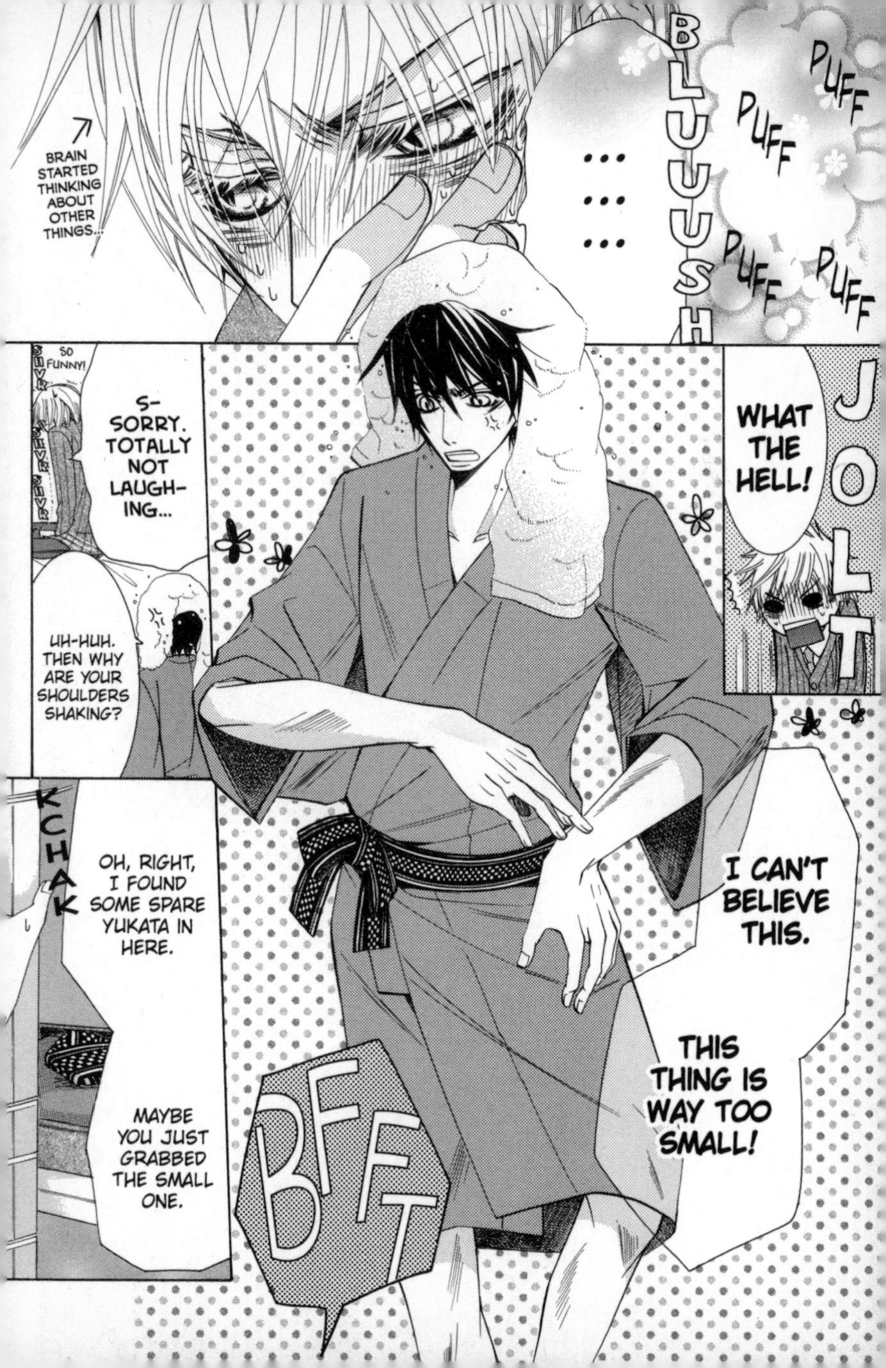
PUFF
PUFF
PUFF
PUFF
BLUUUSH
...
...
...
BRAIN STARTED THINKING ABOUT OTHER THINGS...
JOLT
WHAT THE HELL!
I CAN'T BELIEVE THIS.
THIS THING IS WAY TOO SMALL!
BFFT
SO FUNNY!
SHVR SHVR SHVR
S-SORRY. TOTALLY NOT LAUGHING...
UH-HUH. THEN WHY ARE YOUR SHOULDERS SHAKING?
KCHAK
OH, RIGHT, I FOUND SOME SPARE YUKATA IN HERE.
MAYBE YOU JUST GRABBED THE SMALL ONE.

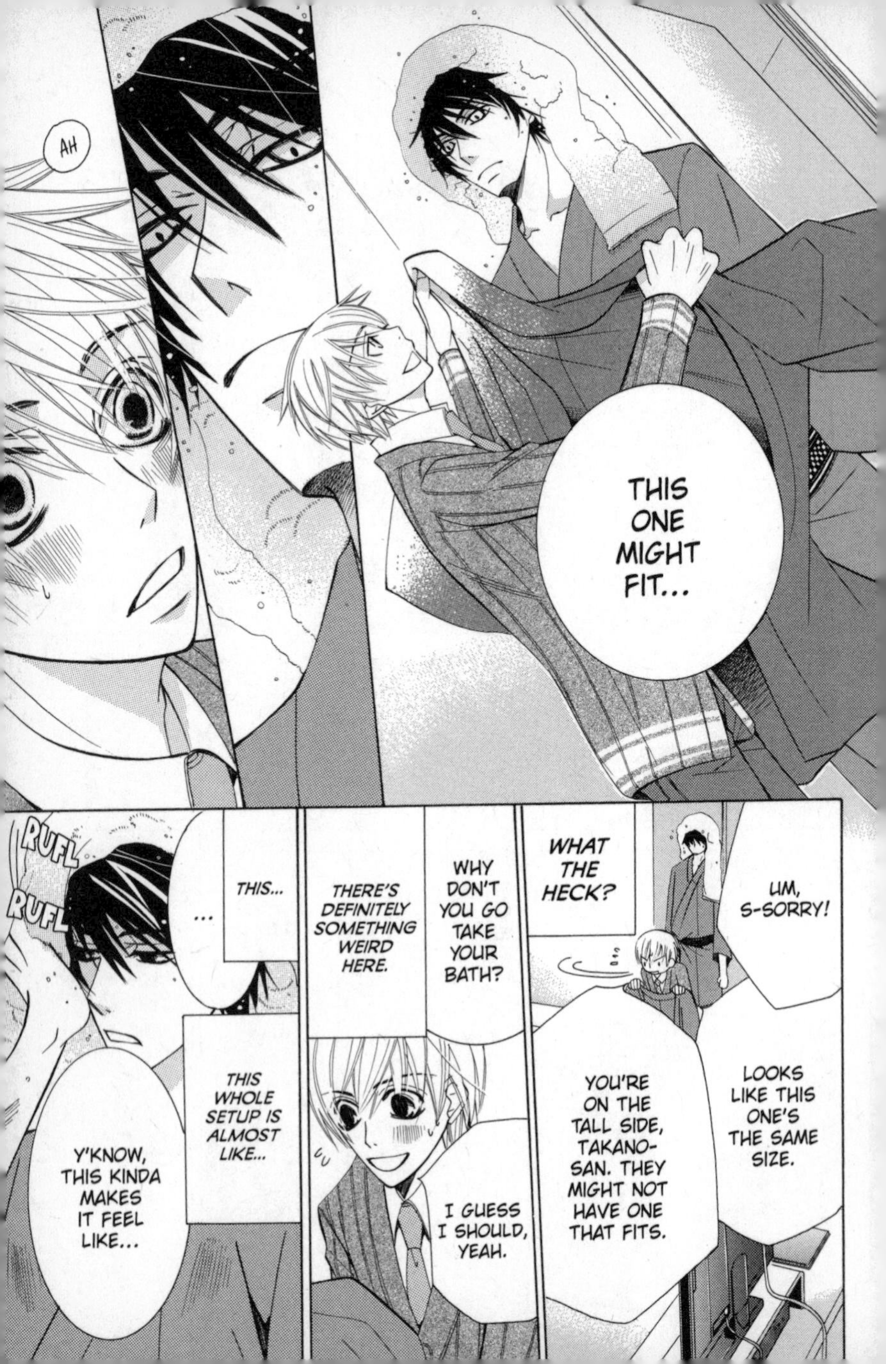
THIS ONE MIGHT FIT...
AH
UM, S-SORRY!
WHAT THE HECK?
LOOKS LIKE THIS ONE'S THE SAME SIZE.
YOU'RE ON THE TALL SIDE, TAKANO-SAN. THEY MIGHT NOT HAVE ONE THAT FITS.
WHY DON'T YOU GO TAKE YOUR BATH?
THERE'S DEFINITELY SOMETHING WEIRD HERE.
I GUESS I SHOULD, YEAH.
THIS...
...
THIS WHOLE SETUP IS ALMOST LIKE...
RUFL RUFL
Y'KNOW, THIS KINDA MAKES IT FEEL LIKE...

...WE'RE ON OUR HONEY-MOON-
NO, IT DOES NOT!
WAH HA HA HA HA!
GEEZ, THE PEOPLE IN THE NEXT ROOM SURE ARE LOUD.
I WISH THEY'D QUIET DOWN. I WANT TO GET SOME SLEEP.
I MEAN, WHEN WE GO HOME TOMORROW, I HAVE TO GO STRAIGHT BACK TO THE OFFICE AND HANDLE ALL THE WORK I PUT OFF TO COME HERE.
I NEED TO SLEEP.
I HAVE TO HURRY UP AND FALL ASLEEP BEFORE...

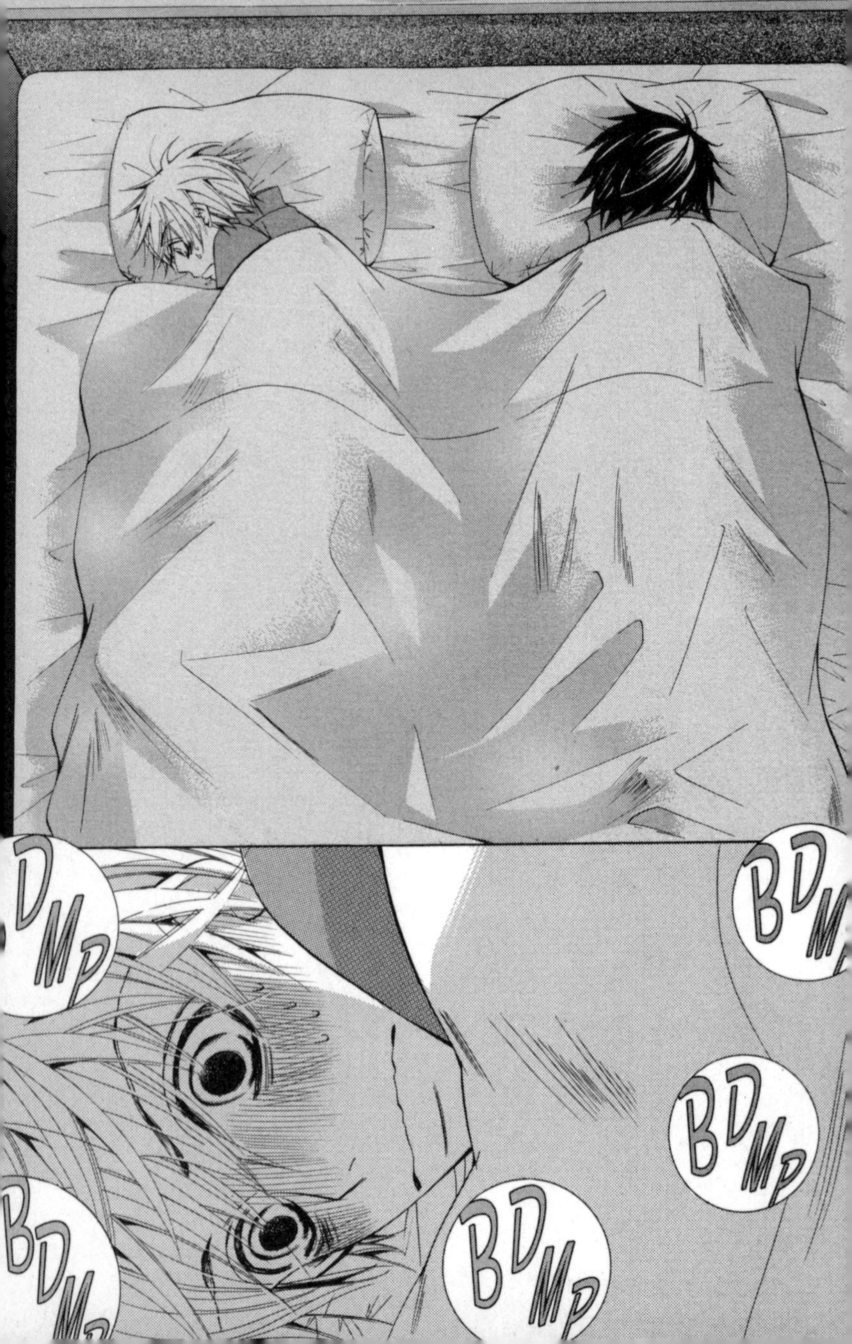
BDM
DMP
BDMP
BDMP
BDM

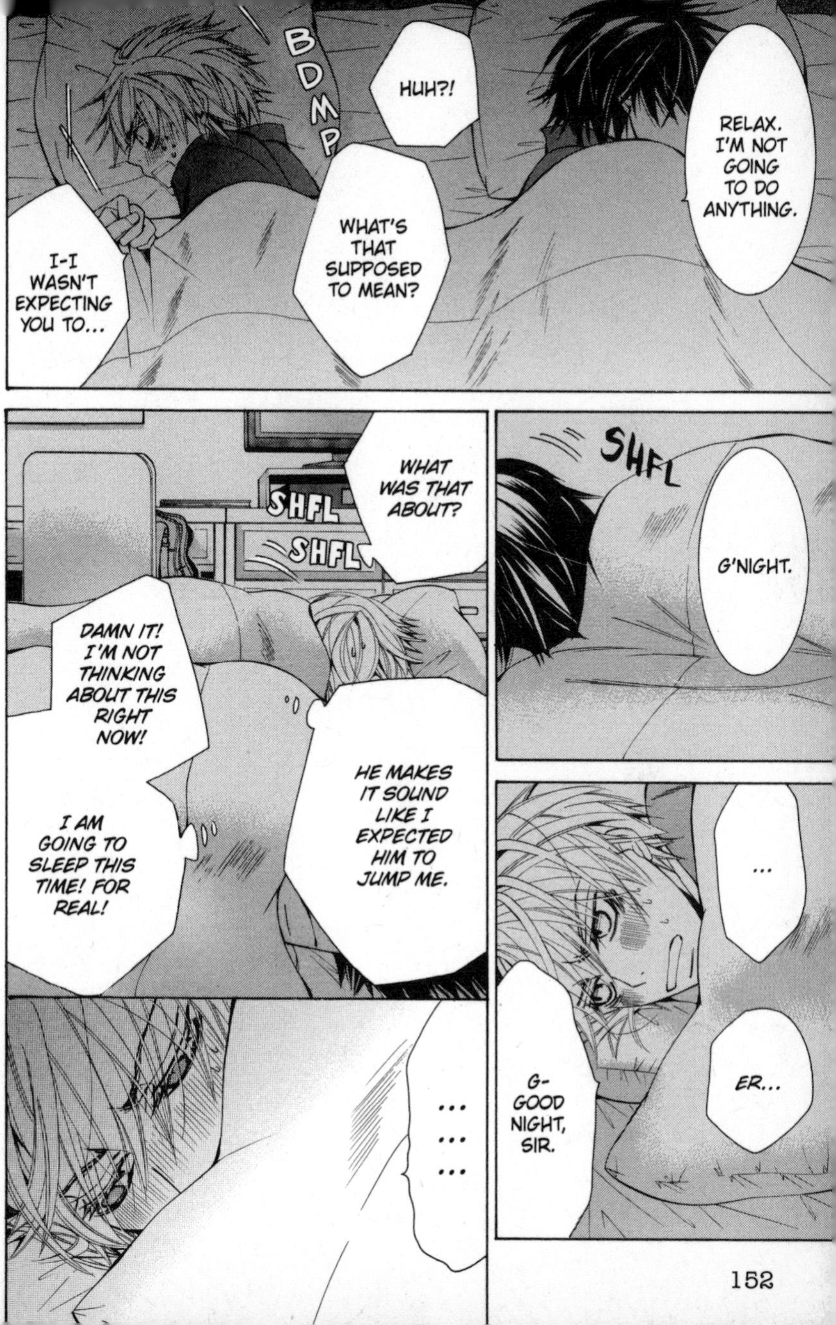
RELAX. I'M NOT GOING TO DO ANYTHING.
HUH?!
BDMP
WHAT'S THAT SUPPOSED TO MEAN?
I-I WASN'T EXPECTING YOU TO...
SHFL
G'NIGHT.
...
ER...
G-GOOD NIGHT, SIR.
WHAT WAS THAT ABOUT?
SHFL
SHFL
HE MAKES IT SOUND LIKE I EXPECTED HIM TO JUMP ME.
DAMN IT! I'M NOT THINKING ABOUT THIS RIGHT NOW!
I AM GOING TO SLEEP THIS TIME! FOR REAL!
...
...
...

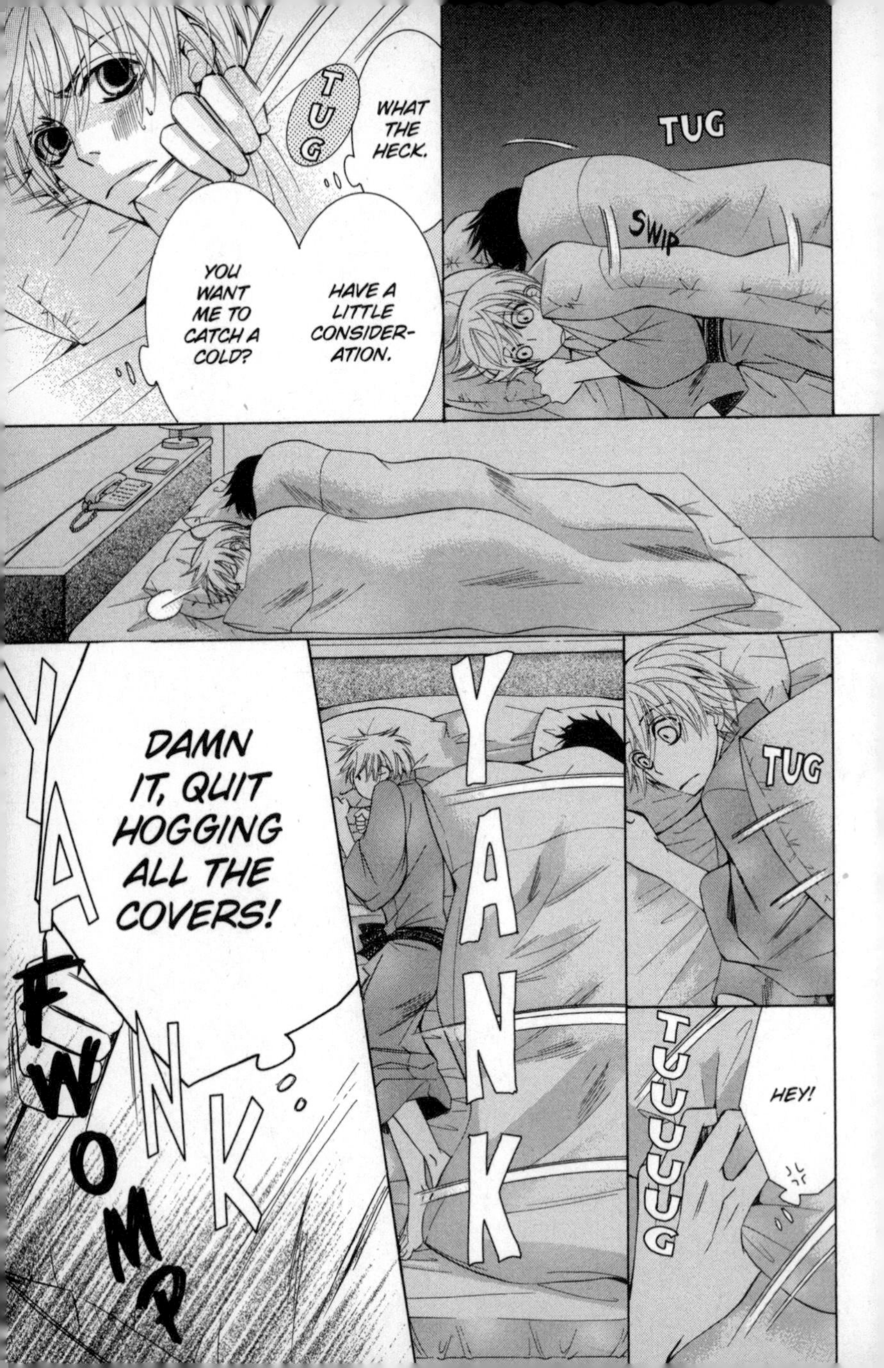
TUG
SWIP
WHAT THE HECK.
TUG
HAVE A LITTLE CONSIDERATION.
YOU WANT ME TO CATCH A COLD?
TUG
HEY!
TUUUUG
YANK
DAMN IT, QUIT HOGGING ALL THE COVERS!
YANK
FWOMP

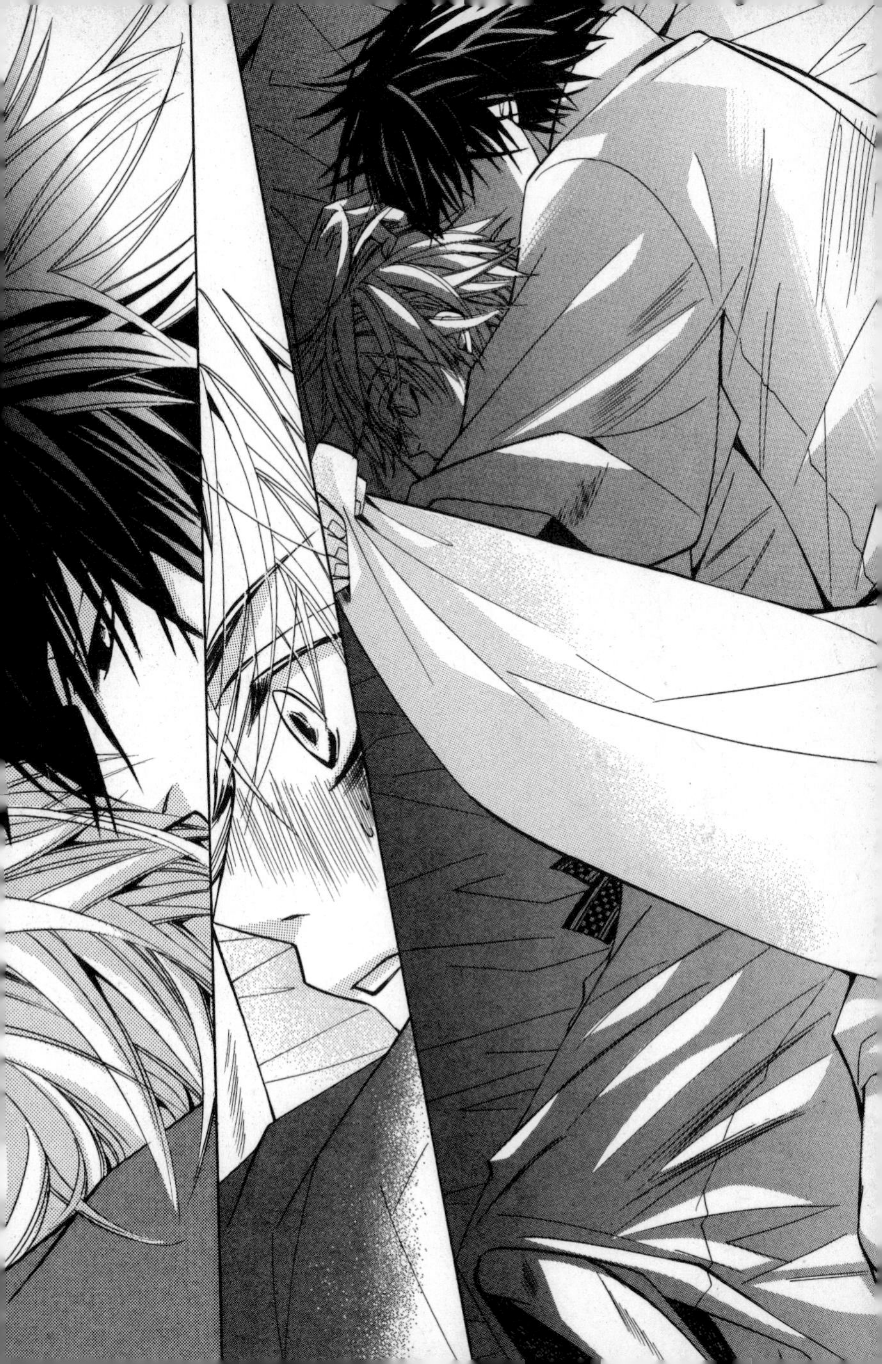

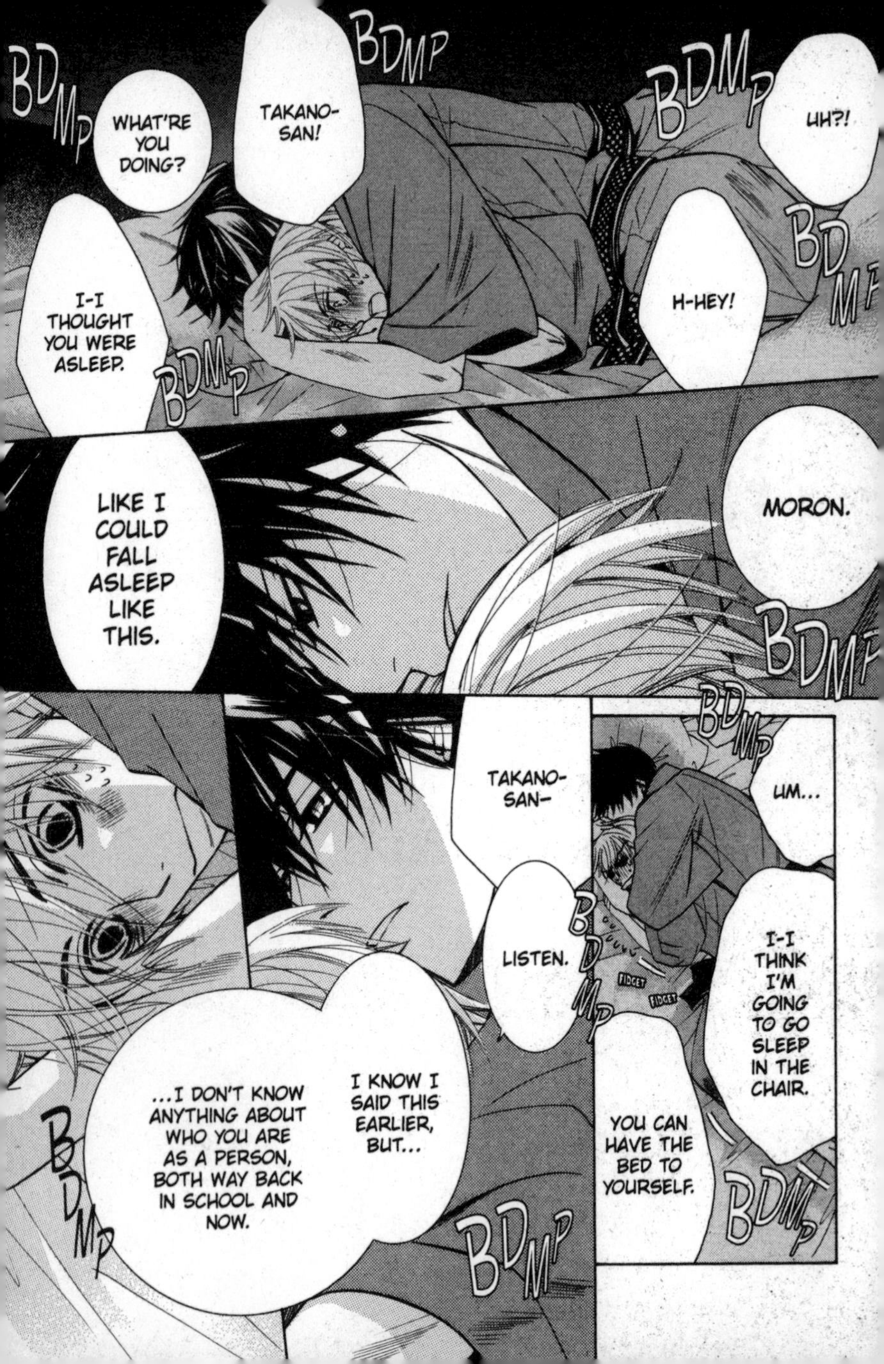
BDMP
UH?!
BDMP
BDMP
H-HEY!
BDMP
TAKANO-SAN!
BDMP
WHAT'RE YOU DOING?
I-I THOUGHT YOU WERE ASLEEP.
BDMP
MORON.
BDMP
LIKE I COULD FALL ASLEEP LIKE THIS.
BDMP
UM...
I-I THINK I'M GOING TO GO SLEEP IN THE CHAIR.
YOU CAN HAVE THE BED TO YOURSELF.
BDMP
FIDGET
FIDGET
BDMP
TAKANO-SAN-
LISTEN.
I KNOW I SAID THIS EARLIER, BUT...
...I DON'T KNOW ANYTHING ABOUT WHO YOU ARE AS A PERSON, BOTH WAY BACK IN SCHOOL AND NOW.
BDMP
BDMP

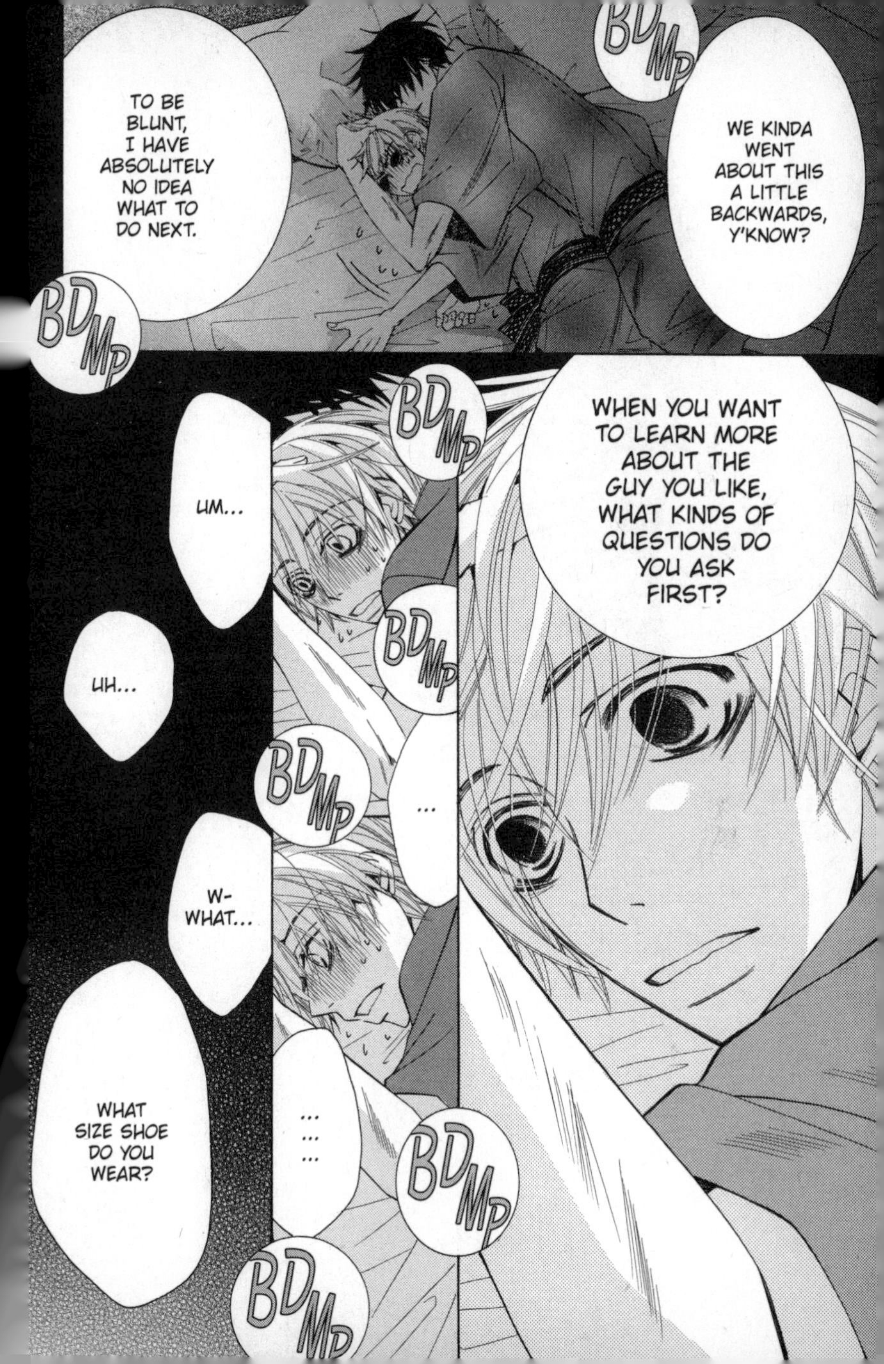
BDMP
WE KINDA WENT ABOUT THIS A LITTLE BACKWARDS, Y'KNOW?
TO BE BLUNT, I HAVE ABSOLUTELY NO IDEA WHAT TO DO NEXT.
BDMP
WHEN YOU WANT TO LEARN MORE ABOUT THE GUY YOU LIKE, WHAT KINDS OF QUESTIONS DO YOU ASK FIRST?
BDMP
UM...
BDMP
UH...
BDMP
...
W-WHAT...
BDMP
... ...
WHAT SIZE SHOE DO YOU WEAR?
BDMP

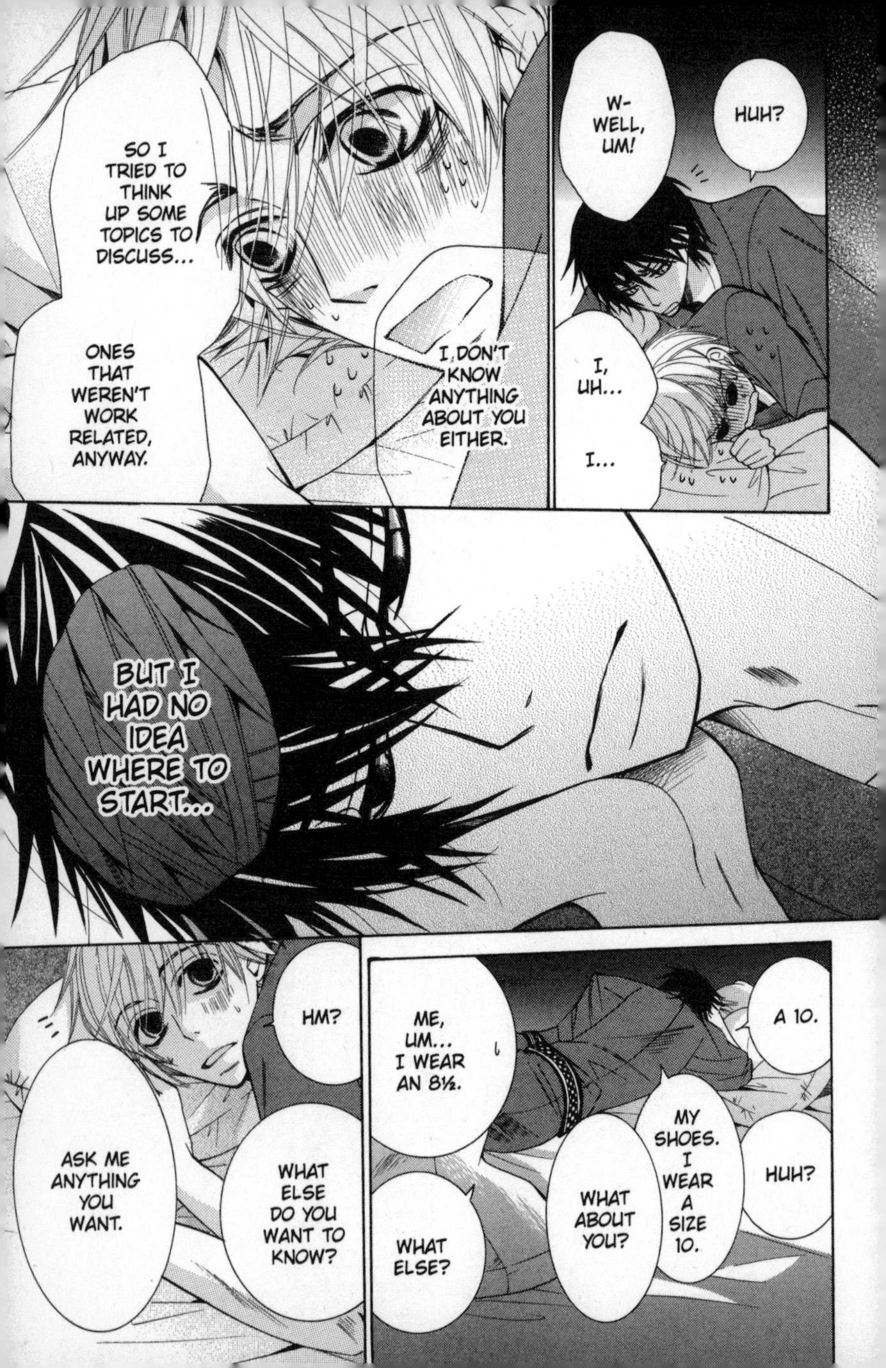
HUH?
W-WELL, UM!
I, UH...
I...
I DON'T KNOW ANYTHING ABOUT YOU EITHER.
SO I TRIED TO THINK UP SOME TOPICS TO DISCUSS...
ONES THAT WEREN'T WORK RELATED, ANYWAY.
BUT I HAD NO IDEA WHERE TO START...
A 10.
HUH?
MY SHOES. I WEAR A SIZE 10.
WHAT ABOUT YOU?
ME, UM... I WEAR AN 8½.
WHAT ELSE?
HM?
WHAT ELSE DO YOU WANT TO KNOW?
ASK ME ANYTHING YOU WANT.

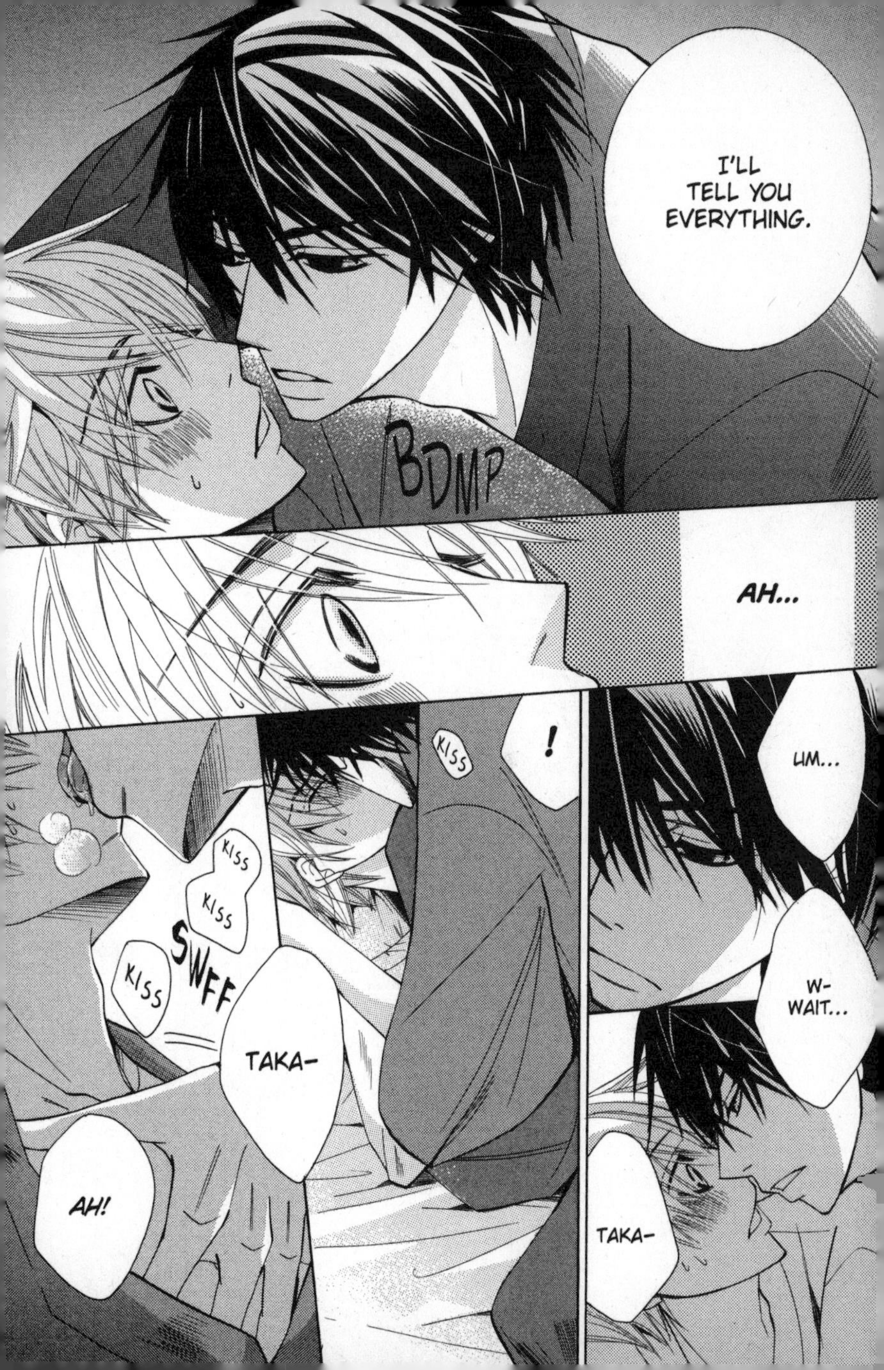
I'LL TELL YOU EVERYTHING.
BDMP
AH...
UM...
W-WAIT...
TAKA-
!
KISS
KISS
KISS
SWFF
KISS
TAKA-
AH!

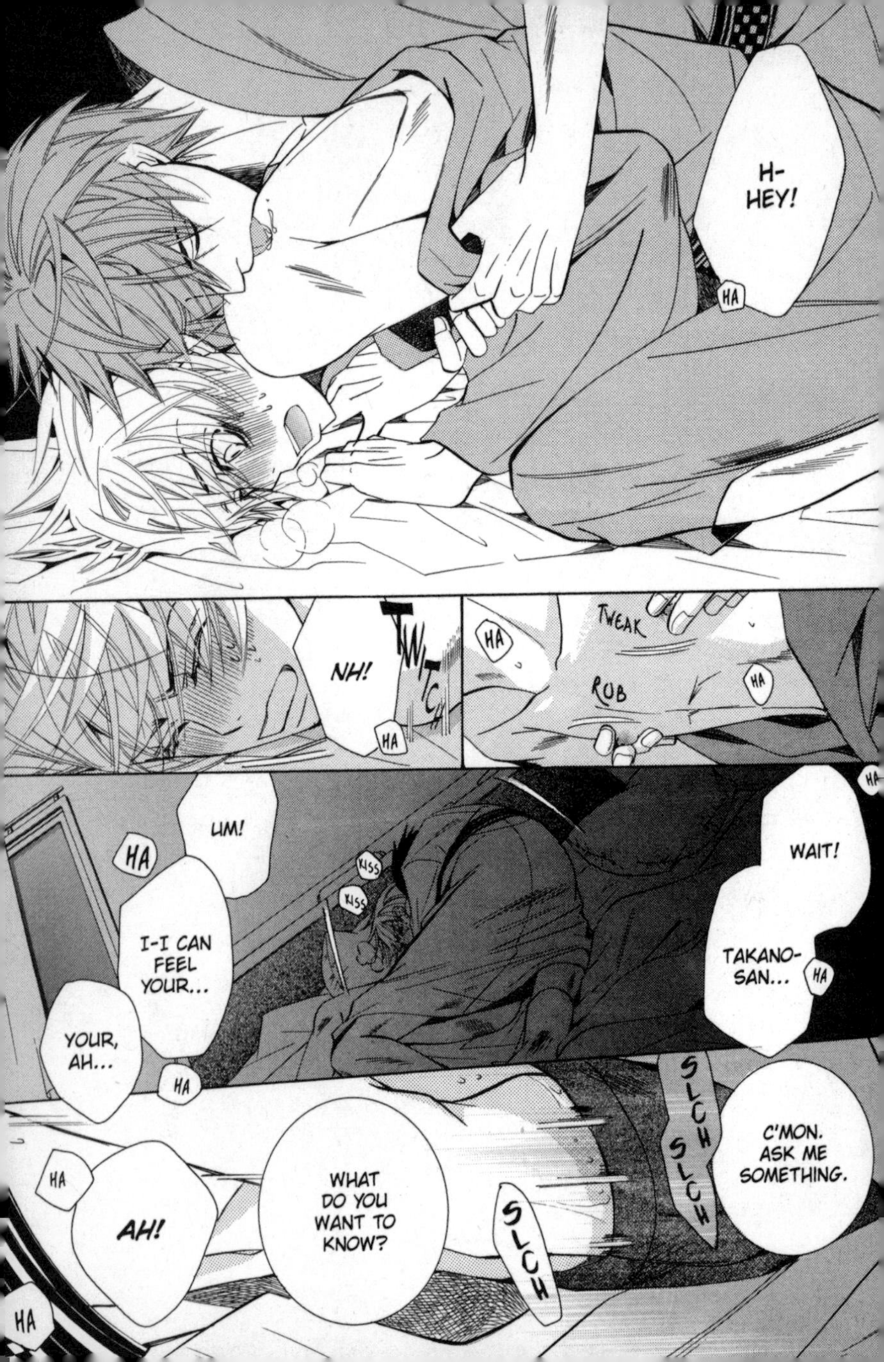
H-
HEY!
HA
HA
TWEAK
RUB
HA
NH!
TWITCH
HA
HA
WAIT!
TAKANO-SAN...
HA
UM!
HA
I-I CAN FEEL YOUR...
KISS
KISS
YOUR, AH...
HA
C'MON. ASK ME SOMETHING.
SLCH
SLCH
WHAT DO YOU WANT TO KNOW?
SLCH
HA
AH!
HA

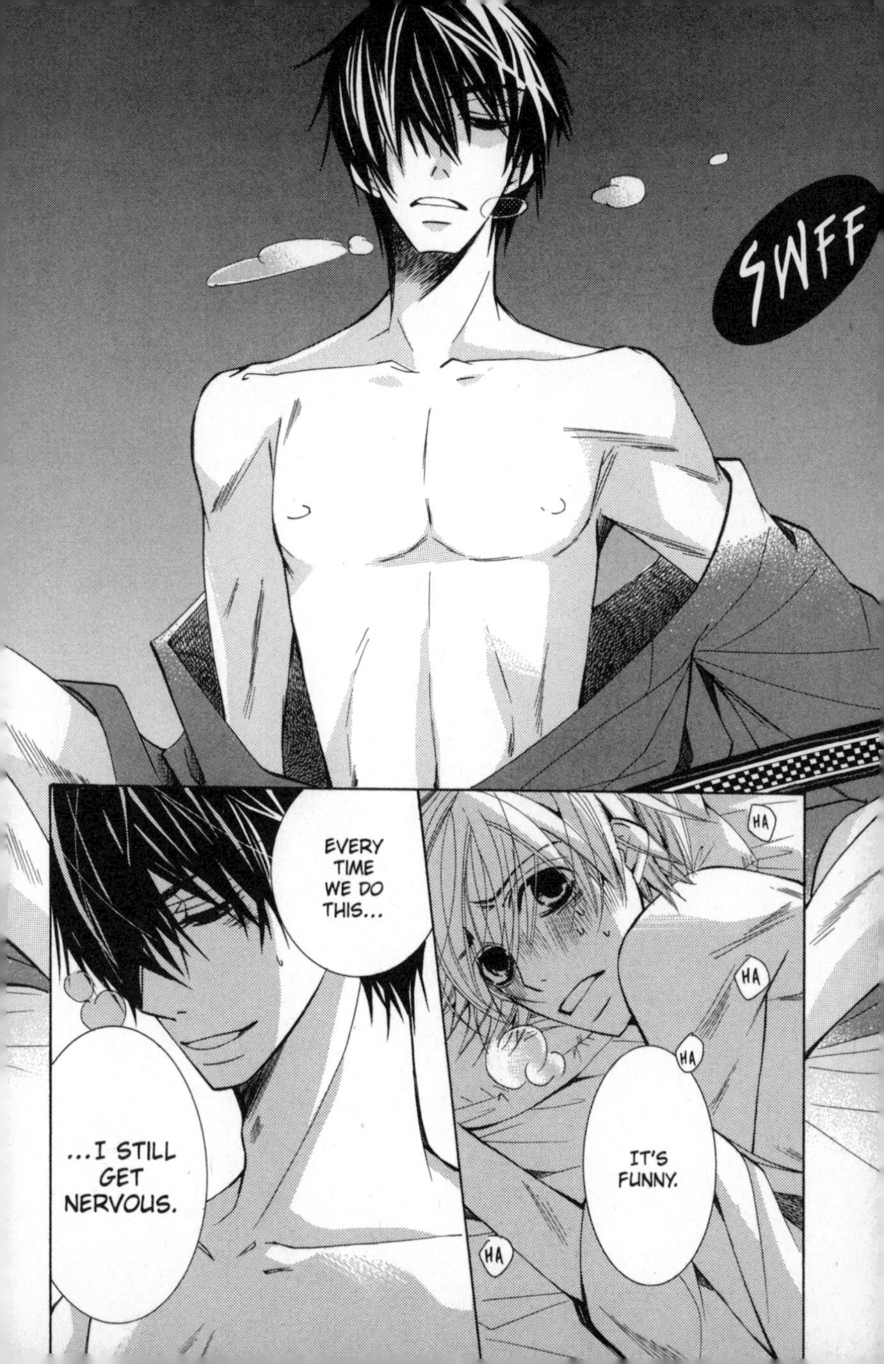
SWFF
HA
HA
HA
IT'S FUNNY.
HA
EVERY TIME WE DO THIS...
...I STILL GET NERVOUS.

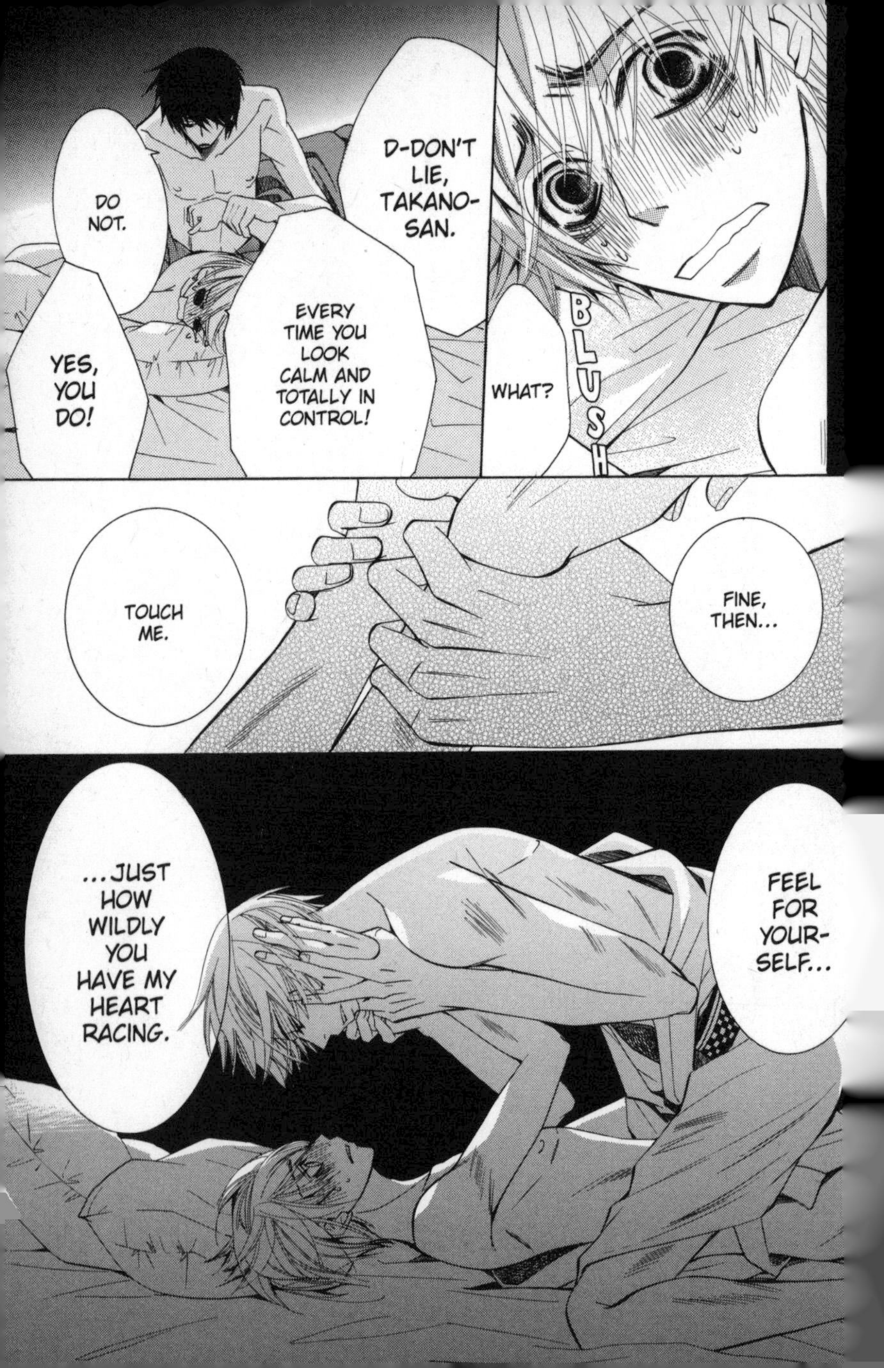
BLUSH
WHAT?
D-DON'T LIE, TAKANO-SAN.
EVERY TIME YOU LOOK CALM AND TOTALLY IN CONTROL!
DO NOT.
YES, YOU DO!
FINE, THEN...
TOUCH ME.
FEEL FOR YOUR-SELF...
...JUST HOW WILDLY YOU HAVE MY HEART RACING.

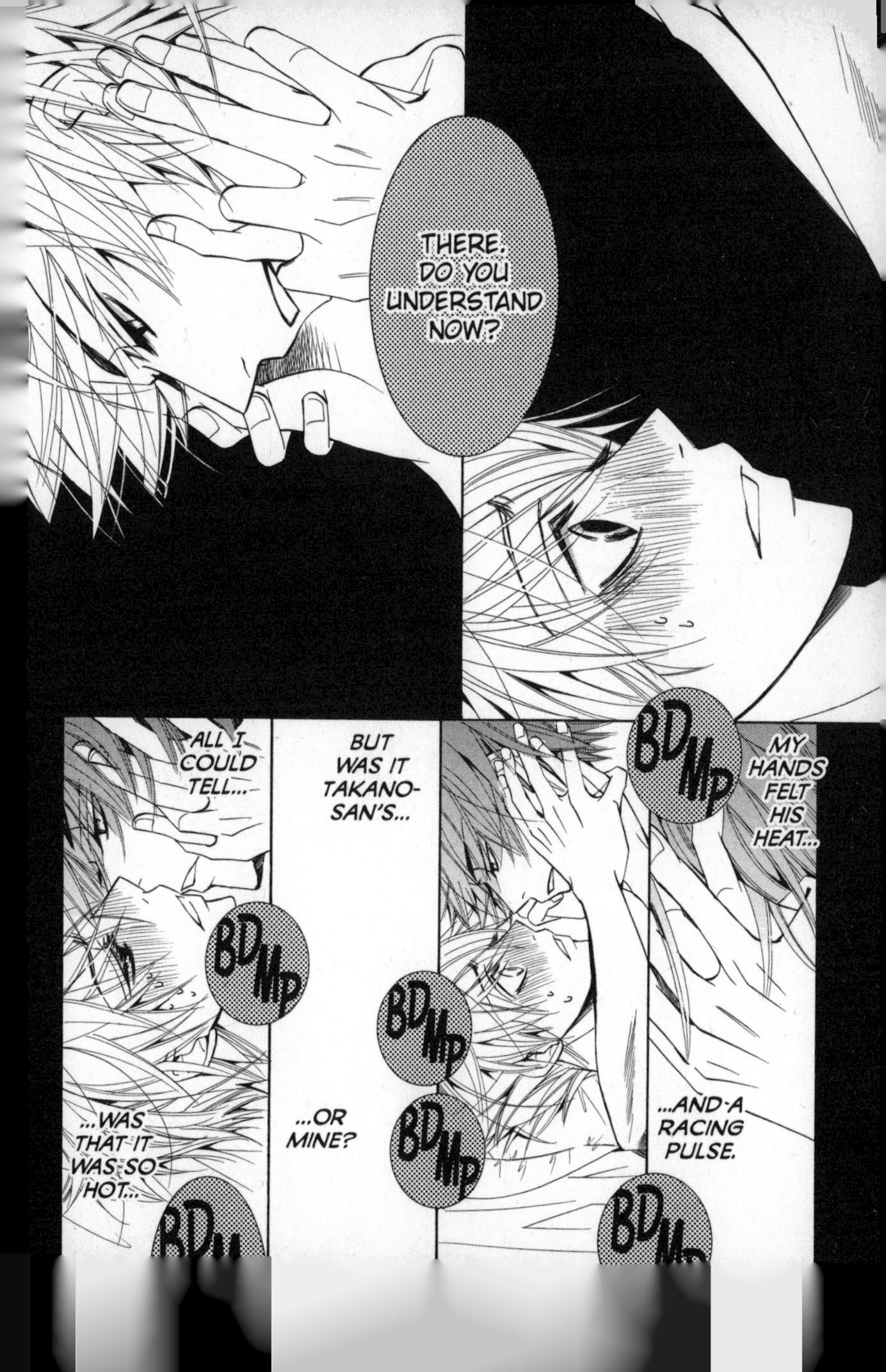
THERE. DO YOU UNDERSTAND NOW?
BDMP
MY HANDS FELT HIS HEAT...
...AND A RACING PULSE.
BDMP
BDMP
BDMP
BUT WAS IT TAKANO-SAN'S...
...OR MINE?
BDMP
ALL I COULD TELL...
...WAS THAT IT WAS SO HOT...

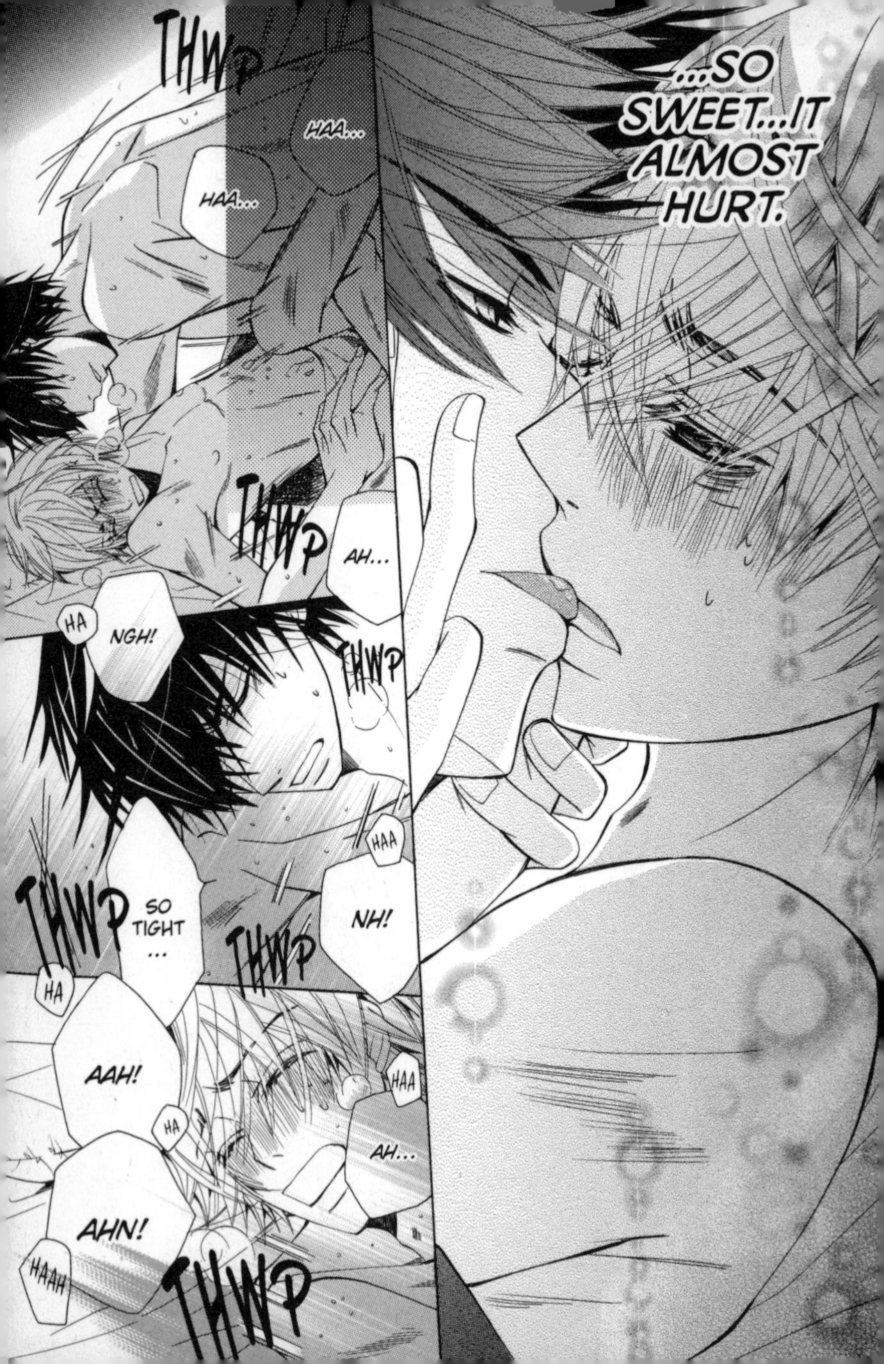
...SO SWEET...IT ALMOST HURT.
THWP
HAA...
HAA...
THWP
AH...
NGH!
HA
THWP
HAA
NH!
THWP
SO TIGHT ...
THWP
HA
HAA
AAH!
HA
AH...
AHN!
HAAH
THWP

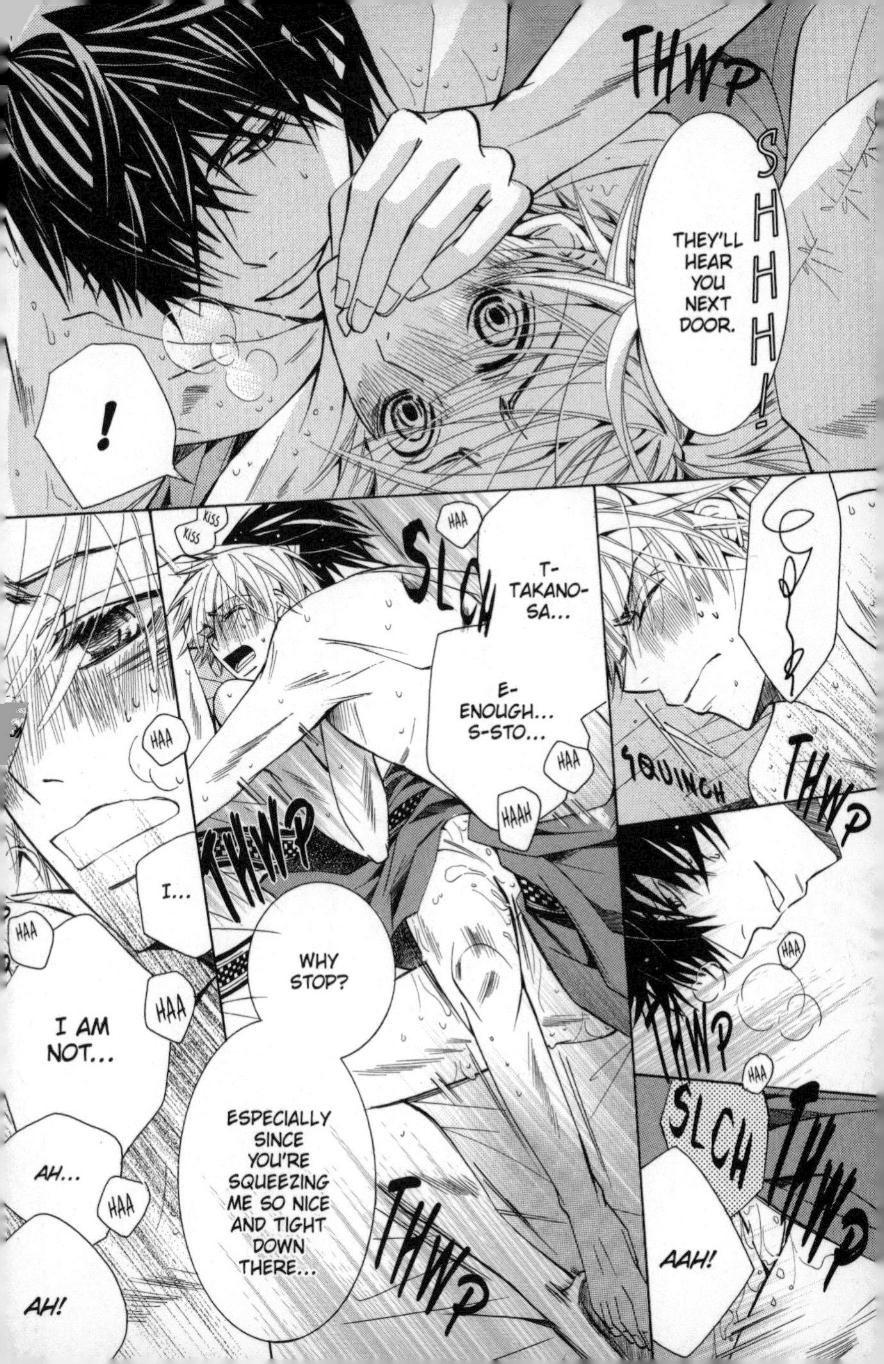
THWP
SHHH!
THEY'LL HEAR YOU NEXT DOOR.
!
SQUINCH
THWP
HAA
THWP
HAA
SLCH
THWP
THWP
AAH!
T-TAKANO-SA...
HAA
SLCH
KISS
KISS
E-ENOUGH... S-STO...
HAA
HAAH
THWP
WHY STOP?
ESPECIALLY SINCE YOU'RE SQUEEZING ME SO NICE AND TIGHT DOWN THERE...
THWP
HAA
I...
HAA
HAA
I AM NOT...
AH...
HAA
AH!

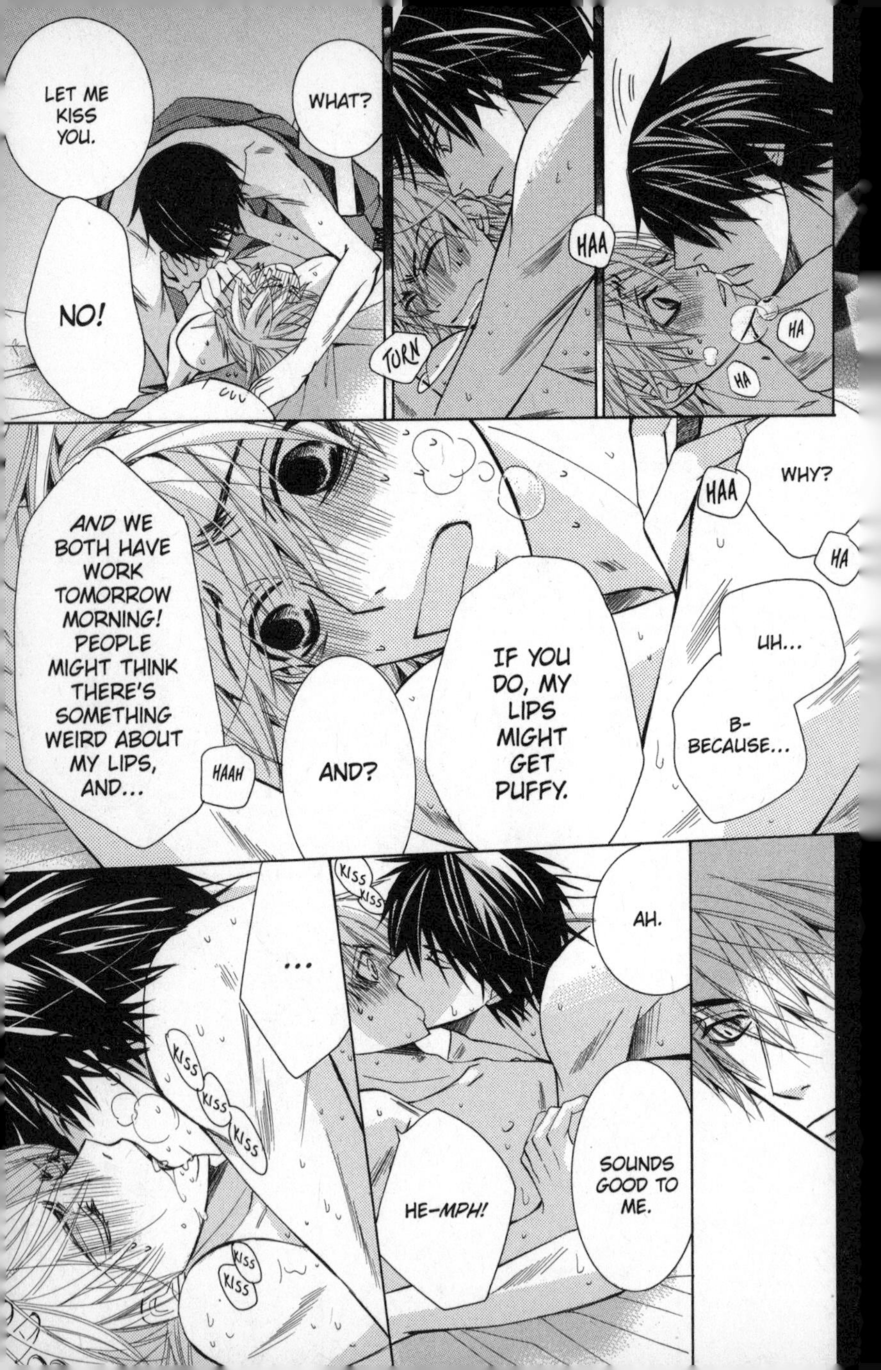
HAA
HA
HA
TURN
WHAT?
LET ME KISS YOU.
NO!
WHY?
HAA
HA
UH...
B-BECAUSE...
IF YOU DO, MY LIPS MIGHT GET PUFFY.
AND?
HAAH
AND WE BOTH HAVE WORK TOMORROW MORNING! PEOPLE MIGHT THINK THERE'S SOMETHING WEIRD ABOUT MY LIPS, AND...
AH.
KISS
KISS
SOUNDS GOOD TO ME.
HE-MPH!
...
KISS
KISS
KISS
KISS
KISS

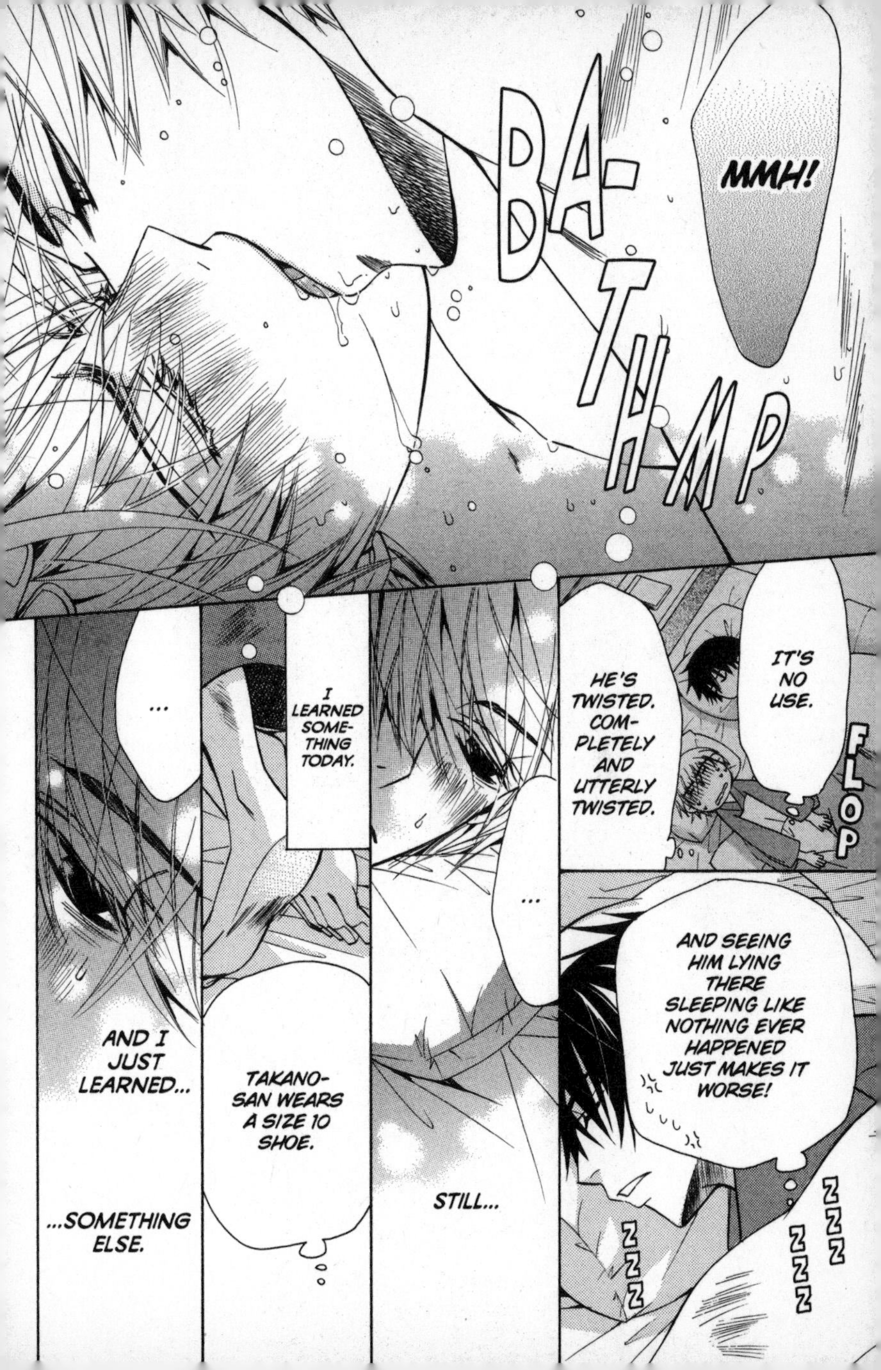
MMH!
BA-THMP
IT'S NO USE.
FLOP
HE'S TWISTED. COMPLETELY AND UTTERLY TWISTED.
AND SEEING HIM LYING THERE SLEEPING LIKE NOTHING EVER HAPPENED JUST MAKES IT WORSE!
ZZZ
ZZZ
ZZZ
...
STILL...
I LEARNED SOMETHING TODAY.
TAKANO-SAN WEARS A SIZE 10 SHOE.
...
AND I JUST LEARNED...
...SOMETHING ELSE.

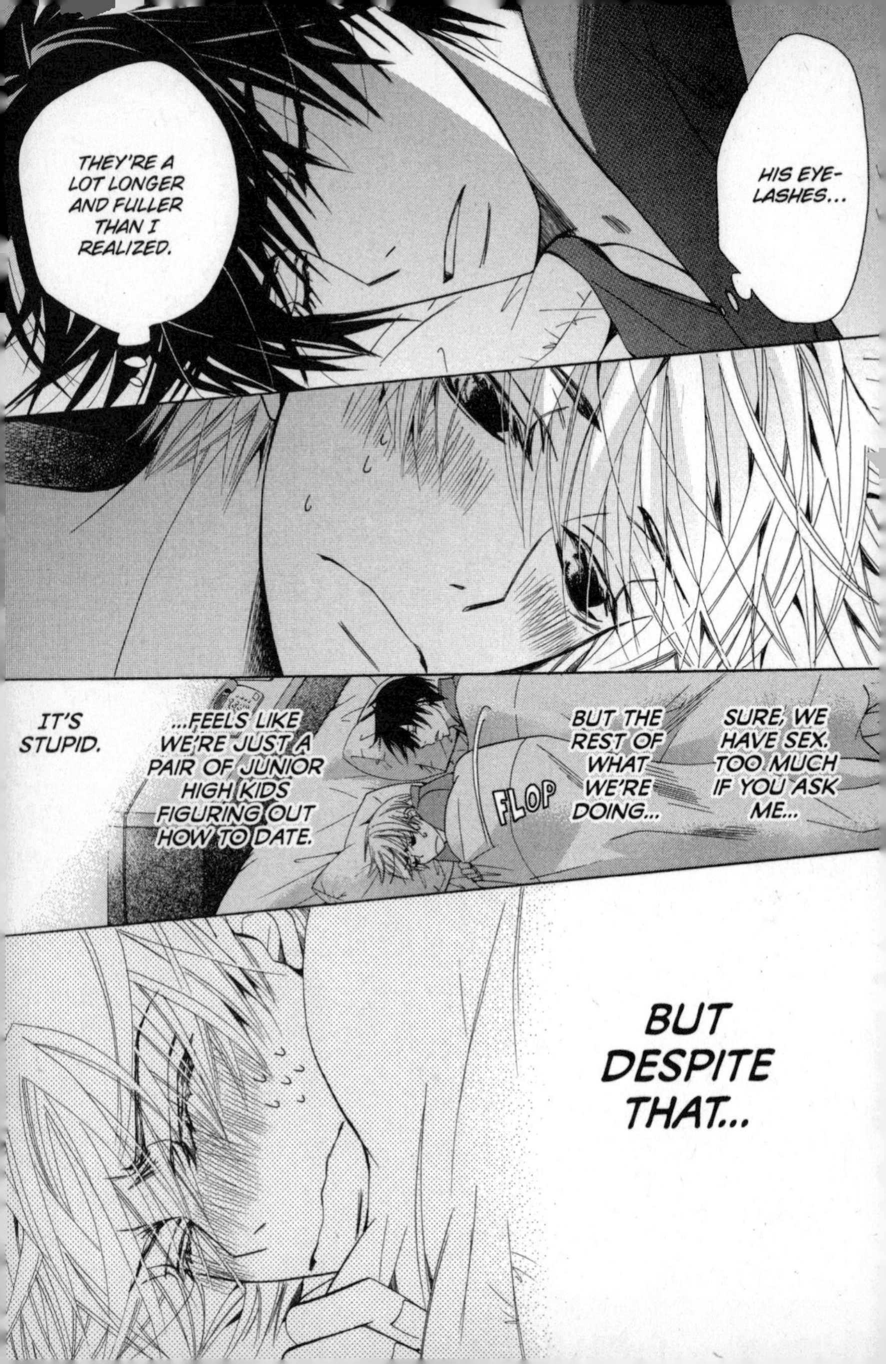
HIS EYE-LASHES...
THEY'RE A LOT LONGER AND FULLER THAN I REALIZED.
SURE, WE HAVE SEX. TOO MUCH IF YOU ASK ME...
FLOP
BUT THE REST OF WHAT WE'RE DOING...
...FEELS LIKE WE'RE JUST A PAIR OF JUNIOR HIGH KIDS FIGURING OUT HOW TO DATE.
IT'S STUPID.
BUT DESPITE THAT...

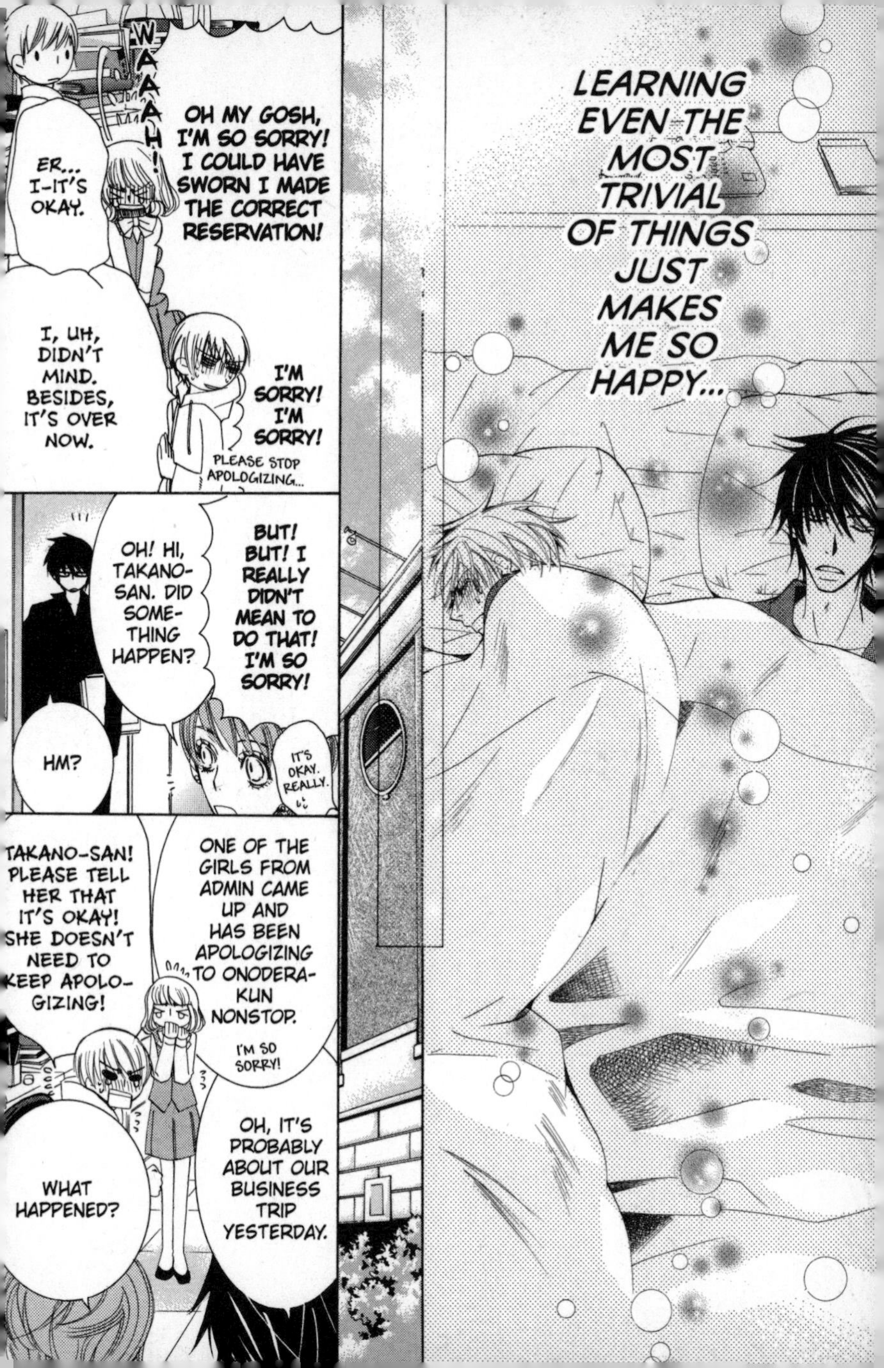
LEARNING EVEN THE MOST TRIVIAL OF THINGS JUST MAKES ME SO HAPPY...
WAAAAH!
OH MY GOSH, I'M SO SORRY! I COULD HAVE SWORN I MADE THE CORRECT RESERVATION!
ER... I-IT'S OKAY.
I'M SORRY! I'M SORRY!
I, UH, DIDN'T MIND. BESIDES, IT'S OVER NOW.
PLEASE STOP APOLOGIZING...
BUT! BUT! I REALLY DIDN'T MEAN TO DO THAT! I'M SO SORRY!
OH! HI, TAKANO-SAN. DID SOMETHING HAPPEN?
IT'S OKAY. REALLY.
HM?
ONE OF THE GIRLS FROM ADMIN CAME UP AND HAS BEEN APOLOGIZING TO ONODERA-KUN NONSTOP.
TAKANO-SAN! PLEASE TELL HER THAT IT'S OKAY! SHE DOESN'T NEED TO KEEP APOLOGIZING!
I'M SO SORRY!
OH, IT'S PROBABLY ABOUT OUR BUSINESS TRIP YESTERDAY.
WHAT HAPPENED?

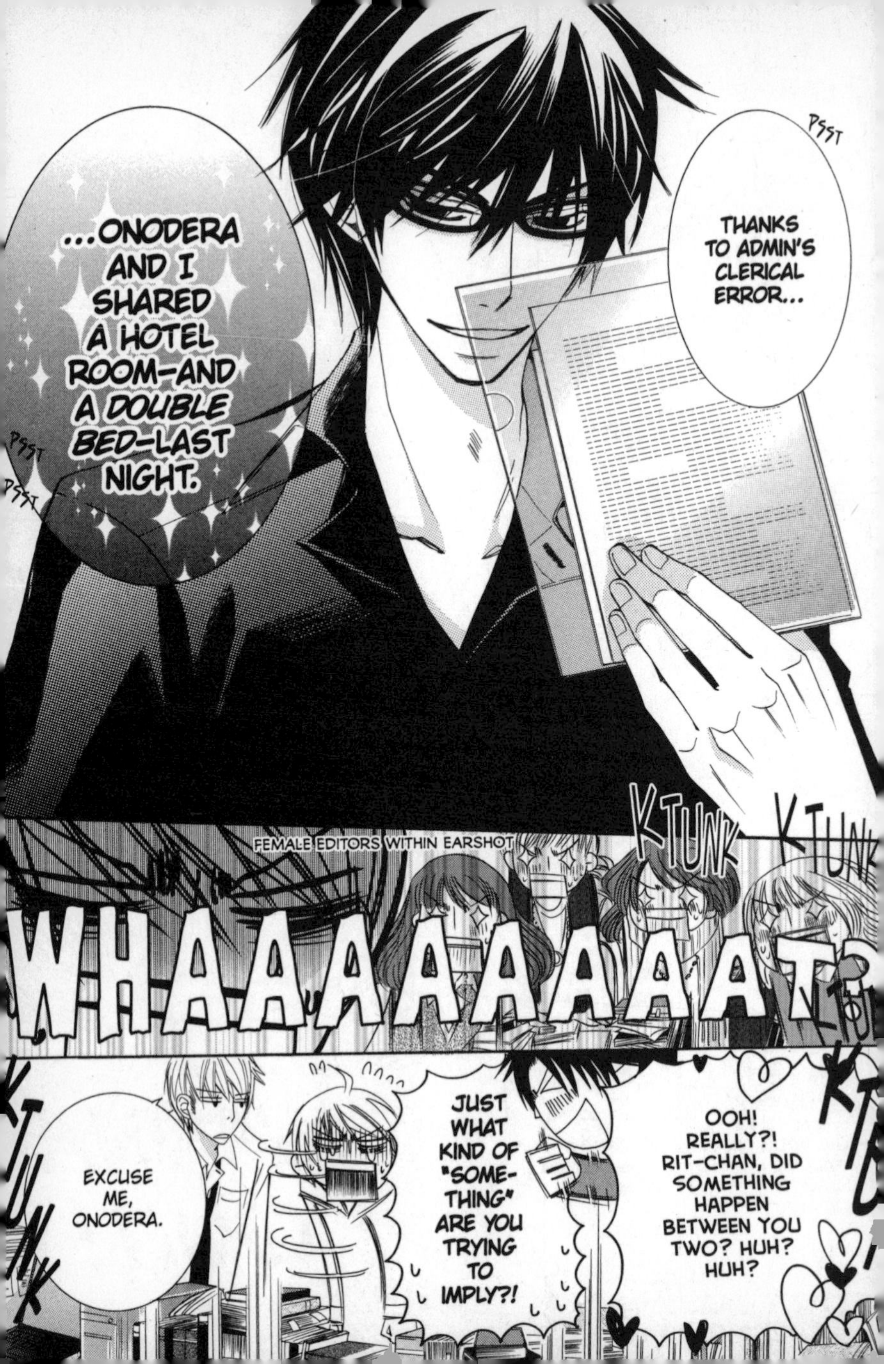
PSST
THANKS TO ADMIN'S CLERICAL ERROR...
...ONODERA AND I SHARED A HOTEL ROOM—AND A DOUBLE BED—LAST NIGHT.
PSST
PSST
KTUNK KTUNK
FEMALE EDITORS WITHIN EARSHOT
WHAAAAAAAT?!
KTUNK
OOH! REALLY?! RIT-CHAN, DID SOMETHING HAPPEN BETWEEN YOU TWO? HUH? HUH?
JUST WHAT KIND OF "SOMETHING" ARE YOU TRYING TO IMPLY?!
EXCUSE ME, ONODERA.
KTUNK

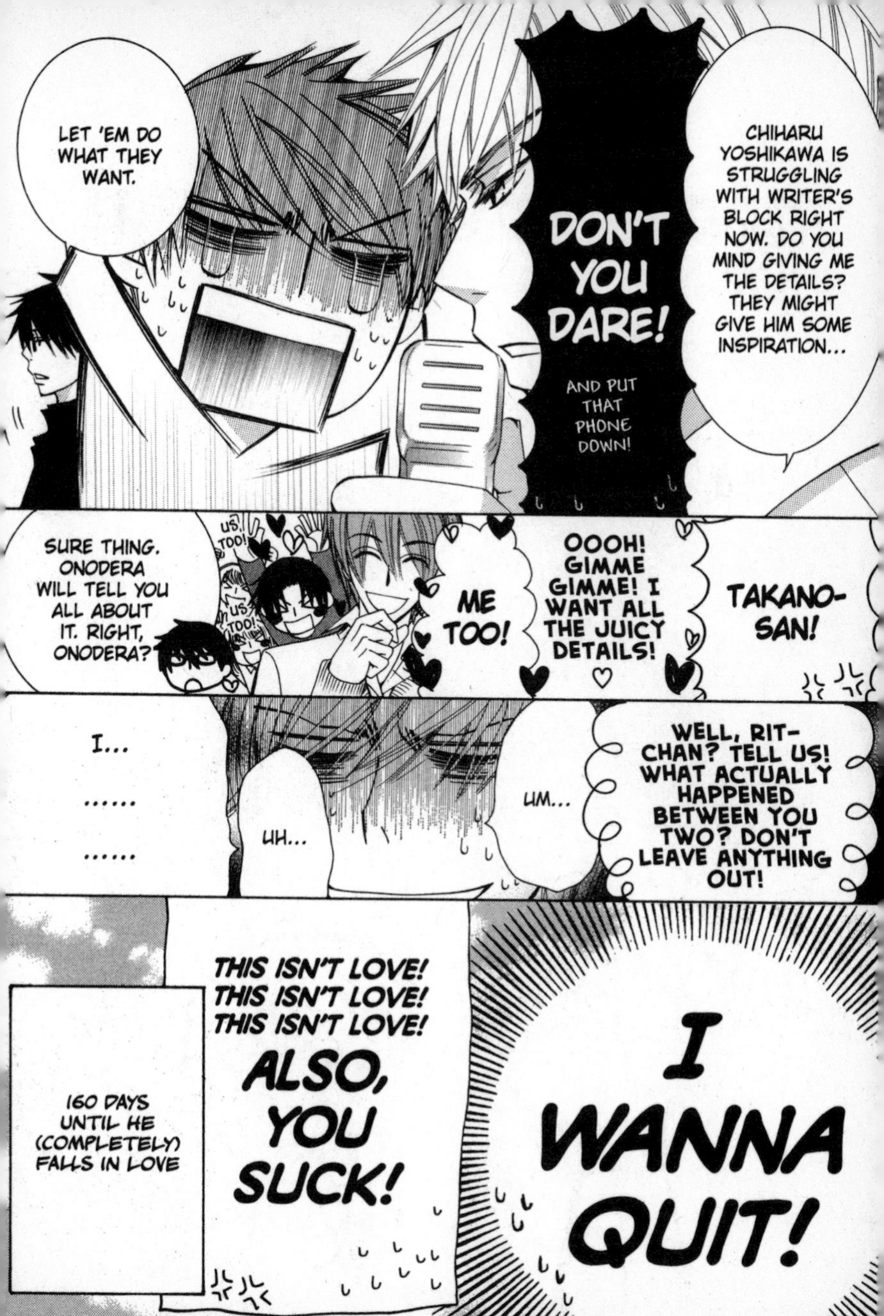
CHIHARU YOSHIKAWA IS STRUGGLING WITH WRITER'S BLOCK RIGHT NOW. DO YOU MIND GIVING ME THE DETAILS? THEY MIGHT GIVE HIM SOME INSPIRATION...
DON'T YOU DARE!
AND PUT THAT PHONE DOWN!
LET 'EM DO WHAT THEY WANT.
TAKANO-SAN!
OOOH! GIMME GIMME! I WANT ALL THE JUICY DETAILS!
ME TOO!
US, TOO!
US, TOO!
SURE THING. ONODERA WILL TELL YOU ALL ABOUT IT. RIGHT, ONODERA?
WELL, RIT-CHAN? TELL US! WHAT ACTUALLY HAPPENED BETWEEN YOU TWO? DON'T LEAVE ANYTHING OUT!
UM...
UH...
I...
......
......
I WANNA QUIT!
THIS ISN'T LOVE! THIS ISN'T LOVE! THIS ISN'T LOVE!
ALSO, YOU SUCK!
160 DAYS UNTIL HE (COMPLETELY) FALLS IN LOVE

The Case of Ritsu Onodera NO.11 END

MARUKAWA PUBLISHING TERMINOLOGY & JARGON (PART 15)

***NOTE:** ALL OF THE TERMINOLOGY LISTED HEREIN IS SPECIFIC TO MARUKAWA PUBLISHING AND MAY NOT BE APPLICABLE TO THE GENERAL PUBLISHING INDUSTRY.

[PROOF PAPER]

PAPER SPECIFICALLY FOR PRINTING OUT GALLEYS, BLUELINES, COLOR PROOFS, AND OTHER TEST COPIES FOR PROOFREADING PURPOSES.

[REDLINE]

THANKS TO THE TRADITION OF USING RED PENS OR PENCILS TO ADD CHANGES AND CORRECTIONS TO A DOCUMENT, EDITED PROOFS ARE SOMETIMES CALLED "REDLINES" AND THE EDITING PROCESS ITSELF "REDLINING."

[RUBI]

IN JAPANESE TEXT, *RUBI* (ALSO CALLED *FURIGANA* OR *YOMIGANA*) ARE READING AIDS ADDED TO KANJI CHARACTERS USING EASIER-TO-READ HIRAGANA OR KATAKANA TO INDICATE PROPER PRONUNCIATION. WHEN KANJI IS VERTICAL, RUBI ARE ADDED TO THE RIGHT OF IT. WHEN IT'S HORIZONTAL, THE RUBI ARE ADDED ABOVE. USUALLY ADDED DURING THE PASTE-UP OR DIGITAL TYPESETTING STAGES, RUBI CAN ALSO BE USED TO CLARIFY OR OFFER AN ALTERNATE PRONUNCIATION FOR CERTAIN KANJI. IT'S SAID THAT *RUBI* COMES FROM THE ENGLISH WORD FOR "RUBY," WHICH WAS A SIZE OF TYPEFACE IN VICTORIAN ENGLAND.

The World's Greatest First Love

The Case of Ritsu Onodera

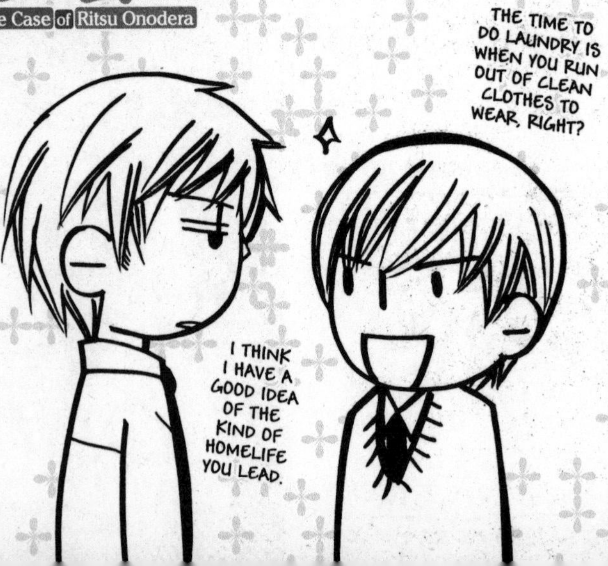
THE TIME TO DO LAUNDRY IS WHEN YOU RUN OUT OF CLEAN CLOTHES TO WEAR, RIGHT?
I THINK I HAVE A GOOD IDEA OF THE KIND OF HOMELIFE YOU LEAD.

SO I SLIPPED UP AND ACCIDENTALLY INVITED HIM TO MY PLACE.

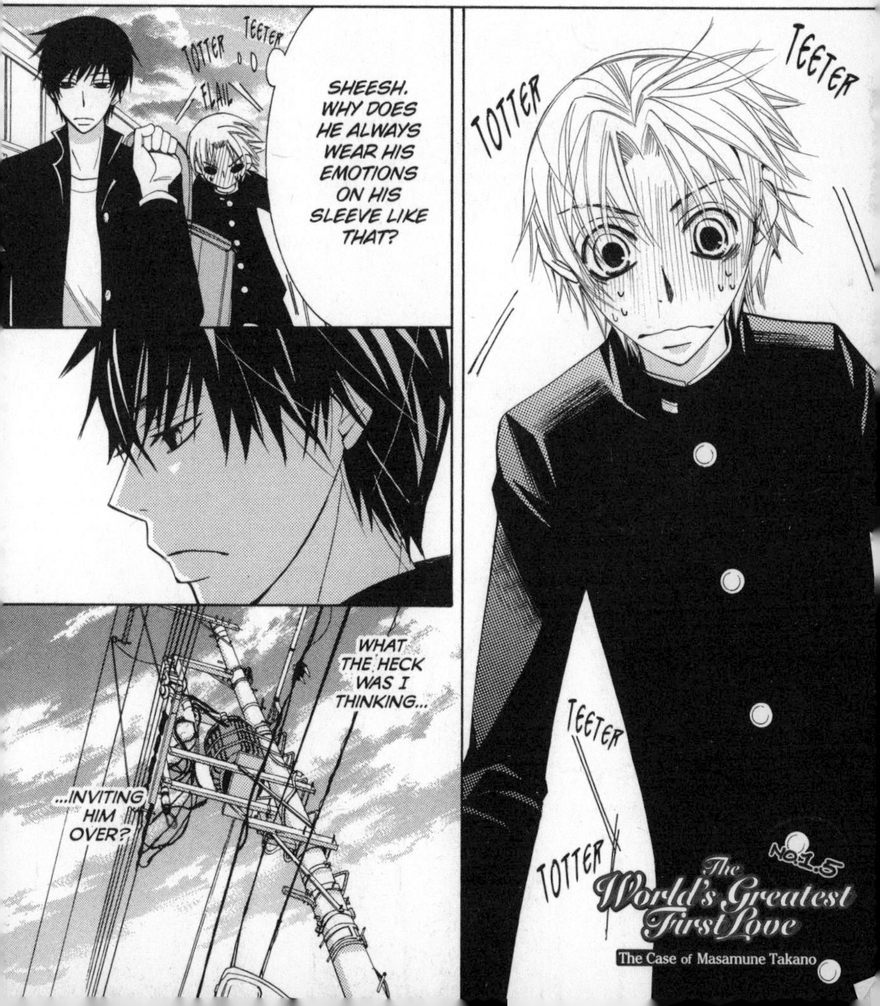
TEETER
TOTTER
TEETER
TOTTER
No.1.5
The World's Greatest First Love
The Case of Masamune Takano
TEETER
TOTTER
FLAIL
SHEESH. WHY DOES HE ALWAYS WEAR HIS EMOTIONS ON HIS SLEEVE LIKE THAT?
WHAT THE HECK WAS I THINKING...
...INVITING HIM OVER?

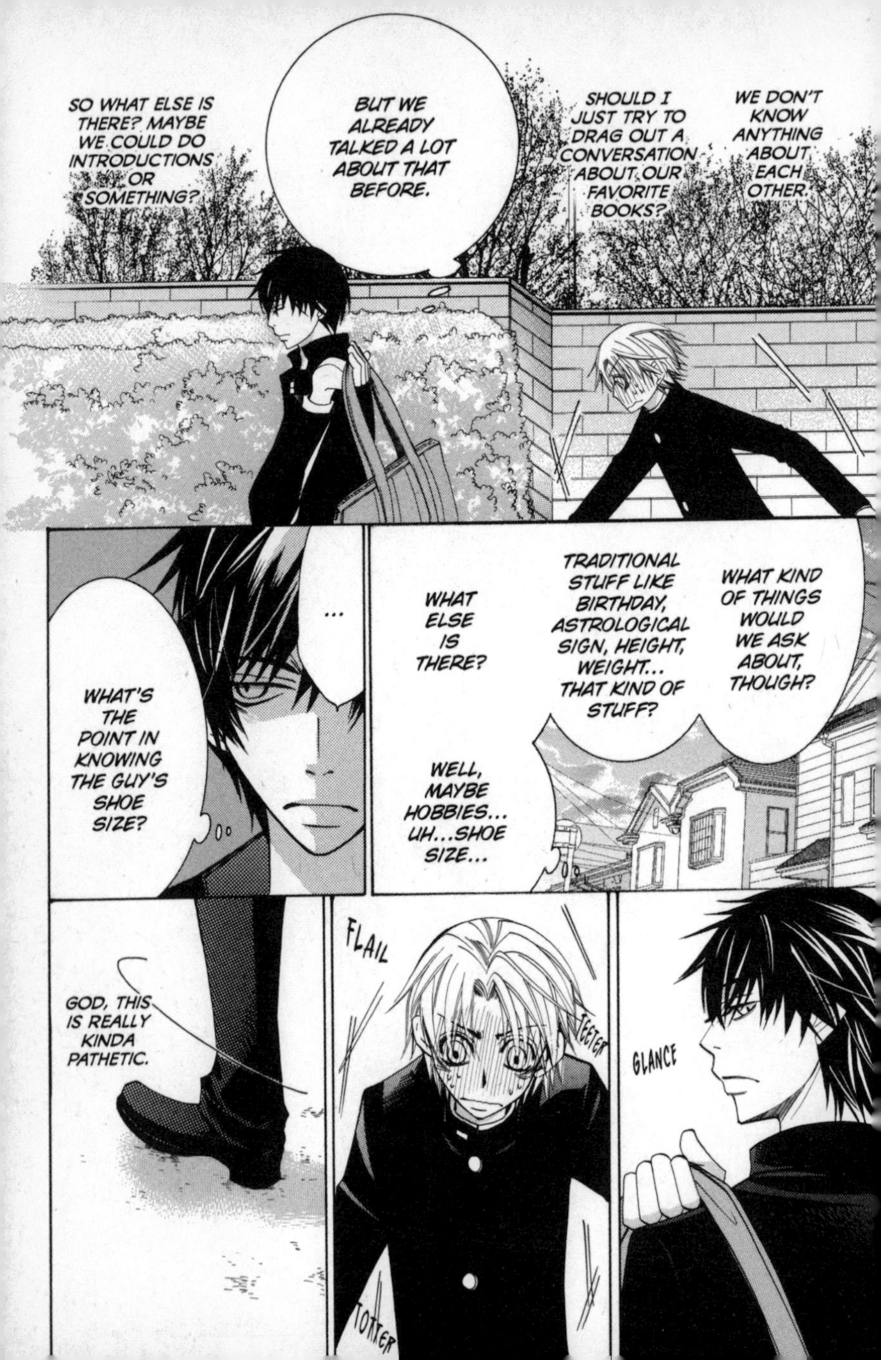
WE DON'T KNOW ANYTHING ABOUT EACH OTHER.
SHOULD I JUST TRY TO DRAG OUT A CONVERSATION ABOUT OUR FAVORITE BOOKS?
BUT WE ALREADY TALKED A LOT ABOUT THAT BEFORE.
SO WHAT ELSE IS THERE? MAYBE WE COULD DO INTRODUCTIONS OR SOMETHING?
WHAT KIND OF THINGS WOULD WE ASK ABOUT, THOUGH?
TRADITIONAL STUFF LIKE BIRTHDAY, ASTROLOGICAL SIGN, HEIGHT, WEIGHT... THAT KIND OF STUFF?
WHAT ELSE IS THERE?
WELL, MAYBE HOBBIES... UH...SHOE SIZE...
...
WHAT'S THE POINT IN KNOWING THE GUY'S SHOE SIZE?
GLANCE
FLAIL
TEETER
TOTTER
GOD, THIS IS REALLY KINDA PATHETIC.

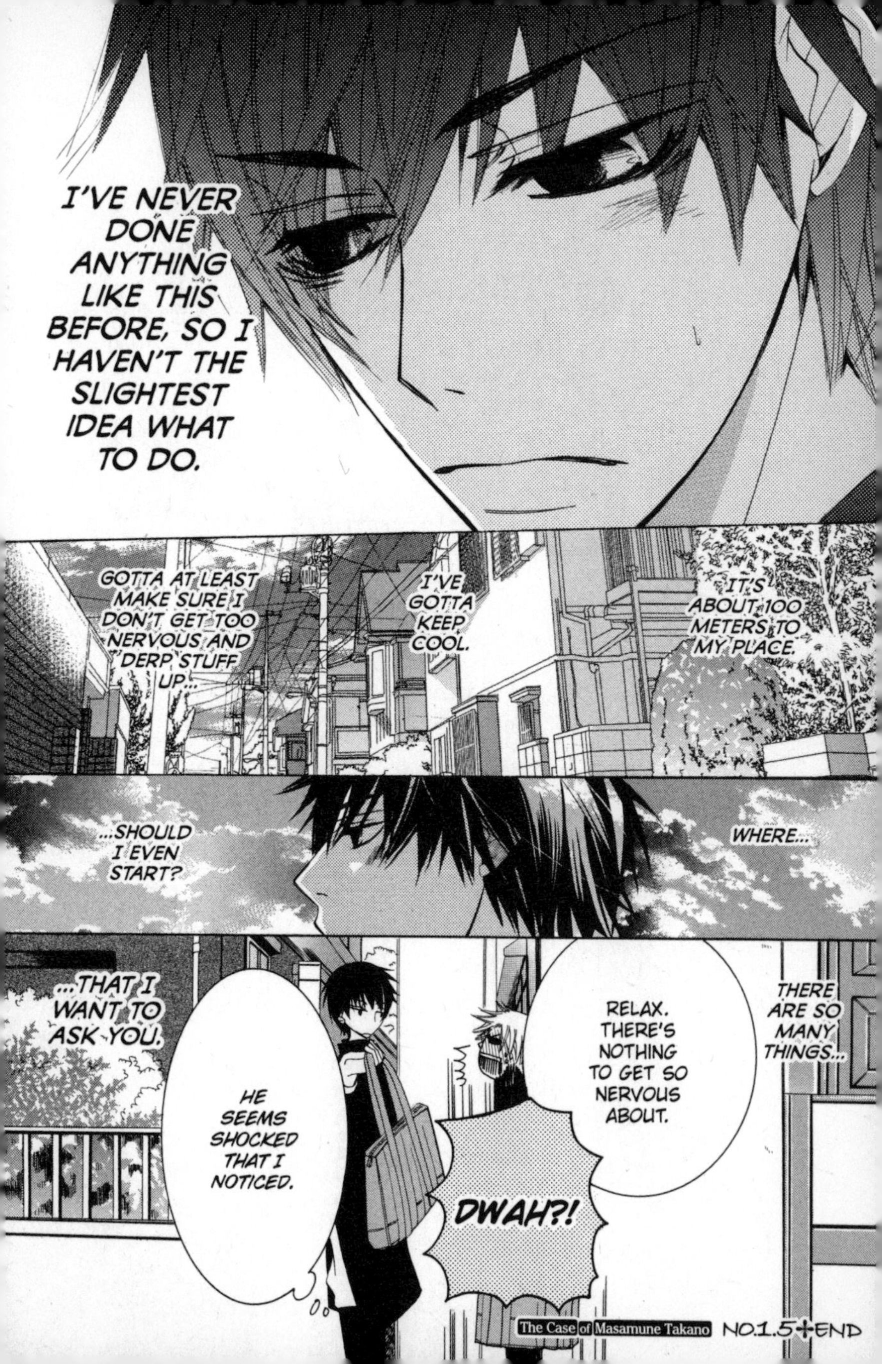
I'VE NEVER DONE ANYTHING LIKE THIS BEFORE, SO I HAVEN'T THE SLIGHTEST IDEA WHAT TO DO.
IT'S ABOUT 100 METERS TO MY PLACE.
I'VE GOTTA KEEP COOL.
GOTTA AT LEAST MAKE SURE I DON'T GET TOO NERVOUS AND DERP STUFF UP...
WHERE...
...SHOULD I EVEN START?
THERE ARE SO MANY THINGS...
...THAT I WANT TO ASK YOU.
RELAX. THERE'S NOTHING TO GET SO NERVOUS ABOUT.
DWAH?!
HE SEEMS SHOCKED THAT I NOTICED.
The Case of Masamune Takano NO.1.5 + END

REMEMBER WHEN I MENTIONED THAT ROBOT THAT CLEANS YOUR FLOOR FOR YOU? IT WAS HALF-PRICE THE OTHER DAY, SO I WOUND UP GETTING ONE.

EHEH HEH...

AH, I SEE. CHIHARU YOSHIKAWA BOUGHT ONE AS WELL.

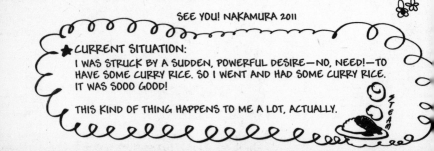

☆ HELLO! IT'S GOOD TO MEET YOU! MY NAME IS SHUNGIKU NAKAMURA. THANK YOU FOR BUYING VOLUME 6 OF *THE WORLD'S GREATEST FIRST LOVE ~THE CASE OF RITSU ONODERA~*!

YAAAY!

☆☆ STARTING IN OCTOBER 2011, THE SECOND SEASON OF *THE WORLD'S GREATEST FIRST LOVE* ANIME STARTS AIRING! I REALLY HOPE YOU CHECK IT OUT. I CAN HARDLY WAIT TO WATCH IT MYSELF.

☆☆☆ RUBY BUNKO IS RELEASING *THE WORLD'S GREATEST FIRST LOVE ~THE CASE OF CHIAKI YOSHINO~*. CHECK IT OUT IF YOU'D LIKE!

☆☆☆☆ THERE'S ALSO *JUNJO ROMANTICA*, WHICH IS CONNECTED TO MARUKAWA PUBLISHING. CHECK THIS ONE OUT TOO IF YOU'RE INTERESTED.

☆☆☆☆☆ IF YOU HAVE ANY THOUGHTS OR COMMENTS, I WOULD LOVE TO HEAR THEM!

SEE YOU! NAKAMURA 2011

★ CURRENT SITUATION:
I WAS STRUCK BY A SUDDEN, POWERFUL DESIRE—NO, NEED!—TO HAVE SOME CURRY RICE. SO I WENT AND HAD SOME CURRY RICE. IT WAS SOOO GOOD!

THIS KIND OF THING HAPPENS TO ME A LOT, ACTUALLY.

STEAM

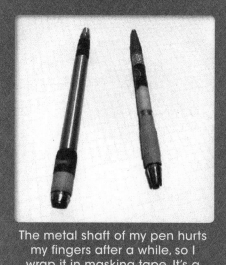

The metal shaft of my pen hurts my fingers after a while, so I wrap it in masking tape. It's a lot softer and comfier now.

About the Author

Shungiku Nakamura
DOB December 13
Sagittarius
Blood Type O